Dear Larry

Thank you so much for all your support, encouragement and friendship over the years.

I really appreciated and valued your advice and editorial assistance in preparing the manuscript.

Warmest regards

SCHOOLING FOR LIFE:
COMMUNITY EDUCATION AND SOCIAL ENTERPRISE

DALE E. SHUTTLEWORTH

Schooling for Life

Community Education and Social Enterprise

UNIVERSITY OF TORONTO PRESS
Toronto Buffalo London

© University of Toronto Press Incorporated 2010
Toronto Buffalo London
www.utppublishing.com
Printed in Canada

ISBN 978-0-8020-9811-5

∞

Printed on acid-free, 100% post-consumer recycled paper
with vegetable-based inks.

Library and Archives Canada Cataloguing in Publication

Shuttleworth, Dale E. (Dale Edwin), 1938–
    Schooling for life : community education and social enterprise /
    Dale Shuttleworth.

    Includes bibliographical references and index.
    ISBN 978-0-8020-9811-5

    1. Community education – Ontario – Toronto – History.
    2. Community development – Ontario – Toronto – History.   3. Social
    entrepreneurship – Ontario – Toronto – History.   4. Toronto (Ont.) –
    Economic conditions.   5. Economic development – Effect of
    education on – Case studies.   6. Community development, Urban –
    Case studies.   I. Title.

    LC1036.8.C32T6 2009   370.11'509713541   C2009-906289-5

University of Toronto Press acknowledges the financial assistance to its
publishing program of the Canada Council for the Arts and the Ontario
Arts Council.

 Canada Council   Conseil des Arts   ONTARIO ARTS COUNCIL
for the Arts   du Canada   CONSEIL DES ARTS DE L'ONTARIO

University of Toronto Press acknowledges the financial support for its
publishing activities of the Government of Canada through the Book
Publishing Industry Development Program (BPIDP).

Contents

Figures

Preface

In reflecting on my career as a community educator, I am reminded of the words of Edmund Burke, the eighteenth-century liberal reformer: 'Those who would carry on the great public schemes must be proof against the most fatiguing delays, the most mortifying disappointments, the most shocking insults, and, worst of all, the presumptuous judgments of all the ignorant upon their designs.'

I was very much a working-class child of the auto industry. My father grew up on a farm near Windsor, Ontario, but had to leave school at the age of fourteen when his elder brothers went off to Europe to fight in the Great War. He was soon doing a man's work and was able to plough a straight furrow behind a team of horses. After a stint as a carpenter's helper and then three years of service in the United States Marine Corps, Harry Shuttleworth joined the industrial age, making tires for thirty-nine years at U.S. Rubber in Detroit. His strong work ethic and his devotion to the welfare of his family meant that he was able to keep a job, even during the Great Depression of the 1930s and the Detroit race riots of the 1940s.

Nearby, in Canada, although the first settlers to cultivate the flat fertile soil of Essex County had been French, and later British, during the twentieth century the newcomers who were drawn to the area in search of employment in the burgeoning auto industry came from central and eastern Europe and the Middle East. Growing up in Windsor, with its multicultural heritage and close proximity to an American lifestyle, was, for me, an immersion in diversity. But what does *diversity* mean? It refers not only to cultural and racial differences but also to diverse social and economic realities and to ideas and values.

My own life options seemed pretty limited: get an education, or seek employment on an auto assembly line at Ford, Chrysler, or General

Motors. After dropping out of school to work in a succession of dead-end and part-time jobs (at a textile plant, in retail sales, at a gas station pump, as a theatre usher), I decided to go back to school to get enough education to qualify as an elementary school teacher. In the 1950s, that meant graduating from high school as well as taking one year at London Teachers' College. In 1960, I was fortunate to be hired by the Riverside Board of Education as a fifth-grade teacher. (At that time, Riverside was a suburb of Windsor.)

As I assumed my teaching career I was also fortunate enough to be able to attend Assumption University of Windsor, mostly part-time. Aside from being steeped in the philosophy of St Thomas Aquinas by the Basilian Fathers, I majored in applied sociology as pioneered by Professor Rudolf Helling, a German immigrant. He encouraged me to pursue experiential learning, including original research in the field. One of my service learning assignments involved more than a year's volunteer work at St Leonard's, Canada's first halfway house for ex-prisoners. I also had the privilege of being taught by Wilson Head, an African American newcomer, who gave me an understanding of poverty and social welfare, human rights, and race relations. It was Wilson who introduced me to the concept of the school-community worker. He became a mentor and a source of encouragement throughout my career.

Graduate studies in the sociology of education followed at the University of Toronto's Ontario Institute for Studies in Education, where I encountered community education and development with James Draper; adult and non-formal learning with Alan Thomas and Allen Tough; and the politics of education with Tom Williams. My 1978 doctoral thesis was entitled 'The Learning Exchange System (LEARNXS): Analysis of a Demonstration Project in Community Education.'

Thus began a career struggle to try to serve as a change agent and a social entrepreneur. From the 1960s to the 1990s I worked for three of the most progressive school boards in Canada – North York, Toronto, and the City of York — but change by its very nature can be a complex, frustrating political process.

I have often thought that public hospitals and public schools have a lot in common. They were both outgrowths of voluntary action, particularly during the nineteenth century in North America. Leadership frequently originated through churches and religious orders, who responded to the needs of the impoverished and disadvantaged for health services as well as literacy and numeracy skills. Before the practitioners in both sectors were professionalized, with standards of performance regulated by the state, volunteers were pressed into service to help the ailing and the illiterate. Over time, a hierarchy developed in the medical field, with doctors employed at the pinnacle of power. They were served by registered nurses, who directed nurse's aides, orderlies, and other support staff, forming a service pyramid known as the medical or clinical model.

Teachers, who were originally volunteers, came to be employed by municipal ratepayers to provide educational services in a mostly agricultural environment. The state soon hired inspectors to standardize centrally developed curriculum and pedagogical practice. As the society became more urbanized, the one-room rural schools were consolidated into multi-classroom facilities to which students travelled by school bus. An administrative hierarchy was created, led by a principal or a head teacher, with a vice-principal, subject department heads, other academic support staff, secretaries, and caretakers.

Both hospitals and schools soon evolved into inward-looking institutional models of efficiency, heavily influenced by the scientific management movement, which fuelled the rise of the industrial revolution. Urbanized mass producers of goods and services, known as factories, were replacing the agricultural artisan-led economy. Hospitals, schools, and factories often became captives of a cult of efficiency, where the drive for increased productivity surpassed concern for the patient, the student, or the factory worker.

Seeing the school as an extension of the community it served, I often found myself caught in the middle, seeking to be responsive to diverse community needs while struggling to survive in the complex political environment known as institutional schooling. This was particularly true in attempting to meet the needs of diverse socio-economic, cultural, and racial minorities in a series of impoverished urban neighbourhoods. The vehicle I employed, to try to make a difference, was the demonstration project, which often involved using alternative sources of financial and in-kind support to demonstrate the need for changes in public policies and programs. However, this career struggle included its share of failures as well as successes. The successes could be incorporated into new policies and programs, while the public body could distance itself from the failures. Success has a thousand parents; failure is an orphan.

In September 2006, I was asked to provide keynote addresses to two conferences in Berlin involving German legislators, educators, and community service advocates. The themes of both conferences focused on the 'educational needs of immigrants and migrants in an increasingly multicultural German society.' The first address, to the Friedrich

Naumann Foundation conference, was entitled 'Pre-School Education for a Multicultural Society – The Toronto Experience.' The RAA (German Association of Regional Offices for Foreigners) federal working groups of the Freudenberg Foundation sponsored the second conference, held at the Canadian Embassy. This address concerned community education for a multicultural society. Although community education has been somewhat out of style recently, the Germans were most enthusiastic to learn more about our past history in community education and development in Toronto, which has been called the most multicultural city in the world. The Berlin experience was really the catalyst that made me decide to write this book.

In so doing, I have endeavoured to present a forty-year inventory of personal experiences, observations, process studies, policy and program initiatives, and alternative strategies in the fields of community education, community development, and community economic development. I have tried to merge these three fields together in a continuous change process to improve the quality of community life, particularly in our impoverished urban areas. The current term, sometimes used to describe this partnership of the commercial, governmental, and voluntary sectors, is *social enterprise.* I believe public schooling can have an essential role to play in promoting the cause of social enterprise. Social enterprise can be defined as a non-profit organization or venture that advances its social mission through entrepreneurial resource strategies.

In the last decade, public schooling and social welfare provisions have been devastated by a harsh and regressive neoconservative political agenda. I believe that a knowledge and appreciation of previous practices can be extremely important, as we continue to struggle to rediscover and renew a social and economic infrastructure that is desperately needed to confront the inequities to be found in our increasingly diverse society. A source of encouragement, however, might be found in such social enterprises as the Learnxs Foundation, the Learning Enrichment Foundation, and the Training Renewal Foundation. These non-profit charitable organizations have partnered with the commercial and governmental sectors to create new social and economic innovations in an attempt to address these inequities. The following chapters will explore, in particular, the origins of these voluntary organizations as part of an ongoing process of community education and development.

Toronto, Ontario, Canada   Dale E. Shuttleworth, PhD

Acknowledgments

During my career I have been privileged to have had a series of influential mentors, including Roy Giroux, Rudolf Helling, Father Neil Libby, Wilson Head, Whit Morris, Bill Quinn, James Draper, Ned McKeown, and John Phillips. I wish to thank the following colleagues and friends who helped in my research for this book: Duncan Green, Judith Jordan-Austin, Charlotte Maher, Elizabeth Hill, Bob Doyle, John Phillips, Rod McColl, Joan Milling, John Rennie, Elaine Vine, Scott Darrach, Rose DiVincenzo, Lesley Miller, Jack Quarter, Julie Mathien, and Ned McKeown. I wish to acknowledge the assistance of Greg McKinnon of the Toronto District School Board who provided access to archival material.

Most important has been the support of the directors of the Training Renewal Foundation: Steven Mould, Fritz Kugler, Larry Hebb, Judith Gabor, Angela Dozzi, Ari Dassanayake, Michele Leroux and Motoyo Kamiya. In particular, Larry Hebb gave invaluable advice and editorial guidance, for which I am very grateful. I also must pay tribute to my friend and colleague Murray Shukyn with whom I have worked since the 1970s. Finally, this book would not exist without the ongoing assistance, advice, encouragement, devotion, and wondrous word-processing skills of my wife, Marilyn Shuttleworth. It was truly a team effort all the way.

Introduction

In November 2008, Roy McMurtry, a former chief justice of Ontario and Progressive Conservative Attorney General, and Alvin Curling, a former Liberal Cabinet minister and Speaker of the Ontario legislature, delivered a report to the Ontario government on the roots of violence involving youth. This came as a result of the 2007 shooting death of a fifteen-year-old in the hallway of C.W. Jefferys Collegiate, which serves the Jane-Finch social housing area in northwest Toronto.

In their report McMurtry and Curling found that 'there is far too much poverty in Ontario and far too few services and supports for those struggling to get ahead.' The report went on to highlight concerns about high concentrations of poverty in certain housing areas; increased incidents of racism; unaddressed youth mental-health problems; a school system that is often unresponsive to the needs of at-risk youth; a lack of mentors for youth and of supports for families; failure to communicate, engage, and respect those of different backgrounds; and the absence of adequate recreation and economic opportunities for disadvantaged young people.

According to the Statistics Canada 2006 Census, Ontario's child poverty rate stands at almost 12 per cent. This means that 324,000 Ontario children – almost one in nine – are living in poverty. In November 2008, Campaign 2000, a national coalition of more than one hundred and twenty organizations, petitioned the Ontario and federal governments to invest in good jobs, higher social assistance rates, low-cost childcare, affordable housing, and better access to post-secondary education and training.

Both the McMurtry-Curling report and the Campaign 2000 petition were issued at a time when the economy was in danger of falling into a recession. How did we get to this state of crisis and despair?

In an attempt to find sources of innovation to address these concerns, I will explore in the following chapters a series of events and policies and programs implemented in the province of Ontario during the past four decades of social, political, and economic development. This exploration will include the following objectives:

1. **To provide a historic overview of events during the period from 1966 to 2006 in Ontario concerning the impact on public education of theory and practice in the fields of community education, community development, community economic development, and social enterprise creation.** This objective represents attempts to introduce to the prevailing traditional culture of institutional schooling the potential for learning opportunities beyond the classroom and the influence that this knowledge might have on the initiation of policies and programs that better reflect social, economic, and political realities.

2. **To provide a political insight into the decision making concerning policy and program development during the above events.** The nature of public education is a complex political process involving decisions of elected representatives at the local and provincial levels. These decisions may also be affected by the informal political influences that exist among parents, other taxpayers, advocacy and labour groups, and individuals who endeavour to shape the nature of public education to reflect their particular needs and interests.

3. **To describe the role of the internal change agent or social entrepreneur in influencing these events.** Those employed by school boards – teachers, administrators, and support staff – have traditionally been part of a top-down hierarchical model of organization insulated from the influences of the community at large. The introduction of a new class of personnel who work both sides of the school-community divide has challenged the nature of institutional schooling. New vocations bearing such titles as school-community worker, community liaison officer, outreach youth worker, and cooperative education teacher have introduced the theory and practice of community education and development as a source of change and innovation to the practice of public education.

4. **To provide a blueprint for social and economic renewal related to the current and future diverse challenges facing public education in the twenty-first century.** The decades from the late 1960s to the late 1990s tended to be a period of growth and innovation in public education. Barriers between school and community were lowered. Community resource learning was not only tolerated but encouraged. Business-education partnerships were forged to improve the relevancy of curricula and programs. The exploration of diverse learning styles and alternative programming to meet the needs of community learners was established. Policies and programs were introduced to better serve impoverished and at-risk children and youth.

A new government, with a neoconservative agenda, came to power in 1995. The result was a dismantling of many of the innovations realized in the previous decades as budgets were restricted and the performance of teachers and administrators was criticized. In the first decade of the twenty-first century, schools and communities now find themselves struggling with concerns of youth violence, child poverty, and race relations in an economy sliding into recession. An exploration of what was learned in the past four decades might provide a blueprint for public education as a vehicle for social, economic, and political renewal.

SCHOOLING FOR LIFE:
COMMUNITY EDUCATION AND SOCIAL ENTERPRISE

1 Embracing Diversity

Newcomers to This Place

According to the Statistics Canada 2006 Census, the City of Toronto has a population of more than 2.5 million, and the Greater Toronto Area about 5 million. The region receives about 110,000 international immigrants each year, the majority now coming from China, southern Asia, the Philippines, the Middle East, and Latin America. Within the next decade more than 50 per cent of Torontonians will be visible minorities.

Toronto has long embodied Canada's commitment to cultural pluralism through its services to immigrants, migrants, and refugees. In 1976, the Toronto Board of Education published a report entitled *We Are All Newcomers to This Place*.[1] Toronto was originally settled by our aboriginal people, who were followed later by the Europeans – first the French, next people from the British Isles, and after the American Revolution a group of dissenting refugees known as the United Empire Loyalists. At the time of the American Civil War, Toronto was a destination for escaped slaves from the south. Wars in Europe and elsewhere in the world have resulted in waves of migrants, immigrants, and refugees settling in Toronto. In the 1960s and 1970s thousands of Americans resisting the Vietnam War fled to Canada to escape military service. Many settled in Toronto, and their influence on the social and cultural environment was profound.

In the nineteenth and mid-twentieth century, newcomers were predominantly Europeans, arriving first from northern regions and later the southern Mediterranean. Beginning in the 1960s more people of colour, from former British colonies in the Caribbean, Africa, southern Asia, and Hong Kong, made up the new arrivals to Canada. Toronto, receiving 40 per cent of total immigration, has also been a refuge for refugees fleeing hunger and war.

In 1976, Canada's adopted a points system whereby people from any part of the world would be considered for immigration depending on their level of education, skills, and money to invest. Multicultural-ism was declared in 1971, giving all Canadians equality before the law, regardless of race, ethnic origin, language, or religion. The year 1985 saw passage of the *Canadian Multiculturalism Act*, recognizing the use of languages other than English or French and the freedom of those who wish to preserve and enhance their cultural heritage.

Social Investment

The decade of the 1960s was a period in the province of Ontario's his-tory of unparalleled personal affluence, when career expectations and concern for social well-being corresponded to a rise in the revenue received from taxation. Consequently, the Ontario government began to spend increasing portions of its budget in the social development areas of education, health, community and social services, and culture and recreation. The post-war baby boom created a further demand for greater commitment to public education as well as other forms of human service.

The decade also became a time of diversity in which to challenge traditional values and human rights and to experiment with different lifestyles and models of organization. Americans fleeing to Ontario to escape the Vietnam War draft often became strong social and political advocates for such changes. This unprecedented growth and experi-mentation had a profound influence on schools and other social institu-tions. Policies and programs were made more flexible. Greater concern was expressed for the needs and aspirations of the individual and the rights of minority groups. There was the beginning of a tendency to move away from traditional, institutional models of service in favour of more outreach, participative, and community-based approaches.

Spending Restraint

The early 1970s saw the height of public concern for more and better human services. However, it also was the beginning of a shift in pro-vincial government spending priorities away from social develop-ment toward more 'hard' services such as transportation, utilities, and energy creation. As a result, in the face of rising expectations, ceilings on spending were imposed, causing an increased sense of frustration and disillusionment among the human services. At about the same time, census data and population projections showed the start of a steady downswing in the birth rate. As most human services are funded on the basis of the numbers of persons served, an ominous message was being sent about the future vitality of the social development sector. In public education this message was often translated as the increased use of all available resources for the mere maintenance of existing services and as a decreased interest in the support of innovative or experimental programs.

Learning about Institutionalization

In the early 1960s I was an elementary school teacher in the town of Riverside, a suburb of Windsor, Ontario, having obtained an elementary teaching certificate after one year of study at a teachers' college. In the evening and summers I studied for an undergraduate degree at Assumption University, majoring in applied sociology as pioneered by a German immigrant, Professor Rudolf Helling. His approach differed from the theoretical approach favoured by most Canadian universities at that time. Dr Helling encouraged me to involve myself in experiential learning, including original research in the field. I can remember taking field trips to the Detroit House of Correction and to Jackson State Prison in Michigan during my course in the sociology of deviant behaviour.

One of my service learning assignments consisted of more than a year's volunteer work at St Leonard's, Canada's first halfway house for ex-prisoners, which was in the process of being founded (much to the dismay of area residents) by Father Neil Libby, an Anglican priest. My job as a volunteer was to be a friend to those who had recently been paroled from prison into St Leonard's. I soon discovered that there were only two types of people in their world: the 'squares' and the 'rounders.' Needless to say, I never did achieve the status of a rounder.

I will always remember watching television one evening with Bob, a grade-seven dropout who had the gift of the gab. He pointed across the living room at Jake, a newcomer to the house. 'See Jake?' he said. 'He ain't gonna make it.' 'How do you know?' I asked. 'He's just too institutionalized,' said Bob with conviction. Sure enough, Jake returned to prison about two weeks later after trying to rob a confectionery store. Bob maintained that prison was the only place where Jake had a sense of identity and felt secure. The outside world had become a pretty frightening and confusing place for Jake. It was then that I began to understand the nature of institutionalization. Both Jake's prison and my elementary school had something in common: they were top-down custodial institutions with a strong commitment to external control and a culture that encouraged dependency. I also began to ponder the question of whose needs were really being served in such institutions.[2]

Schools as Institutions

For most of the twentieth century, institutional schooling seemed to be more involved with the manipulation of buildings, administrative structures, human timetables, and programmed teaching aids than with a real concern for the encouragement of learning as a basic life skill. For example, teacher training programs traditionally concentrated on pedagogy as a technical, custodial process related to classroom management rather than on developing an overview of the teacher as an encourager of lifelong learning through the provision of information, attitudes, and enquiry skills. I recall my first day in the Classroom Management class in 1959 at London Teachers' College. The master entered the room with a yardstick, which he slammed down with a loud bang. 'Have I got your attention?' he shouted. 'Remember, don't smile until Christmas. To be a successful teacher you must learn to control the class.'

Educational philosopher John Dewey has identified two conflicting aims for modern education: 'the first would be to preserve the status quo; the second to act as a preparatory system for social change.'[3] It is my belief that the former has shaped our actual behaviour while the latter has fuelled the rhetoric of countless reformers but has been seldom practised by educators – the preservationists versus the anticipators.

The justification for teacher as technician has been the provision of basic literacy (for example, the three Rs) as preparation for the needs of the economic system. In other words, formal schooling provides the only legitimate pathway to maturity and fulfilment. The flaws in this assumption emerge when the overall level of schooling rises while the economy fails to keep pace by providing meaningful employment or indeed enough jobs of any kind to go around. What then is the role of public education? If it is no longer purely a preparatory system for the economy, is it then a holding system to keep people out of an overburdened underproductive work force?

It is my belief that the impending challenge to our civilization will not be how to cope with the future shock of a rapidly developing technology of material abundance but, rather, how to live with less. The pre-eminence of institutional schooling, either as a form of moral suasion to inculcate the masses in the age-old values or as a human assembly line feeding the economy, must give way to the learning needs of individuals struggling to reorient their lifestyles. This reordering of priorities will produce the most profound sense of change our society has experienced since the Great Depression.

Agents of Change

I believe that our present system of schooling by technician must give way to a new concept of teacher as change agent. This person will continue to stress literacy as a basic life skill, a fundamental on which to build patterns of lifelong learning. However, other basic skills must include cooperative problem solving, social and emotional fulfilment, and the ability to identify, analyse, develop, and use resources as part of a process of learning to cope with continuous change. As stated in article 26 of the United Nations Universal Declaration of Human Rights, 'education shall be directed to the full development of the human personality and to the strengthening of respect for human rights and fundamental freedoms.' But change is a political process. The teacher as change agent must learn the political skills of survival.

The current institutional structures and attitudes on which schooling is based seem incapable of adequately delivering basic life skills to learners as individuals or in groups. These structures are largely dependent upon previous practice and pre-packaged materials, which do not reflect the realities of the life space in which we live. For example, if a key issue in today's learning environment is understanding how to combat a growing sense of racism, the answers will not be found by sending directives to the teachers to be more multicultural in their attitudes or by sprinkling a few ethnic stereotypes among the basal readers. The state of current structures is a concern so vital to our future that we must seek answers in the dynamics of our day-to-day interpersonal relationships if teachers are to be agents of change in an increasingly diverse society. However, social diversity is not limited to race, religion, or culture; it also encompasses differences in learning styles, beliefs, patterns of thought, gender, sexuality, and the ways we deal with change.

Community Education and Development

The alternatives movement in public education has identified some of these concerns and has begun to experiment with a variety of strategies, which may ultimately transform institutional schooling and teacher behaviour. Educational theorists, such as Mario Fantini, have seen this movement as 'a lifeline to the future for a system of human service, which has become stagnant, no longer accountable to the needs of the people it professes to serve.'[4]

One such theory of innovative exploration has been *community education and development*, which stresses 'a cooperative outreach approach to better utilize community and public education resources to produce a more relevant and vital learning experience for persons of all ages.' This concept was not to be confined just to institutional schooling; it cuts across formal organizational lines to encompass the fields of library science, health, recreation, social service, cultural affairs, and economic development, including the voluntary sectors of citizen participation. Elements of this general theory are to found in a series of demonstration projects, policy statements, and programs that have emerged during the period from the 1960s to the 2000s. An objective of this book will be to reflect on my own personal experiences as a social entrepreneur in a quest to introduce the processes of community education, community development, and community economic development – basic elements of social enterprise – to change the traditional nature of public schooling as it struggles to respond to the needs of an increasingly diverse society. This is not a theoretical analysis but rather a historical overview of the events over four decades that influenced the creation of original policies and programs in these fields of endeavour. In the 1960s, as Canada's first school-community worker serving the Lawrence Heights housing project in North York, I discovered the meaning of institutional poverty, while attempting to meet the diverse needs of children, youth, parents, teachers, and other human-service personnel in a challenging, socially and economically disadvantaged area.

In the 1970s, as a result of the Lawrence Heights experience, I found myself in Toronto immersed in the politics of education as part of a special task force on inner-city schooling, which explored the process of how decisions are reached and changes implemented in a complex and politically charged urban environment. Consequently, a series of new policies and programs was created in such fields as urban and compensatory education; community use of space and school-based childcare;

multicultural education and race relations; community resource learning and alternatives in education; cooperative education and youth employment; community education; and social enterprise.

The Toronto experience provided a foundation for my work in the next two decades as a school superintendent in the Borough of York (later known as the City of York) where school-community relations, adult and continuing education, community economic development, and business-education partnerships were added to the inventory. From 1995 to 2008 my original work developing such innovations as the Learnxs Foundation and the Learning Enrichment Foundation resulted in the Training Renewal Foundation, a new social enterprise to serve the training and employment needs of at-risk youth, social assistance recipients, immigrants, and refugees.

2 Education for Community Living

Community as Classroom

In the early 1960s a rather inexperienced teacher undertook a learning project with his grade-seven class concerning the economy of Essex County in south-western Ontario. Of particular interest was the fact that this area had once been the bed of a great inland sea, resulting in a flat topography and a rich sandy loam ideally suited for agriculture. In addition, the comparatively mild climate in this southern-most section of Canada supported the establishment of a large greenhouse industry capable of producing market vegetables in the winter months.

The best way to illustrate these features to the students, it seemed, was to organize a field trip by bus along Highway 3 to the town of Leamington. Besides passing through the heart of farming country, the route included the village of Ruthven, which was the highest point in the county, overlooking the aforementioned greenhouses and affording a view of the Lake Erie shoreline to the south. The final destination would be the food-processing plant of H.J. Heinz, the major employer in Leamington. School-board officials, however, did not meet this proposal with much enthusiasm. Such a long trip (thirty miles) was seen as particularly risky from a student safety standpoint. How could one ensure adequate supervision? There was no money in the budget to hire a bus. Besides, such an excursion was of questionable educational value, anyway. After considerable debate and much dogged determination on the part of the teacher, permission was finally granted with the following provisos: (1) the cost of hiring the bus was to be met by students and their parents; (2) another class and its teacher were to go along to ensure more supervision; and (3) the teacher who organized the trip was to be held responsible for the safety and well-being of all concerned. The field trip, as a learning experience, was a resounding success, but it left the teacher feeling rather disillusioned at the prospect of any further field trips.

I was that teacher, and over the intervening years I have witnessed a great transformation of curriculum and program priorities. Teachers in some jurisdictions are now expected to participate with their classes in a certain number of field trips each year and to encourage small groups and individual students to use out-of-school learning resources. What caused this transformation of attitudes and learning styles? How and by whom was this change of philosophy being implemented? What would the future bring?

The late 1960s and early 1970s in Ontario saw the beginning of a radical shift in public education policies away from a tradition of centralized curriculum development and regimentation in classroom management toward a new emphasis on decentralization and flexibility to meet the individual needs of students. A series of reports and guidelines were issued, beginning in 1968 with the Hall-Dennis Report[5] in the elementary field which proposed a more child-centred approach, stressing learning activities, continuous progress, and social development skills. Its counterpart at the secondary level, in 1972–3, was the HS 1 curriculum credit system,[6] which allowed each student to choose part of his or her own program from a variety of courses offered by the local school. In 1972 the Commission on Post-secondary Education[7] in turn envisioned a much more open access to educational opportunities for adult learners. Although the overall intent of these guidelines and recommendations has never been fully realized, they were most influential in shaping education in the early to mid-1970s and beyond.

The changes coincided with a dramatic increase in the school population as a result of the post-war baby boom. Many schools, as a way of accommodating increased numbers of students, saw a liberalizing of the curriculum and a broadening of educational opportunities. This spirit of reform, however, was not met with universal acclaim across the province of Ontario. Many teachers and parents did not appreciate the need for such changes. Little time had been spent in communicating with the public or in developing a process to assist teachers in adopting the changes. Discontent focused on a fear that academic standards were being lowered and that basic skills were not being taught. The back-to-the-basics movement, which continues to be a major political issue, is an outcome of this lack of adequate communication and preparation for change.

One aspect of the liberalization of curriculum and program has been a greater emphasis on *out-of-school learning* for individuals and groups. This approach has really addressed itself to two areas: a concern for the relevancy of curriculum materials and sources of information, and a recognition that learners may respond to a variety of learning styles including small-group activities and self-directed methods.

Community Resource Learning

Consequently I have viewed learning as one or more personal experiences that shape the perception of reality and strengthen the ability to absorb or reject information as it affects the personal need for growth and fulfilment. Education is seen as an organization of these learning experiences into some systematic pattern in order to achieve certain preconceived goals or results. Such organization can be carried out by either a single individual relating to a need for personal development or a group process influenced by an external force (for example, a teacher, group leader, school, or agency).

People, places, and organizations that surround the individual learner or the educational facility are seen as potential sources of enrichment for the learning experience. The *Dictionary of Education* provides this definition of a practice in education that uses learning resources in the community: 'a reality-centred concept of education which assumes that the learning process is given vitality by the utilization of community resources in the education program.'[8]

Most twentieth-century authors who wrote about the community learning resources concept emphasized its effects on students and schools. One of the most profound influences on the growth and direction of public education has been John Dewey. In his widely read text *The School and Society* he condemned the institutional school of the nineteenth century for its sense of isolation from the social, economic, and physical realities of life experience.[9]

The Community School

Dewey's writings on elementary education stressed the need for concrete examples of life experience as a source of motivation in institutional schooling. One educator who was strongly influenced by Dewey was Edward Olsen. As an advocate of the community school approach, Olsen proposed five goals for a school offering life-centred education:

1. Operate as an educational centre for adults.
2. Utilize community resources to invigorate the conventional program.
3. Centre the curriculum in a study of community structure, processes, and problems.
4. Improve the community through participation in its activities.
5. Lead in coordinating the educative efforts of the community.[10]

Olsen merged the life-experience philosophy of Dewey with his own model of the ideal school. His *community school* model was not the inward-looking educational clinic, which had been the tradition, but rather a facility that gets involved in quality-of-life issues. Olsen's model dealt with the basic aims of community education by proposing an organizational structure that would focus on community needs, identify and mobilize resources in school and community to satisfy these needs, and serve as a learning centre for people of all ages to acquire the necessary information and skills for community problem solving.

Community Education

Community education is a process, which is most difficult to define as it covers such a wide spectrum of belief. Jack Minzey, in an article entitled 'Community Education: An Amalgam of Many Views,' provided this definition:

> An educational philosophy, which has concern for all aspects of community life. It advocates greater use of all facilities in the community, especially school buildings, which ordinarily lie idle so much of the time. It has concern for the traditional school program, seeking to expand all types of activities for school-age children to additional hours of the day, week and year. It also seeks to make the educational program more relevant by bringing the community into the classroom and taking the classroom into the community. It includes equal educational opportunities for adults in all areas of education: academic, recreational, vocational, avocational and social. It is the identification of community resources and the coordination of these resources to attack community problems. And finally, it is the organization of communities on a local level so that representative groups can establish two-way communication, work on community problems,

develop community power and work toward developing that community into the best it is capable of becoming.[11]

It is curious that while the literal meaning of *community education* would be 'education in the community,' the definition has been extended to a whole range of issues with a strong emphasis on the utilization of school buildings. It does, however, speak of relevancy by bringing the classroom into the community. It also refers to the identification of community resources to attack community problems.

I propose the following working definition for community education: an approach to education that advocates the identification and utilization of human, physical, and organizational resources in the community to enhance the learning process and to respond effectively to human needs in order to improve the quality of both personal and community life.

Community Development Process

William W. Biddle and Loureide J. Biddle defined community as 'whatever sense of common good people can achieve.'[12] Their approach to social change involved a *community development* process. Community development was defined as 'a process of social action in which the people of a community organize themselves for planning and action; define their common and individual needs and problems; execute these plans with a maximum reliance on community resources; and supplement these resources when necessary with services and materials from governmental and non-governmental agencies outside the community.'[13] According to Biddle and Biddle, the community development process refers to 'a progression of events that is planned by the participants to serve goals they progressively choose. The events point to changes in a group and in individuals that can be termed growth in social sensitivity and competence.'

Responsibility for the process may rest upon just one person or upon several. Biddle and Biddle referred to the role of the *community developer* as a special type of political change agent who encourages indigenous participant growth, using the demonstration project as a change mechanism.

Organizational Interdependence

Using Biddle and Biddle's theories, I designed a process model for organization interdependence between governmental and non-govern-mental organizations in the interests of common overall goals.[14] The major stages are as follows:

Stage 1: Identification. A particular need or problem is identified that relates to both public education sectors (that is, governmental) and community interest sectors (for example, non-governmental). A group of public educators and community people meet informally to further define the need. (This could be initiated from either the public educa-tion or the community interest side). Out of these informal meetings emerges a sense of commitment to alleviate the need or to solve the problem. A joint work group of committed persons with a variety of interests and skills is established.

Stage 2: Exploration. One or more persons within the work group assume the role of encourager or community developer. Surveys (for example, interviews, questionnaires, informal meetings, and data search) are undertaken to clarify needs, collect ideas, and further identify potential resources (for example, influence leaders, volun-teer workers, seconded personnel, funds, goods, and services) among organizations and individuals within the public education and com-munity sectors. Proposed alternatives and volunteers are appraised, and needs, ideas, and potential resources are documented.

Stage 3: Formulation. The first draft of the project proposal, includ-ing an implementation schedule and an evaluative design, is prepared for discussion within the work group. As a result of these discussions the first draft is revised, usually more than once. Through consultation with selected influence leaders in public education and the community at large, a tentative proposal is prepared and submitted to the work group for consideration. The work group then approves a final pro-posal as a basis of submission to support sources.

Stage 4: Application. The work group approaches a variety of pos-sible enablers in both the governmental and the non-governmental sectors to create a support environment and to assess their degree of potential involvement (for example, boards of education, municipal councils, federal and provincial governments, foundations, service clubs, and community organizations). On the basis of this survey the final proposal is restructured to reflect different types of emphasis and application procedures. Formal applications are submitted to sources of single and shared funding and other means of support (such as goods and services).

Stage 5: Promotion. Informal promotional activity is undertaken to organize support for the applications among decision makers and influence leaders. This promotional activity might also be formalized through the establishment of, or referral to, an ongoing support organization, which could take the form of a non-profit charitable foundation with the legal status required to receive funds (and/or goods and services) and issue tax-credit receipts to donors. Smaller grants received might be used to form the basis (that is, upfront money) of new applications to other sources that only provide support through matching funds.

Stage 6: Implementation. An adequate level of support (short or long term) is received to begin to implement the proposal in its final form. At this point the original work group might disband to be replaced by a task group or a steering committee of influence leaders and resource persons who would guide, support, and evaluate the implementation of the proposal as an ongoing project.

Stage 7: Evaluation. Evaluation of the project according to its original objectives would be undertaken through the evaluation process and/or participant observation. This could result in the reassessment and redefinition of the original objectives and sources of support for the project (for example, action research design).[i]

Stage 8: Continuation. As a result of the evaluation procedures and/or spin-off activities from the original project, new needs might be identified, and the process model as described above would repeat itself.

The concepts of community resource learning, the community school, community education, and development and organizational interdependence will provide the theoretical framework to develop partnerships in support of education as a focus for social enterprise and economic renewal.

---

i Action research is an ongoing study of a social process and its results where accumulated findings are used to guide and correct the decisions of the continuing process.

3 Learning in the Heights

Housing the Poor

Low-income migrants, immigrants, and refugees are often drawn to an inner city in search of relatively inexpensive accommodations that will accept children. They usually find crowded conditions, shared facilities, exorbitant rents, and indifferent landlords. What is anticipated to be a short transitional period while one finds a job and gets to know the city becomes a prolonged reality of failure and suffering. As so-called urban renewal takes place, even these humble dwellings are knocked down to be replaced by commercial development or high-rise apartments whose opulence, limited space, and astronomical rents are hardly designed for the people they so rudely displace.

In an attempt to solve this problem, urban planners have embraced the concept of public or social housing where large low-income projects are constructed and their rent subsidized by the government. Some such developments have been built in the inner city, but they have often been only modern reproductions of the type of housing they supplanted. While there may be some decrease in horizontal crowding, it is replaced by vertical, sterile columns of concentrated humanity. Land in the inner city has become so valuable that this type of housing is the only economical use of space. While better shelter has undoubtedly been provided, one wonders whether there has been any attempt to alleviate the social problems inherent in slum living, or one type of socio-economic ghetto has just been exchanged for another.

One attempt to find a solution to this problem is to relocate inner-city and other low-income families to housing developments in the suburbs. Crowding is not such a problem there, and the attitude has been that the access to more advantaged groups might allow these people to see 'the error of their ways' and aspire to be more middle class, a way station in the process of upward social mobility. There are other advantages to relocation: vacant land is cheaper and more available in the suburbs; existing inner-city units that were poorly designed or uneconomical may be bought at a good price; unattractive slum conditions in the inner city can be cleansed in favour of more functional and profitable edifices; inner-city services once saddled with the dependency of the poor can now share the burden with their more affluent neighbours.

The disadvantages of this largely economic solution to the problems of low-income housing have also been dramatic. The solvent suburbanites have not looked kindly on the intrusion of these 'welfare people' into the symbols of their success and consider that the behaviour required to survive in the poverty subculture hardly has a place in the quiet neighbourhoods, schools, hospitals, shopping plazas, recreation centres, and churches of the proponents of the puritan ethic. Social service workers, educators, receptionists, police officers, librarians, and medical personnel may be hard pressed to understand their own roles in this changing environment. Planners and developers who have attempted to use housing as a means of cultural integration are now faced with the reality that they may have created islands of institutionalized poverty in a suburban sea.

The Lawrence Heights Experience

In the fall of 1965, I left my position as a grade-seven teacher with the Riverside Board of Education to accept a job as a teacher-counsellor at Flemington Road Public School, which serves the Lawrence Heights community in the Metropolitan Toronto municipality of North York. I went from a school governed by a school board with about sixty elementary teachers to a school with more than sixty teachers on staff from junior kindergarten to grade six. I am sure I was hired because I had taken a course in social service techniques towards my bachelor of arts degree at Assumption University. My professor had been Dr Wilson Head, a part-time lecturer who was also research director for United Appeal in Windsor. A black educator, born and raised in the American south, he became a mentor and a source of inspiration to my future career.

The Lawrence Heights low-income housing development was created in 1957 as a discreetly concealed public housing enclave in Metropolitan Toronto. Constructed at the crossroads of Lawrence Avenue and the Spadina Expressway (now Allen Road), this community should be considered a segregated geographic unit. Patterns of access from within the community to the surrounding neighbourhood were limited by physical barriers: to the north, a major thoroughfare; to the south, the institutional buildings along the north side of Lawrence Avenue; to the west and east, a fence containing the project population from the neighbouring single-family dwellings of a middle-class, predominantly Jewish community. The Spadina Expressway divided the project into two fairly equal areas. There were only four routes of access into the community: two from the north, and two from the south.[15]

All housing was rented and administered by the Ontario Housing Corporation. Rent was set at approximately one-third of a family's monthly income. Admission was restricted to low-income families, depending upon priority of need. There were 1,081 units, including one- to three-bedroom walk-up apartments and three- to five-bedroom row or semi-detached units. The low-rise nature of the community could be attributed to the fact that it was on the glide path to the Downsview airbase.

The total population of the development was about five thousand persons, three thousand of whom were school-age children and preschoolers. Many of the families had been relocated from substandard housing in the city's inner core, often on an emergency basis. Almost 30 per cent of the families were one-parent (mother) led. The families receiving social welfare financial assistance ranged from 20 per cent to 40 per cent depending upon economic conditions.

The family problems found here were no different from those that could be found throughout Toronto, but they were more highly concentrated due to geographic segregation and population density. For some families the major struggle was for survival because of their low income and the resulting burdens of debt and other accumulative family problems. A large number of families came from the inner-city slum areas. Some were recent immigrants or migrants from Atlantic Canada in particular. Although their housing problems had been solved, new problems were created as a result of the loss of such amenities as familiar neighbourhoods, second-hand stores, a corner pub, and easy access to hospital clinics. The Conroy Hotel near the development once had the largest draught-beer gallonage sold in Canada. Some complaints, which also came from within the community, were that 'children are allowed to run wild, parents do not care about their children, or families on welfare spend their money on drink.'[16]

Those inhabiting the neighbouring residential area and those service and trades people visiting the community most often conveyed a negative image of the project. Such terms as *the jungle, poverty village,* and *the camp* were commonly used. This stigma hurt personal pride, made residents feel inferior, and produced the depressing feelings of hopelessness that are common attributes of alienation.

Flemington Road Public School

Not only was Lawrence Heights the first low-income public housing area to be built in a Canadian suburban setting, but Flemington Road Public School was the first school to serve such an area exclusively. It grew with the community, reaching an enrolment of almost 1,300 students by 1967, in junior kindergarten to grade six, plus special education classes.

During the late 1960s Flemington Road was transformed from a traditional, status quo institution into a thriving experiment in compensatory education designed to break down the barriers between school and community. Throughout this crucial developmental period the school was fortunate to have a most outstanding principal in the person of W.K. 'Whit' Morris. Mr Morris had participated in a study group organized by the Ford Foundation, which toured inner-city schools in the United States to learn about education for the 'culturally deprived.' At the time, it was felt that inner-city children suffered from cultural deprivation because they lacked the cultural amenities afforded middle-class children – especially access to reading materials and a stable home environment. The term *compensatory education* was coined to describe programs introduced to compensate for these deficiencies.

Whit Morris petitioned the North York Board of Education for additional resources to support a demonstration project in compensatory education. As a result, additional staff members were allocated to the school, including the services of a reading-improvement teacher, a special adjustment teacher, a teacher-counsellor, and two vice-principals with extensive experience in educating slower-learning children. In addition, Flemington Road housed a full-time dentist, a dental assistant, and a public health nurse, Evelyn McKelvie. The National Council of Jewish Women, led by Marilyn Gross, provided classroom volunteers at the primary level and, at their council centre, a preschool enrichment program for mothers and children.

Role of the Teacher-Counsellor

When I joined the staff at Flemington Road in the fall of 1965, the role of *teacher-counsellor* was described as follows: 'This person is a resident staff member serving Flemington Road Public School and the Lawrence Heights community exclusively. He provides a counselling and consultant service to members of the teaching staff who seek his aid; is called upon to organize in-service training related to his area of specialization: interprets school policy and educational techniques to parents and the public; carries a constant case load which must be served on a continuing basis; and frequently fulfils a liaison and public relations role.'[17]

Problems of low status and self-esteem among residents, which plagued Lawrence Heights from the beginning, were in some respects also the problem of the teachers in relating to their professional community ('Oh no, you're not going *there* to teach!'). Consequently, there was a constant turnover of teachers. Of eight beginning teachers hired in September, say, at least four would have left by Christmastime.

Besides the challenges of teaching literacy and numeracy, teachers had to cope with disruptive behaviour and social and emotional problems in the classroom. It was my belief that before the three Rs (reading, 'riting, and 'rithmetic) could be relevant, the three Ss of shelter (housing, clothing, et cetera), sustenance (nutrition), and social and emotional well-being had to be met.

The mental health of teachers was an ongoing concern of the principal. During the late sixties there was an average of one suicide attempt among teachers per year (one of which was successful). Because the principal and vice-principals were seen as line evaluators, Mr Morris would refer teachers experiencing mental health problems to the teacher-counsellor for non-threatening and confidential social and emotional support. I had to learn to be a good listener, and in addition to ongoing counselling assistance and referrals I developed a series of professional development activities for Flemington Road teachers.

Professional Development

I believed that it was essential for teachers in a disadvantaged area to have a thorough knowledge of the cultural background and lifestyle of the community that they served. This seemed a definite prerequisite in developing a meaningful curriculum that reflected the needs of students and parents. At Flemington Road we experimented with several different approaches to the problem. One of the first involved school and community seminars where discussions were led by workers from other agencies serving the community (for example, Children's Aid Society, the North York Department of Welfare, Big Brothers, the Juvenile and Family Court, and the School of Social Work). While this resulted in a kind of academic understanding, some of these people reinforced the detached attitude of the dominant culture. Another approach saw small groups of teachers visiting selected homes, accompanied by a social worker. While this was an improvement and offered insights into the physical environment, it was also an artificial and almost patronizing exercise.

A breakthrough came when we started to use parents as group leaders and resource persons, under the assumption that no one knows poverty as well as someone who lives it. Not only did a much more relaxed and informal atmosphere develop, but also the group leaders found a feeling of importance and fulfilment. Out of this experience grew the whole coffee-party movement. One mother, Barbara Aoki, began by holding a number of coffee parties in her home in the evenings and inviting teachers and parents. Later, other parents hosted similar get-togethers involving their neighbours and teachers from several of the schools serving Lawrence Heights. General discussions were held related to the school and the community. Some parents who never visited the school soon became active participants in coffee parties. A new sense of human awareness emerged in both groups.

For many residents, the coffee parties served as a springboard for involvement in a variety of community betterment projects. For the teachers, a new, more positive community image was projected, which resulted in more interest in home visits. Representatives of other community agencies and politicians soon attended as observers, and a new model of communication based more on humanity than on status began to emerge.

Therapeutic Services

The child with a problem in the socio-emotional area has always been of critical concern to education. In any school there are gifted teachers who possibly provide the best treatment available anywhere; however, too often schools have chosen to avoid responsibility for these children by declaring them unmanageable and forcing them out of the school, hopefully into some sort of treatment program. Unfortunately, because of the serious shortage of appropriate mental health services for children, their treatment could be anything from perpetual home instruction to a training school for juvenile offenders.

The disturbed child from a lower socio-economic background has a particular problem. Not only must he adjust to the school environment, but also, and perhaps more important, consideration must be given to his relationships with adults and peers at home and in the community. The conflict comes when the dominant culture, which shapes the treatment program, is at variance with the community subculture.

A prime responsibility of the teacher-counsellor was to provide therapeutic services for children experiencing social and emotional problems. I developed a behavioural checklist, which was distributed to teachers who then referred students to me for counselling. About 10 per cent of the students at Flemington Road were identified as experiencing behavioural problems in the classroom or schoolyard. Many boys were also involved in theft, vandalism, and acts of violence in the community, which resulted in police charges and appearances in juvenile court. Due to a lack of after-school activities, older (often 'latchkey') children gravitated to the nearby Yorkdale Plaza (Canada's first indoor shopping mall), where they might be arrested for shoplifting.

At first, I tried to work with teacher referrals by using Carl Rogers' non-directive approach, but it often proved ineffective because many children were non-verbal, at least initially. It was only after I adopted an activity-based approach (for example, model building, puppetry, and games) that some sort of rapport could be established.

Home Visiting

Another of my responsibilities was to visit the homes of Flemington Road students. This was of importance for parents who would not or were not able to come to the school, owing to disabilities or childcare issues. Some parents saw schools as a symbol of authority or a painful reminder of their own lack of success in the academic world.

I also served as the school's attendance officer. I recall one situation where Molly, a grade-six student, was missing a great deal of school time. When she did attend, she was often very withdrawn and non-responsive. I spoke to our public health nurse in order to get some background on the family before my visit; Mrs McKelvie was a vital source of information about the needs of area residents and an invaluable support to me in my work. It turned out that Molly's mother was a single parent and a holocaust survivor who was experiencing mental health problems. She was originally from Poland, and her English was limited. When I arrived for a visit, Molly's apartment was in disarray, with chunks of plaster missing from the walls. When I questioned Molly, she said that her mother often threw knives into the walls of the apartment. She also said that her mother would send her off to school in the morning, then chase her in the street, and drag her back into the apartment.

Needless to say, I was most concerned about Molly's safety and approached the Children's Aid Society to see if she could be taken into care for her own protection. They said that they had no accommodations in their group homes or treatment facilities. My only option was to have Molly's mother charged with failure to compel her daughter to attend school. When the case was heard in juvenile and family court, the judge asked the Children's Aid Society to find a treatment setting for Molly. After some consultation they came back and said that it was not possible. At this point the exasperated judge replied, 'I order you to take this child into care.' Molly was admitted to the Browndale treatment facility, where she was found to suffer from serious mental health problems that required long-term care. I felt more than a little disheartened and apprehensive because Molly's mother was now alone and, I am sure, blamed me for the loss of her daughter. I hoped that she would get the treatment she obviously needed, but remembering her fixation with knives, I kept looking over my shoulder during yard duty.

Lawrence Heights Family and Child Services

One innovation to improve relations between the school and community service agencies was the creation of Lawrence Heights Family and Child Services, a joint venture of the Family Service Association and the Children's Aid Society. The new agency, located in a small plaza adjacent to the school, attributed its inception to the active role assumed by the school in the Lawrence Heights community.[16]

Social Development Groups

Activity Group Therapy was conceived and developed in the United States by S.R. Slavson. It utilized a distinctly permissive atmosphere to provide a healing, corrective, and maturing experience for personally disturbed and socially maladjusted children. Small groups of five to eight members met weekly for two-hour sessions in a simply furnished meeting room where a variety of arts and crafts materials, tools, and group games were available. In an attempt to find a better method to serve Flemington Road students, I visited agencies in Detroit (Michigan) and Windsor (Ontario) who were offering the program in school settings.

Utilizing the Slavson model and with assistance from our school psychologist, Dr Birute Januskevicius, I introduced *social development groups* as a form of preventive therapy for boys, with emphasis on activity in order to develop non-verbal and verbal skills geared to the lifestyle and subcultural traits of the community. Therapeutic interaction was created through a kind of primary peer group relationship of balanced personality types (for example, two aggressives, two withdrawns, and two isolates). From the beginning, group members learned planning and decision-making skills that were directly relevant to their life space. The emphasis was on identity, for experience had shown that all these children suffered from an inadequate self-image, which had caused them to choose negative pathways of expression leading to a failure identity. The social development group was a form of educational experience where a child received support in developing skills, which led ultimately to better social adjustment and a more successful identity for the child in the environment and subculture in which he or she was forced to live.[18]

Owing to the very limited space at Flemington Road, group meetings were held in a tiny storage room under a stairwell on the way to the boiler room. Activities included model building, clay modelling, puppetry, role-playing games, and visits to the gym for more active games. Field trips consisted of hiking in the neighbourhood as well as excursions by car to museums (such as the Ontario Science Centre) and parklands (including the Toronto Islands and the Board of Education's outdoor education facility).

Group solidarity was encouraged, and those showing withdrawn behaviour learned to interact positively with those having an aggressive personality. The aggressives developed more self-control from their interaction with the withdrawns, who were often victims of bullying in the schoolyard. The isolates learned social skills from the other personalities and a sense of belonging, often for the first time. Group identity became a very important therapeutic component. At any given time, four boys' groups were in operation at both the primary and junior levels, involving twenty-four participants.

A particular group excursion to Centre Island was memorable. After a ferryboat ride across the harbour we soon arrived at the lush green island park with its animal farm and small collection of amusement rides. Charley, a grade-six student and an aggressive, was known for his violent hyperactive outbursts. (On a previous field trip, to the Ontario Science Centre, we lost Charley, and one of the volunteer fathers found him sitting belligerently, twenty feet in the air, atop Miss Supertest, Canada's famous hydroplane. He certainly craved attention.) In the days before the Island trip Charley had been pestering me for the promise of a canoe ride; finally he wore me down, and I agreed that this might be one of our activities. I then quickly forgot about it, but Charley did not. When we reached the lagoon where canoes could be rented, he demanded that I honour my promise – an issue of trust.

I knew virtually nothing about canoes but hoped that Charley did. After donning life preservers we set out, paddling awkwardly. When we reached the middle of the small lagoon, I noticed that Charley had turned rather pale and seemed to be shaking with fear. 'How do you like canoeing?' I asked. 'I ... I've never been in a canoe in my whole life!' gasped Charley. 'Please don't stand up,' said I. I had never seen him so quiet and attentive. We really had to trust each other. By the time we returned safely to land, a new sense of mutual rapport had emerged between Charley and me.

Special Adjustment Centre

To complement individual counselling services and social development groups a new resource was created: the Special Adjustment Centre, located in a small tutorial room that was equipped with study carrels and a variety of learning materials. The individual in charge of its operation could perhaps best be referred to as a crisis teacher. To be effective, a crisis teacher had to be experienced, familiar with the curriculum for the school level served, and knowledgeable of the scope and range of individual differences in exceptional children. A good teacher who was provided with ample facilities and time was not sufficient. Much more was demanded of a person placed in such a position. Humanistic awareness and sensitivity to the feelings and needs of troubled children were primary requisites. A crisis teacher had to be capable of accepting these pupils as they were, and possess the ability and skill to maintain a consistent attitude and atmosphere.

The classroom teacher, with the approval of a member of the administration, decided who would visit the Special Adjustment Centre. Children were never the decision makers where the centre was concerned. When a child's behaviour was deemed to be too disruptive to the learning environment, the teacher could request that the teacher-counsellor or an administrator remove the child for placement in the centre. Children removed from the classroom often expressed violent behaviour (such as kicking, biting, and swearing) and had to be physically restrained until they regained self-control. In fact, most children who visited the centre did so because of disturbing or aggressive behaviour. Each child was dealt with on an individual basis dependent upon the source and nature of the immediate problem, the age, the emotional state, and the frequency of previous visits.

A sincere attempt was made to maintain an atmosphere of quiet control. All children who visited the centre were exposed to an attitude of firm kindness. They were neither punished nor pampered. Usually the children were assigned writing work that was supervised, marked upon completion, and then returned for correction. It was always explained individually to the children that they did not belong in the Special Adjustment Centre and that their proper place was in the classroom with the teacher, who was concerned about their academic progress and correct social behaviour. An attempt was also made to help the children realize that it was their duty, as members of a class, to cooperate to the fullest extent so that the teacher could teach and the other children learn. Many approaches were tried in an effort to reintegrate the child into the class as quickly as possible. In some instances this could be done after a short time, whereas in others it involved a much longer period.

The Special Adjustment Centre was not a remedy for classroom problems or social maladjustment. It was hoped that it was, however, a teacher-pupil aid that could be used to relieve teachers in times of stress and prevent a difficult situation from becoming worse. It was also hoped that the centre would help the children who visited it to gradually develop a degree of inner control that could be used to prevent the recurrence of similar problems. Not only was an improved academic climate maintained in classrooms and throughout the school, but also a sincere effort was made to provide a therapeutic environment for troubled children.

The Social Services Project

In 1966 the role of teacher-counsellor was expanded, and a new position of chairman of social services was created. There had been an established need for a person on staff at Flemington Road Public School who combined both teaching experience and training in the social sciences, notably social work, and this position had borne the classification of teacher-counsellor. However, the position had evolved to a point where distinct differences had arisen, such that the former classification had become somewhat ambiguous.

As a resident staff member serving Flemington Road Public School and the Lawrence Heights Community exclusively, the teacher-counsellor was involved not only in the treatment of crises as they arose but also, to a much larger extent, in the important function of protection and prevention. Moreover, the nature of the Lawrence Heights community necessitated the extension of some of the school's existing services into the community and the development of many unique new services;, and someone would be required to play an active role in program development and social planning. In addition, owing to contacts with the home, social welfare agencies, other educators, other professional personnel, and the public in general, the teacher-counsellor often fulfilled a liaison and public relations role. Within the school this person provided a counselling and consultant service to members of the teaching staff who sought his or her aid. He or she was called upon to organize in-service training related to his or her area of specialization. The teacher-counsellor was asked to interpret school policy and educational techniques to the public and a constant caseload had to be served on a continuing basis. It was also expected that this person might become involved in research projects devoted to assessing problems or evaluating results in order to facilitate adequate future planning.

Therefore, it was recommended that this position be reclassified and, owing to its unique properties, given a new title. My proposal was for Social Services Consultant; however, the first position approved by the Board was Chairman of Social Services, which was later changed to Social Services Consultant. I proposed specified duties and responsibilities for the new position, oriented to the beneficiaries as follows:

1. The Child
   a) Individual counselling
   b) Group therapy and group activities
   c) Referrals to other professional services
   d) Casework techniques
   e) Protection service
   f) Charitable administration

2. **The Teacher**
    a) Consultant and counselling services
    b) In-service training programs
    c) Interpretation of data and information
    d) Liaison between parent and teacher
    e) Provision of information related to individual children, families, and environmental conditions.

3. **The Parent**
    a) Counselling services
    b) Parent-oriented group therapy
    c) Interpretation of school policy and educational techniques
    d) Provision of information on social welfare assistance
    e) Liaison between parent and teacher

4. **The Agency**
    a) Provision of information related to individual academic progress and emotional and social adjustment
    b) Provision of referrals related to individuals and families
    c) Interpretation of school policy and educational techniques
    d) Coordination of services related to individuals and families

5. **The Community**
    a) Cooperation with agencies and individuals devoted to community betterment
    b) Participation in program development and social planning related to educational and community advancement
    c) Participation in research projects designed to facilitate better the above objectives

While, to some, these preceding aims might constitute an overview, they are indicative of the increasing leadership role that the school must assume as the most well-established and socially acceptable institution serving the community.[19]

Social Service Team

The *social service team* was composed of educational personnel with different professional skills who united their abilities, training, insights, and judgments to help those students who were troubled by academic, personal, environmental, or social problems. The team might include the principal, the chairman of social services, a public health nurse, and the school psychologist. Certain additional personnel might be invited to attend specific conferences: for example, a classroom teacher, community social workers, a police youth bureau, Children's Aid Society, juvenile court staff, and clergy. Each team member had a specific role in furthering the aims of the team.

The *principal* was at the helm of the school and might serve as chair of the team. As the representative of authority within the school, he was responsible for discipline, attendance, class placement, and general school policy. In this capacity the principal bore the final responsibility for all team decisions.

The *chairman of social services* represented the counselling and group therapy services within the school. He also provided a liaison with the home and social welfare agencies within the community. Direct avenues of referral and communication were maintained through his knowledge of community resources. The chairman of social services reported on the academic and behavioural progress of the child.

The *public health nurse* had access to all community health resources. She interpreted the health situation of the pupil and the pupil's family, investigated and followed through on health problems, and gave support to the individual pupil and family as they worked out problems caused by temporary or permanent physical impairment.

The *school psychologist* interpreted test information and provided an intellectual and emotional assessment. He could aid in implementing team decisions through his consultant service to the classroom teacher.

The social service team membership was often supplemented by individuals who possessed specific knowledge or exercised specialized skills.

Meeting weekly, or on call, the social service team reviewed the list of student cases that had come to its attention during the previous week. The list might include such problems as social adjustment, the habitual absentee, the hostile transfer, the emotionally disturbed, the underachiever, the delinquent, and the pre-delinquent. Within the team each case was reviewed. Background information regarding the child's siblings, home conditions, school activities, and academic progress was carefully considered, and decisions were made on the basis of all available information and the overall consensus of the disciplines represented.

Inter-agency Coordination

Since its inception Lawrence Heights was served by a multitude of community service agencies and groups. Most of these organizations were located outside of Lawrence Heights and visited their clients on an intermittent 'day-tripper' basis. Services for families and children included casework, family counselling, child protection, public health, recreation, public welfare and housing, a police youth bureau, social planning, homemaking, and volunteer assistance.

As the largest resident service organization in Lawrence Heights, Flemington Road School enjoyed the confidence of a great majority of the community's citizens.[15] Early in 1966, Principal Morris and I decided to convene a series of inter-agency meetings of service providers at the school to discuss better means of coordinating the services, with the aim of improving the quality of life in Lawrence Heights. From the beginning it became apparent that even though all these agencies were providing services, often to the same children and families in the community, many of the workers did not know each other. The coming together of these agencies with the school as focal point was the beginning of a process of inter-agency coordination. One outcome was the *interdisciplinary team*.

The Interdisciplinary Team

As a complement to the social service team, the concept of an interdisciplinary team evolved. This team constituted a unified approach to child and family problems. It represented a collaboration of services between the school (represented by the principal, social services staff, and public health nurse) and the Lawrence Heights Family and Child Services. In addition, representatives of other agencies were invited to particular conferences held on a monthly basis. However, interdependence was maintained through informal daily contact. Decisions were made on the basis of all available information and the consensus of the disciplines represented.[20]

Research Studies

As an integral part of the role of the chairman of social services, several research studies were undertaken that influenced the future development of the social services project. The following are excerpted from two of these studies.

A Survey of School Attitudes and Occupational-Educational Expectations in Culturally Different Areas

Method. A questionnaire was developed and designed to incorporate a two-fold purpose. First, to evaluate and measure expressed data related to particular school-oriented attitudes: (1) the school, (2) education in general, (3) the role of the teacher, (4) parental influence, and (5) rules and discipline. Second, the questionnaire was complemented by the addition of three questions designed to explore the areas of occupational choice, occupational preference rating, and educational expectations.

The questionnaire was administered to three separate groups of twenty-five grade-six pupils. The first two groups, one from Flemington Road Public School and the other from Tumpane Street School (a more advantaged area), were matched according to sex and IQ and were considered average students. The third group was drawn from a cross-section of grade-six students from Flemington Road Public School who might be classified as either social adjustment, emotional, delinquent, or behavioural problems. This was referred to as the Atypical group.

Conclusions. There seemed to be little significant difference in overall school oriented attitudes between the two average groups. Highly positive attitudes were expressed toward the school and the value of education. Teachers were seen as being quite receptive to individual needs and, for the most part, just in relating to their pupils. Rules were felt to be quite necessary to the maintenance of the school. Parental interest and influence was expressed as being quite high.

The Atypical group agreed with their counterparts with reference to: the school, value of education, and parental interest. Some negative feeling toward authority was expressed along with a trend toward mistrust of teachers. This corresponded to a feeling of injustice as related to punishment. The frequency of neutral response within the Atypical group seemed to suggest some degree of general indifference.

In the area of occupational educational expectation, the two average groups expressed hopes for higher education and occupations requiring a high level of training. The Atypical trend, on the other hand, was toward low education and low skill jobs.

My research seemed to indicate that there was no appreciable difference between the school oriented attitudes and the educational occupational expectations of the two average groups even though their environments were in fact quite different. Either environment or socio-economic status had little effect on attitudes or expectations or some equalizing force had offset these effects. It was my contention that the school has been a significant factor in equalizing the attitudes and expectations of these two groups. But what of the Atypical group? They had been exposed to the same forces. Why had their attitudes and expectations not approached those of the average groups in several respects? These were the children who had not adjusted to the learning situation. They were often the outsiders, the isolates whose social integration had been impaired by a variety of internal and external factors. The frustration they felt had resulted in acts of aggression and defiance, which had effectively formed a barrier to social adjustment, to academic achievement and to cultural integration. It was my assertion that programs of cultural enrichment within the school do not significantly influence some children due primarily to personality and environmental factors.

The noted Canadian sociologist Dr Rudolf Helling made the following observation at a seminar: 'Those lower-class children who drop out at the minimum permissible age have frequently dropped out mentally a few years earlier. To them, schools have become painful experiences.'[21]

It was my opinion that many school dropouts emerge from the lower strata of our society and that these students had mentally resolved their fate in the elementary school in anticipation of their sixteenth birthday. It was my belief that the marshalling of school and community resources to affect attitudes of this atypical group would be a positive step toward stemming the tide of dropouts from our educational system.[22]

The Effect of the Multi-problem Family on the Educational Process

Method. Two groups of fifty families were selected from the student body of Flemington Road Public School. The first group was identified as multi-problem while the second was a more stable control group. The eldest student in the school from each family was chosen, except when the sex ratio of about 60 per cent boys and 40 per cent girls was threatened. In relation to each of these students, their classroom teacher completed a Pupil Behaviour Inventory. This instrument explored the following dimensions: classroom conduct, academic motivation and performance, socio-emotional state, teacher.dependency and personal behaviour. Resulting data was compiled and comparisons drawn between the two groups.

Conclusions. The data indicated that children from Multi-Problem Families had particular difficulty in the dimension of *Classroom Conduct* as compared to their counterparts from more stable families. In fact, 48 per cent of the MPF group might be classed as definite behaviour problems in the classroom due to the fact that they received a below average rating on each of the twelve items on the rating form. By comparison, only 12 per cent of the Stable group received this classification. It was of interest that of the Stable group 74 per cent were considered to have above average classroom conduct, compared to 24 per cent of the Multi-Problem group.

Another area of wide differential was *Socio-Emotional State*, which gave some indication of the emotional stability and social adjustment of the student. The Multi-Problem group scored considerably lower with 40 per cent of the students in the below average range compared with only 8 per cent in the Stable group. By further comparison, the Stable group placed 56 per cent in the above average group while the Multi-Problem group had but 20 per cent.

It was my belief that Classroom Conduct and Socio-Emotional State were likely to have the most effect on academic progress. This opinion seemed verified in the *Academic Motivation and Performance* dimension where the findings seemed to parallel the other two dimensions. For example, 50 per cent of the Multi-Problem Family group had below average Motivation and Performance compared with 8 per cent of the Stable group. On the other hand, only 8 per cent of the Multi-Problem Family group was above average in contrast to 44 per cent of the other group.

The rate of differentiation was least in the area of *Teacher Dependence* (0.9) but 40 per cent of the Multi-Problem Family group was quite dependent while only 8 per cent of the Stable group had this weakness. Seventy per cent of the Stable group had above average non-dependence along with 24 per cent of the Multi-Problem Family group. However, I did not consider it a failing to have some degree of dependence on the teacher in an academic setting.

The dimension of *Personal Behaviour* was obviously rather difficult for the classroom teacher to rate. Therefore, I did not feel that it was always as valid as the other dimensions. Ninety per cent of the Stable group was felt to have above average Personal Behaviour as compared with 54 per cent of the Multi-Problem Family group.

The data seemed to indicate that children from Multi-Problem Families had behavioural, emotional, and social adjustment problems, which tended to impede their academic progress. Further, due to their behavioural problems MPF children tended to be disruptive to the atmosphere in the classroom and thus have a derogatory effect on the educational process.

MPF children, due to their emotional and social adjustment problems, were in need of more supportive services than children from stable homes. Therefore, schools with above average numbers of multi-problem families in their educational population should build in extra ancillary services to meet the atypical supportive needs of these children.[23]

Outcomes and Reflections

The role of the teacher-counsellor was established primarily to serve the needs of students, teachers, and parents, particularly with regard to classroom behaviour. One-to-one counselling, social development groups, the Special Adjustment Centre, and the social service and interdisciplinary teams were new services created to meet the needs of students. Professional development activities and other supportive services focused on the needs of teachers. Parent involvement, however, was too often centred on concerns about child behaviour at school and in the community, particularly the delinquency problems involving the youth bureau and the juvenile and family court. Other agency referrals concerned child protection, family counselling, and public health and treatment services.

The creation of the position of chairman of social services was the beginning of a recognition that the school was but an extension of the community it served. Factors such as poverty, low self-esteem, multi-problem families, and limited recreational opportunities were often the root causes of school-based problems. Thus began the evolution of the school as a major resource in community education and development. In order to begin to deal with causes and not just effects, a new partnership of citizens and service organizations was forged. The focus for this partnership became the Flemington Road Community School.

4 Flemington Road Community School

Education and Social Change

John Dewey, an advocate of education as an instrument of social change, made the following statement: 'The desired education cannot occur within the four walls of a school shut off from life. Education must itself assume an increasing responsibility for participation in projecting ideas of social change and taking part in their execution in order to be educative.'[9]

Nowhere have the challenges of public education been more apparent, or the problems more acute, than in our cities. Urbanity has indeed become a way of life for the great majority of our families. The heterogeneous nature of urban life, the density and diversity of population, the problems of adjustment to a new lifestyle, and the inability of some individuals to compete economically or cope emotionally have led to a major dilemma. Suddenly, traditional, time-honoured methods no longer apply. It is our ability to differentiate between the needs of diverse segments of the population and to plan effective programs to promote equality of opportunity that is in question.

Education has borne the brunt of problems associated with social disorganization, but it is just one of the many institutions that shoulder the burden. Many other groups are intensely involved and frustrated by the problems of the poor and disadvantaged. Educators cannot isolate themselves from this reality but must begin to extend themselves in many directions – to meet, to discuss, to understand. Social welfare, public health, recreation, education, and – most important – the people themselves must become common partners if this urban crisis is ever to be resolved at the community level.

A Community School Philosophy

Beginning in 1966 with the creation of the social services project, the *community school* philosophy was adopted at Flemington Road Public School as part of a holistic program of compensatory education for children and parents in a disadvantaged area. In the belief that the school and the educational opportunity it represented could not be separated from the community it served, the school endeavoured to extend itself as a partner in community development. Other equal partners included the citizens of the community and the governmental and service agencies devoted to community betterment.

To guide the program and provide a forum for matters of mutual concern, we organized the Community School Advisory Council. Membership included area residents and representatives from groups actively involved or providing organizational support, for example, North York Board of Education, North York Council, North York Social Planning Council, North York Department of Public Welfare, North York Department of Parks and Recreation, Lawrence Heights Family and Child Services, North York Public Library, National Council of Jewish Women, Big Brother Movement, the Neighbourhood Association, Lawrence Heights Sports Committee, St Phillips Church, Ontario Housing Corporation, Seneca College, Mennonite Brethren Church, and senior citizens. The chairmanship rotated from meeting to meeting among community residents. Thus, many resources were brought together under the umbrella of the community school in a coordinated effort to improve the quality of community life.

A Community-Focused Curriculum

As an extension of the community it served, the school began to view the community as a resource for the enrichment of the curriculum and program. Other community resources helped to determine the kinds of learning experiences that children could have. Thus, in the development of a more relevant curriculum, the neighbourhood and the larger city became a vast classroom of learning experience. Teachers were exposed to the lifestyles of the community through home visits, coffee parties, and a variety of professional development activities involving community workers and parents as resource persons. Through participation in extended day activities, teachers met parents on an informal basis, which led to greater mutual understanding and respect. Teachers began to understand the environment and value systems of their pupils and to gear the learning process to developing strengths and compensating for deficiencies. To quote from an article that I wrote in James Draper's book *Citizen Participation Canada*:

> A curriculum committee was formed on a volunteer basis, representing all educational levels. This group is directing its efforts to writing a curriculum that reflects the particular needs of the community. A further objective is to develop a systematic progression of learning experience through the school. Language programs are studied to evaluate their appropriate use in the setting of Flemington Road School. Field trips are organized and rated according to their learning objectives. Real life experience becomes a key to unlock the mysteries of reading, mathematics, science, and social studies. An effort is made to meet the child at his level and to develop a relationship that enriches patterns of educational growth.
>
> Through these experiences, teachers may develop a greater sensitivity to the social, emotional, and physical needs of their students. Certainly a teacher learns that he must meet these basic needs before the academic realm has any meaning for the child. An empathetic rather than a sympathetic relationship must evolve while the teacher continues to enrich the educational environment. Under these circumstances, teachers become need oriented rather than program oriented.[20]

A Centre of Community Living

One outcome of regular Community School Advisory Council meetings was an ongoing process of community needs assessment. Research studies and consultations with service providers and citizen groups identified services that were not being met, such as insufficient recreational activities for children, teens, and adults. The small community centre was inadequate for group games (for example, basketball). The fact that youth and children were involved in antisocial behaviour (for example, theft, vandalism, and assaults) could be attributed to a lack of supervised activities and boredom.

A study that I conducted on the lifestyle of pre-adolescents in public housing in Lawrence Heights included the following observations for boys and girls from the ages of nine to twelve.[24]

1. Enormous blocks of time were spent by children of both sexes watching television. This amounted in many cases to as much as

six hours per day, or more than the time spent in school. The rate escalated even further on the weekends. Television viewing must be considered the primary activity of this age group.

2. There was a lack of self-directed organization by children in the before-school and recess periods, particularly in the area of games and sports. This was contrary to my experience with children of schools in more advantaged areas.

3. There was a general lack of reference, particularly among the girls, to any of the activities that were highly espoused by the dominant culture for example, music, dancing, and art lessons. Besides going against the grain of the subculture, these could be ill afforded by most families.

4. Yorkdale Plaza (an indoor shopping mall) was predominant in their life both for shopping and leisure activity. The exposure to this symbol of affluence in Canadian society must certainly have brought feelings of anxiety to many children. In addition, many parents seemed to shop there although it was common knowledge that the prices were inflated, particularly for groceries and specialty items.

5. The parental practices seemed adequate, although the absence of parental figures at meal times, particularly the father, and during the week might have been a disadvantage.

6. There seemed to be a higher degree of socialization among boys than girls, possibly because they were either more outgoing by nature or could cope better with the environment.

7. There was a high incidence of church attendance among girls as compared to boys.

8. Reading was not high on the preference list among these children although this would seem to be a top priority in a disadvantaged background.

9. There was a strong undercurrent of negative feeling towards identification with the stigma surrounding public housing (for example, the description of the neighbourhood by some as 'the jungle,' a moderate to strong wish to leave, and the spending of leisure time outside the project).

10. The absence of playground facilities was a concern. Some had been installed in the building courts by the housing corporation, but they were later removed because it was felt that they constituted a hazard when unsupervised.

11. The major concern of the children involved being around the negative behaviour (for example, quarrelling, swearing, and fight-

ing) of people in the community. This validates a previous study done with adults who had the same priority of concern.
12. There seemed to be a lack of suitable recreational activities for girls, with more emphasis on activities for boys (for example, organized sports).

In response to these consultations and studies the North York Board of Education in October 1966 approved the sum of thirty-four hundred dollars to establish an after-four program in cooperation with the North York Parks and Recreation Department. Emphasis was placed upon developing the fullest use of the physical facilities of the school by various community groups. This was facilitated by the development of the community school framework whereby the school retained direct responsibility for the use of the building through the principal and myself as community school director. The school benefited through the supervision of facilities; thus their use was coordinated, and morale problems with both teachers and caretakers were avoided. Participating groups benefited through the use of equipment and facilities under the favourable image that the school enjoyed in the community. The community school programs included the following:

After-four Activities. The program began in October 1966 with activities for boys and girls on Monday, Wednesday, and Thursday evenings from four to seven o'clock. Activities included team sports (such as floor hockey), gymnastics, crafts, quiet games, music lessons, ballet, storytelling, science, and judo, as well as social adjustment groups. A successful recorder group taught by a teacher spawned the beginnings of a school instrumental band. Marilyn Gross of the National Council of Jewish Women organized a music shower among council members to donate brass instruments for the band.

Walter Molnhuber, a recent immigrant from Austria who loaded transport trucks at night, approached me to set up a judo program for his sons. When I told him that I knew practically nothing about judo, he loaded me into the family car to visit a judo facility in the more affluent suburb of Willowdale. He told me that a judo instructor named Jim McNeilage lived in Lawrence Heights and might be interested in forming a club if space were available. One of the school's gymnasiums seemed to be the perfect spot, but mats would be required to cushion the hard floor. One of the vice-principals, Mac Fairfield, who used to be in the Board of Education's Physical Education Department, told of discarded gym mats sitting in a warehouse. He and Walter went to see them and chose the best of the lot, and we had a beginning. Then Walter said that we would definitely need a canvas cover to hold the mats in place, and our school trustee, Saul Cowan, came to the rescue with a company that was prepared to donate a mat cover. Next, Walter was concerned that participants would not have the proper judo uniforms or gis to wear because they were quite expensive. We took a sample to Eldon Comfort, the principal at nearby Yorkdale Vocational School, and soon their industrial sewing training program was turning out gis for club members. Before long, boys and girls from the Lawrence Heights Judo Club were winning medals in competitions across the province – a great boost to community self-esteem.

Another agency, Bathurst Heights Public Library, which was located outside of the community, expressed concern that they were not attracting children from Lawrence Heights to borrow books. This was important as many children were behind in their reading levels. One of the librarians, Phyllis Goldman, began story-time sessions as part of the after-school program. Later, librarians loaded books into their cars and handed them out in the housing courts. Some parents then volunteered to host court libraries in their homes so that people of all ages could access reading materials.

Adult Programs. The adult programs took root much more slowly. School staff first met different groups of community residents to discuss the concept and develop ideas for programming. Booths were set up at School Open House to disseminate information and gather further ideas. School administrators met representatives from community agencies to discuss the program and later to gain their active support. From these meetings, interviews, and conferences, a blueprint of cooperative effort was drawn.

Finally in February 1967 the program got underway on Monday and Wednesday evenings from seven to ten o'clock. Lawrence Heights Family and Child Services developed informal adult get-acquainted sessions. The Parks and Recreation Department began fitness programs for men and women. Gradually, interest groups were spawned. A rod-and-gun club, a soccer club, and a neighbourhood association met regularly. The National Council of Jewish Women provided leadership for craft and dramatic groups. Early in 1968, Thursday evening was established as 'Family Night,' with childcare provided. Activities included a family-life film series, a homemakers' group, a men's club, a TOPS (Take Off Pounds Sensibly) group, and English improvement classes. Resident Barbara Aoki organized coffee parties where parents and teachers enjoyed a social evening to discuss educational programs and community needs.

Youth Activities. It soon became apparent that one important segment of the community had been overlooked. Lawrence Heights had a large population of young people without recreation facilities. Many were dropouts with nothing to do at night but hang around the local fish-and-chip shop in the small plaza next to the school. Alcohol and solvent abuse was rampant among these role models for Flemington Road schoolchildren.

When youth became aware that the school was open in the evening, they were soon pounding at the door and demanding to participate. As a result the corridor and adjoining rooms at the front of the school served as a drop-in centre on Tuesday and Thursday evenings. Music was provided from teen record collections for dancing and listening. The adjoining gymnasium hosted basketball, floor hockey, and murder-ball games. Table tennis, crafts, discussion groups, and a television lounge were added. An elected board of teenage monitors helped in the development of policies and in the supervision of activities. It was very much a youth-organized program.

Yet, something was missing. The young people wanted to play snooker, and a pool table was not a piece of equipment to be found in an elementary school. If permission were granted, where would the money come from to purchase such an expensive item? Again the Community School Advisory Council came to the rescue. We discovered that Lawrence Heights' tenants had had to provide a security deposit (one month's rent) when taking up residence. With more than a thousand households, this amounted to a large sum of money being held in trust. The advisory council asked what happened to the interest on the security deposits. We soon had funds, donated by the Ontario Housing Corporation, for a pool table and other recreational equipment.

Interest Groups. Small interest groups for youth began meeting on Wednesday evenings for activities such as a girls' fitness class, a snooker club, a charm club, a film series, and several special projects. Youth from the drop-in centre began to assist me with social development group sessions. This was of particular importance because these unemployed young people often served as role models for Flemington Road students. At one time, dropouts could be seen next to the schoolyard, sniffing nail-polish remover from plastic bags. The involvement of street youth as volunteer assistants in counselling and group work activities in the school during the day provided them with a new sense of positive identity. The solvent-sniffer problem soon disappeared.

I can remember one occasion when I was called to a classroom to remove a student, Kyle, because of his violent anger and out-of-control behaviour. As I marched down the hall, holding a struggling Kyle from behind, we met Dave, one of the drop-in boys, who was arriving to assist me with a group session. As Dave came forward, Kyle suddenly lashed out and kicked him square in the mouth. Now Dave was also known for his violent outbursts, and Kyle soon realized that he was in serious trouble. After a menacing look, Dave smiled, said that that was not a nice thing to do, and took over restraining Kyle, who immediately calmed down as he was led to the Special Adjustment Centre.

Job Improvement Corps. As a demonstration project, the Job Improvement Corps was launched in the winter of 1968 as an outgrowth of the drop-in centre. It offered unemployed boys who had left school an opportunity to improve their education while gaining skills to aid in their employability. It was a joint venture that brought together the resources of the Board of Education's Work Study and Adult Education departments and the facilities of Yorkdale Vocational School and Flemington Road Community School. The concept included evening classes in English, mathematics upgrading, and auto shop (for example, building go-karts) provided through Yorkdale's principal, Eldon Comfort. I operated guided group interaction sessions at Flemington Road. Jack Ulan, Director of the Work Study Office, was responsible for sourcing job opportunities for Job Improvement Corps participants. A follow-up survey of the status of the twenty-four boys who had entered the program produced these results:

Presently employed	14	58%
Back in school	7	29%
In reformatory	1	4%
Presently unemployed	2	9%
Total	24	100%

Challenges

Not everyone was supportive of the use of school facilities at Flemington Road. One day, in 1968, I received a telephone call from a reporter at the *North York Mirror* who had previously written articles describing the progress of the community school program. He said that he had received an accusation that the community use programs had caused extensive damage to the school (for example, broken windows and the destruction of classroom projects). My first reaction was to state that I had no knowledge of any excessive damage, and I added that the use of classrooms for the community was avoided wherever possible. I further added that the problem was one of a 'credibility gap depending on one's philosophy of education. There has been a 75 per cent reduction in juvenile delinquency in the Flemington school area since the community program started. The school has one of the smallest rates of vandalism of any school in North York.' At this point I remembered to ask who had made such accusations. The reporter replied that Albert Boddy, who had replaced Whit Morris as principal of Flemington Road in 1967, had approached him. These were the headlines on the front page of the *Mirror* for 18 December 1968: 'Educators clash on damage.'[25]

Needless to say, the senior administration of the school board was not pleased. Mr Boddy and I soon found ourselves 'on the carpet' in separate interviews before Dr Fred Minkler, Director of Education. With trepidation I told my story of how I thought I was protecting the reputation of the school and community. Dr Minkler listened intently, and when I was finished, he took off his dark-framed glasses and stated, 'I make at least ten major decisions each day. I'm lucky if one turns out to be correct.' I was not privy to Dr Minkler's conversation with Mr Boddy, but soon afterwards, the principal announced his retirement for the following June. I was soon promoted to become the Board of Education's first social services consultant, reporting to Mel Prideaux, the supervisory officer for the area. My duties at Flemington Road continued, but I also provided consultative support to other schools in North York that served public housing areas. The new principal at Flemington Road, Jim Montgomerie, stated in an address to the Special Senate Committee on Poverty when it met at the school in 1970, 'Our school can only do one thing first, and that is what the teachers try to do in this school, and that is love the children ... I think in our work in the community that is what we try to do to make people see that they are people of value and worth.'[26] (Flemington was known as the hugging school during Mr Montgomerie's tenure.)

The Community-Service Function

As the best-established and most socially accepted resource in the community, Flemington Road was prepared to assume an active role in community and social planning. To improve the conditions of life in the community, efforts were made to coordinate the activities of many agencies with the school's program. Thus, the school assumed a leadership role in community education and development.

Flemington Road housed a number of services that benefited the whole community. The social services staff represented supportive and therapeutic services within the school and provided a liaison with the home and social agencies within the community. The public health nurse interpreted the health of the pupil and his or her family and investigated and gave support in combating problems related to physical or emotional health. Remedial reading specialists, a library-resource teacher, and a speech therapist were available to provide assistance in the language area. A full-time dentist and dental nurse provided dental services for children of the community. A psychologist and a psychometrician visited the school to provide an assessment and consultative service in regard to educational and behavioural problems. The interdisciplinary team constituted a unified approach to child and family needs. This team represented a collaboration of services between the school, the social services staff, the public health nurse, and the Lawrence Heights Family and Child Services. The Lawrence Heights Family and Child Services, led by Dorothy Hahn, chose to locate in the plaza next to the school as a result of the community school partnership.[27]

Supervision and training was provided to the many volunteers who assisted with activities. Seneca College and York University used the Flemington Road Community School as a field placement. Workshops and seminars were provided to citizens' groups, teachers, and students of both social work and public health nursing. In addition, large numbers of community service personnel and educators from other schools made casual visits and fact-finding tours.

The Community School Advisory Council became the focus for community development in Lawrence Heights. It never became structured into a traditional executive hierarchy, and the chairmanship rotated from meeting to meeting among community residents. Decisions were reached by consensus. Ad hoc work groups were formed spontaneously to respond to issues, and later they reported their progress back to the council. Meetings were open for all to attend and participate, whatever might be their interests or political views. A sense of trust grew among people sharing a common philosophy of community action. The Community School Advisory Council spawned several special projects:

Volunteers Unlimited. The Volunteers Unlimited project involved senior students from three North York secondary schools in the Lawrence

Heights area (Bathurst Heights, Fleming, and Boylen). Students volunteered with social service agencies for up to three hours per week and then met once a week with a staff adviser to discuss their placements and to share ideas and perceptions. Applications to participate in the program were made through each school's guidance department. In setting up this service program, the following plan of action was followed:

1. A faculty adviser was appointed in each school to supervise the formation of a separate student organization responsible to the principal and affiliated with the student council.
2. Each student member was classified according to his or her individual interests (for example, medical, social welfare, recreational, or educational).
3. A list of institutions and agencies interested in making use of youth volunteers was compiled: for example, hospitals, social welfare agencies, mental health agencies, recreational and educational bodies, institutions of rehabilitation and convalescence, residential treatment, and care centres).
4. Each agency accepting volunteers was responsible for orientation, instruction, placement, and supervision.
5. Each agency operated its own autonomous program while maintaining liaison with the faculty adviser.
6. A fellowship of student volunteers was maintained within the school and provided an unstructured forum for the sharing of ideas, experiences, and philosophies.
7. Operational costs were minimal and were underwritten through student council grants.

Both the staff advisers and the students in the program felt that the experience was very positive. The students were highly motivated and sincerely interested in the problems of the people with whom they were dealing. In general, they felt they were really doing something worthwhile. There appeared to be no conflict with academic performance, and in some cases there was an improvement due to attitude change.[28]

Junior Big Brothers. This project was initiated on an experimental basis between Bathurst Heights Secondary School and Flemington Road Public School. The Big Brothers organization wished to extend its services to the 30 per cent of Lawrence Heights families who were single-parent (mother) led. However, they were experiencing a shortage of volunteer Big Brothers to provide a supportive service to boys

without an active father figure. Joyce Bradley of the guidance department at Bathurst Heights and I, as part of Volunteers Unlimited,
recruited senior students from Bathurst Heights to be matched to those
boys from Flemington Road who were on the Big Brothers' waiting list.
Bathurst Heights senior student volunteers received training and ongoing supervision from Big Brothers personnel. Each Junior Big Brother
agreed to spend a minimum of four hours per week with Little Brothers
in a variety of activities, using the school, public library, community
centre, swimming pool, sport facilities, theatres, et cetera.

From discussions held with Junior Big Brothers, mothers, and Little
Brothers, there was a consensus of opinion that this was a worthwhile
project that should be extended. The senior students, for the most part,
related well to the challenge of the situation. The concern that they might
be overinvolved with the home situation did not prove to be a problem.[29]

Emergency Day Care. Parents with preschool children often had to
leave the community for medical or social service appointments or to
attend family court several miles from Lawrence Heights. School-age
children were often kept home to care for their younger brothers and
sisters. Through the Community School Advisory Council, an emergency day-care program was established – the first of its kind in Metropolitan Toronto. The community centre of the Department of Parks and
Recreation, which was down the road from the school, donated space
for the program. Parents needing to use the facility would first visit the
public health nurse for a check-up. Peter and Betty Balzer, Mennonite Central Committee volunteers from Vancouver, provided staffing
through the Mennonite Brethren Church. As they did not have Early
Childhood Education qualifications, staff from the North York Welfare
Department who operated a nursery school in the same building supervised the Balzers. The Family Service Association made available toys
and equipment for use. Food was prepared by students from Yorkdale
Vocational School and transported to the site by Peter Balzer, using the
car of Pastor Issac Tiessen from the Mennonite Brethren Church. The
container in which to transport the food was donated by the Tri-Bell
Ladies Auxiliary through the National Council of Jewish Women.

The success of the emergency day-care program led to the later establishment of a licensed day-care centre, which was eventually relocated
to the school as space became available.

Hot Lunch Program. The catering for the day-care program from
Yorkdale Vocational was expanded to provide a hot-lunch program

for Flemington Road students at a cost of fifty cents per day. The program included active games and other recreational activities during the lunch period, with supervision provided by Peter Balzer and other agency volunteers.

Legal Counselling Service. A group of students from Osgoode Hall Law School was led by Al McChesney, who described the group's role in an address to the Special Senate Committee on Poverty: 'I am with a group from Osgoode Hall Law School known as the community and legal aid service program ... People in areas such as Lawrence Heights were missing out on the valuable things that a lawyer could do for them, not only after they were in trouble but also in preventing trouble from happening, things like drawing up wills ... Since it costs money, these people have to think twice about doing it.'[26]

Grocery Cooperative. With the assistance of Father David Clarke of St Philip's Anglican Church and Reverend Issac Tiessen of the Mennonite Brethren Church, a non-profit direct-charge cooperative grocery store was opened. Memberships were drawn from Lawrence Heights residents, and each member in the cooperative paid a fee in order to raise money to build the inventory of groceries. Overhead costs were shared among the members, who enjoyed a saving of 20 per cent on the average grocery bill. At first, the program began in donated space at St Philip's Church because there was nothing available within Lawrence Heights. The cooperative later shared accommodation with the Family Service Association's used clothing store in the local plaza.

Police Relations. Youth in Lawrence Heights had long complained of being picked off the streets at night by police, put into patrol cars, and taken behind factories outside the community to be beaten. Matters came to a head one Saturday night when a teen drop-in centre at the community centre was being operated by staff of the Addiction Research Foundation and parent volunteers. After some words had been exchanged between young people outside the centre and police in a cruising patrol car, a police riot ensued. Police in cars and on motorcycles soon converged on the centre and began to assault youth, Addiction Research staff, and volunteers. An emergency meeting, called the following day at the centre, was attended by Community School Advisory Council members including Alderman Paul Godfrey and School Trustee Saul Cowan; the regional superintendent of the Metropolitan Toronto Police Service represented the police. Accusations flew thick and fast, but when the smoke had cleared, it was agreed that non-uniformed community officers would be assigned to Lawrence Heights to work with youth, service agencies, and community volunteers. These officers worked most effectively with young people in the community school and other recreation programs. The incidence of arrests in the community soon decreased, and no longer were police cars to be seen cruising through Lawrence Heights to 'see what they could pick up.'

Community on the Move. Meeting at the community school, the Community on the Move organization combined the efforts of volunteers who lived in Lawrence Heights and those who lived outside the community. Some projects of Community on the Move included:

1. A community newspaper, providing a forum in which to exchange information and ideas with neighbours. Yorkdale Vocational donated printing, and Flemington Road students distributed the papers.
2. A questionnaire to assist in recruiting people to serve the community in both paid and voluntary capacities, which was circulated by Flemington Road students.
3. The Family Store, which was operated by the Family Service Association and area resident volunteers, who collected good used clothing from schools in North York to be sold at minimum prices. The funds were used to purchase at wholesale those items that were most in demand, which were then sold at cost. Space in the clothing store, which was located in the local plaza, was later shared with the new grocery cooperative.

Lawrence Heights Neighbourhood Association. The Lawrence Heights Neighbourhood Association was a tenants' organization that appeared before the provincial task force on housing to criticize the existing system of rents, the building maintenance, and the general attitude of the Ontario Housing Corporation towards public housing tenants. It called for tenants to have the opportunity to purchase their own units.[30]

Outcomes and Reflections

Therapeutic Community

The community school represented but one approach in an overall community education and development plan for Lawrence Heights.

The concept of the interdisciplinary team evolved into an overall strategy to further integrate services in order to produce a more self-sufficient therapeutic community. Mental-health services were expanded through the extensive use of volunteers, many drawn from Lawrence Heights itself. A coordinating body known as the Volunteer Council was formed with the goal of canvassing all households to identify needs and mobilize human resources. This produced a range of services such as an information centre, home visitors, emergency childcare personnel, classroom volunteers, foster parents, and Junior Big Brothers and Sisters in support of a community-oriented treatment program.

One outcome was that, from 1966 to 1968, the number of children appearing in juvenile court decreased by more than 90 per cent. During 1966, I made thirty-five court appearances in support of Flemington Road children; by 1968 there were but two such visits. Whereas at one time a term in the detention home or training school was seen as a status symbol ('They have a fridge filled with food'), problems were more often dealt with by the use of community resources in general. Since the Children's Aid Society was less likely to take children into care as a result of a family breakdown caused by medical or mental-health problems, Lawrence Heights residents often opened their homes, acting as foster parents or providing short-term placements until family life improved.

Lawrence Heights resident volunteers began serving as resource people to other communities – some of which were much more advantaged – in establishing community school and community development programs. One such volunteer was Barbara Aoki, a truly gifted volunteer leader who was responsible, among other projects, for the coffee-party staff development concept. Another was John Cadieux, who addressed the Special Senate Committee on Poverty on his work with youth in the community as follows: 'I am working in the capacity of a detached worker in Lawrence Heights. I live in the community. I have all this time because I am on dependent father's allowance myself with my wife and children. I was on the verge of a nervous breakdown so I decided to find something for myself to do, and I started working with my protégés here. I enjoy the work very much and I am sure that it means something to them, although I don't know what it is.'[26]

It was not unusual to have parents and youth volunteers sharing the staffroom during the day with Flemington Road teachers, much to the chagrin of some teachers ('Now we can't gossip about parents and students').

Compensatory Education

In the summer of 1968, I was asked by Bob Thomas of the Ontario Department of Education to become a member of the Curriculum Committee on Compensatory Education. Its duties were 'to prepare guidelines for the adaptation of school programs to meet the special needs of disadvantaged students and to make recommendations pertaining to the curriculum and organization of a proposed Departmental Summer Course in Compensatory Education.'[31]

Part of the work of the Curriculum Committee was to visit inner-city schools and review their education programs in major Ontario cities including Toronto, North York, Hamilton, London, Windsor, and Ottawa. The experience of developing the Flemington Road Community School proved to be unique in the province. In seeing the school as an extension of the community, the Flemington model was influential in policy development by the Department of Education.

Another outcome of the committee's work was the initiation of the first professional development summer course in compensatory education, in 1969. Eighty-six teachers, whose pupils came from disadvantaged areas across the province, spent five weeks at the Duke of York School in inner-city Toronto. They learned about the community as well as curriculum development, language arts, and learning materials. There was demonstration teaching, with regular Duke of York students making up the classes. In the afternoon, teachers served as volunteers with a number of existing agencies, not only learning the roles played by these organizations but meeting the people who lived in the neighbourhoods.[32] I served as coordinator for this program and for subsequent departmental summer courses in compensatory education and community school development.

New Services

In the early 1970s, services in Lawrence Heights continued to develop with the establishment of a health services clinic, first in the community centre and later in its own building, which replaced the small strip plaza adjacent to the school. The community centre burned down and was replaced by a much larger facility to accommodate basketball games. Residents, working with Alderman Paul Godfrey, petitioned the North York Borough Council and were successful in having an ice arena built just outside Lawrence Heights. (This campaign also

resulted in two arenas being built in other areas serving public housing projects.)

Letting Go

In 1970, I was accepted as a doctoral student at the Ontario Institute
for Studies in Education (OISE) at the University of Toronto, majoring in community education and development. Area residents Barbara
Aoki and John Cadieux then shared my position as community school
director.

Unfortunately there was not a happy ending to the community school
story. In the early 1970s, the Ontario Department of Education introduced ceilings on educational spending by school boards. It severely
limited the amount of money that could be raised through residential
and commercial assessment. Budgets were restricted, and one of the
first items to go was funding for community school activities at Flemington Road and other schools implementing the Flemington model.
The North York Board of Education turned the programs over to the
Department of Parks and Recreation. Parents employed in the community school programs were subsequently terminated and their positions
given to sons, daughters, and other relatives and friends of Parks and
Recreation personnel.

A concern voiced by some critics was that the concentration of services might be inhibiting the involvement of citizens in solving their
own problems. Questions arose: Were the professionals and resident
volunteers creating a dependent community? Was this a form of institutionalized poverty, which discouraged social action and citizen discontent? Was the school academic performance really improving, and
were children and their parents really developing the skills necessary
to escape a life of poverty?

It was with a feeling of sadness and uncertainty that I left my work in
Lawrence Heights. My time there, from 1965 to 1970, had represented
a profound series of learning experiences that had irrevocably transformed my life and my career path from classroom teacher in the small
town of Riverside, Ontario, to change agent in the emerging field of
community education and development in Canada's largest and most
diverse urban centre. It was also my introduction to the internal and
external politics of change in the world of educational decision making.
I will always be grateful to Whit Morris for his vision, leadership, and
encouragement in making it all possible.

5 Politics and Education

Seeking New Challenges

It was with a real sense of apprehension in the spring of 1970 that I applied for a leave of absence from my position as social services consultant with the North York Board of Education in order to enter the PhD program in the Adult Education Department at OISE. With a wife and two small children to support, I was not sure we could survive on a graduate assistant's salary. Nevertheless, I knew that I had to find a way to translate all the profound learning and experience gained through five years in Lawrence Heights. Not only had I discovered a new vocation, but I had learned to work in two different worlds – the school and the community.

I was drawn to the study of andragogy because my mentor, Dr Wilson Head, had received a doctorate in adult education from Ohio State University. I was also inspired by a course in my master's program on the theory of adult education, which was taught jointly by doctors Alan Thomas and Allen Tough. In particular, I was fascinated by Tough's concept of *non-formal learning* (now known as intentional learning).

In his 1971 book, *The Adult's Learning Projects,* Tough reports on a survey of adults, adolescents, and children concerning learning episodes and learning projects. An episode is 'a period of time devoted to a cluster or sequence of similar or related activities, which are not interrupted much by other activities. Each episode has a definite beginning and ending time. The activities during an episode include all of the person's experiences during that time ... A learning project is a series of clearly related episodes.'[33]

In a study conducted in 1970 among sixty-six adults from a variety of backgrounds, Tough discovered that 98 per cent of the group had participated in at least one learning project during the previous year. Only 7 per cent of these learning projects were for credit. A survey of out-of-school learning projects among sixteen-year-old boys and ten-year-old girls produced results similar to those of the adult study. However, the sixteen-year-olds had conducted more learning projects than had the adults, while the ten-year-olds had acquired a far greater variety of knowledge and skill in relatively short learning episodes.

Tough's work seems to indicate that learning and schooling are not necessarily synonymous. Persons of all ages may be involved in self-directed learning exclusive of any contact with formal educational procedures.

Community: Involvement or Control?

In the 1960s, citizens in Toronto had begun to organize around the issues of new expressways and urban renewal. Both were proving grounds for social action, a workshop for budding politicians to learn their trade. Some of these politicians directed their activities to Ward 7, which was located just east of the central core and included the traditionally impoverished neighbourhoods of Cabbagetown and the north and south Regent Park public housing projects. Both John Sewell, who sought election in 1969 as a city alderman, and Gordon Cressy, as a school trustee, were community organizers who had trained in the methods of Saul Alinsky in the United States.

Beginning in the 1930s, Alinsky developed his strategy of community organization and power politics, which included techniques that, he acknowledged, had been influenced by the power struggles of organized labour and the Chicago Mafia. Alinsky preached that, for the impoverished, the name of the game was power and the method was organization in order to improve their social and economic life. He also maintained that it took the active support of no more than 5 per cent of the population to mount an effective base from which to wield community power. Toronto-based organizations created by disciples of Alinsky included PRAXIS, Just Society, Stop Spadina, and the Greater Riverdale Organization, all dealing with issues of poverty and urban renewal.

There was growing evidence that one of the next targets of community politics, and certainly the most vulnerable, would be the schools. Organizers brought together parents and teachers to form the political action organization known as Citizens' Committee for Change in

Schools, as well as the Community School Workshop and the publication *This Magazine Is About Schools*. Their stated objective was 'a shift of responsibility and authority from the hands of principals and senior Board administrators to the school community of teachers, parents, and students.' The concept was commonly called *community control*. Organizers from very advantaged backgrounds began to move into the slums of the Cabbagetown neighbourhood to begin to build their power base. It was not enough for school personnel to just be more involved with the community; they were required to cede control to parents and their organizers.

Learning to Function in the Middle

During the summer of 1969, the *Toronto Globe and Mail* published three articles criticizing the special education program of the Toronto Board of Education, with particular emphasis on Opportunity Classes.[34] These special classes were for children who, on the basis of academic performance and intelligence ratings, were judged to be incapable of making adequate progress in regular age-graded classes.

On 2 September, the management committee of the Board of Education requested that the director of education report on 'how children are admitted to Opportunity Classes, what special education is provided, and the desirability of reducing the number of Opportunity Classes or abolishing them.'[35] The issue was picked up by a number of persons who were seeking to become trustees in the November election. Among the group of new faces were several aggressive and very determined candidates, including Gordon Cressy in Ward 7, who had been endorsed by the Citizens' Committee for Change in Schools. Those candidates who were elected became known as the reform caucus.

A major plank in their platform had been the proposed replacement of the retiring director of education, Graham Gore, with John Bremer, an educational innovator from Britain who had recently directed the much-publicized Parkway project in Philadelphia. The final three candidates for the position were Ronald Jones, Academic Superintendent with the Metropolitan Toronto School Board; Archie Milloy, Superintendent of Secondary Schools with the Toronto Board; and John Bremer. The voting was very close, but it finally resulted in a run-off between the conservatives' candidate, Mr Milloy, and the reform candidate, Mr Bremer; the final vote was 10-8 in favour of Bremer. A new roadblock, however, was created. According to Ontario law, a senior administrator had to have either an inspector's certificate or a secondary school principal's certificate. Mr Bremer had neither, and the minister of education refused to bend the regulations. The decision was then thrown back to the trustees, and in a two-way ballot between Mr Jones and Mr Milloy, Ronald Jones, a veteran of thirty-three years with the Toronto system, was declared the new director.

Mr Jones inherited a divided house, both among trustees and senior officials. One of the first challenges to his leadership was the Opportunity Classes issue. On 10 February 1970, a report from the Board officials, which supported Opportunity Classes, was presented to the management committee. A community group from Ward 7 known as the Trefann Court Mothers disputed this report. It soon became evident that they had the support of the reform caucus, and the officials' report was sent back to be rewritten.

The Trefann Court Mothers were a group of homeowners living in the Park School area who had withdrawn their children from the public system and established a private school called Laneway. They, along with a group of community organizers, continued to criticize the Toronto Board of Education, having a variety of concerns related to reading, special education, and school discipline in the inner city. Wolfe Erlichman, a transplanted organizer from suburban Downsview, led the Trefann Court Mothers' group. The brief presented by the group stated that placement in Opportunity Classes was the outcome of social discrimination and that they failed to help children learn and prepare for the world of work. However, it is questionable that the erudite literary style, presentation of data, and general theoretical information could have been the work of five mothers from Trefann Court, an area immediately south of the Regent Park housing project. The highest level of education among the mothers was grade ten. It soon became apparent that the brief was in fact the work of George Martell, an organizer from a well-to-do Halifax family who was associate editor of *This Magazine Is About Schools*. A regular contributor to the magazine was Loren Lind, author of the previously mentioned series of articles in the *Globe and Mail*. George Martell was also a close confidant of Gordon Cressy, who was now the chief spokesman for the reform caucus and the trustee for Ward 7. Mr Cressy had been raised in the wealthy Lawrence Park area of North Toronto.

Special Task Force on Education

On 15 July 1970 the Board of Education's officials produced a second report, which was presented to the trustees sitting as the committee of the whole. The basis of this report was the proposed establishment of a special task force to study and report on matters having to do with inner-city problems, educational programs, and community relationships in Toronto schools. Problems to be dealt with by the Special Task Force on Education were the following:

1. Early childhood education and the feasibility of instituting a nursery school program for preschool children, beginning at three years of age, in the inner-city schools.
2. The community school and community involvement.
3. The involvement of community agencies who were concerned about problems outside of the school having a significant effect on school achievement.
4. Pre-service and in-service teacher training. (Should every teacher in the inner city be required to take specialized courses, and should a salary allowance be paid for the successful completion of such courses?)
5. The use of lay personnel.
6. After-four, evening, and weekend programs.
7. Summer programs.
8. Day care.
9. Pupil mobility.
10. A thorough study of the strengths of inner-city families in order to develop models of the characteristics of those who have achieved upward mobility.
11. The closer involvement of parents in the education of their children.
12. Educational television, particularly programs like *Sesame Street*.
13. Mini-schools in portables, trailers, and houses, for example.
14. The establishment of a new inner-city school category for schools that have six or more pluses on the current seven-criteria evaluation scale (these schools would receive additional resources, for example, teachers, supplies, and equipment).
15. Liaison with Metropolitan Toronto School Board's Inner City Committee (which included representatives from six area boards), which would conduct a re-examination of the criteria used for the designation of a school as inner city.[36]

The Globe and Mail reported that the official primarily responsible for the task force recommendations was Dr Edward 'Ned' McKeown, Inspector in Charge of Special Education. It seemed that the man who was most under attack around the Opportunity Class issue was chosen to invent the cure. Had the officials accepted the Trefann Court Mothers' definition of the problem, the rational decision would have been to direct the task force to focus on the curriculum and program of Opportunity Classes. The first proposed candidate for the position of chairman of the task force was Dr McKeown, whose appointment was strongly opposed by the reform caucus. On 10 September 1970 the Board of Education approved the appointment of William J. 'Bill' Quinn to act as the group's chairman; known as a gentle reformer, he was seconded from his position as inspector of public schools in the inner city. He was to be assisted by a part-time professional staff of four persons, which included the following areas of expertise: human relations, community development, school neighbourhood relations, and research and curriculum development. Chairman Quinn was to report directly to Ron Jones concerning the work of the task force. Consultations with community groups and Board of Education staff strongly supported the idea of an action team (as opposed to a study group). Therefore, the special task force chose to be not merely an information-gathering unit but rather a working group that was able to initiate and develop a number of demonstration projects in response to concerns identified as a result of school-community interaction. Some of the projects undertaken were community development of a new school, a school community council, services for youth, community health centres, a community school program, and programs for new Canadians.[37]

Joining the Task Force

I believe that my involvement in the Board of Education's special task force came as a result of a presentation I had made to the Commission on Emotional and Learning Disorders in Children (CELDIC), which was chaired by Ron Jones. I had also worked with Bill Quinn on the Ontario Department of Education's Curriculum Committee on Compensatory Education. Mr Quinn realized that my role as a graduate student at OISE afforded me some discretionary time. In 1970 he proposed that I become an occasional member of the task force initiation team, specializing in school neighbourhood relations, and Ron Jones agreed. The next year, I was appointed assistant chairman of the Special Task Force on Education, at the pay level of a public school principal of an A-level school. However, this proved to be a most controversial decision. The Public School Principals' Association and some senior officials strongly opposed my appointment. First of all, I had not progressed through the ranks as a teacher and vice-principal in the Toronto system (that is, 'paid my dues'). Second, owing to my Lawrence Heights experience I was seen by some principals, officials, and trustees as a radical who was not to be trusted in a time when the system was under attack. Mr Jones used his political clout and silenced the naysayers within the system with the statement 'I am the Director of Education.'

The organizers and reform politicians in Ward 7 were also after my hide. I was seen as a threat because I came from a working-class background and had served as a school-community worker in Lawrence Heights. I did not fit the profile of the reactionary bureaucrat. Ongoing strategy meetings were held, some in Trustee Cressy's home, to either block my appointment or attack my credibility in order to have me removed from the task force. These efforts were duly reported by the task force supporters from Regent Park who attended the meetings. Needless to say, it was a very stressful period for me.

Task Force Initiation

The original task force initiation team consisted of secondments from various departments of the Board of Education. In addition to Bill Quinn, a secretary, and myself, other members included Dr Stewart Wilson, a psychologist from the Child Adjustment Centre who specialized in organizational development training; Bob Marino, a social worker from the Attendance Department who had worked on the establishment of the new Kensington Community School in Ward 6; and Dr Seymour Trieger of the Research Department.

Headquarters for the task force were found in a semi-detached house that the Board of Education owned at Oak and River Streets, directly across from the north Regent Park housing project. The site had gained notoriety as an organizing focus for Alderman John Sewell's attack on urban renewal. The task force's house at 203 Oak Street was half of the last residential building left standing in the Oak-Cornwall neighbourhood, the rest having been purchased or expropriated by the Board of Education as the site for a new school. Sewell, along with organizer Wolfe Erlichman, was part of the T-Cup Community Organization in the Trefann Court area.

Task Force Progress Report

The work and deliberations of the task force initiation team were not always harmonious, recognizing the disparate interests and disciplines represented. There was also a certain sense of paranoia ('Who is after us today?'). We felt ourselves to be between a rock and a hard place. Owing to provincial ceilings on educational spending, funds for the task force were in doubt. Life in the middle was a frightening place to be. What soon became apparent, however, was that if the task force was to survive, it had to shed traditional bureaucratic behaviour and become much more political. I remember, after conversing with a trustee outside of a Board of Education meeting, I encountered the superintendent of secondary schools who admonished me by stating, 'The only time I speak to a trustee is across the Board table.' It was obvious that we had to learn how to lobby trustees, officials, parents, community groups, and political factions to gain support for the role of the task force. Politics was indeed the art of compromise.

On 25 February 1971 the Board of Education received the progress report of the Special Task Force on Education and approved the following recommendations:

(a) i. That it be the policy of the Board to encourage the development of, and the functioning of, school community councils among the secondary and elementary schools, wherever possible.

ii. That all school community councils be included in the operations of the Task Force, if desired by each council.

(b) That approval be given to the Director of Education for implementing the intent of the Task Force proposal as approved by the Board on 15 July 1970, subject to present limitations of staff, budget, and resources.

(c) That wherever possible, personnel from the Board staff be redeployed on a full or part-time basis, and that facilities and resources within the Board be re-allocated as needed to carry out the work of the Task Force.

(d) That residents of the City, such as the Trefann Court Mothers and others who are not professional educators, be included as participants on the Task Force.

(e) That approval be given to the involvement of resource specialists, scholars, consultants, teachers and students, and representatives from organizations and agencies both inside and outside of the Toronto school system.

(f) That continued use of the Board house at 203 Oak Street as the Task Force office be approved.

(g) That the Director of Education be authorized to solicit and accept funds from outside organizations and foundations for use in setting up special projects.

(h) That, as time and the availability of personnel permit, the Chairman of the Task Force be authorized to continue work on approved projects.

(i) That priority be given to the Trefann Court Mothers' concern for the teaching of reading by the Task Force involvement in:

  (1) an analysis of pupil progress and teaching methods, in language development and reading in selected Inner City schools;

  (2) (a) the organization of a special language development and reading program in Park Public School.

    (b) That the Board approve, in principle, that the Special Program be instituted under the direction of the Park School Community Council, and that prior to the program being implemented, the Park School Community Council present recommendations on the specific costs of the program.

    (c) Working with the Park School Community Council in assisting the development of the project and in obtaining needed resources and funds.

(j) That a survey and analysis be made of where children go from Inner City schools, e.g., high school, university, dropout.

(k) That two members of the Task Force, one to be experienced in educational research, be assigned to work full time with the concerns outlined in sections (i) and (j) above.

(l) That the Chairman of the Board name at least four trustees to serve with the initiating team in establishing the Task Force and to explore ways and means of involving interested trustees in specific projects.'[38]

During the months that followed, the task force continued to pursue its mandate, ever mindful of some of these ongoing issues:

1. Community organizers such as George Martell and Wolfe Erlichman continued to attack the task force, and me personally, in public meetings and behind-the-scenes political lobbying.

2. The Ward 7 trustees Gordon Cressy and Graham Scott continued to support the organizers 'community control agenda.'

3. Park School Community Council and Oak Street Community School Project became the battleground in promoting this agenda.

4. There was a split in allegiance between Regent Park parents and youth who tended to support the work of the task force and the Trefann Court Mothers and their organizers who strongly opposed it.
5. An organization in Ward 8 known as the Riverdale Youth Project, led by organizer Harry McKay, was locked in a struggle with the principal of Riverdale Collegiate concerning the need for a school community council.
6. Senior officials at the Board of Education were lukewarm, at best, to the work of the task force even though it was strongly supported by the director of education (they resented the fact that Bill Quinn reported directly to Ron Jones).
7. After observing the goings-on in Ward 7, many local school administrators across the system were not in favour of more community involvement and were fearful of the prospect of mandated school community councils and any form of community control.
8. Budgetary cutbacks were on the horizon owing to the provincial ceilings on educational spending introduced by the government.

Drafting the Final Report

During the fall of 1971 the task force initiation team began to draft its next progress report to the Board of Education. By then, the team consisted of Chairman Bill Quinn, myself as assistant chairman, Stewart Wilson, Seymour Trieger, as well as two community practice interns (Sheine Goldstein and John Hayes, students from the School of Social Work). (Bob Marino had left to resume his duties in the Attendance Department.) In addition, a trustees' committee had been established to guide the work of the task force, comprising Mary Fraser, Fiona Nelson, Dock Yip, and Gordon Cressy. It transpired that this was the final report of the Special Task Force on Education.

During this time, numerous meetings were held with trustees, senior officials, principals, teachers, school community groups, and service organizations. As we addressed each item in the task force mandate, we sought consultation from groups and individuals affected by the issues. Most notably, we sought to demonstrate progress in the following areas.

Park Public School Projects. A school community council made up of school administrators, teachers, parents, community organizers, trustees, and task force staff was convened. It was a fractious group, with some parents (particularly from Trefann Court), organizers such as Wolfe Erlichman and George Martell, and some staff from the school attempting to control the agenda. This tended to polarize other parents, teachers, and administrators including Junior School Principal Helen Sissons, Senior School Principal Doug Inglis, and Area Inspector Helen Banks. The task force representative, Seymour Trieger, was seen by school administration as favouring the radical community faction. Some contentious issues were the council's role in teacher evaluations, a new language development and reading program, and a special parent-participation funding proposal to the Donner Foundation. The situation reached a climax when the school administration directed teachers to pack council meetings in order to control the agenda and outcomes. The role of Dr Trieger was under attack, and attempts were made internally to have him removed from participation in the council.

The Park School Community Council accomplished the following:

1. A remedial program for grade-eight students to prepare them for secondary school.
2. Thirteen parent volunteers working in classrooms to assist pupils with special reading needs.
3. Additional language development instruction for senior students.
4. A teacher and two parents employed in a remedial demonstration class for Park pupils, which was part of my Department of Education's Compensatory Education summer course for teachers, held at the Duke of York School.
5. A major proposal to the Donner Foundation, which was prepared by a special parent and teacher committee of the school community council and the task force team, to fund a parent project, which would be carried out over the next two years.

Oak Street Project. Since June 1971, the Special Task Force on Education had been working from its office at 203 Oak Street, endeavouring to involve Regent Park North parents and area schools in the decision-making process on the future of the Oak Street site. In many ways, the Oak Street house and a portable classroom on the site had become an extension of Regent Park North, providing space for meetings, a youth centre, and a baseball diamond. Intern Sheine Goldstein was particularly effective in working with parents.

The Toronto Board of Education had originally approved a kindergarten-to-grade-eight school for the Oak Street site. The Oak Street Citizens' Committee was asked to review this decision through a process of community consultation. The Citizens' Committee meetings were often a focus for conflict, with Regent Park North residents squaring off against Trefann Court Mothers and their organizers, Erlichman and Martell. The parents most affected (those with children in portables) developed and conducted a survey of parents in the proposed attendance area. This infuriated the Trefann group who were not from the attendance area. They tried to go door to door with their own survey, preaching their own community control agenda. Some Citizens' Committee surveys that had been completed even 'disappeared' from a committee member's home. When the smoke had cleared, 77 per cent of the questionnaires favoured a kindergarten-to-grade-eight school incorporating community and recreational facilities; these could include participation by the City of Toronto, Ontario Housing Corporation, and the Regent Park Community Improvement Association.

Trustee Gordon Cressy, who had promised a secondary school, was forced to support the decision of the Citizens' Committee. Lobbying of trustees by both sides continued, but on 20 January 1972 the Board of Education voted to approve the building of a kindergarten-to-grade-eight school on the Oak Street site in consultation with local residents – much to the chagrin of some senior officials, particularly the superintendent of public schools, who opposed community involvement. In addition, a work group of the Oak Street Citizens' Committee, including Janet Ross, Connie Chatten, Dorene Fenton, and Intern Sheine Goldstein, was awarded a federal Local Initiatives Program grant to assist in developing the Oak Street project – to the dismay of the Trefann group.

The Oak Street portable was used as a centre for community meetings and professional development of teachers. It also served as a drop-in centre for area young people and was converted into a theatre for presentations by a drama group of youth led by volunteer professionals. In addition, the portable was the setting for a parent and preschool children demonstration project that was organized by area parent Ginny Pettipas, with leadership from George Brown College and Regent Park United Church. Supplies were made available through the Board of Education's Kindergarten Department.

The house at 203 Oak Street, besides serving as an office for the task force, was a meeting place for parents, teachers, and students. It was also the headquarters for the Green Summer Day Camp. Led by Regent Park resident Dave Stanley and other young people in the area, the camp served more than six hundred children in the Regent Park neighbourhood. Other services in the house included a professional library for teachers; an information centre for parents, teachers, and students; and assistance for several youth in getting back into school.

Riverdale Collegiate Community Groups. The Special Task Force on Education served as a resource to Riverdale Collegiate, Riverdale Youth Project, and other groups and individuals interested in school community involvement. I was instrumental in bringing together Ward 8 Trustee Ted Matthews, Principal Ken Turner, and Secondary School Superintendent Archie Milloy to focus on the school issues raised by organizer Harry McKay of the Riverdale Youth Project. Task Force Intern John Hayes was assigned the difficult task of working as a liaison between McKay and Riverdale staff. The previous Riverdale principal had suffered a heart attack, which was attributed to stressful confrontations about the community response to student discipline issues.

A new openness to community involvement at Riverdale Collegiate resulted in the SHARE summer project in 1971. The project received a grant from the Board of Education's Drug and Related Social Issues Committee to involve students and teachers in a program of social and recreational activities. In November, a meeting of parents and teachers was held to assess the needs and interests, as a beginning step in a process of involvement. The SHARE Project was resumed in January 1972 with financial assistance from the Board and the City of Toronto. A community youth program operated during three nights per week, using collegiate facilities and serving the needs of more than two hundred youth from the Riverdale area. In February 1972, an advisory committee was formed, composed of students, teachers, administrators, and local residents.

Citizen Participation. The Special Task Force on Education involved five community representatives in its work by employing them as staff members in my Department of Education Compensatory Education winter course for teachers. The major emphasis was on parent participation and the community school. Community staff included Noreen Gaudette (Trefann Mothers), Janet Ross (Park School and Oak Street), Nellie Williams (Blake School), Dave Stanley (Oak Street), and Murray Starr (Kensington).

New Canadians. The task force worked closely with Noel Bojovic, senior social worker and chairman of the Inter-Cultural Council, to build a firm relationship between the Toronto education system and communities of new Canadians. The Inter-Cultural Council, made up of more than twenty ethnic nationalities, held meetings with the Board's New Canadian Committee to demonstrate its desire and readiness to strengthen Board of Education relationships with cultural groups in the city in order to bring home and school together.

Ward 7 School Community Council. Several meetings were held by a group of concerned persons to explore the feasibility of establishing a Ward 7 school community council. It was decided that there was not sufficient interest, at the time, to maintain such a council.

Report Summary

On 22 March 1972 the director of education forwarded to the trustees a progress report from the chairman of the Special Task Force on Education to be considered at the Board of Education's meeting of 13 April. The following was the report's executive summary.

From the beginning, the Task Force was faced with a number of disadvantages. The series of incidents and issues leading up to the establishment of the Task Force had created a barrier of fear and distrust. The complex nature of the problems which were to be studied and worked on precluded easy or quick solutions. Budget restrictions prevented the hiring of community representatives and made it difficult to obtain help from the system. In addition, the question of whether the Task Force was to be a 'reporting' or a 'working' body caused repeated delays and attacks. A few individuals questioned whether in fact members of the system should, or could, do anything about the concerns facing the system.

Because the original Task Force proposal did not spell out a method of working on the issues, which had been raised, people viewed the Task Force in various ways. Some saw this group as a means of changing the system, while others saw it as a 'cooling out' device. The resulting conflict left the Task Force team in the impossible situation of trying to satisfy two opposing groups. On any given day the team could be called by a school to help it deal with a threat from the parents or community, and on the same day be summoned by the community, demanding to find out how to make the system accountable to its needs and wishes. Therefore, the Task Force team has been forced into the position of listening to both sides and often being the messenger between the sides. The obvious need was to get both sides together. However, no clear-cut machinery existed to do the job, nor did attitudes of trust exist to allow such a cooperative solution. Thus, it is felt that until communication links and connections between the educational system and the community are established, little progress will result.

Community involvement refers to the set of relationships that exists between a school and the community it serves. As every school community has a unique social, cultural and economic identity, the degrees and levels of involvement will vary. What is essential is that the decision that shapes this involvement be reached cooperatively among parents, students, teachers and administration. One method to insure that the needs and interests of community residents will be respected has been the self-survey. This opinionative or interview schedule is developed cooperatively to explore needs and assess resources. A survey conducted by citizen volunteers of all households, or at least a random sample, forms the basis of future planning and decision making. Community involvement must be an educational process for all concerned parties, not a snap judgement for reasons of political expediency. This process must be on-going with a clear set of stated goals and objectives, a step-by-step operational plan and built-in machinery for evaluation.

Therefore, it is recommended that a School Community Development Team from within the system should now be appointed to replace the Task Force. In the light of budget limitations and the lack of credibility that seems to exist in the public view of education, the only hope for the future lies in building skills and processes within the system to accommodate needed changes. In reorganizing to do the job, goals and objectives must emerge to develop a strong thrust and achieve a unity of purpose. Retraining and redeployment of existing personnel is needed to implement these goals. The system must get together as a united force to bring about rational change.

As a result of the experiences gained from becoming involved in some of the problems facing the Toronto system, and considering the needs outlined above, it is now clear that work must be continued on the projects already begun. However, the major responsibility for carrying these projects forward must be assumed by the appropriate part of the educational system, rather than by the Task Force. In addition, it is proposed that the system mobilize itself to begin to work on a number of other concerns, which were originally assigned to the Task Force, but because of limitations of time, staff and budget were not dealt with.

Since it is felt that change can best be accomplished by focusing on emerging needs, the proposed School Community Development Team should now begin to serve as a resource by setting up one or more groups to work on specific problems and issues which are described later in this report. Work groups would bring together capable individuals from the system and the community to work on problems of mutual concern. Characteristics of such a group would be: clearly defined goals, flexibility, integration of skills, strong sense of commitment, collaboration and the facility to disband as soon as the task is complete. Each 'work group' would have a cross section of people from the school system and the community. The involvement of staff members from the system would not be compulsory but would be based on their individual level of skill, expertise and commitment as required by the task undertaken. Each person would be expected to get an agreement from his school or department to be released from his regular duties, a maximum of five hours per week, and to match this with an equal number of hours of his own time. Terms of involvement would coincide with the life of the work group but would not exceed six months without review. Such involvement would be open to any member of the staff who could satisfy the above guidelines.

To enable the system to become involved with the community at the local level, the proposed School Community Development Team should also assume the responsibility of staff development, to mobilize facilities and people in the interests of cooperative problem solving and shared decision making. Thus, through the provision of information and skills, the system will be enabled to cope with the top priority issues of accountability and reorganization.'[39]

Outcomes and Reflections

What were the implications of the work of the Special Task Force on Education? Here are some thoughts that come to mind.

A group of community organizers who were following the teachings of American activist Saul Alinsky introduced the politics of polarization to the City of Toronto using inner-city Ward 7 as a launching pad. The Trefann Court Mothers, led by Wolfe Erlichman and George Martell, became the instrument to confront the school system on the issues of literacy and Opportunity Class placement. They promoted their 'community control agenda' through publications of the Community School Workshop, *This Magazine Is About Schools*, and *Globe and Mail* articles by education reporter Loren Lind.

The task force was seen as a threat to this community control agenda because we did not remain entrenched in the system bureaucracy but ventured forth to meet and consult with parents and other citizens of the community. The fact that the task force took a decidedly political stance by actively promoting a process of community involvement to get trustees, parents, community groups, and school personnel to work together was a radical departure from the traditional educator role. This change in role was strongly opposed by the community organizers and their supporters. The confrontational politics of polarization does not work well when the opposition will not stand still to be confronted. The task force kept getting in the middle.

On a personal level, my involvement in the task force was particularly opposed by organizers Erlichman and Martell and Trustee Gordon Cressy. At a meeting with Cressy on 14 February 1972, convened by Trustee Mary Fraser and including Bill Quinn and myself, he declared his personal opposition to my approach.[40] He said he saw me as a 'fly-by' who was using the situation to enhance a career. He also felt that as a community worker I was making too much money and that I was manipulating the Oak Street situation to suit my personal interests, not the interests of the people. I countered by saying I had been very aware since coming to the task force that some saw me as an interloper and that I would have to gain respect through my present actions, not my past performance. I was also aware that Gordon's reference group, especially Martell, tended to be in opposition to my developmental method and saw it as a real threat to their agenda. I saw myself primarily not as a community worker but as a community educator who assumed a broader, more encompassing role in shaping the total learning environment, rather than working with a specific age group. As a teacher I felt entitled to the level of financial reward paid to teachers and administrators with my education and experience.

Gordon Cressy said that he had trouble understanding this feeling because he had been born into comparative affluence but had rejected materialism to try to help the less fortunate. In my reply I indicated that I had grown up in a working-class home and had a great deal of empathy for people who had no alternatives; it had been my aim to make sure that people had these alternatives, at least through their educational experience. I was also responsible to my family for providing an adequate and secure lifestyle. If I could not do so, then I felt that I had failed them.

Cressy said that he was really 'middled' by having George Martell and company as friends and by having Trefann, and especially Erlichman, as allies. He saw that Wolfe Erlichman's problem with me was competition: Wolfe had worked for four years as a community worker with minimal success, and in four months I had been able to rally people around the Oak Street project. Cressy finished by saying he felt a bit jealous that I had achieved success by pursuing a route that he himself had felt he had rejected; he had not really ever been able to totally accept that rejection in his own mind.

However, the Special Task Force on Education also felt middled. It seemed that the original rationale for its creation was to divert attention from the true target of Martell's Trefann brief, which was special education, literacy, and Opportunity classes in the inner city. The original focus had been Park School, but the whole system felt under attack. It appeared that Ned McKeown, the inspector chiefly responsible for special education, had diverted public and political attention from his domain by proposing the task force as a 'working group to initiate and develop a number of demonstration projects in response to concerns identified as a result of school community interaction.' To the task force's mandate was added a whole series of contentious issues. By then, the senior officials below the director of education, especially superintendents of public and secondary schools and many school administrators, saw the task force as a body that had been created to critique their performance. We had become the outlaws, caught in the middle.

The idea of shared decision making and service delivery through a process of community involvement was totally foreign and threatening to the bureaucratic hierarchy, which was most concerned with preserving the status quo. Consequently, its members often did what they could to passively resist the work of the task force. This was ironic because the Ministry of Education had recently convened its own governmental task force to develop provincial policy on school community involvement. This Ministry task force toured the province to observe exemplary community use and community involvement programs. Flemington Road Community School, Kensington Community School, and the proposed Oak Street Community School were highlighted in the provincial survey.[41]

Just at the time when the Ministry was developing policy on community involvement and community schools, the Toronto Board of Education was locked in a bitter struggle over community control that tended to polarize relations between school and community, between parent and teacher. The sense of fear and mistrust was a serious setback to the cause of community education and development, which would take years to heal.

Our task force report proposed the establishment of a school community development team to replace the task force. The mandate of the new team would be to build skills and processes within the system to accommodate needed changes. This was to be accomplished through the retraining and redeployment of existing personnel to form a unity of purpose. The key to this strategy was a release plan, where Board of Education personnel would be released from their duties for a maximum of five hours per week to participate with community members in work groups to resolve problems of mutual concern. The success of the work group process depended on the availability of funds to cover the release time and on agreement from the school or department to have the personnel released from their regular duties. Therefore, the process was really dependent on financial considerations and the support and goodwill of administrators and department heads.

In actuality, the provincial ceilings on educational spending led to budget cutbacks that determined the fate of our task force and its final recommendations. The school board also underwent a drastic restructuring. When it finally dealt with the task force report on 27 July 1972, Bill Quinn was redeployed to become area six superintendent in north Toronto. I remained as principal on special assignment in the director's office to follow up on task force recommendations.

On 24 February 1972 the then superintendent of public schools had telephoned me to say that he had received a letter from the Ministry of Education stating that before the Oak Street school could be approved, the Board of Education must undertake a detailed house-by-house study in order to assess the school accommodation needs for the area. This would include Sprucecourt, Lord Dufferin, Park, and Regent Park schools, as well as St Paul School which was operated by the Metropolitan Separate School Board. This must have pleased the superintendent because he had never supported the application to the Board by the Oak Street Citizens' Committee for a kindergarten-to-grade-eight school. A combination of declining enrolment and cutbacks due to ceilings on educational spending ultimately proved to be the death knell for Oak Street Community School, which was a bitter disappointment for the Oak Street Citizens' Committee, who had been meeting with architects and senior officials to develop plans for the new school.

Finally, a tribute must be paid to Bill Quinn, the gentle reformer. Bill had been a former principal of the Duke of York School and a campaigner for inner-city education and school-community involvement. The media portrayed him as a dynamic leader. He was later promoted to inspector in the Kensington Market area during the development of the Kensington Community School. Needless to say, Bill's high profile did not go down well with some of his more conservative colleagues who saw him as an opportunist. He was also seen as a threat to other bureaucrats who had their eyes on promotion once the Board of Education's organization was restructured. Bill had assumed the role of task force chairman with a great deal of courage and compassion. To walk the line between conservative, progressive, and reform trustees and Board administrators was enough of a challenge. Add to these the citizen concerns about the quality of education in inner-city schools, special education streaming, and concerns about the plight of the poor, immigrants, and other newcomers to the community. This was all happening in a revolutionary political climate of community control and urban reform. It would have been an almost impossible assignment even at the best of times with unlimited resources.

These were not the best of times. Director Ron Jones, to whom Bill reported, had not been the choice of many reform-minded trustees. He was in his own struggle for survival. Budget limitation meant that people and other material resources could not be spared for the task force. With the exception of myself – the outsider – other appointments to the task force team were often seen as 'push outs' from different departments and lacked credibility in the system. In spite of this, Bill showed amazing political skills in being able to work effectively with the different factions, using a totally new style of educational leadership. I found Bill to be a man of outstanding integrity, creativity, resourcefulness, and compassion. For me, he was a great role model and a wonderful mentor.

6 Work Group Process

Implementing the Task Force Report

The Special Task Force on Education was unique in the history of the Toronto Board of Education because it represented an admission that problems and criticisms facing the system could not be dealt with internally. While some community activists saw this as a ploy to defuse the confrontation that had grown up around the Trefann Court issue, the task force did represent a potential mechanism to open up the system and make it more responsive to the needs of minorities within both the schools and the communities they served. The whole question of the use of community resources to support learning and the initiation and maintenance of alternative programs was an area of special concern.

The task force departed radically from existing Board practices in that it actively solicited opinion from community interests and established various demonstration projects to attempt to alleviate some of the problems identified. This method of operating, however, put the task force at a decided political disadvantage. It was often seen by the more conservative elements within the system (certainly, the majority of administrators) as being somewhat disloyal and therefore not to be trusted. The reform trustees and community activists also viewed the task force with suspicion and distrust, particularly as it began to affect their sources of organizing strength and political power bases.

In September of 1972 I found myself assigned to assist the new director of education, Duncan Green, on the second floor of the Education Centre, 155 College Street. The location was quite a change of scene from the task force house at 203 Oak Street, being in the centre of downtown Toronto and removed from any housing projects. As a principal on special assignment, I was responsible for implementing the task force recommendations. On 27 July that year, the Toronto Board of Education had approved the formation of *work groups* as described in the final report of the Special Task Force on Education: 'Work groups would bring together capable individuals from the system and the community to work on problems of mutual concern. Characteristics of such a group would be clearly defined goals, flexibility, integration of skills, strong sense of commitment, collaboration, and the facility to disband as soon as the task is completed.'[38]

The process began in October with the convening of a planning work group in order to share information, set priorities, and further develop the process. Spin-offs from the Planning work group included the following work groups: School Community Communications, Volunteers in the Schools, Early Childhood Education, Inner City Schools, Cooperative Education, and Community School Development.

The initial membership for each work group consisted of a broad cross section of persons representing trustees, senior officials, local school administrators, teachers, unions and federations, consultative staff, Ministry personnel, community service organizations, business and industry, colleges and universities, and other citizens of the community. As for staff to operate the work group process, I was given Joyce Wry, the former task force secretary. Eventually I was able to secure the services of Murray Shukyn, who had been lead teacher at SEED Alternative School until being reassigned to Blake Street Junior Public School, from where he had been placed on sick leave.

The work group process was one outcome of the task force that legitimized the involvement of teachers, students, parents, and other lay persons in a process of shared decision making and policy formulation and implementation. Work groups were often influential in introducing new demonstration projects and program proposals, which helped to shape future Board of Education policies. The following are profiles of the achievements of selected work groups.

Volunteers in the Schools Work Group

On 26 April 1972 a group of Board of Education staff and parents met with Trustee Judy Jordan to discuss the use of volunteers in the schools. From this initial meeting, a work group was formed, consisting of parents, teachers, consultants, school administrators, superintendents, and community organizations.[42] A number of schools were visited to discuss volunteer programs, and interviews were conducted among staff and volunteers. Available information about volunteer problems in Toronto and other areas was surveyed and discussed in subsequent meetings. The work group found that the presence of volunteers in classrooms had several beneficial effects on the learning situations in those classrooms; their presence might improve the quality of teaching by making it possible for pupils to receive more individualized attention; it might strengthen communication between the school and the community by affording more adults a first-hand experience in the day-to-day operations of a school, thus improving community support for the school; and volunteer presence might allow schools to adapt programs and activities more closely to the needs, interests, and abilities of individual students by making available the resources and skills of more than one adult.

On 21 June 1972, Bill 128 to amend the *Schools Administration Act* was passed by the Ontario Legislature. Section 33, paragraph 6, states, 'A Board shall make provision for insuring adequately the buildings and equipment of the Board and for insuring the Board and its employees and volunteers who are assigned duties by the principal against claims in respect of accidents incurred by pupils while under the jurisdiction or supervision of the Board [effective 1 January 1973],' and section 34, paragraph 2b continues, '... permit a principal to assign to a person who volunteers without remuneration such duties in respect of the school as are approved by the Board and to terminate such assignment [effective 23 June 1972].'

The work group submitted the following proposals:

1. That a volunteer be recognized as a person who, without remuneration, gives support and assistance to a teacher.
2. That a volunteer be recognized as a responsible person who performs tasks, as determined by the principal of a school, which do not involve any of the actual processes of teaching such as planning, diagnosing, or evaluating. These tasks should be performed under the guidance of a teacher, but not necessarily under her or his direct supervision.
3. That individual schools be invited to plan an orientation and training program for volunteers.
4. That the work group be authorized to compile a resource list of people available to assist the development of a volunteer program.

The report of the Volunteers in the Schools work group was influential in shaping both Board and Ministerial policy.

Early Childhood Education Work Group

Membership in the Early Childhood Education work group included trustees, principals, teachers, and representatives of the Kindergarten Department, Psychological Services, and Plant Operations, the Ministry of Education, the Ministry of Community and Social Services, Metropolitan Toronto Social Services, the Social Planning Council of Metropolitan Toronto, and interested parents. The group was later expanded to include representation from the Parent Cooperative Preschool Council, the Day Care Coordinating Committee, and the Oak Street Parent and Child program. Its objective was to explore possible relationships between day care and early childhood education in the school.[43]

Proposals affecting the Duke of York Day Care Centre were discussed within the work group as a model for policy development. The centre had operated since 1967 as a charitable group structured under the *Ontario Corporations Act*. As a day-care service for school-age children, the centre had been licensed under provisions of the *Day Nurseries Act* and had received a subsidy for children of families in need from Metropolitan Toronto Social Services. The proposals would extend this program to include a day-care service for preschool children and infants.

The planned ultimate capacity of the program was fifteen infants below the age of two years and thirty children aged two to five years. It was anticipated that the program would begin with up to twenty children, aged fourteen months to five years, during the summer and then increase slowly until the maximum of forty-five children was reached. The centre would be open from 8:00 a.m. to 6:00 p.m. from Monday to Friday throughout the entire year. Parents using the centre would pay the daily fee-for-service or would be subsidized by Metropolitan Toronto Social Services on a sliding scale. The admission policy, insurance coverage, and overall funding would be the responsibility of the board of directors. The parents would assume a cooperative relationship as volunteers in the day-to-day operation of the school, as resource personnel for maintenance, clerical duties, and fund raising, and as elected representatives on the board of directors.

The regulations required that at full capacity the centre was to provide four persons who were especially trained or experienced in the care of infants, while an additional four trained staff would be needed for the preschool program. The supervisor of the centre, who could be one of the eight, had to be trained and experienced in early childhood education as required by the *Day Nurseries Act*. If volunteers were used in place of regular assistant staff, there had to be two volunteers to cover each assistant staff position. Staff selection would be the responsibility of the board of directors of the day-care centre. It was understood, however, that the principal (or designate) as a member of the board of directors would also be a member of any hiring committee.

Experience gained in the Duke of York Day Care Centre model led to the following general policy, which I submitted to the work group, for a day-care centre in an elementary school. This turned out to be influential in the formulation of a policy for the school board.

The need for neighbourhood-based day care for children of working parents has long been expressed, especially in low-income areas of the city. Such a service, besides ensuring adequate care, should also include a comprehensive developmental program of learning experience and language enrichment geared to the individual needs of each child. Present population trends are indicating a declining school enrolment, providing potential space for day care and early childhood education. A combined service located in the school would result in a smooth transition into kindergarten and provide for continuity in the learning process.

The objective was to establish a facility for early childhood education and day care for two- to five-year-olds, using available space in an elementary school serving a neighbourhood where such a need is apparent.

Schools with empty classrooms (preferably kindergarten) would be identified, and those interested would survey their area by questionnaire and/or consultation with citizen groups and agencies to determine the degree of need for such a service. A series of meetings would be called involving interested parents, school staff, and service agencies to further explore the feasibility of such a centre. A letter of intent would be drafted and circulated. Upon receipt of signed statements from at least fifteen families, a Board of Directors would be elected to include parents using the proposed centre and representatives from the school and the Department of Health. The Board of Directors would then enter into negotiation with the Toronto Board of Education for use of the space; the Day Nurseries Branch of the Ministry of Community and Social Services for licensing; Metro Social Services for possible per diem funding; and other sources of financial support to assist with establishment costs. The Board of Directors would become legally responsible for the setting and administration of a budget, the establishment of the facilities, the development and maintenance of a program, and the hiring of staff according to the provisions of the *Day Nurseries Act*. Liaison with the school program would be ensured by the presence of one or more staff members on the Board of Directors and the ongoing consultative services of the Kindergarten Department of the Toronto Board of Education.[44]

Community School Development Work Group

The membership of the Community School Development work group included principals, area superintendents, and Scott Darrach, a Ministry of Education official. I proposed the following action profile to the group as a demonstration project to influence policy development.

The Funding and Coordination of Extended Day Programs for Adults in the Elementary School

The Toronto Board of Education has been offering academic upgrading courses for adults, leading to a high school graduation diploma. Some elementary schools have been used for the same purpose (e.g., Jesse Ketchum). Due to curricular changes a growing number of non-credit interest-centred courses have been offered. Interest in initiating such courses may be part of the curriculum plan of a new school or of the community involvement program of an existing school. These needs, coupled with an increased demand for community use of facilities by the public, may result in administrative problems, especially with regard to the development, coordination, and maintenance of these activities.

Objectives for the project would be

- to provide a stable source of funding for adult education activities, and
- to coordinate these activities as part of a total administrative plan for community-use of the school.

Adults interested in courses and/or activities to be offered in the local elementary school would approach the Principal for assistance in the planning process. Each application, including a course description and a list of at least fifteen potential participants, would be submitted to the Assistant Superintendent of Extension Programs. When the number of approved courses reached ten, a Coordinator, responsible to the Principal, would be appointed to develop, coordinate, and maintain the community use program of the school.

Possible implications of the project might see representatives of groups using the school, service agencies, and community organizations forming an Advisory Council to work together with the Principal, the Coordinator, and interested teachers in developing a cooperative process of community involvement.

The Advisory Council would serve as a continual means of evaluation for the overall program. The direct relationship between degree of need and the source of funding would also serve an evaluative function.[45]

Continuing education was very much controlled by secondary school principals who used night-school appointments as an incentive to teachers when competing among themselves to fill regular teacher vacancies. The provision of adult education classes at the elementary school level was strongly opposed by secondary school principals. (This proposal did, however, become the model for my future career in the City of York. See chapter 12).

Inner City Schools Work Group

Membership in the Inner City Schools work group included trustees, principals, teachers, area superintendents, and representatives from the Toronto Teachers Federation, University of Toronto, COSTI Immigrant Services, and the Social Planning Council. Work group members developed action profile proposals for demonstration projects to influence Board of Education policy in several areas.

School Development Fund. As a work group member I submitted the following proposal.

There is a need to create a stable source of funding to support innovative program and practice at the local school level. Such a fund would make research and development seed money available to initiate projects designed to alleviate specific problems as identified by the school and/or community. There is a growing consensus that an alternative approach to the allocation of resources to Inner City Schools (e.g., Metro School Board) is needed.

The objective would be to reallocate existing sources of funding to establish a development fund for school-based problem solving.

At present, there are sixty-one schools in Toronto designated as Inner City. Besides extra staff allocation, each Inner City School receives an additional per classroom grant of $50.00 for supplies and $50.00 for equipment.

If this sum (e.g., total number of classrooms) times $100.00 were diverted into a School Development Fund, it would represent a considerable source of money to be used to provide grants to specific schools in support of innovative projects.

Each school would be required to present a proposal, including such items as problem definition, objectives of the project, operational plan, method of evaluation, and future implications. A Special Review Board would select proposals to be funded. One criterion for selection might be that the proposal be developed as a cooperative effort of a work group including principal, teachers, parents, and possibly students. Each project would be funded for a one-year period.

Progress reports and evaluations of individual projects would be circulated to all the schools. Successful projects might be incorporated as an integral part of the curriculum and program of the school. A series of projects in a developmental sequence might be undertaken as part of a long-range plan.[46]

The proposal was influential in providing extra funding to inner-city schools that presented submissions for innovative demonstration projects.

A Transition Program for Young Children. The following proposal was submitted by teacher Tony Grande, a work group member.

Children from ethnic communities experience learning difficulties in school settings. They lag behind in achievement mainly because their oral command of English is not as far developed as that of a child who comes to school from an English-speaking environment. Nevertheless, these children have linguistic and cultural experiences, which, if properly utilized, can work to the child's advantage and hence facilitate the introduction of the English language. The basic principle inherent in this approach is that the school begins from 'where the child is' and with what the child has learned prior to formal schooling.

The primary objective of the special program is to help the ethnic child learn to read and write in English to the best of his ability.

It is suggested that children be selected for the special program on the basis of a similar non-English cultural and linguistic background. The teacher should be fluent in both English and the child's mother tongue. It is suggested the teacher remain with this group of children for more than one year to allow for flexibility and continuity in the program. It is anticipated that the child's mother tongue would be dominant in the first year with English being added slowly at first as it arises out of the child's experiences. The child would be introduced to reading and writing in his mother tongue while at the same time oral language development in English would be accelerated in an atmosphere that is relatively secure from the point of view of the child.

Curriculum content such as Social Studies, Science, and Mathematics would remain the same as with those children speaking English. There will be a time when all oral communication is in English and the children would have grasped the principles of reading and writing in their mother tongue. At that time, reading and writing in English will be introduced and shortly after the complete programme will be in English only. It is anticipated that the pace of learning to read and write English will be considerably accelerated due to the fact that the pupils have grasped the principles of reading and writing in the mother tongue, until the students will be functioning better, or at least as well as their English-speaking age-mates.[47]

Tony Grande's proposal formed the basis of a research and development proposal for Italian students that was undertaken by the research department at General Mercer Junior Public School. Tony later became the Member of the Provincial Parliament (MPP) for Oakwood in the Ontario Legislature.

Social Policy Subcommittee. This proposal was submitted by Marvyn Novick, program director at the Social Planning Council and a work group member.

Inner city schools cannot be abstracted from the social environments in which they are situated. Therefore, an exclusively institutional or network approach to the inner city school (e.g., more teachers, more specialists, more parents, more hardware) runs the risk of tampering with mechanisms without addressing itself to the negative social forces which persist and undercut a child's learning and achievement potential. Insufficient family income, inadequate housing, poor employment prospects, and malnutrition are among some of the contributing factors to social environments which destroy children and which invariably affect the ability of inner city schools to educate effectively.

The primary purpose of a 'Social Policy Subcommittee' would be to create inter-network linkages between this group of educational planners and other organized planning efforts, which are attempting to initiate policy changes affecting the social environment of the inner city school. Such groups include voluntary agencies, grass roots community organizations, and public and private planning bodies.

Linkages could be established by the subcommittee in the following manners:

1. Identification and contact with allied planning efforts in the community for purposes of preliminary exchange, and to inform this planning group of such efforts.
2. Public endorsement by this planning group of policy changes being sought by other planning efforts, e.g., higher payments to Family Benefit recipients. This process would work two ways where it would be useful for this group to enjoy wide community acceptance of its work.
3. To serve as a catalyst to secure official Board of Education endorsement and support for social policy positions related to the inner city being pursued by other groups in the community.
4. To conduct joint research and promotion efforts with other planning groups where there is an immediate area of mutual interest and concern, e.g., financial support to enable 16- to 18-year-old students to complete secondary school.[48]

Marvyn Novick later was the author of the very influential *Suburbs in Transition* report from the Social Planning Council, and he became professor of social work at Ryerson University.

A Plan to Use Out-of-School Indigenous Youth as Lay Assistants in Working Class School Classrooms. Teacher Ruth Johnson, a work group member, submitted the following proposal.

It is necessary to consider some new approaches to solving some of the learning problems in working-class elementary schools by recognizing:

a) That the cultural economic gap between middle-class teachers and their students may be one of the factors preventing more successful results in the classroom and that an increase in awareness and sensitivity is desired.
b) That the influence of older youths on elementary school children is a strong one.
c) That there is a strong need for educators to establish credibility in the

working-class community, e.g., to educate the children to their highest potential, resulting in an increase in professionals coming from the community itself.

d) That some solutions for elementary school learning problems can be found within the community itself.

Objectives of the project would be:

1. To improve the educational experience and academic results of elementary school children in working-class areas by giving them an opportunity to be exposed to their 'own kind' of people in a school environment, rather than just middle-class outsiders.
2. To offer another opportunity to indigenous youth to choose and prepare for a career in teaching or a related field.

In-service training for youth would consist of an operating group (teachers and youth) meeting regularly to continually evaluate the program. Youth would be made aware of any upgrading programs and contacts for admission to university.

Possible implications of the project might be:

1. For the students:
   • an improvement in academic results as well as the development of a more positive attitude to school, where needed. To be on the receiving end of constructive influences by the older youths.

2. For the youth:
   • successful experiences helping younger children from the community;
   • another opportunity for intelligent indigenous youths to consider a career in teaching or a related field.

3. For teachers:
   • learning from the youth assistant and improving his/her teacher's sensitivity and affect attitudinal change in their students and his/her self;
   • finding some successful approaches to class learning problems;
   • increasing awareness of the school's community and its problems;
   • improving credibility in the community that the teaching profession

is interested in encouraging working-class youth to choose a professional career.

4. For the community:
   • to see one effort amongst many being made to help solve their children's learning problems and to also provide a career model for
   adults and children in the community;
   • to see that the educational system is willing to look beyond the
   experts, to the community, for some help in seeking solutions.[49]

Ruth Johnson's proposal went to the Learnxs Foundation for funding. She later mounted successful cross-cultural curriculum projects:
Pinocchio for All People (Italian) and *Anansi the Spider* (West Indian).

A Cultural Immersion Program for Teachers in Immigrant Areas. As
a work group member I submitted this proposal.

Schools in areas of the city with a large proportion of immigrant families may have difficulty in relating their curriculum and program to the
needs of children and parents. One approach to bridging this gap might be
through a better appreciation, on the part of teachers, of the cultural heritage which these people bring to their new homeland. Another consideration would be an understanding of the attitudes, customs, and values,
which affect their lifestyle in the context of the neighbourhood in which
they live.
   Objectives of the program would be:

1. To develop a learning program for teachers and prospective teachers in
   order to provide an intensive exposure to the culture and lifestyle of a
   selected immigrant group.
2. To involve members of the immigrant community in the development,
   organization, and maintenance of such a program.

The program would be approached in three phases:

1. Involvement of social and cultural groups within the immigrant community in working together with Board of Education staff to develop
   introductory courses for teachers in experiential learning around such
   areas as family life, art forms, language familiarization, cuisine, and
   cultural history, as well as problems of integration into a new culture.

Such a course might be organized so as to qualify for credit through the
Ministry of Education or a university.

2. An outgrowth of phase one would be the organization of a Charter tour
to the particular country and region from which a majority of immigrants within a group have come, e.g., Calabria in Italy. Such a tour
might include billeting in private homes, visits to schools and other
institutions, and discussions with parents, teachers, and students. This
experience would also provide an opportunity to develop learning
materials for the classroom, e.g., films, slides, tapes.

3. As a follow up to phase one and/or two, interested teachers would
involve themselves in an intensive program of self-directed and/or
small group learning in conjunction with a facilitator, which might
include language instruction, cultural activities, and a broader sociological perspective of the needs of the individual within the immigrant
group.[50]

The proposal was implemented in the fall of 1973, beginning with a
series of seminars on Italian culture and followed by a study tour, during the winter break in 1974, to the Abruzzi region of Italy.

Cooperative Education Work Group

One of the community groups that had approached the Special Task
Force on Education during its lifespan had been the Metropolitan
Toronto Labour Council, which identified the need for a work study
project involving secondary school students who would spend time
in business, industry, and other work situations as part of their school
day. As a result, the final report of the task force had recommended
'that the Director of Education be authorized to set up a "Work Study"
work group composed of trustees and staff of the Board of Education,
representatives from the Department of Education, the Department of
Labour, the Labour Council of Metropolitan Toronto, and business and
industry to report on the desirability and feasibility of establishing a
work study program in the secondary schools.'[51]

Another community group, known as the Riverdale Youth Project,
had approached the task force concerning their Work Experience Education program, which had involved about twenty secondary school
students working one day per week in business and industry. On 29
May 1972, the Board of Education received a progress report from this
project and adopted the recommendation 'that the Director of Educa-

tion be requested to meet with representatives of the Riverdale Youth Project to discuss details with respect to possible continuation and expansion of the work study aspects of the Project during the 1972–3 academic year.'[52]As a result, a liaison committee consisting of the area superintendent, principals, and myself as the director of education's representative was established to involve the Riverdale Youth Project and secondary schools in the Riverdale area. The committee became a reference group concerning the task force's recommendation on work study.

On 27 July of that same year, the Board, after consideration of the final report of the task force, approved the recommendation 'that Work Study projects referred to in the Task Force Report ... be implemented at the discretion of the Director of Education.'[53] I was asked by the director of education to implement this recommendation.

As a result of meetings of the liaison committee of the Riverdale Youth Project held on 12 and 20 September, it was proposed that the new work group on work-study projects should be known as the Cooperative Education work group. This new group would incorporate concerns identified by the Riverdale Youth Project within the broad terms of reference of the relationship between the school and learning resources in the community.

The first meeting of the Cooperative Education work group was held on 30 October and was attended by persons from business and industry (Imperial Oil, Canada Life, and Consumers' Gas), the Ministry of Education (the departments of Curriculum Services, Commercial Education, and Technical Education), the Riverdale Youth Project, and the Toronto Board of Education (superintendents of Areas 4 and 5, Business Education, Technical Heads' Association, and the Office of the Director of Education). Regrets had been received from the trustee (Ward 8) and the Metropolitan Toronto Labour Council (United Steelworkers of America). The meeting began with a statement of the terms of reference for the work group, followed by a progress report on the second year of the Riverdale Youth Project and a general discussion about the meaning of work experience and cooperative education. There was a consensus within the group that schools should make better use of community resources, but a concern was expressed that such resources might not be able to accommodate the demand should academic as well as commercial and technically oriented students become involved.[54]

The second meeting of the work group was held on 21 November, and reports were received from several technical schools concerning their work experience programs. A discussion followed around the relationships between education, work, and life experience. The feeling was expressed that there was a need for change in education to prepare students better for the future. Education should be a cooperative venture between school and community as a preparation for life experiences.

Another concern expressed by some work group members centred on the needs of students who go directly from secondary school to the world of work. They require an orientation to the work place and a source of money to help them stay in school until graduation. The Riverdale Youth Project was directed to this type of problem. The point was also made that all students should have an opportunity to pursue out-of-school learning, which could provide a sociological experience, opportunities to scan alternatives, and an introduction to the adult world rather than the school world, for example, by having student works one day per week in business and industry.

It was decided to establish two action committees (or subcommittees). The first would investigate the possibility of organizing a broad cooperative learning project to extend HS 1 (the secondary school curriculum) into the community. The second would focus on the need to reach kids who are not able to function in the school system.[55]

Work Experience Subcommittee

As a result of the deliberations of the Cooperative Education work group, a subcommittee of the Board's School Programs Committee was authorized on 8 February 1973 to consider proposals from the work group and to serve as a source of policy formulation in order to guide the growth of work experience as a cooperative relationship of business and industry, labour, the Board of Education, and the community at large. On 3 May 3 the Board approved the following proposal:

> The Students in Business Project is designed to build upon the knowledge and experience gained through the Riverdale Youth Project, in order to provide a solid base for the future growth and development of the work experience concept.

> There are two primary goals of the proposed Students in Business Project:

> 1. To prevent premature dropouts from the secondary schools through

the creation of (a) supportive social relationships in order to raise the level of aspiration of the student, and (b) a source of financial assistance through part-time employment.
2. To strengthen the employability potential of the student through on-the-job experience.

Ground rules for the Project will include:

1. A standard set of selection criteria to be worked out jointly through the schools and employers participating in the Project;
2. An ongoing system of evaluation which would include (a) the performance of the student in school and on the job, (b) an assessment of the value of the experience to the student and the employer, and (c) an overall evaluation of the Project by an external source, e.g., the Research Department of the Board;
3. A common procedure for defining and communicating job descriptions; and
4. Consistent compensation and benefits including working conditions agreed upon by participating employers.

It is recommended that:

1. The Toronto Board of Education adopt the Students in Business Project as a Cooperative Education program during the 1973–74 school year.
2. The Director is authorized to designate a staff member as a liaison resource person to coordinate the Project with the selected schools.[56]

The Students in Business project influenced both Board and Ministry of Education policy in the area of cooperative education. A result was the introduction of Ministry curriculum guidelines on the cooperative utilization of community resources.

Outcomes and Reflections

When the Special Task Force on Education was officially dissolved in July 1972, the intent was to continue to work on identified issues through the establishment of a school-community development team. Provision was made for staff release time to participate in the work group process. I was assigned to the director's office, with the assistance of a secretary and later the services of a seconded teacher who had both elementary and secondary school experience. This was the extent of the development team. However, I was most fortunate to be able to recruit, as work group members, a large, diverse group of trustees, senior officials, parents, teachers, local school administrators, central office staff, and representatives from business and industry, community service organizations, school-community groups, and post-secondary institutions. This extended team represented a whole new concept of shared decision making and working relationships.

The work groups mounted a variety of demonstration projects and proposals that helped to focus and influence policy directions in several key areas, including volunteers in education, day care in the school, adult and continuing education, support for inner city schools, community resource learning, and alternatives in education. The work group process later became the model for a whole series of administrative and trustee-initiated committees that largely transformed decision making at the Toronto Board of Education, for example, work groups on vocational schools, student rights, and multiculturalism.

The Cooperative Education work group established an action committee to investigate the possibility of organizing a broad cooperative learning project to extend HS 1 into the community. The next chapter will present the committee's response to this objective as an action research study.

7 Learning Exchange System

As previously stated, action research is an ongoing study of a social process and its results, where accumulated findings are used to guide and correct the decisions of the continuing process. The following is a case study of such an action research process.

Community Learning Resources

On 18 December 1972 the first meeting of the Cooperative Education work group's action committee on school community learning resources was held in the Inno-Space Centre at the Ontario Institute for Studies in Education.[i] Attendance at that initial meeting consisted of persons from Adult Education, OISE; Inno-Space; and Metropolitan Toronto Planning Review; as well as Area 5 superintendents, representatives from the Department of Business Education and Central High School of Commerce, and myself from the director's office of the Toronto Board of Education.

The committee examined the problem of how to identify resources in the community to support learning. One example used was the Greater Riverdale Organization, where potential resources had been identified to improve the quality of life in the community. Another approach discussed was the *Yellow Pages of Learning Resources*,[57] a publication using the telephone directory as a format to catalogue and organize sources of community learning. The committee recognized that trying to educate the masses on an individual tutorial system was almost an impossi-

---

i · Inno-space was a learning centre for people to develop, share, and test new ideas for innovations in education.

bility. Schools were no longer the only source of knowledge, and there was a need to educate the public on how to learn from their own experience.

Concern was expressed about the problem of storing and accessing information about learning resources. Two examples, which used computer technology, were the Educational Resources Information Centre (ERIC) system for cataloguing research data on education in the United States, and Metro Doc, a directory of adult education activities in Metropolitan Toronto.[ii]

It was agreed that any school utilizing a community-learning-resources approach would have to have a radically different style of operation than one currently existing. For example, the program would have to be based on independent study with freedom of movement in the community. It might require the creation of a new alternative program specially designed to accommodate the community-learning-resources model. Consequently, it was decided to prepare a proposal that would incorporate a learning resources bank, an information retrieval system, and an alternative program to extend HS 1 (secondary credit system) into the community.[58]

On 12 and 19 January 1973 the action committee held informal brainstorming sessions to discuss the first draft proposal, which was entitled 'Learning Exchange System, the Learnxs Project.' (I had conceived the Learnxs concept during a family camping trip while travelling across Saskatchewan.) The proposal was to be presented to the next meeting of the Cooperative Education work group, on 25 January. As a result of the committee meetings, sections of the first draft were greatly expanded and an introduction and an implementation plan were added. Since this proposal was being prepared for eventual submission to the Toronto Board of Education, references and examples reflected Ministry of Education policies (for example, HS 1) and school-related analogies as opposed to a broader community education perspective.

The introduction began with reference to the curriculum needs of the current population of students. Allusion was made to the HS 1 secondary school guidelines that spoke of the potential of community-based learning resources as well as individual and small group research and problem solving. The need to identify, develop, and record materials, experiences, and human resources that would support spontaneous (that is, non-formal) as well as programmed learning was expressed.

---

ii   Diana Ironside, the Adult Education Department representative, had previously worked for ERIC in Syracuse and had designed the Metro Doc project in Toronto.

Finally, the specific aims or tasks of the project were stated: to collect and catalogue potential sources of learning experience in the community; to develop a system of access to share this information among learners; and to organize an alternative school project to use and evaluate these learning resources.

The Objectives and Rationale section of the second draft included the general objectives of the project with accompanying explanations. The first objective stressed the value of using community resources in individual and small group learning as part of the curriculum and program of the school. The second objective expanded the learning environment to include the sharing of information and skills among individuals and community groups (for example, teachers, librarians, receptionists, and adult educators). The concept of joint planning and policy development among these groups was also proposed. The third objective dealt with the need to explore alternate approaches to the achievement of educational goals. These could include traditional group learning techniques as well as more informal, experiential, self-directed approaches. The fourth objective aimed to find alternative sources of human, financial, and material support to encourage educational development. The final general objective involved an information-sharing and retrieval system to provide better access to learning resources. A variety of media were mentioned (such as print directory, filing system, computer, telephone, radio, television, and newsletter).

The Method section proposed a work group process whereby a group of interested and committed individuals with different skills and affiliations would form a joint action committee to oversee the work of task groups in the following areas:

1. Learning Resources Exchange – This would involve the identification and compilation of a directory of community learning resources.
2. Information Sharing and Retrieval System – This task group would investigate a variety of media and technological applications to establish a retrieval system for the Learning Resources Exchange.
3. Subway Academy: The task group would seek to establish an alternative public secondary school in order to encourage a flexible approach within a learning environment, stressing the utilization of community resources, independent study, and shared decision making. (For the Board's alternatives in education policy, see chapter 8.)

The Implications section stated that while the proposal was directed to the secondary school setting, the overall objective would be to involve younger and older learners within a process of continuing education.

It was envisioned that the project would be evaluated by an external source, using an action-research type of design, and that funding for the project would consist of support in goods and services from participating organizations. In addition, longer-term funding would be sought from the Ministry of Education, as would special grants from other sources to finance specific tasks.

The implementation strategy consisted of a description of the process by which the different tasks would be undertaken, involving the formation of task groups, the acquiring of project personnel, the implementation of the programs, and the communications and interrelationships among task groups.

Debate within the action committee on school community learning resources generally focused on the need to reflect a community perspective while maintaining the relevance of the proposal to formal education. It was recognized, however, that although non-formal learning played an important part in the daily life of the learner, the credits and certificates of formal education were still valued by the majority of people. Therefore, the proposal that went to the Cooperative Education work group was somewhat of a compromise.

On 25 January the Cooperative Education work group met to consider progress reports from the two subcommittees School Community Learning Resources and Work Experience. The work group first considered the presentation of the School Community Learning Resources subcommittee (or action committee) concerning the Learnxs proposal (second draft). Possibly because the majority of work group members were school-related people, the discussion focused on the Subway Academy section of the proposal, in particular the degree of flexibility of HS 1 to respond to students' needs, and the relative need of students for alternative programs.

The opinions of the work group were divided as to the value of and the need for alternative schools. Some Board administrators and teachers and the representatives from the Ministry of Education expressed the opinion that the HS 1 curriculum provided adequate flexibility for existing secondary schools to relate to students' needs without the establishment of separate alternative schools. For example, the Ministry suggested that it should be possible to extend the school day so that some students could work part time and still continue their studies.

At this point in the meeting I presented a verbal report that compared the traditional group-oriented, textbook-based education to a more individualized approach that stressed the need for continuous access to current information. I also provided a five-year survey of the dropout rate in Toronto secondary schools during the school year.[iii] This presentation made the points that there was more than one valid style of learning or approach to teaching and that comparatively large numbers of students were already choosing an alternative by leaving school before graduating.

Another concern was raised as to whether or not the existing SEED alternative school already satisfied the needs of students who wished this type of education. It was pointed out by a group member that SEED had been established as a free school, operating as independently as possible from the Toronto Board of Education's administrative practices; the emphasis had been on bringing in resources to enrich the learning environment. Conversely, the Subway Academy concept would utilize the administrative and other support services of the Board. Students would be encouraged to seek their own sources of learning to support their course work by drawing upon both in-school and community-based experiences.

Alternative schools, such as Subway Academy, do not deny the need for a more traditional approach for the majority of students. However, they recognize that changing lifestyles have created a need for more meaningful learning experiences for certain students.[iv] Subway Academy would have been one way of testing the validity of these students being involved in developing their own program under HS 1 through the use of a variety of learning resources.

The work group decided to study material on existing information and learning support systems (for example, Metro Doc and those of the University of Toronto's Faculty of Library Science) and then reconsider the proposal at a future meeting.[59]

On 22 February the work group met to reconsider the Learnxs proposal. After a general discussion concerning the feasibility of the project, it was decided that the proposal should be approved for implementation. The Learning Resources Exchange and the Information Sharing and Retrieval System were to be dealt with as one project, and a joint task group was to be formed to further refine the proposal and seek

---

iii This report had been prepared by work group members from IBM, Consumers' Gas, and the Director's Office who met informally to respond to questions raised at previous meetings concerning the relative need for alternative programs.

iv A copy of the speech delivered by Mario Fantini at the Wingspread Conference on Educational Alternatives had been sent to members of the work group.

alternate sources of support. It was agreed that the Subway Academy phase should be presented to the Toronto Board of Education for consideration as a new public alternative school. Work group members, area superintendents George Hayes and Harold Kitney, and I were asked to meet with the director of education to discuss procedures for presenting this proposal to the trustees and to gain support for the concept within the Toronto Board of Education system. It was necessary to take the Subway Academy phase to the Board because, as a new public alternative school, it required Board approval. Also, if the school were to open in September 1973, the proposal had to go to the trustees as soon as possible.

Implementation of Learnxs

After approval was gained from the Cooperative Education work group, we were faced with two main options in seeking support for implementation of the Learnxs proposal. The Toronto Board of Education seemed to be the obvious source of support for the project. However, as the Province of Ontario had recently imposed ceilings on school-board spending, it was doubtful that the trustees would look favourably on the proposal unless it could be tied directly to the instructional process. Also, if the Board were the prime funding agent, it could conceivably control the growth and direction of the project. This might seriously inhibit the project's sense of innovative flexibility, particularly with relation to non-formal learning for persons of all ages and its objective of serving the broad community education sector including libraries and social and recreational services. To fund the project from sources external to the Board would preserve its sense of autonomy but could limit its degree of access and acceptability in Toronto Board schools, which would be its largest potential constituency. Certain services of the Board could also be important to the success of the venture, for example, information and publications, computer services, and teaching aids.

Therefore, it was decided to seek a mix of internal and external support. For example, Subway Academy as an alternative school could attract students who had left school, who were dissatisfied with their current situation, or who came from other jurisdictions in Metropolitan Toronto. These new students would generate ceiling dollars to justify the added expenditure. The Learnxs directory could be developed by grants for the use of external short-term community employment in the initial identification and cataloguing of learning resources. A similar arrangement might be used for the promotion and distribution of the Learnxs directories and the maintenance of an information service. The information-retrieval function of the project required access to an electronic system of data processing. As the costs of such a system would be prohibitive for an outside organization, a cooperative relationship with the Toronto Board of Education's Computer Services department would be essential for testing the feasibility of the concept.

The following sections provide a chronology of the events that grew out of the cooperative utilization of support sources.

Subway Academy

When the Cooperative Education work group disbanded in February 1973, it was recognized that to establish Subway Academy as an alternative secondary school opening in September that year would require almost immediate Board of Education approval of the concept, with particular reference to staffing and accommodation. Therefore, it was necessary to pursue this phase of the proposal first. The recommended Subway Academy was to be hosted by an existing secondary school that was located in close proximity to the subway line. The ad hoc subcommittee had been delegated by the work group to consult with the director of education to find a secondary school principal who might be most receptive to the concept while maintaining credibility with his or her colleagues in the Toronto Secondary Schools Headmasters' Association.

The subcommittee met on 13 April with Aubrey Rhamey, the principal of Eastern High School of Commerce, who was also president of the Headmasters' Association. It had been decided to approach Mr Rhamey for the following political and logistic reasons: he had a reputation as a progressive administrator; as president of the Toronto Secondary Schools Headmasters' Association, he held the esteem of the other principals and was in a position to actively influence their level of cooperation; and his school was located one block south of the Donlands subway station in the east central section of Toronto.

There were several key elements in the presentation that influenced his decision. First of all, the director of education had approached him informally about the proposal, and Mr Rhamey`s area superintendent (Area 5) was one of the persons making the presentation. Enrolment at Eastern Commerce had declined to the point where it was in danger of losing its third vice-principal; by agreeing to be the host principal for Subway Academy, Mr Rhamey was assured of maintaining this position for at least another year. In addition, he would have the opportunity to discuss the proposition with his staff, and should they collectively decide not to participate, this decision would be viewed without prejudice by the senior administration.

Mr Rhamey responded enthusiastically to the proposal, particularly when he was assured that he would be in charge of the program. After discussing the idea with his staff during the following week, he formally agreed to serve as the host principal of Subway Academy.

On 15 May the Subway Academy proposal was incorporated into a report from the director of education to the School Programs Committee of the Toronto Board of Education as follows:

The following proposal is submitted as an outgrowth of deliberations of the Cooperative Education Work Group:

Introduction
As new curricula are developed to meet the needs of today's students, the wealth of practical knowledge and experience available in the community becomes increasingly apparent. The potential of community-based learning resources is being appreciated not only as a complement to H.S. 1 but also as a vehicle for individual and small group research and problem solving. The new directions encouraged by the Ministry include curricula based on student interests, and the increasing emphasis on multi-disciplinary subject areas. In order to incorporate these aspects of learning into a visible pilot project, the following model is suggested:

Objectives
1. To develop learning experiences and materials using the community as an extension of the school, and to encourage the greater use of community resources for individual and small group learning projects.
2. To encourage the sharing of information and skills among individuals and groups, such as teachers, librarians, and other co-professionals, interested in incorporating the learning environment into the community.
3. To explore and evaluate alternative patterns of learning. (Because there is awareness that there are different levels of need and styles of learning, experiments should be undertaken with different approaches to existing guidelines such as H.S. 1 as well as exploring the needs and interests of people who wish a more experimental and self-directed program.)

4. To allow the business and general community to participate in and contribute to the learning process in a more meaningful and direct manner.
5. To establish a model which can be studied and researched in an attempt
   to document new directions in learning.
6. To develop a training model so that concepts and practices developed
   through community-based learning can be made available to the wider
   learning community.

Method

This project would be developed and guided by a task group consisting of
Board representatives and community people, including students, assisted by an advisory board invited for assistance on specific aspects of the
program. The space to be used would be that already available in an existing school, located in close proximity to the subway line. Staffing would
be accomplished within the existing staff complement for the city, through
the cooperation of the area superintendents and the principal involved.
Curriculum would be within the existing guidelines, except where permission is granted for the establishment of experimental courses. This
program would not be an additional real cost to the Board, but rather a
re-deployment of existing resources to establish an alternative program
for 60 secondary school students.

The task group would develop a program linked with the most concentrated source of learning resources in the city, e.g., the subway corridor. Such a program might develop a curriculum around a central theme
(e.g., transportation and communication) but stress individual guidelines.
It would utilize administrative and clerical services of the host school but
encourage curriculum and program development to be a shared responsibility of students, teacher facilitators and parents. A student might arrange
his program to take advantage of credits available at several different
schools along the subway line. Another approach would extend H.S. 1
into the community so as to encourage individual and small group learning projects using community resources. A third option would include
work experience as an integral part of the learning plan. A fourth possibility would be a combination of the other three approaches. The individual
programs would reflect the individual needs and interests of the students.

It is recommended:

a) That approval is given, in principle, to the establishment of the 'Subway
   Academy' in September 1973, for up to 60 secondary school students.

b) That the host school be Eastern High School of Commerce.

c) That a task group be established consisting of six members of the teaching and administrative staff, two parents, two community people, four students and two trustees to be named by the Chairman of the School Programs Committee, to begin to develop the direction and means of implementation of the 'Subway Academy.'

d) That appropriate materials be developed for distribution to the schools through normal channels within the next two weeks so that an immediate indication of interest can be ascertained.

e) That the task group, through the Director of Education, report back to the School Programs Committee on June 5, 1973, on its plans for implementation and the interest generated by the information bulletin, and the estimated budget which will be necessary to operate the project.

f) That tentative applications are gathered from students.

g) That tentative applications for the positions of teacher facilitators are invited from the existing citywide staff.

h) That retiring teachers be contacted to ascertain their interest in volunteering some time without remuneration to work with students.

i) That the Ministry of Education be requested to cooperate in this venture.

j) That negotiations are started with post-secondary institutions with a view to ensuring their cooperation regarding admission of graduates.

k) That the College of Education, the Ontario Institute for Studies in Education, and the University of Toronto be approached regarding the possibility of incorporating their students into the program as volunteer resource people.

l) That a method of identifying and gathering information regarding community resources be investigated to ensure their availability for the academic year 1973–74, e.g., Learning Resources Exchange phase of Learnxs Project.[60]

At the regular meeting of the Board on 24 May, the Subway Academy proposal and recommendations were approved in principle. The following day, a notice was sent out from the director of education to principals of secondary schools announcing the Board's approval of the program, that the principal of Eastern High School of Commerce would be in charge of administering and organizing the project, that all students should be informed that they were eligible for admission to the program, and that application forms were available for September 1973. On 21 May a notice in the *Weekly Circular* to all public and secondary schools had invited applications for staff positions at Subway Academy. On 5 June the director of education reported to the Board that about 50 per cent of required student applications had been received, and it was decided to extend the deadline for applications to 15 August. On 14 June the Board formally approved the establishment of Subway Academy.

Subway Academy commenced operations on 4 September, using three portable classrooms on the playing field of Eastern High School of Commerce. Staff consisted of two full-time teacher facilitators and a half-time unassigned teacher, Murray Shukyn, who had been loaned through the director's office. By the end of the first week there were fifty-two students enrolled.

The Subway Academy task group decided to confine its role to overall policy decisions and program evaluation, while the day-to-day operations would be left to the students, staff, and administration of the school. Although a separate entity, Subway also had the right to draw upon the secretarial, guidance, and library services of Eastern High School of Commerce.

Learnxs Foundation

On 14 June the Toronto Board of Education had also recognized that further implementation of the Learnxs proposal in the areas of the Learning Resources Exchange and the Information Sharing and Retrieval System would require funding support from other than the Toronto Board. If the Learnxs Project was to receive such funding directly, it would be a distinct advantage to be legally incorporated and to have a charitable taxation number. On 16 June the following report was presented to the School Programs Committee:

> On June 14, 1973, the Board at its regular meeting adopted the following resolution: 'That alternative sources of funding be investigated for extension of the Learnxs concept, e.g., alternative forms of learning, and that a definite proposal be prepared for the next series of meetings.'
>
> In keeping with the intent of this motion, the following proposal is submitted:
>
> *Introduction*
> As budgets become strained and pupil enrolment decreases, a clear direc-

tion for the future is emerging. Boards of Education, in order to maintain the numbers of students, must become responsive to the needs of their potential and actual clientele. Inflation has accentuated the effects felt under the constraints of the present policy of educational spending. The Toronto Board of Education has a tremendous amount of experience in alternative modes of learning, responsive to community needs. This may be one area in which additional students may be brought back into the school system. One of the major problems in this area is the lack of short-term funding.

Rationale

There is a need to create a stable source of short-term funding to support innovative program and practice at the local school level. Such a fund would make research and development seed money available to initiate projects designed to alleviate specific problems as identified through schools and/or communities within the Toronto Board of Education. Since the present educational budget seems hard pressed to provide basic services, it is proposed that the community be encouraged to become involved in education through a foundation to be established for the above purposes.

The funds required for this type of project could be solicited from industry, foundations, service clubs, and private individuals. By setting up a foundation, funds can be solicited, direction given, and projects implemented. The foundation would also act as a buffer zone between donor and recipient. Co-funding and multi-donor funding of single projects can also be considered under the umbrella of a foundation. Since foundations can be set up to conform to the regulations of the *Income Tax Act* (sections regarding charities), monies donated to a foundation could be used more efficiently, taking advantage of the provisions for deduction of donations. There is also the possibility of cost-sharing arrangements with various levels of government to increase the purchasing power of the foundation's dollar (e.g., Canada Assistance Plan). This flexibility in itself is a unique aspect of this type of short-term funding.

Objective

To establish a foundation to be called the Learnxs Foundation which will solicit funds from private and public sources, for the purpose of providing short-term funding for innovative programs within the Toronto system. The fund will encourage each program to build in a research aspect to document the developmental process by providing additional funds specifically for research.

Fund raising will be carried out in two phases. The first phase will be the soliciting and administering of funds from established funding sources. This phase will enable the Foundation to establish credibility and gain acceptance as a funding source. The second phase will be the accumulation of sufficient capital to begin making grants from earned interest. This phase will require a wider base of grants, e.g., bequests, grants from community groups, etc. For this phase to be successful, the Foundation must have established credibility and a proven administrative record. Once this is accomplished, the Foundation will have both a stable source of continuing funds and the flexibility of interim grants.

Advantages
a) Money channelled for innovative programs would no longer reduce funds available for on-going programs.
b) Funded research components could be built in to each project so that projects could seek long-term funding as documented, evaluated, on-going projects.
c) The Foundation could assist schools and community groups in the development of program plans.
d) The Foundation could begin to develop skills among people in the schools and community familiar with alternative funding possibilities.
e) The Foundation could maintain an up-to-date data bank of funding sources and maintain regular contact with them.
f) The Foundation could coordinate funding appeals.

Possible Projects
Although the initiative for projects will come through schools and/or their communities, it is possible to cite several possible categories of projects, which may arise:

a) City Wide Projects – e.g., Learnxs Project; Students in Business Project; multicultural programs, cultural immersion courses for teachers; volunteer training.
b) School-based Projects – e.g., School-based Day Care Establishment costs.
c) Innovative Projects – e.g., Science School and Art School.

Proposed Method
a) The establishment of an incorporated charitable foundation to be called The Learnxs Foundation, through the cooperation of the Toronto Board of Education's Legal Department.

b) The formation of an interim nine-member Board of Directors composed of three representatives of the Board of Education staff (appointed by the Director), three trustees (appointed by the Chairman of the Board) and three representatives of the community (appointed by the Social · Planning Council), augmented by a non-voting advisory board.

c) The preparation of a brief and prospectus to be distributed to various foundations and private sources of funding. This is to be an appeal for support and tentative funding, dependent on requests for support from school and/or community groups.

d) Distribution of a brief prospectus and explanatory material to all schools through normal channels. Schools will then be invited to prepare submissions to the Foundation for help in possible funding.

e) The Board of Directors will rate submissions as to priority, budgets established, research components added, if necessary, and the completed document resubmitted to funding sources, which have indicated willingness to cooperate, for funding.

f) The Foundation will administer funds for projects, contract, if necessary, for research and documentation, and gather interim reports.

g) The Foundation will prepare semi-annual reports for distribution to schools and interested parties so that the progress of each project will be visible.

Recommendations

1. That the Toronto Board of Education assist in the establishment of the Learnxs Foundation as an incorporated charitable foundation as outlined in the proposal.

2. That staff time be allocated so that staff members be able to sit on the Board of Directors.

3. That one staff member [myself] be seconded from the Toronto staff on a part-time basis for a period of one year to assist in the establishment of the Foundation.

4. That the Solicitor of the Toronto Board of Education be allowed to assist in the legal work involved in this project.

5. That the Toronto Board of Education endorse publicly the concept of the Learnxs Foundation.

6. That staff and community groups be encouraged to begin work on programs that might fall within the purview of the Foundation and submit them to the Interim Board of Directors.

7. That staff of the Foundation be requested to prepare quarterly reports during the first year for the information of the Board, the officials, and other interested parties.

8. That the Toronto Board of Education absorb the costs involved in printing and distributing the brief and prospectus and the quarterly reports
for the first year of operation.[61]

At its regular meeting on 5 July the Board approved this report and
its recommendations. The Board's solicitor was asked to prepare objects
and by-laws for the proposed foundation. On 6 December the interim
board of directors held its first meeting to consider these objects and
by-laws, to discuss the directors' role as members of the board, and to
hear a progress report on the Learnxs Project. Membership on the board
of directors consisted of Kay Brown, Executive Secretary, Inter-agency
Council for Services to Immigrants and Migrants; June Callwood, a
journalist, media personality, and social activist; Burleigh Leishman,
a community volunteer appointed by the United Community Fund;
Judith Jordan, Chairman, Toronto Board of Education, and Trustee for
Ward 11; Charlotte Maher, Chairman, Community Programs Commit-
tee of the Toronto Board of Education, and Trustee for Ward 10; Dan
Leckie, Trustee for Ward 6, Toronto Board of Education; Dr Edward N.
McKeown, Associate Director, Toronto Board of Education; Mitchell
Lennox, Superintendent of Curriculum and Program, Toronto Board of
Education; and myself, Special Assistant to the Director of Education,
Toronto Board of Education.

The choice of members reflected a need to ensure visibility and credibility both within the Toronto Board of Education and increasingly in
the community at large. Each person represented a certain constituency or area of interest or influence. For example, within the Board of
Education, the associate director and budget chief (Ned McKeown)
wielded considerable power in the organization, and his support of
the Learnxs directory and future innovative projects would be almost
essential. The superintendent of curriculum and program (Mike Lennox) had the most influence over the Board of Education's curriculum
content and program support to the schools. This was also the department that became involved in the establishment of new alternative
programs.

On the trustee side, the chairman of the Board of Education (Judith
Jordan), representing North Toronto, had a track record of support for
community involvement with particular interests in school volunteers,
the after-four program, and day care. The chairman of community
programs and a social worker (Charlotte Maher) was also from North
Toronto. The Ward 6 trustee (Dan Leckie), representing an inner-city

area, was a prominent member of the reform caucus among trustees; he had been very active in student politics at the University of Toronto during the late 1960s and now taught a course there in alternatives in education.

The community representative from the Inter-agency Council for Services to Immigrants and Migrants (Kay Brown) was also a social worker with considerable experience in the areas of fund-raising, information services, and programs for immigrants. The United Community Fund representative (Burleigh Leishman) had experience as a community volunteer. The other community representative (June Callwood) was a well-known author, journalist, television and radio personality, and social activist, particularly in the area of human rights.

In April 1974 the Learnxs Foundation received its charter of incorporation from the Province of Ontario. A charitable number from the federal government was also received to ensure tax-exempt status for contributors to the foundation.

While the Learnxs Foundation was created in response to an original objective of the Learnxs proposal (fourth version), the work of the foundation was seen as a general support mechanism for innovation in community education. Therefore, a variety of other demonstration projects were considered by the foundation aside from the Learnxs directory project, which reported to it regularly through representations by the Learnxs task group. The following is a detailed step-by-step description of the Learnxs developmental process.

Learnxs Directory

With the disbanding of the Cooperative Education work group, members of the Subcommittee on School Community Learning Resources continued to meet concerning the implementation of the proposal. Subway Academy became the first priority because of the need to implement the program by 1 September 1973, and the other phases of the original proposal were held in abeyance. However, trustees and staff were informed of the existence of these phases as an appendix of the Subway Academy report, and the following motion was approved on 24 May 1973: 'That a method of identifying and gathering information regarding community resources be investigated to ensure their availability for the academic year 1973–74, e.g., Learning Resources Exchange phase of Learnxs Project.'[62] As community information gathering had not traditionally been seen by Board of Education officials and trustees as a legitimate part of the classroom learning process, it was not considered appropriate to use funds from the Board's instructional budget to create such a resources exchange.

The summer of 1973 was viewed with a sense of alarm in the political and economic communities because of a serious shortage of summer jobs for students. The Ontario government had established a youth secretariat, and one of its first programs was a job creation scheme for students known as Experience '73. Each ministry in the social development sector was given a sum of money to create summer employment. The Ministry of Education announced to school boards the availability of grants for student employment, to be known as Students Participating in Community Education or SPICE.[v]

A SPICE application from the Toronto Board of Education on behalf of the Learning Exchange System was prepared for the compilation of 'a list of all the resources, human and physical, in the East End of Toronto (Yonge Street to the eastern boundary).' It was decided to confine the project to east Toronto because it was anticipated that Subway Academy would be established at Eastern High School of Commerce. Also, if the grant application were successful, no more than four workers could be hired for a period of eight weeks. Early in June it was announced that the project had received a grant of $3,183. For a chart concerning the implementation of this phase, see figure 1. Four persons were hired, two each from the University of Toronto and Sheridan College.[vi] An orientation kit was prepared for each worker, detailing the objectives of the project, an organizational plan. and a procedure for the identification, collection, and recording of data.

By the end of August, a loose-leaf binder comprising about three hundred typed and handwritten pages identifying learning resources in the east Toronto area had been produced. The next problem was to find a method of indexing this material. The model proposed was the *Continuing Education Directory* (Metro Doc), which had been compiled to inform citizens of Metropolitan Toronto about the educational and

---

v   SPICE, or Students Participating in Community Education, was an attempt by the Ministry of Education to promote its policy of community schools and community education among boards of education.

vi The four workers included a graduate of SEED who was a first-year University of Toronto student, an MA student in history, and two media arts students from Sheridan College.

Figure 1. Learning Exchange System: Phase One

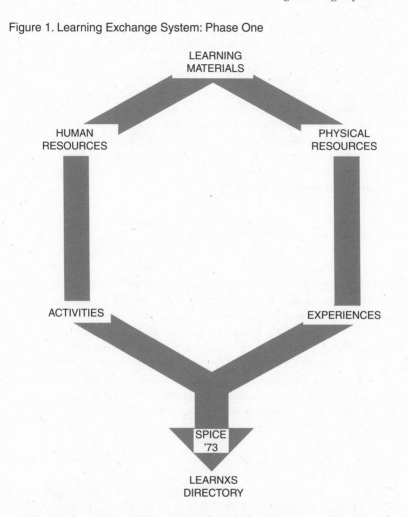

recreational courses and activities for adults that were offered by institutions and organizations on a part-time basis or by correspondence. It was thought that each community resource from the Learnxs directory could be given a subject heading and resource number from the *Continuing Education Directory* so that the two systems could be interrelated. Therefore, by using the two directories, it would be possible for a learner to gain access not only to traditional courses but also to community-based resources.

On 23 October 1973 the following progress report on the Learnxs Project was submitted to the School Programs Committee.

For eight weeks during July and August a grant was received from the Ministry of Education under its S.P.I.C.E. program for student employment. As a result of this grant, a directory of community-based learning resources has been compiled for the area of the city east of Yonge Street. The directory is now being assembled and indexed and it is hoped that the Ministry of Education will print a limited number of copies. The Learnxs Summer Project was chosen to represent all S.P.I.C.E. projects throughout the province at the Experience '73 Showcase held at Queen's Park on September 25th.

It is anticipated that students of Subway Academy will use the directory, initially, but it will be made available to all interested schools if sufficient copies can be printed.

Another outcome of the summer project has been the preparation of an information booklet on the entire Learning Exchange System or 'Learnxs,' which includes the directory, a retrieval system, Subway Academy and the Learnxs Foundation.

To further develop the Learnxs Project a proposal entitled 'Resource Bank for Community Learning' has been submitted to the Federal Local Initiatives Program for funding. The Resource Bank would (1) update and extend the Learnxs Directory; (2) develop resources to encourage the greater use of volunteers; (3) organize a support system by identifying alternative sources of funds, materials and services; and (4) provide an information service in the general area of out-of-school learning resources.[63]

On 1 November, the Board of Education approved the following recommendations:

1. That the Toronto Board of Education endorse the Local Initiatives Program proposal entitled 'Resource Bank for Community Learning.'
2. That space for an office be made available to the project from 3 December 1973 to 31 May 1974 without charge.
3. That sufficient copies of the Learnxs directory be printed to distribute to interested schools.
4. That discussions be undertaken with the Computer Services Department to explore the feasibility of developing a computer program to incorporate the Learnxs directory, and that a report be

made to the School Programs Committee before the end of December 1973.

On 11 December the Learnxs task group was convened to form a learning cooperative, consisting of interested persons from the Toronto Board of Education, the Ontario Institute for Studies in Education, Toronto Public Libraries, the Metropolitan Toronto Library Board, the Volunteer Centre of Metropolitan Toronto, the Addiction Research Foundation, the Inter-agency Council for Services to Immigrants and Migrants, and the community at large. The group discussed the results of the summer project and the best way to organize the material so that it might be published as a directory and distributed to schools, libraries, and community organizations. The problem of funding an indexing system was considered, and it was agreed that at this time the index from the *Continuing Education Directory* would provide a very comprehensive framework for the Learnxs directory. The next step would be to have the material typed and organized into a directory format for printing and distribution in the east Toronto area. Group members saw the directory as an important informational tool, primarily for teachers and librarians. However, it was agreed that an evaluation procedure should be built in to assess the directory's use (for example, its action research design).

As future support for the Learnxs Project would have to come from alternative sources, a Local Initiatives Program (LIP) proposal entitled 'Resource Bank for Community Learning' had been prepared and submitted to the federal government by myself as the secretary-treasurer of the Learnxs Foundation on behalf of the project. It was agreed to explore other means of handling the material in the directory (for example, media and computer applications) in order to expand the information-sharing and retrieval aspects of the original proposal. Finally it was decided to establish an evaluation subcommittee to consider means of creating feedback mechanisms for the directory.[64]

The Local Initiatives Program proposal contained the following objectives and activities:

Objectives
To identify, record and catalogue potential sources of learning, as an assist for schools, libraries, social agencies and citizen groups in developing non-formal learning experiences and utilizing resources in the neighbourhood outside of existing institutions.

Activities

1. To update and extend an existing resource directory produced during the summer of 1973 as part of the Learning Exchange System of the Toronto Board of Education.
2. To compile a talent list of volunteers with particular skills, interests or experiences who would be willing to share same with schools, libraries, social agencies, hospitals, etc.
3. To prepare and distribute a manual on the effective use of volunteers in an educational setting.
4. To prepare a directory on alternate sources of funds, materials and services to support the ongoing project and provide a financial base for future development of the Resource Bank.[65]

On 7 January 1974 the project of the Resource Bank for the Community Learning received a grant of $18,720 from the Department of Manpower and Immigration of the federal government to employ a manager, three researchers, and two clerk typists. A telephone and office space were provided by the Toronto Board of Education in the Computer Services section on the third floor of the Education Centre. On 8 January, the manager and staff of the project were introduced to the Learnxs task group. It was agreed that the priorities for the project should be completing the directory for distribution, updating the directory, and obtaining alternate funding.

In its report, the Evaluation Subcommittee made the following recommendations:

1. That an evaluation form should be developed.
2. That the Learnxs directory should be delivered in January 1974 and an evaluation made in June 1974.
3. That directories should be numbered for identification and distributed to public and secondary schools in east Toronto (Areas 4 and 5), libraries, resource centres, and information centres.
4. That the approach taken should be personal contact by staff, with verbal instructions followed by written explanatory material.
5. That updating of material must be a continuing process, with carbonized forms included with the directory so that changes can be made and a copy forwarded to the office.
6. That a tally form should be placed in the front of the directory so that a record of who is using it and which sections are being used can be kept by the person in charge.

7. That self-addressed, stamped postcards should be provided with the directory so that users can report on the success of their contact and the accuracy of information.

It was decided that January to June should be a test period and that distribution should be on a contractual basis to those user centres ordering the directory. The centres would be assured that lost copies would be replaced, to ensure that directories were kept in full view rather than put away for safekeeping. User centres would be encouraged to also provide access to other information directories in order to establish their own vertical file.

A mock-up of the directory cover was presented and met the approval of the task group. It was decided that a sample directory should be prepared for demonstration to a cross section of potential users, who could provide feedback on its possible use and distribution.

Several options were discussed for recovering costs during the test period. As this was an experimental project, it was agreed that directories should be provided without cost but that a service fee should be assessed to each school, library, agency, or group receiving them. A set of guidelines for users was to be prepared, detailing the services available from Learnxs staff and the level of cooperation expected from the user or agents.[66]

The next meeting of the task group was held on 21 January. A progress report on the project indicated that a full complement of staff had been hired, a vertical file was being assembled with the assistance of the Board's library services, and copies of the introduction, preface, and index were now available. The Evaluation Subcommittee's suggested format for user evaluation cards was reported, and the task group decided that it wanted the following basic information about the directory and the user: topic of interest, availability of information, validity of information, degree of follow-up, and agreement to a more in-depth interview. Tally sheets to be attached to the directory included sections for date, topic, age level, and sex. The use of evaluation cards and tally sheets was to be a condition of the agreement with agents, who were also to be asked to make general evaluations. In addition, a poster was to be placed with the directory, saying, 'We want to make the Directory more useful and accurate. Your help in completing these cards and tally sheets would be appreciated.' It was suggested that each centre set up a Learnxs area with a sign, a map of the designated area, and vertical file materials to go with the directory. It was reported that the cost to produce each directory was $3.10. By charging $5.00 as a service fee, it would be possible to recover costs.[67]

At a meeting on 14 February the task group learned that one hundred directories were ready for distribution and that a slide-tape presentation had been prepared to illustrate the Learnxs concept. Staff had met with Area 5 principals (East Toronto) and found that the attitudes ranged from sincere interest to open hostility, with the majority either somewhat curious or completely disinterested. There were sarcastic remarks about such entries as the 'Tattoo Parlour' and the 'Hare Krishna' sect. One senior school principal exclaimed, 'I control everything my students learn, and I wouldn't want them to have access to some of the information in that book!' However, several principals were interested and came forward afterwards to ask how they could get copies for their schools. The staff had also met with the Volunteers in Education work group, and this group of parents, teachers, principals, and consultants was generally enthusiastic about the directory as a source of enrichment for the school curriculum. They were particularly excited at the prospect of the project producing a volunteers' kit.[68]

At the 14 February meeting, sample copies of the tally sheets, evaluation postcards, guidelines for agents, and project business cards were distributed for approval. To assist in promotion, a Learnxs reception was planned for 18 and 19 February to introduce the Learnxs Project and to advertise the directory. Many potential agents such as schools, libraries, and community organizations, and funding sources had been invited. As visual aids, a videotape of the summer project and Lori Learnxs, a special doll, were created. A press conference would also take place on the afternoon of 18 February.

The next item on the agenda concerned the second phase of the Learnxs proposal, the information-sharing and retrieval system. Originally, it had been planned to establish a separate task group to consider its implementation. However, because of limited resources and the degree of overlap with the learning resources exchange phase, it was decided to integrate the work of the two phases. Task group members had prepared the following draft report.

On January 7, 1974 the Resource Bank for Community Learning received a grant of $18,720 from the Federal Government under the Local Initiatives Program to 'identify, record and catalogue potential sources of learning as an asset for schools, libraries, social agencies and citizen groups in developing non-formal learning experiences and utilizing resources in the neighbourhood outside of existing institutions.' The project represents an extension of work previously done under a Ministry of Education S.P.I.C.E. grant of $3,183 during the summer of 1973.

The Resource Bank for Community Learning with a staff of six persons is located in an office on the third floor of the Education Centre. In the short time that the office has been established, it has become the focal point of an information dissemination service using the Learnxs Directory. The Directory has now been printed in sufficient copies for distribution to interested parties.

The Learnxs Directory contains about five hundred entries of learner accessible resources and shares the same indexing system as Metro Doc – a directory of existing courses for continuing education. In this way, it is possible for a learner to gain access not only to traditional courses but also to community-based resources.

The Learnxs Directory has been guided in the interim period by a task group which forms a 'learning cooperative' consisting of interested persons from the Toronto Board of Education, the Ontario Institute for Studies in Education, Toronto Public Libraries, the Metropolitan Toronto Library Board, the Volunteer Centre of Metropolitan Toronto, the Addiction Research Foundation, the Ministry of Education and the community at large. This cooperative has been actively involved in future planning for the use of the Learnxs Directory. The size of the Directory makes storage and retrieval a problem that requires investigation of methods other than the printed page.

In discussions with the Computer Services Department, it was decided to explore the computer application in three phases:

Phase One

This phase refers to an immediate set of goals, which can be implemented during the next six months (March to August 1974). A major concern with the Directory is that it will continue to be updated and corrected to meet the needs of its users. To ease access to the various entries and permit rapid retrieval and correction, it is proposed that the computer be used for indexing. The ability of the computer to manipulate data quickly would allow several types of indexes to be produced without the time required for manual manipulation.

Storage of books in excess of 500 pages represents a serious problem; however, the book could be stored on several microfiche cards and read with the aid of a microfiche viewer. It is proposed that this type of storage facility be investigated in preparation for the possible expansion of the number of entries, as further information is discovered. If the text can be recorded on computer tape, microfiche copies could be easily and inexpensively obtained.

Since the Learnxs Directory is a relatively new learning tool, some type of ongoing and term evaluation is necessary. The Learnxs Task Group is beginning to discuss ways and means of accomplishing this task; however, the statistical work becomes far easier if the survey and other research tools are developed in cooperation with the Research Department and the Computer Services Department. This will enable the raw data to be processed using the Toronto Board's computer and the existing statistical programs.

The most important aspect of this phase will be the development of a structure within which the Learnxs Directory will expand. It is proposed that systematic planning procedures be developed with the Computer Services Department and the Learnxs Task Group to allow for a smooth transition from print to more sophisticated media.

Phase Two

This phase will encompass short-term goals and should require a time period of between six and eighteen months beginning in September 1974. Experience gained during Phase One will be used to structure the information in a form suitable for storing and accessing using electronic means. It is proposed that an experiment be undertaken to test the potential for direct access to a central information bank using an online computer terminal.

To offset developmental costs, it will be necessary to secure alternative sources of computer time, as well as systems analysts and programmers, possibly through cooperative relationships among similar projects (e.g., Metro Doc, Student Guidance Information Service) or with private industry through the proposed Learnxs Foundation. This will allow for a truly integrated system to share information and resources to better serve the needs of the learning community.

Phase Three

This phase directs itself to the 'long-term implications' of phases one and two. Using the results of evaluative research among users of the system and experience accumulated through the various approaches to the storing and accessing of information, this phase will continue to assess the potential of this form of technology as an aid to the individual learner. The overall success of the venture can only be gauged by its degree of acceptance; and the merit ascribed to it among the people it purports to serve.

Therefore it is recommended:

1. That the Toronto Board of Education explore the possibility of a student employment grant from the Ministry of Education for the summer of 1974 to further consolidate and extend the Learnxs Project.
2. That permission be granted to provide office space for the Learnxs Project until the end of August 1974.
3. That the Computer Services Department allot sufficient computer time and manpower during the next six months (March to August 1974) to allow for the indexing of the Learnxs Directory using the computer and for related projects, such as the investigation of the utilization of microfiche.
4. That the Research Department and Computer Services Department continue to cooperate with the Learnxs Task Group in establishing evaluation procedures for the Learnxs Directory and that some computer time and staff be allotted for statistical analysis in non-peak periods.
5. That the Computer Services Department be allowed to cooperate, in an advisory capacity, with the Metro Toronto Library Board, the Ontario Institute for Studies in Education and the Ministry of Education in conducting an experiment for online computer access to the Learnxs Directory.
6. That alternative sources of support and funding be investigated to continue work in this area of the Learnxs Project.[69]

After considerable discussion about the best means of storing and updating Learnxs material (for example, computer tape or microfiche), it was decided to send the report on to the Toronto Board of Education's School Programs Committee meeting of 19 February. (The Toronto Board subsequently approved this report on 28 February). For conceptual charts of the information-sharing and retrieval system, see figures 2 and 3.

The task group meeting on 8 March 1974 considered progress reports on the Learnxs reception and presentations to schools, groups of librarians, psychologists, and principals by project staff and task group members. It was agreed that the response had been generally favourable, and orders for the directory were increasing steadily.

The following chart, figure 2, provides a graphic depiction of the

Figure 2. Information-Sharing and Retrieval System

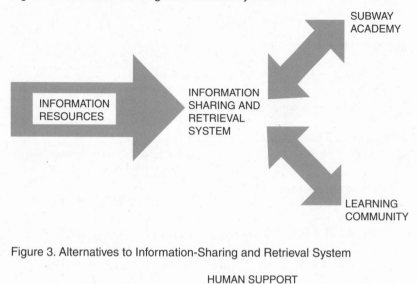

Figure 3. Alternatives to Information-Sharing and Retrieval System

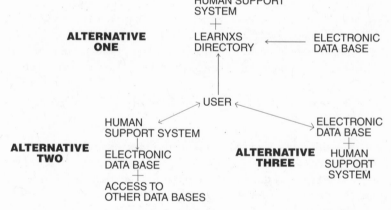

information-sharing and retrieval system for the distribution of community learning resources through both the Learnxs directory and Subway Academy. Figure 3 offers three alternatives that can be used as catalysts to encourage community resource learning.

A concern was expressed about the future of the project after the expiration of the LIP grant. It was decided to establish a funding committee to investigate possible sources of ongoing support.

The need for a learner centre in the Education Centre building was discussed. Such a facility could provide better access to materials such as Learnxs and the *Continuing Education Directory*, as well as provide information about Toronto Board of Education services. It was decided to explore possible models for such a learner centre and report back to the task group.[70]

On 30 May the task group learned that a total of eighty sites had received the *Learnxs Directory*: junior schools; senior public schools or junior high schools; high schools; public libraries; community centres or storefronts; media; boards of education; government; and post-secondary institutions. Applications for several alternate sources of funding to maintain the project were submitted. The Experience '74 summer employment program for students provided $7,889 for two projects:

1. SPICE – to update the directory, evaluate its use and produce a talent bank, a volunteers' manual, and alternate funding supplements, as well as a media presentation for Learnxs.
2. PEOPLE (Preservation and Exploration of Ontario's Past a Learning Experience) – to survey the local histories (including oral histories and archival research) of three schools that were celebrating centennials in the east Toronto area.

A funding proposal and prospectus, 'Learnxs 1974,' had been produced, and an application for interim support submitted to the United Community Fund.

A proposal entitled 'A Toronto Learning Centre as an Integrated Service within the Education Centre Building' was presented. This facility was seen as providing a model for informational learning centres in large institutional settings. If implemented in the Education Centre, it could be directly related to the information-sharing and retrieval system phase of the Learnxs Project. It was agreed that the proposal should be submitted to the Toronto Board and other funding sources.

An outcome of the SPICE grant had been an investigation of computer indexing systems so that an electronic database for the directory could be established. The Information Retrieval Management System (IRMS) was deemed to be the most suitable indexing system for efficient storage of Learnxs information and satisfied one of the long-term goals of Learnxs – to make information in the directory immediately accessible to direct requests at a computer terminal.

A slide-tape media presentation was also prepared to be used by staff to accompany the directory in order to illustrate the Learnxs method to potential users of the directory.

On 19 September 1974 the Board of Education approved the following recommendations from a progress report on Learnxs summer projects. As proposed by participants in the Learnxs Project, it was recommended that the Learnxs Project continue to utilize office space and telephone facilities at the Education Centre, receive the cooperation of the Computer Services Department in extending the computer program and retrieval system, and cooperate with the Information and Publications Department in the distribution of the *Learnxs Directory* and the Learnxs supplements.[71]

Second Edition of the Learnxs Directory

At a meeting of the Learnxs task group on 18 September the members considered the implications of the results of the summer project. The media presentation was discussed and approved for use as a promotional device. Evaluation data was considered, and it was decided to proceed with a second edition of the directory.

The second edition of the *Learnxs Directory*, with revised and updated entries and an index, represented a considerable improvement in form and efficiency of use as a direct outgrowth of the information gained from the evaluations of the first edition. In addition, progress had been made in converting the directory to readable computer form. A system using key words (such as location and subject) had proven that the *Learnxs Directory* met all the requirements for storage and retrieval. The ultimate goal was to make the information more accessible through a terminal, provided there was online computer time. However, this system was not user oriented, would require a trained interpreter-counsellor to access information, and would be quite expensive to operate. It was decided not to pursue a computer-assisted system until adequate financial support was available.

Four supplements to the directory were published:

1. *Introduction to Special Libraries in Toronto* – a list of private and business libraries and special collections, with details of availability and contact people.
2. *Volunteers in Education* – a resource kit for setting up a school volunteer program.
3. *A Cast of Thousands: Peoples' Talents* – a list of people willing to bring

their talents and skills into schools, libraries, hospitals, and community centres.
4. *Learning about Labour Unions* – a resource kit with a list of contact people and a number of labour publications.

The Learnxs task group was notified that the Learnxs Foundation had received a grant of $2,000 from the J.P. Bickell Foundation to further the work of the Learnxs Project. These funds would keep the office open from September to December 1974. Fees consisting of $10 for the second edition of the *Learnxs Directory* and $3 for each of the supplements would be charged, with revenue used to cover future printing costs. During the period from September to December 1974, two part-time workers staffed the Learnxs office. Their primary responsibility consisted of the distribution of the second edition of the directory and the four supplements. However, they were also able to maintain a limited information service to users and to continue fund-raising activities.

A second proposal entitled 'Learning Exchange System – Learnxs' was drafted for submission to the Local Initiatives Program on behalf of the Learnxs Foundation. This proposal included the following objectives:

1. To further research and refine the directory.
2. To further develop an orientation program to assist individuals and groups in using the directory.
3. To maintain an information central office to assist users and to distribute directories and supplements.
4. To further develop a program designed to put the directory into a computer retrieval system.
5. To develop a manual that would document the Learnxs process for other groups who wished to establish their own directory and system.
6. To continue to explore sources in order to make the project self-sufficient.[72]

Early in December 1974, the foundation was notified that a sum of $21,372 had been approved to employ six workers from January to June 1975, led by Ian Scott. The staff began by examining material from previous evaluations and then embarked on an extensive series of interviews of all agents to discover how the directory could be improved.

The Learnxs task group met on 19 February 1975 in the new Learnxs office accommodation, which had been established on the first floor of the Education Centre, adjacent to the Information and Publications Department. Members were introduced to the LIP project staff, and a report was given on their activities since 6 January.

Third Edition of the Learnxs Directory

On 13 June 1975, the Learnxs task group met to receive a progress report from the project staff. The third edition of the *Learnxs Directory*, consisting of 213 pages and including six introductory pages describing the philosophy and use of the directory, had been completed. This edition contained 313 fully described contacts and over two hundred partially described resources. A table of contents was placed at the beginning of the book, and an eleven-page index at the back. The index listed the name of every resource in the directory, as well as subject references, which would greatly facilitate information retrieval. Within the directory's thirteen large colour-coded sections (such as Media and Health) were fifty-nine subsections dealing with specific aspects of the topics. Each large section had its own table of contents listing its subsections. The page format of the directory allowed for a clear identification of the name, address, telephone number, contact person, and description of each entry. As well, cross-references were included in some entries in order to direct users to additional information in other portions of the directory.

From the end of March until the middle of June more than two hundred directories had been distributed. The layout and the breadth of information had been very favourably received by the agents, as evidenced by the informal comments received by the staff. In the area of promotion, information flyers and order forms had been sent to schools, libraries, social services, and community groups in Metropolitan Toronto. Directories were hand delivered to all new agents within the city of Toronto, who also received a detailed explanation of the directory and the services (for example, the information service and vertical file).

During the project, the following other publications were initiated:

1. *A Field Trip Supplement* containing information on field trips for students in the Metropolitan Toronto region. There were 150 field trip possibilities arranged in fourteen subject areas, with an index.
2. *How to Compile a Directory of Educational Resources*, a detailed thirteen-page guide to assist people who wished to compile their own Learnxs type directory.

3. *Learnxs Directory Fact Sheet* containing information on the purpose and history of Learnxs as well as specific information about the third edition.
4. *A Short Guide to Fund Raising,* a five-page guide to assist community groups in fund-raising activities. It contained information about funding handbooks and government and private grant agencies.

The task group was informed of approaches made by the Learnxs Foundation for project funding to such organizations as the Ontario Ministry of Education, the Ontario Ministry of Culture and Recreation, the Canada's Secretary of State Department, Metropolitan Toronto, City of Toronto, and Metropolitan Toronto Library Board. As a result, a sum of $12,000 was received by the foundation from the miscellaneous fund of the Minister of Education for the continuation and development of the Learnxs Project.

As an Experience '75 grant would sustain the project during the summer months, it was proposed that a portion of the $12,000 grant be used to employ two persons from September to December. There was also some likelihood that Learnxs would receive another Local Initiatives Program grant in January. A decision was reached to employ two workers for the time period (at $150 per week) with the option of hiring a third person if the need arose.

A discussion followed on the future of the Learnxs Project. Should it terminate as a demonstration project in December 1975 or seek new directions for the concept? It was thought that the field trip supplement had definite potential for commercial sales beyond the traditional Learnxs constituency. The publishing of materials with general appeal to the community at large might be a source of revenue for Learnxs in the future. The project's other function, that of an information service on community learning resources, had not produced a stable source of revenue, and there was a concern that short-term grants to support this service would not be available in the future. Therefore, it was decided to explore the feasibility of developing a publications policy to produce and market materials using the Learnxs method.[73]

On 16 July 1975 three task group members met with a well-known author, a representative from a publishing company, and a bookstore operator to investigate the potential of Learnxs becoming a publishing source for innovative educational materials. Using the field trip supplement as an example, it was agreed that this book should have a market with teachers, parents, and recreationists. However, it would be essential to reach as wide an audience as possible in Metropolitan Toronto. It also might be possible to do some form of survey to assess need. If the book were turned over to a commercial publisher, they would require a run of at least three thousand copies selling at five times the cost of production. This publisher would then assume the costs of advertising, marketing, and distribution.[74]

Application had been made to the Experience '75 student employment program for funding of community education resource kits. Early in May, the Ministry of Education announced that this project had been given a grant of $5,000 to employ four persons. During June, July, and August, considerable research was done in the areas of community school development, alternatives in education, and multicultural programs, and this material was to form the basis of a future publication.

On 11 September 1975 the Learnxs Foundation submitted an application to the Local Initiatives Program entitled 'Community as Classroom Publications.' The objectives of the proposed project were

> to publish and distribute material which serves the informational needs of the community at large. The publications would include material previously prepared by the Learnxs Directory, as well as other community education projects. This material falls into three basic categories: (1) information that constantly changes and needs to be updated, such as a Guide to Field Trips in Metro Toronto; (2) kits that provide resource material on specific subjects, such as day care and labour unions; and (3) material that has been produced by short-term projects which could not be then published through lack of time, money or because the material was directed towards a special interest group.'[75]

In the fall of 1975 the Learnxs staff (consisting of two persons in September, increasing to three in October and November) continued with the promotion and distribution of the third edition of the *Learnxs Directory* and its supplements. The *Metropolitan Toronto Field Trip Guide* was added to the list of supplements, development work continued on alternatives in education and multicultural programs, and research began on a new topic – historical survey techniques. It was also recognized that the 8½ x 11 size of the field trip guide was not appropriate for production in volume, and the format was changed to the size of a pocket book with perfect binding.

In the area of fund-raising, two new possibilities were investigated. The Learning Materials program of the Ministry of Education was providing development and production grants to encourage the publishing of Canadian materials, and the Wintario program of the Ministry of Culture and Recreation was offering funds to match 50 per cent of the development costs of new publications. Both seemed viable sources of support should Learnxs move into the publishing field.[76]

Learnxs Press

On 1 December 1975, the Learnxs Foundation received a grant of $18,000 from the Local Initiatives Program to employ four workers to operate Community as Classroom Publications. For practical reasons, this title was soon changed to Learnxs Press. The overall objective of the press was to develop an ongoing publishing house of innovative educational material. A promotional campaign focused on the introduction of the *Metropolitan Toronto Field Trip Guide*. On 29 January 1976 the Learnxs Foundation convened a wine and cheese reception at a local art gallery to announce the establishment of Learnxs Press.

During the period from January to June 1976, three new publications were completed:

1. *Learnxs Directory*, fourth edition, with a revised, updated, and redesigned format that discarded the loose-leaf binder in favour of a perfect-bound catalogue.
2. *Discover Your Neighbourhood Heritage*, a resource kit for teachers, students, and community groups interested in historical research in the local area.
3. *Resources for Multicultural Programs*, a how-to-do-it book to assist school and community groups in organizing programs to preserve their cultural heritage.

This period also saw development grants received from the Learning Materials program of the Ministry of Education and from Wintario. By the spring, revenue from sales had reached a high of almost a thousand dollars per month. Learnxs Press was indeed a reality.

Outcomes and Reflections

The key internal and external elements in the Learnxs implementation procedure were the relationship of the Learnxs Project to the Toronto

Board of Education. There were certain differences between Learnxs and regular programs of the Toronto Board. As a demonstration project, Learnxs chose to seek its own sense of direction and developmental autonomy rather than become just another program of the Toronto Board and subject to the dogmatic constraints and financial limitations of such a large organization. However, it recognized the need to maintain an ongoing support relationship with the Board in terms of goods and services while seeking alternate sources of financial support. In addition, Learnxs chose to define its service network from a broad community education perspective, including schools, service organizations, and other groups across Metropolitan Toronto, rather than the limited constituency afforded by the schools and support systems of the Toronto Board of Education.

As a result, a form of political interdependence emerged between the two organizations. For example, Subway Academy, as a phase of the Learnxs proposal, provided a controlled setting in which to explore the community learning resources concept at the secondary school level. However, as an alternative school of the Toronto Board, Subway Academy added new students and grant dollars while providing a potential model for other secondary schools to develop in-house alternative programs.

Trustees of the Toronto Board of Education had shown responsiveness to proposals from parents, teachers, and students for establishing alternative school programs. For example, SEED (1970),[vii] ALPHA (1971),[viii] and CONTACT (1972) were all proposals external to the regular programming mechanisms of the Board. Each program emphasized the use of community learning resources and shared decision making as a central focus in their organizational plan.

Subway Academy (1973), as a phase of the Learnxs Project, followed in the tradition but with certain specific differences. It sought a hosting relationship with an existing secondary school in order to receive the administrative and support services that such a small program would not normally generate. Subway also stressed the importance of the use of teachers and facilities in regular schools as part of its total bank of community learning resources. From the beginning, it did not seek isolation from the regular schools, as had its predecessors, but rather it was recognized as a potential demonstration model for developing alterna-

---

vii SEED stands for Shared Experience, Exploration, and Discovery (see chapter 9).
viii ALPHA stands for A Lot of People Hoping for an Alternative (see chapter 9).

tive programs within regular secondary schools. In these respects, Subway Academy was seen by administration and trustees as a potential change agent to introduce greater flexibility to the system.

The choice of the principal of Eastern High School of Commerce as principal of Subway Academy was a key political decision, which was to reflect very favourably on the future success of the program. His reputation as a progressive within-limits administrator gave degrees of credibility to the program from the very beginning. The high regard in which his colleagues held him was to prove invaluable in opening the doors of other secondary schools for Subway Academy students to use as learning resources.

The fact that Subway Academy, as phase three of the Learnxs proposal, came to the trustees as a report from the director of education was also a key political element in the decision-making process. The director had a reputation as a progressive administrator, which he needed to reinforce, particularly among the reform caucus of trustees. The fact that he supported the proposal could not help but enhance his reputation with this group. In the same respect, when the notice went out to secondary school principals concerning the establishment of the program, the support of the director was essential to gain cooperation in communicating the existence of the program to potential students and teachers. This was particularly crucial considering the fact that the proposal was not approved in principle until 24 May 1973 and that regular classes ended in early June.

Once the decision had been made to maintain phases one and two of the Learnxs proposal as a community education project separate from the Toronto Board of Education, but drawing upon its facilities and services, there was a need to establish an external funding base for the project. Potential funders of community projects (such as government, charitable foundations, and business and industry) usually require that the recipient have a charitable registration number, sometimes to ensure that the donor qualifies for tax-exempt status. It is also often a distinct advantage for the receiving organization to be incorporated.

There had been examples in the United States and Canada (in New York and Winnipeg) of municipalities establishing charitable foundations in order to raise money to support worthy projects that could not be funded exclusively through the tax base. These foundations could often qualify to receive private funds that were unavailable to the public body. This was the rationale behind the establishment of the Learnxs Foundation as a community organization that was legally independent but required by its objects 'to apply the resources of the Corporation by gift or grant to the Board of Education for the City of Toronto or its successors and to other organizations and groups working in cooperation with the said Board of Education or its successors for the development and advancement of pre-school, elementary, secondary, and adult educational programs, particularly of an innovative or experimental nature.'

Again, the Learnxs Foundation reflected this sense of political interdependence whereby the Learnxs Project could solicit funds (or goods and services) through the foundation, but the foundation could also be used to receive funding to support worthy projects of an innovative or experimental nature that were identified by the Toronto Board or related groups.

The board of directors of the Learnxs Foundation reflected a cross section of influential people among the staff and trustees of the Board of Education and the community at large. While each of the persons sat as a private citizen, his or her other affiliations and interests could obviously prove beneficial to the future work of the foundation. The mix among directors was also designed to attempt to ensure that the foundation would not become just an extension of the administration or trustees of the Toronto Board of Education but would function as a community education-oriented organization.[ix]

As was previously mentioned, action on the Learning Resources Exchange phase of the project was temporarily postponed to allow for the establishment of Subway Academy before the end of the school year. The more important reason, however, was a lack of funds to proceed with this part of the proposal. To the rescue came the SPICE program of the Ministry of Education, which was intended to encourage the employment of students and the involvement of boards of education in community education projects. (Special recognition should be extended to Ministry official Scott Darrach, who had a real appreciation of the importance of community resource learning owing to his experience as a 'recreationist.') The SPICE grant allowed for the employment of four post-secondary students who were interested in the general concept and appreciated the need for such resources for individual and classroom studies. The summer project operated out of the Ministry of Education's Community School Development summer course (of

---

ix This goal was further strengthened in 1976 when two community members were added to the Learnxs Foundation's board of directors.

which I was course director) and was assisted by the staff and participants in that course. One staff member, Murray Shukyn, a former coordinator of SEED, provided invaluable assistance in the organization
and implementation of the project.

A rough draft of the first edition of the *Learnxs Directory* was completed by the end of August 1973. It was decided to use the index of the
Continuing Education Directory because no staff time was available to
create a separate index and it was hoped that the two directories could
be interrelated.

The progress report to the Board of Education in October 1973 pub-
licized the achievements of the summer program in order to increase
the visibility of the Learnxs Project among trustees and administration
of the Board and to attain the following objectives: endorsement by the
Toronto Board of the LIP proposal from the Learnxs Foundation, thereby enhancing its potential to be funded; approval of office facilities for
a new project beginning in December; printing of sufficient copies of
the *Learnxs Directory* for distribution to interested schools; and support
from the Computer Services Department to proceed with phase two
of the original Learnxs proposal (that is, the information-sharing and
retrieval system).

During the period from the dissolution of the Cooperation Education
work group and the convening of the Learnxs task group, the work
of the project was carried forward by an informal group of interested
persons from the original Subcommittee on School Community Learning Resources and myself. As the directory had been completed in draft
form, and approvals gained to proceed with phases one and two of the
project, it was decided to convene the Learnxs task group, as described
in the original proposal.

Membership in the Learnxs task group consisted of some members
of the original subcommittee and a few persons who, through their
own interests or the interests of their organization, might enhance the
work of the Learnxs Project. The task group served as a sounding board
to evaluate progress and to formulate policy for future directions. Task
group members also participated in the process of lobbying for financial
support from the Local Initiatives Program and other potential funding
sources.[x] From the beginning, they were particularly concerned with
the day-to-day promotion, distribution, and evaluation of the use of the

---

x   For example, one task group member was also on the Local Initiative Program Con-
    stituents' Advisory Group for the Spadina riding.

directory in a variety of settings. Policies were developed, and the staff delivered progress reports at three-week intervals.

The second progress report to the Toronto Board of Education, in February 1974, included an introductory section to bring the administration and trustees up to date on the establishment of the Resource Bank for Community Learning and the Learnxs task group. However, the main purpose of this report was to make a case for the continued involvement of the Computer Services Department, including staff and computer time, in testing the feasibility of phase two of the original Learnxs proposal. In this regard, permission was granted to explore a second student employment summer grant, the use of office space was extended, and the cooperation of the Computer Services Department was assured for another six months. The involvement of the Computer Services people was vital to the completion of phase two. Although there had already been limited cooperation from this department, it was seen as politically essential to have them officially identified with the project to ensure their active participation in the future. The fact that this department reported to Associate Director Ned McKeown (a director of the foundation) was also a definite advantage.

The first evaluation of the *Learnxs Directory*'s first edition (used mostly by schools) had caused considerable concern among staff and task group members. As a result, the poster, tally sheets, and postcards were discarded. Even though agents had been individually visited and the guidelines explained to them, the evaluation confirmed the suspicion that they were not understanding the potential use of the directory by individuals and thus were relegating it to the status of just another resource guide for teachers. Finally, the potential use of the Learnxs office and vertical file for updating information was not recognized. (Often the directory was not readily accessible to learners but was kept locked up in an office.)

The second evaluation had been conducted among agents who operated during the summer. Previous concerns about the value of posters, tally sheets, and postcards were confirmed. Most agents either did not understand or were not communicating the potential uses of the directory. The index continued to be a source of dissatisfaction. Again, the Learnxs office was not generally being used as an information source.

With these comments in mind, the summer project team had produced the second edition of the *Learnxs Directory* with its own indexing system, published the four supplements from the previous project, completed a feasibility study of a computer-assisted retrieval system, and prepared a slide-tape presentation to illustrate the Learnxs concept. Early in September 1974, a third progress report was taken to the Toronto Board of Education to highlight these accomplishments. As usual, a series of recommendations accompanied the report to extend the use of office facilities and continue the relationships with the Computer Services Department. As there were no funds available at that time to maintain the Learnxs office, approval was also given for the Board's Information and Publications Department to assist with the distribution of the directory and supplements.

At the September task group meeting, it was decided to discontinue work on phase two of the Learnxs proposal. Although it proved quite feasible to place the directory into a computer-assisted storage and retrieval system, a major infusion of funds and computer time would be required to complete this phase.

The publishing of the four supplements represented a distinctly new direction for the Learnxs Project. The directory itself had always been seen as primarily a service to encourage the greater use of community learning resources. The supplements were in fact spin-offs from the directory and the involvement of staff with users and agents. Not only were they a potential new source of revenue, but they also demonstrated the capacity of the project to publish innovative materials in response to community needs. The decision to publish the supplements was to have a profound effect on the future of the project.

Although considerable fund-raising activity had taken place among foundations, business, and industry, the only grant received had been $2,000 from the Bickell Foundation. This key contribution, however, bridged the gap between the summer and winter grants and at least kept the office open. The fact that two people were able to share one position successfully was also a first for the Learnxs project.

The final item of importance was the changing role of the task group. During the first year, when staffing was uncertain, task group members had been very active in the day-to-day operations of the project. With a greater continuity of staff involvement, the role of the volunteers changed to that of advising on major policy changes.

The second Local Initiatives Program grant brought a new level of proficiency to the project. Owing to the difficult employment conditions and generally favourable publicity about the project, there was an abundance of comparatively well-educated and experienced personnel from which to choose.[xi] To acquaint themselves better with the work of the Learnxs Project, the new workers studied the evaluation reports of previous staff members and then embarked on a series of interviews with agents in the field. As a result of these explorations, they chose to propose a revised format for the directory, which would include network pages, a table of contents, a new cross-referenced index system, colour-coded sections, graphics and cartoons, and extensive coverage of the resources throughout the city of Toronto. At the task group meeting in February 1975, after considerable debate, it was decided that the staff should proceed with the changes. Although the directory might lose some of its informality and be less geared to individual interests, the format would be much more attractive and render the directory easier to use. There was also recognition that the directory was being used increasingly as an aid to program planning, as opposed to its original purpose as a resource guide for individual learners. Rather than disputing this trend, it was decided to encourage a broader spectrum of uses to support both individual and group learning projects.

In June 1975 task group members discovered that during the spring, over two hundred copies of the third edition had been distributed in the Metropolitan Toronto area. Staff visits to new agents in the city had encouraged effective use of the directory and had increased circulation. A guide to field trips in Metropolitan Toronto was also produced because of a strong need expressed by some agents and users.

An important decision was then reached concerning the future of the Learnxs Project. There were enough funds available to continue the project until the end of December 1975 as a demonstration in the use of community learning resources, and it could be officially completed by that date. However, the Learnxs Project had begun to assume a new role as a publisher of innovative materials, while its potential, as a service project, to continue to receive short-term grants was questionable. Therefore, it was decided, for economic reasons, to begin to wind down the service function and pursue a future of publishing innovative materials.

Community as Classroom Publications, the Local Initiatives Program proposed by the Learnxs Foundation in the fall of 1975, was the first concrete step in this new direction. For all practical purposes, the

---

xi The new staff included a community worker, a history graduate who had written a book on canoeing, a secondary school English teacher who had also taught at ALPHA, an Honours English graduate, and an experienced bookkeeper.

Learnxs Project as a service to promote the use of community learning resources had officially terminated. In its place was Learnxs Press, a publisher of innovative materials of a regional nature, whose publications would include the *Learnxs Directory*.

The Learnxs Project had included an action research design[xii] whereby the use of each edition of the directory was evaluated through some form of survey of the agents who had ordered it. The results of these surveys were then fed into the decision-making process of the task group, which established future directions for the project.

---

xii Action research is an ongoing study of a social process and its results where the accumulated findings are used to guide and correct the decisions of the continuing process.

8 Learnxs and Community Education

Learnxs as a Demonstration Project

The demonstration project has traditionally not enjoyed a position of respect in either public education or the human services field in general. This type of project has often been identified with short-term funding from external sources, and, therefore, there has been a tendency to dismiss its usefulness as a legitimate method of influencing social policy and program development. This was particularly true of job creation schemes in the 1970s such as the federal Local Initiatives Program (or its successor, Canada Works) and the student employment programs of the Province of Ontario. These programs generally were initiated out of community interest and dedicated to the identification of local needs and the creation of alternative service patterns. They were often resented by the public service sector for creating expectations of new services and identifying gaps in existing service patterns that municipal government may later be asked to fill. As a result, many public administrators viewed them as a nuisance that must be tolerated but never appreciated or encouraged.

This was not the case, however, among private and voluntary service organizations that had tended to use such projects to supplement their relatively meagre budgets and to serve as an informal research and development source to guide their future programming. This method of organic planning was a form of action research. Information gained through surveys to identify needs and to assess user attitudes was translated into new program directions through the creation of new resources or the reallocation of existing ones. The relatively small size and limited scope of operation of these organizations enhanced this sense of flexibility and responsiveness.

The same could not be said of the public service sector, where a tiny fraction of the overall budget might be devoted to research and development, while the majority of resources were allocated to maintain and extend existing service patterns. This often led to a lack of responsiveness to community needs and a sense of program rigidity. The situation was further exacerbated in a time of declining revenues and fiscal restraint where energies may be directed toward retrenchment and systems maintenance, resulting in organizational stagnation.

It was in this type of climate that the value of the demonstration project as an action research method to encourage internal growth, external responsiveness, and mutual cooperation among public and private organizations became apparent. The Learnxs Project focused on community resource learning as an area of need, which had been originally identified in educational theory but had more recently surfaced in government policies and community interests. Owing to financial restraints and other program priorities, the Toronto Board of Education was unable to allocate resources to respond to this need. The creation of Learnxs, as a community-based demonstration project using an action research design, represented a solution with an alternative approach.

Learnxs began with the hypothesis that the creation of a directory of community resources, to be utilized by schools and other service organizations, could be a way to demonstrate the relative importance of that portion of community education theory known as *community resource learning*. As a result, the demonstration project incorporated an action research design to test this hypothesis, by initiating a new type of relationship between two organizations, one in the private sector and the other in the public education arm of municipal government (a form of organizational interdependence that will be explored later in this chapter).

The strength of action research design is the creative problem solving and flexibility, which is an integral part of the process. Therefore, the means of achieving the objective may, in the final analysis, be more important than the end result. It was my opinion that the establishment of a demonstration project could result in a special focus of energies and resources that normally were completely unrelated. This form of energy sharing and creative communication could also result in a variety of spin-off activities and other outcomes, which might ultimately eclipse the original intent of the exercise.

Figure 4 represents the developmental process of Learnxs from the Special Task Force on Education in 1972 to the creation of the Learnxs Foundation in 1974, followed by Learnxs Press in 1976.

Figure 4. The Development of Learnxs

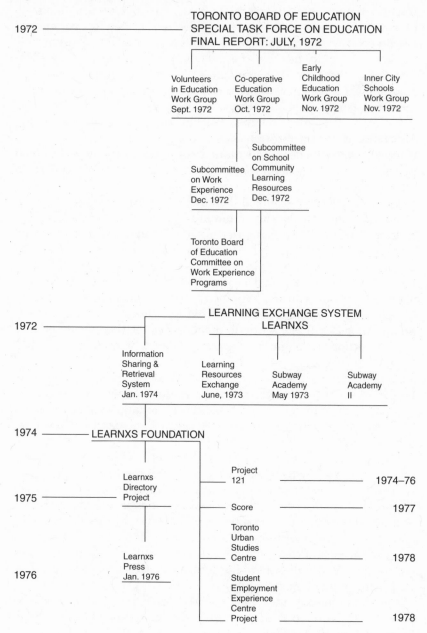

TORONTO BOARD OF EDUCATION
SPECIAL TASK FORCE ON EDUCATION
FINAL REPORT: JULY, 1972

1972

Volunteers in Education Work Group Sept. 1972

Co-operative Education Work Group Oct. 1972

Early Childhood Education Work Group Nov. 1972

Inner City Schools Work Group Nov. 1972

Subcommittee on Work Experience Dec. 1972

Subcommittee on School Community Learning Resources Dec. 1972

Toronto Board of Education Committee on Work Experience Programs

LEARNING EXCHANGE SYSTEM
LEARNXS

1972

Information Sharing & Retrieval System Jan. 1974

Learning Resources Exchange June, 1973

Subway Academy May 1973

Subway Academy II

1974   LEARNXS FOUNDATION

Learnxs Directory Project

1975

Learnxs Press Jan. 1976

1976

Project 121   1974–76

Score   1977

Toronto Urban Studies Centre   1978

Student Employment Experience Centre Project   1978

Outcomes of Learnxs

There were several important outcomes from the Learnxs Project as a result of spin-off activities. The third task of the original proposal, concerning the creation of an alternative school designed to use community learning resources, resulted in the establishment of Subway Academy. While community resource learning was the original focus, Subway's greatest contribution to the alternatives movement was an organizational model to prove the viability of independent study, contract learning, and the flexible use of school resources by the system at large. It was estimated by the Board of Education's comptroller that it cost about one-half as much to educate a student in Subway as in a conventional secondary school. This was primarily due to Subway's very modest physical requirements and its use of a variety of external resources (including teachers from other schools) to support the learning process – a most important consideration in an era of diminishing budgets.

An outgrowth of the Subway model was Subway Academy II (1976), which maintained the operating style of the original program but developed a visual and performing arts theme as a result of its location and association with the Three Schools, an independent non-profit, non-credit arts college for adults. However, even more important was the process of its evolution. When the Subway task group met to consider the problem of how to handle enrolment demands while preserving Subway Academy's small size, a new process known as *swarming*[i] was developed by the task group. The school population, which at that point numbered about seventy-five students and three teachers, would be allowed to increase to one hundred students when a fourth teacher was added. At that point, two of the teachers and fifty of the students would have the opportunity to choose to re-establish themselves as a new unit on the subway line west of Yonge Street. Thus, a solution to the problem of how to handle growth was accomplished with a minimum of personal inconvenience and program disruption. It was this second unit that formed Subway Academy II.

Another important outcome from the Learnxs Project was the establishment of the Learnxs Foundation. The fourth objective of the original proposal had involved the development of 'additional sources of

---

i   This term comes from nature. When there are two queen bees in a hive, one queen and part of the population break away to form a new hive.

human, financial, and material support to enhance and further develop the existing education process.' As a result, the Learnxs Foundation was established as a non-governmental community organization, which was eligible for external funding that was not available to the Toronto Board of Education. However, the foundation continued to maintain an indirect relationship with the Board, as stated in the objects contained in its charter. This form of organizational interdependency, in support of programs of an innovative or experimental nature, represented a new source of educational finance in a time of declining enrolments and budget restraint. Alternate funding from governmental and private sources could be brought to bear to support demonstration projects involved with problem solving and future planning. Such funding is vital to public education bodies struggling to maintain themselves while facing diminishing financial support.

An important feature of the Learnxs Foundation as a community-based organization was its ability to relate directly to community needs and interests. Owing to its small size and inherent flexibility, the foundation was very approachable and had the potential to respond to current issues (provided there was a source of funding). As a community-based organization devoted to innovation and change, it could also maintain credibility with external funding sources and the community at large.

Besides the *Learnxs Directory*, the foundation undertook several other demonstration projects.

Project 121

From 1974 to 1976, Project 121 was the manifestation of a concern of parents, educators, and members of the community in Area 6 of the Toronto Board of Education who had become aware of two factors. First, there were children who were having difficulties in their school work and, as a result, were falling behind. Second, because of the budget ceilings imposed on education by the provincial government, there were not the funds to provide additional help in the classroom to the children who were not eligible for service from the Special Education Department; to be eligible they would have to have been seriously handicapped educationally. At this time, classroom numbers were increasing, resulting in even more difficulty for the teachers and for the youngsters with simple learning difficulties.

Concern was first expressed at People and Organizations in North Toronto (POINT) in 1973/74 and resulted in the organization establishing a steering committee 'to find out how to respond to the recognized needs of children in early grades who were potentially at high risk educationally.' The committee found that 'there was an interest among members of this community (Area 6) to become trained volunteers and help children learn on a one-to-one basis' and recommended that a program, Project 121, be established, with volunteers to help children on a withdrawal basis.

Like all creative endeavours, Project 121 did not develop out of thin air. There already existed in some schools in Area 6 a volunteer program to help children with their schoolwork. In fact, an Area 6 resource team had given considerable leadership in the effective use of volunteers. However, such volunteers had little opportunity for out-of-classroom training. The steering committee believed that each volunteer should be carefully selected and given pre-service training. To ensure success, there should be a half-time paid coordinator of volunteers' service who would look after the many details concerning not only the volunteers but also the students, the teachers, and the principals of the schools.

An extremely vital element in the establishment of Project 121 was the support of the Junior League of Toronto. In the spring of 1974 the league was presented with a brief from the steering committee requesting that the league endorse Project 121 by providing volunteers, one of whom would give administrative support, and funds with which to pay the salary and expenses of a coordinator. The league responded to this request and promised a grant of $15,000 for two years, September 1974 to August 1976. Six volunteers from the league also agreed to work with the project, and one became a member of Project 121's advisory board.

The Junior League of Toronto's proposal was presented to and approved by the Board of Education in August 1974. An arrangement was made between the Board of Education and the Junior League whereby the latter would pay money to the Learnxs Foundation to meet the expenses of Project 121. Thus, Learnxs became the vehicle for legitimizing the project in Area 6 of the Board of Education. The Learnxs Foundation, as a charitable fund, cooperated with the Board of Education in the development and advancement of school community programs of an innovative or experimental nature. (I represented the Learnxs Foundation on the advisory board.)

The steering committee selected a coordinator in September 1974. Following the terms of its original brief, it then selected an advisory board to whom the coordinator was responsible. Many members of the advisory board were members of the steering committee, and they continued to generate the same enthusiasm and hard work as had been evident when Project 121 was initiated. The advisory board included staff members of the Board of Education and members of the community. Some of the community members represented organizations such as POINT, the Association for Children with Learning Disabilities (ACLD), and the Junior League of Toronto.

An evaluation of Project 121 was conducted in 1976 by the Board of Education's Research Department and listed the following accomplishments of the demonstration project.

1. It has developed better community responses to the call for volunteers, via:
   a) More volunteers from the Junior League;
   b) Volunteers in greater numbers from universities and colleges;
   c) More volunteers from within certain school communities.
2. It has brought together teachers from neighbouring schools for valuable discussions among themselves and with volunteers.
3. It has organized training sessions for volunteers.
4. It has done much to stimulate the use of volunteers throughout the Area, particularly to help children with learning problems.
5. Through the Advisory Board, and in other ways, it has brought together community representatives, which in turn, has increased interest and understanding in education.
6. According to the best evidence collected from teachers, volunteers and parents, it has provided significant help for children described as having simple learning difficulties.[77]

Artsjunction

Artsjunction was a demonstration project in the visual arts proposed by community volunteer Sheila MacTaggart. Discarded materials from business and industry were collected and made available for craft programs in school and recreational settings. The Learnxs Foundation provided funding while the Toronto Board of Education donated space.

Community Learning Resources Consultant

From 1976 to 1977 the Community Learning Resources Consultant was a joint project of the Toronto Board of Education and the Learnxs Foundation, utilizing Community School Development grants ($17,000) from the Ministry of Education to employ a resource person to work with schools and community groups in developing local projects that used community learning resources. The job description of the position included the following objectives:

1. To work with teachers, principals, other Board staff, parent volunteers, and community groups in initiating community education programs such as:
   a) out-of-school learning for individuals, for example, *Learnxs Directory*;
   b) field trips for groups, for example, using the *Metropolitan Toronto Field Trip Guide*;
   c) community learning projects, for example, community service in secondary school, and Pinocchio for All People;
   d) neighbourhood learning resource files;
   e) alternatives-in-education projects.
2. To develop a resource bank of information on community learning opportunities, for example, existing directories, guidebooks, and information systems.
3. To be knowledgeable about Toronto Board programs, services, and facilities.
4. To work in close liaison with Learnxs Press.

School Community Organization to Revitalize Education

School Community Organization to Revitalize Education (SCORE) was a three-year research and development project in nine schools, beginning in 1977. The mission of the project was to use community resources to improve inner-city education. The design consisted of a research component and the following intervention programs:

1. *Appraisal for Better Curriculum (ABC)* – This was a cooperative program of Toronto Board of Education's Psychological Services and its Curriculum Division, which combined the regular early identification and psychological screening of grade-one children with an intensive curriculum consultation involving the classroom teacher, the psycho-educational consultant, and a curriculum consultant.
2. *Preschool Registration* – A survey took place in April, May, and June among children eligible to register in kindergarten in September. It

included an intensive medical examination (sight, hearing, respiratory, and structural components plus a behavioural check list), a social history, a classroom tour to assess social and behavioural adjustment, and a follow-up (concerning general and specific finds) by a nurse, teacher, and educational assistant.

3. *Nutrition* – This involved a program of parent education, in-service training of school personnel, and the provision of nutritional snacks as a supplement for children in junior and senior kindergarten and grades one and two.

The SCORE Project was sponsored by the Learnxs Foundation through the funds received from the Atkinson Charitable Foundation and matched by the Toronto Board of Education (for a total of $300,000 per year over three years). Each January, the $150,000 received from each of the two organizations was invested in term deposits, which yielded up to $40,000 per year; this interest was used by the Learnxs Foundation to fund other demonstration projects.

Toronto Urban Studies Centre

The idea of an urban studies centre had been proposed within the Toronto Board of Education since 1969, but a major lack of funding had prevented its emergence. In early 1977, several interested staff members, including representatives of the Geography Heads Association, the Boyne River Natural Science School, and the Board of Education's Curriculum Division, met on numerous occasions as a planning committee to prepare a submission that would seek sources of staffing and funding for a pilot project.

The planning committee approached the Learnxs Foundation to act as one potential source of funding and was warmly received. The foundation agreed to solicit funds on behalf of a Toronto urban studies centre and was successful in gaining a grant of $10,000 through the Ministry of Education's Community School Development program, covering the period from 1 January to 31 December 1978. The planning committee decided to use the money to start a pilot project to assist teachers and students to use the city as a classroom to bring immediacy and relevance to the existing curriculum. The curriculum could be altered to promote a better understanding of the urban environment.

The planning committee asked Gordon Stewart, Superintendent of Area 3, to initiate the program. Charles Hopkins, Director of the Boyne River Outdoor Education School, was asked to supervise the program of the centre with assistance from the staffs of Boyne River and Island Natural Science schools. The centre was located initially in the Area 3 office at Grace Street Public School and offered the following to area schools:

1. Information on historic buildings and sites in both Area 3 and old Toronto.
2. Assistance to teachers and students in researching information regarding their community (for example, library searches and land and title searches).
3. Assistance to teachers in employing the new environmental studies guidelines in an urban setting, both from a subject-matter point of view and in a skills development program.
4. Conceptual frameworks, with specific examples of how cities originate, grow, and in time change. (Toronto was the focal point, but information on other major cities provided comparative models.)
5. Research on and layout of town trails or neighbourhood walks, which allowed teachers to guide students on exploratory walks in their own locale.
6. Contact with various resources to make them available to classes. (These resources included industry, small business, politicians, and public utilities.)
7. A small core of expert staff who assisted the classroom teachers, both in the field and in their own school, for a period of up to two weeks.
8. A library and resource centre of current literature on urban studies, which was available to the teachers in Area 3.

Student Employment Experience Centre

The Toronto Board of Education's Research Department in their study *Patterns of Dropping Out* estimated that the dropout rate in Toronto secondary schools was 24 per cent, or almost eight thousand students per year. Two of the largest groups within this population were the work oriented and the family supporters. Their main reasons for leaving school were to assume employment, either as a demonstration of their need to feel more mature or to help support their families in times of crisis.

Each year there were also about six hundred fourteen-year-olds and fifteen-year-olds seeking employment through the Leaving School Early (LSE) program. A survey of these students indicated that most did not like school and failed to see any value in formal education. Their reasons for wishing to leave school were related to financial need or problems of a family or personal nature.

The Research Department concluded that the dropout problem in Toronto was of staggering proportions. In fact, only 40 per cent of the students entering grade nine would graduate from grade twelve, and only 20 per cent from grade thirteen.[78]

The severity of this problem to society became even more acute when the employment situation in Metropolitan Toronto was examined. A report from the Social Planning Council observed that in the Metropolitan Toronto census area, during the first quarter of 1978, there were 14.5 unemployed persons for every available job. The rate of overall youth unemployment (ages fifteen to twenty-three) in the Toronto area stood at 15 per cent, while a special survey of youth unemployment in Regent Park, in July 1977, had revealed the rate for that area to be 51 per cent.[79] Therefore, at a time when thousands of young people were choosing to leave school to seek a place in the world of work, there were very few employment opportunities available, even of a short-term or marginal nature. The result could be an increased sense of failure and disillusionment among unemployed youth, contributing to serious social problems.

The profound impact of this trend was also felt in the schools where as many as four hundred teachers would be displaced. (Early school leavers plus overall declining enrolment meant that fewer teachers were needed.) When this situation was coupled with the beginning of a natural decline in the number of students entering secondary schools, the problem took on crisis proportions, affecting teacher employment as well as the use of educational resources.

Traditional attempts to quell the dropout rate had involved the provision of school programs based on the premise that an academic vocational-preparation system was the only valid approach. However, youth tended to be better informed about social and economic realities. There was a realization that job experience might be more important to future employment stability than might academic credentials. It was time to consider a non-institutional educational alternative that focused on work and used academic skills to support the needs that would emerge through experience on the job.

One such approach was a demonstration project known as the Student Employment Experience Centre (SEEC) Project, which was established in July 1978 by the Learnxs Foundation. The project provided full-time employment at the adult minimum wage for fourteen- and fifteen-year-olds who had left school under the Leaving School Early program of the Ministry of Education; it also provided part-time employment for older students who were considered to be potential dropouts.

Applicants for the LSE program, fourteen- and fifteen-year-olds who did not want to attend school, were screened by committees of trustees and school-board personnel from each area. The program advisers who were assigned to assist these young people found that they were handicapped in finding employment because of their age, disadvantaged backgrounds, lack of realistic expectations of themselves or the work place, and fears resulting from a poor self-image and little self-confidence. Only the most hard to serve were ever referred to SEEC.

The SEEC Project received financial assistance from Employment and Immigration Canada for up to three years to employ at least eighteen student workers and five management personnel (with industry and small business experience). In addition, the Toronto Board of Education contributed surplus space, equipment, and materials, which resulted in the creation of several cottage industries or micro enterprises:

1. Mario's Place, a cafeteria and restaurant, used a vacant kitchen facility at Eastdale Collegiate (a former vocational school for girls) to provide a food service for students, staff, and area residents.
2. Mario's Community Kitchen, a catering service, provided food for day-care centres, meals-on-wheels delivery for senior citizens and disabled people, as well as food for meetings, conferences, and special events on a contract basis.
3. The Creative Wood Shop, located in a shop facility at Eastdale Collegiate, produced a line of wooden novelty items from pine (for example, wall racks, candle holders, and bread boxes), which were distributed across Canada.
4. The Strip Joint, located in the basement of Contact Alternative School, refinished surplus wooden classroom furniture to be sold as antiques and memorabilia. Individual pieces of furniture were also received from the public to be refinished on a contract basis.
5. The Paper Chase salvaged waste paper from the Education Centre (the administrative offices for the Toronto Board of Education and the Metropolitan Toronto School Board) and other office buildings for resale to the paper manufacturing industry.

Each of these enterprises was designed to operate as a small business on a cost-recovery basis. Revenue from sales was used to defray expenses in order to eventually make the project self-sufficient and provide capital for further expansion of the concept.

It should be stressed that SEEC did not offer work experience where students took time out from their school-based academic pursuits to gain some experience in the workplace. It was a community-based job creation program for at-risk dropouts, with an informal academic component built in to support the learning needs of the workers. Ideally, such a program would have focused on groups of youth organized into working parties (of ten to fifteen members) or work projects, using a small business or cooperative enterprise model. Each party would have had a manager with small-business experience and an academic skills coach who would have been drawn from the ranks of surplus teachers. The academic skills coach, as a working member of the enterprise, would also have been responsible for developing remedial programs and other educational activities according to the learning needs of the workers.

Unfortunately, SEEC as a demonstration project did not have a happy ending. It proved to be extremely difficult to recruit managerial personnel to the project who combined business acumen and social development experience. In the second year, a candidate was interviewed for the position of production coordinator. Although he possessed an MBA, he had been unemployed and living in poverty for some time; however, he came highly recommended by the Board's director of school-community relations (John Piper, a former community organizer and confidant of Trustee Gordon Cressy). As secretary-treasurer of the Learnxs Foundation, I interviewed this individual for the position and was then required to make a recommendation to the Learnxs Foundation's directors regarding his possible employment. He asked if he could visit SEEC to get to know the project better. I mistakenly agreed, and he proceeded to alienate the SEEC managers with his unruly behaviour during a subsequent visit. Consequently, the Learnxs directors did not support his appointment. When the individual received the news, he initiated a campaign to discredit the project. Linking up with Howard Fluxgold, a reporter from the Globe and Mail, he began to organize the student workers to go out on strike against their employer, the Learnxs Foundation. Several articles were published in the newspaper, targeting SEEC and me personally. As a result, the project was terminated by the federal government, and the staff and student workers lost their jobs.[80]

Learnxs Press Publications

Another important outcome of the Learnxs Project was the establishment of Learnxs Press as a non-profit publishing and distribution source for innovative materials in community education. The following titles were published or distributed by Learnxs Press: *Metropolitan Toronto Field Trip Guide, Learnxs Directory* (fourth edition), *Volunteers in Education, Learning About Labour Unions, Discover Your Neighbourhood Heritage, Resources for Multicultural Programs, Youth Resources Handbook, Project 121 Report, So You Want to Be a Social Worker, Toronto the Green, Toronto in a Nutshell, Life Options Catalogue, Arts Metro, Parenting Handbook, Neighbourhood Geography, Neighbourhood Service Curriculum, Public Alternative Schools in Metro Toronto,* and *Discover Southern Ontario.*

Funding was received from the federal and provincial governments, private foundations, fees for service, and revenue from sales. The Toronto Board of Education had provided facilities and services. Learnxs Press also became the publishing source for a selected list of materials from the Curriculum and Program Division of the Toronto Board.

All projects undertaken by the Learnxs Foundation involved external funding as well as financial and/or goods and services support from the Toronto Board. Therefore, by providing upfront money, the foundation was able to secure a matching source of support from public education. In each case, the public body also had a sense of commitment to the project, which might influence policy development.

Outcomes and Reflections

Existing studies of learning patterns among adults have clearly indicated that 80 per cent or more of their learning is of a non-formal, self-directed nature; that is, adults rely upon their personal contacts with individuals and groups as well as on their access to various types of learning materials. There is also a strong indication that similar patterns of 'informal' learning exist for youth and children.[ii]

If this form of non-institutional learning is so pervasive, is there a need to actively support its growth and development? It is my opinion that our traditional method of institutional schooling has been largely devoted to the creation of learning dependencies rather than the enhancement of the natural tendency of students to be non-formal,

---

ii The use of the term *informal* in this context does not mean 'without form' but rather that the individual learner creates his or her own form within the learning process, as opposed to relying upon some external force to direct it.

independent learners. This reliance on patterns of dependent learning (for example, a student dependent upon a teacher for content) may have seriously inhibited whatever innate abilities teachers have to be encouragers and facilitators of student learning in all elements of their life. If the function of the brain is to organize individual experience, the development of enquiry skills among teachers and students is essential to maximize their potentials as non-formal lifelong learners.

A major prerequisite of non-formal learning is access to new sources of information and skills. The creation of systems to access learning resources (such as the Internet) will increase the access of non-formal learners to a wide variety of learning options. These people, places, objects, and media materials represent a learning process in themselves as each contact tends to identify other sources and the enquiry becomes more extensive.

Schools, libraries, and social and recreational agencies represent a major socializing influence on our society. The people who administer these institutional settings should be made more aware of non-formal learning theory and practice. Further opportunities should be found to modify existing curriculum and program so as to sharpen enquiry skills and enhance the flow of information about learning resources in the community. If these resources can become a legitimate part of the formal (as well as the non-formal) learning process, the true potential of lifelong learning may begin to be realized.

The *Learnxs Directory* represented a valid model to achieve this goal. Students and other learners could be involved in the process of identifying, recording, and cataloguing learning resources as a community project. This process was itself a learning experience, which developed enquiry skills and increased the flow of information among community members. The end product formed an informational network, which could be updated regularly and used as a resource for individual learning and interest group programs. It was my opinion, however, that more research needed to be done on this model to assess further its potential use as a renewable information system in a variety of settings involving both print and electronic applications. In addition, more research should be done on the non-formal learning patterns of children and youth.

The establishment of a private charitable foundation, as a non-governmental body that develops cooperative interdependence with a large governmental organization, can be an important source of support for demonstration projects in a period of austerity and fiscal restraint. Through the pooling of public and private resources, it might still be possible to ensure a sense of creative activity and program excellence while public organizations are struggling to maintain themselves. The Learnxs Foundation became a model for similar ventures in North York, York, East York, and Ottawa-Carleton in Ontario, and Nanaimo in British Columbia.

A private foundation attached to a public body can also serve as a vehicle for committed persons from the public body and the community at large to participate in joint problem solving and collective action. Additional research could be done, however, on the potential effect that this organizational interdependence might have on public decision making. The Learnxs Foundation, utilizing a community education and development process, was able to provide financial and in-kind support to a variety of innovative demonstration projects.

In summary, Learnxs was developed around the hypothesis that community resources could be better utilized to enhance learning among individuals and groups. The results of the Learnxs experience support this hypothesis both in terms of the availability and use of community resources for learning and the development of a process model for a demonstration project in community education. As we enter a new era in our history, which some have described as the conserver society, these findings seem not only important but vital to the future of public education.

Institutional schooling will probably continue to be the predominant means of formal education, but there must be a recognition that technological change, the information explosion, and the spiralling costs of traditional schooling, in an economy with a decreasing sense of financial commitment to human services, will eventually lead to a radical redefinition of the role of public education in our society. It is essential that educators begin to direct their efforts to creating their own futures instead of falling victim to political and economic expediency.

Unfortunately, not enough is being done currently to prepare students, teachers, and parents to cope with these changes. Learnxs attempted to demonstrate the viability of an approach to learning that stressed the right of the individual to grow and develop using all available resources. The Learnxs Foundation continues to this day as a resource to provide financial support for innovative projects in community education.

9 Alternatives in Education

Alternative School Programs

Subway Academy, as an outgrowth of the Learnxs Project, was but one example of the alternatives-in-education movement that influenced policy development at the Toronto Board of Education. With the termination of the Special Task Force on Education in June 1972, I had been assigned to the director's office as a principal on special assignment to implement task force recommendations. In 1978, I was named Coordinator of Alternative and Community Programs in the Curriculum and Program Division, responsible for community education policies and programs in the following areas: inner-city schools, community school development, multiculturalism, day care in the school, community use of facilities, parallel use of vacant educational space, neighbourhood schools as multiservice centres, school-age day care, lunch and after-four programs, volunteers in education, and alternative school programs.

The period from 1968 to 1973 had seen the emergence of a variety of innovative school projects and experimental programs in North America as alternative approaches to a mainstream or predominant method of public education. The growth of the alternatives-in-education movement had been seen as the education system's reaction to the free schools of the 1960s, particularly in the United States.[81] During this period, Toronto became home to thousands of Vietnam War resisters from the United States, who often brought with them counterculture ideals and experiences. Many had been influenced by the writings of authors such as A.S. Neill, his Summerhill demonstration school in England, and the de-schooling theories of Ivan Illich (which had a major influence on Learnxs).

Ivan Illich, in his 1971 article 'Education Without School: How It Can Be Done,'[82] proposed a radical departure from the present system of formal education, a departure that was influential in the creation of the Learning Exchange System. According to Illich, learning resources would be divided into four learning exchanges: things, models, peers, and elders. Access to the four sets of resources would be assured through the provision of four networks:

1. *Reference services to educational objects*, which facilitate access to things or processes used for formal learning. Some of these things can be reserved for this purpose and stored in libraries, rental agencies, laboratories, and showrooms such as museums and theatres; others can be in daily use in factories, in airports, or on farms but made available to students during apprenticeship or on off-hours.
2. *Skill exchanges*, which permit persons to list their skills, the conditions under which they are willing to serve as models for others who want to learn their skills, and the addresses at which they can be reached.
3. *Peer matching*, a communicative network, which permits persons to describe the learning activity in which they wish to engage in the hope of finding a partner for the enquiry.
4. *Reference services to educators at large*, who can be listed in a directory giving the addresses and self-descriptions of professionals, para-professionals, and freelancers, along with the conditions of access to their services.

Illich created a theoretical model to separate the learning needs of individuals from current educational practice. His proposals did not deal with the question of how to introduce community learning resources into the current system of public education. Instead, he envisioned a completely new educational information system, geared to the needs of the individual learner, which would replace institutional schooling. By identifying, cataloguing, and disseminating information on learning resources, each individual would be able to develop his own program.

Illich operated on the premise that public schooling had become an expensive anachronism and should be replaced by his system of universal access to learning resources. However, schools have existed in one form or another for thousands of years, and the cultural tradition of institutional schooling will continue to exist, at least in the foreseeable future. This does not preclude, however, the fact that learners can continue to seek out learning opportunities on a non-formal basis. Illich, through his four information networks, provided an alternative approach to learning that could complement the current system of institutional schooling. The following alternative demonstration projects, including Subway Academy, were influenced by Illich.

Parkway Program. One alternative approach was the Parkway program in Philadelphia, conceived by John Bremer, who later became the reformers' candidate for director of education in Toronto (see chapter 5). The Parkway program was conceived as a solution to the problem of overcrowding in Philadelphia high schools. As there was very limited money for new school construction, it was proposed that organizations around the Benjamin Franklin Parkway (such as the Academy of Natural Sciences, the Philadelphia Museum of Art, the Franklin Institute, and the Free Library) be approached to donate meeting space and to provide resource personnel. The Philadelphia Board of Education approved this concept in February 1968.

Students were chosen randomly from each of the school districts to ensure that the student population was representative of the city's population. By January 1969 there were about five hundred students with thirty faculty and thirty interns from the University City neighbourhood. As a school without walls, Parkway did not have a formal building of its own, but it used a wide variety of cultural, scientific, and business institutions.[83]

Metro School. In February 1970 the Chicago Board of Education established the Chicago Public High School for Metropolitan Studies (the Metro School) as an alternative model for high-school education. The program of the school was built on two premises: students must have control over the direction of their own learning; and the resources of the entire city, including its businesses, cultural institutions, and community organizations, must become a laboratory for learning.[84]

The school began with 150 students drawn from all sections of Chicago, representing the total academic, geographic, racial, and economic diversity of high-school youth. With the admittance of a freshman class of 500 students, chosen by lottery each September, it was projected that the school would stabilize its enrolment at 1,500 to 2,000 by 1973. Staffing included a combination of teachers from Chicago public schools, interns from local universities and the Chicago Teacher Corps, volunteers, and representatives of participating organizations. The school used business and institutional facilities and drew public support from the Board of Education and private support from Chicago's business community. Support from either quarter took the form of dollars, facilities, personnel, materials, or services, or some combination of these resources.

Core Project. In the spring of 1972 three teachers from the Edmonton Public School Board proposed an urban core involvement program.[85] Drawing inspiration from the various schools-without-walls projects, the authors suggested a program to make greater use of the potentially rich educational environment of Edmonton's urban core. The format consisted of an integration of four curricular areas: Social Studies, English and Communications, Sociology, and Special Projects. It was proposed that the program operate during afternoons only, with students participating in the regular high-school program during the morning.

These three programs were examples of a growing trend in public education across the continent. However, such programs were seldom initiated in response to the learning needs of individuals. Parkway was established, originally, to ease a problem of overcrowding, because there was not enough money available to erect a new building. The Metro School served as a magnet to lure more suburban students downtown to ensure a balanced, racially mixed constituency. The Core Project became a half-day option to enrich the program of an existing secondary school. In each case the program was quite large (five hundred or more students) and established by educational officials for reasons more organizational than curricular.

During this period there were also alternative school programs being proposed in Metropolitan Toronto.

Summer of Experience, Exploration, and Discovery (SEED). In the Spring of 1968, Fiona Nelson, a reform trustee of the Toronto Board of Education, proposed a summer enrichment program for secondary school students who were unable to find employment during July and August. The program was to be housed in existing school buildings that were vacant during the summer and to be staffed by resource personnel from the city's community as well as volunteer teachers. In June of that year the Board approved the SEED proposal.

That summer Les Birmingham, an elementary school principal, and Murray Shukyn, an elementary teacher, volunteered to coordinate a program composed of a variety of topics of personal interest to the six hundred young people who enrolled. Participants grouped themselves according to interests and met for informal discussions, field trips, and other activities. Meeting space and several telephones were provided in the Education Centre building.

The program continued during the summer of 1969, with a greater variety of studies, as more people from the community volunteered their services. By this time people had begun to look upon the SEED program as an alternative to traditional secondary school education. As a result, the students and volunteer instructors continued the program in the evening during the 1969/70 school year. In the winter of 1970, a committee of students, teachers, catalysts (as the resource volunteers were called), and other interested people formed a committee to prepare a proposal to the Toronto Board of Education that SEED be established as an experimental alternative to the regular secondary school program.[i] The Board, in turn, formed a special committee to study the proposal, which reported to the Management Committee of the Board of Education, and on recommendation of the Management Committee,[ii] SEED was officially established as a part of the regular Toronto school system.

The program commenced in September 1970, with an enrolment of one hundred students, under the direction of coordinator Murray Shukyn and a core staff of four teachers who gave instruction in English, a foreign language, science, and mathematics. Vacant quarters were found in the Young Men's Hebrew Association (YMHA) building at the corner of Spadina Avenue and Bloor Street West, which offered advantages such as handball and badminton courts, ballet practice rooms, a swimming pool, and other athletic facilities. The location was central to the city, on the subway line, and close to the University of Toronto, the Ontario Institute for Studies in Education, various libraries, and other facilities that these institutions offered. It was also reasonably close to the homes, offices, and laboratories of the many catalysts who were donating their services.

Besides the concepts of an educational program built by students for students, all learning was self-motivated and student initiated. Another concept of the SEED program was the use of the resources of the city community. SEED was to be a community school, interacting and coop-

---

i   The word *SEED* in this case stood for 'Shared Experience, Exploration, and Discovery.'

ii   The Management Committee was one of the four standing committees of the Toronto Board and dealt with curriculum and program matters.

erating with those in the city. By being forced to go out and find resource persons who would volunteer their time and expertise, students were able to obtain an education in their area of interest without additional education expenditure. Many of the catalysts were professors at the University of Toronto and York University, while others were professionals working in medical research, advertising, journalism, broadcasting, painting and sculpting, psychiatry, and many other fields.[86]

School of Experimental Education (SEE). Also in September 1970, the Education Committee of the Etobicoke Board of Education approved the resolution 'that an ad hoc committee consisting of three members of the Board and three members of the staff be appointed to consider proposals related to the establishment of a less structured secondary school program designed to meet the special needs of some of the students of the Borough, and that this committee report to the Education Committee.' Membership on this ad hoc committee included (beside the three trustees) a teacher, a regional superintendent, and an administrator from the central office.

After hearing presentations from principals, teachers, students, and parents, the committee formed three subcommittees on community resources, selection, and communications. As a result of their deliberations, a proposal was drafted to establish a school of experimental education (to be known as SEE). The section on curriculum contained this statement: 'Much of the resources for the curriculum will be found in business, industry, laboratories, lecture halls, libraries, and any other human resource that the community is prepared to offer.'[87]

A survey conducted by the Subcommittee on Community Resources produced an interest or commitment from York University, Department of Urban Studies; University of Toronto, School of Social Work; Erindale College; Humber College; administrators and field workers in almost all the social services; professional staff in large industries, such as Bell Telephone and Xerox Corporation; and individuals in the arts and political, journalistic, legal, engineering, and medical fields.

In September 1971, the SEE proposal was implemented by the Etobicoke Board of Education, utilizing space at the former Humber Bay Public School, near the Queensway at the Humber River, which was a facility easily reached by public transportation.

Alternative and Independent Study Program (AISP). In the fall of 1970, the North York Board of Education appointed a program leader to conduct a feasibility study concerning the need for an alternative and independent study program at the senior high-school level. In March 1971, the North York Board received an interim report containing observations drawn from discussions among parents, teachers, and students as well as from fact-finding visits to existing programs.[88] In a suggested course of action, the report proposed that suitable quarters for the new learning community be found in a central location in North York, which would be accessible to students from all areas of the borough, who would pay for their own transportation. It should be adjacent, as far as possible, to cultural institutions, businesses, and social agencies of the community. While core subjects for students requiring diplomas would be offered at this central location, every attempt would be made to provide learning environments in offices, factories, laboratories, and cultural institutions of the metropolitan area.

The school would be staffed by certificated teachers who were concerned with independent study and with providing a new environment for learning. In addition, the school would seek to enlist suitable teacher catalysts from varied walks of life in the community. Enrolment would be limited to a hundred and sixty students during the first year, which, within the pupil-teacher ratio guidelines, would permit the school to be staffed with nine certificated teachers.

In September 1971, AISP was established as an alternative high school, occupying vacant space in the former administrative building of the North York Board of Education, near Yonge Street and Highway 401.

Alternative Policies and Programs

One of the responsibilities of my position as principal on special assignment, and later as coordinator of alternative and community programs, was to work with parents, teachers, and students in developing new innovative programming. The Toronto Board of Education was unique in the field of alternatives in education owing to its bottom-up approach to policy development. The first group of parents with whom I worked, many of whom were professionals and war resisters, wanted to establish Toronto's first alternative elementary school. This involved numerous town hall meetings where educational theories and ideologies were debated, often with great emotion. I represented the school establishment and, at least initially, was not to be trusted; I became the apologist for everything that was wrong with institutional schooling. I found this to be rather ironic, considering all that I had been through in Lawrence Heights and with the task force. The final result of all the meetings and debates was the drafting of a proposal to be presented to the Board of Education.

A Lot of People Hoping for an Alternative (ALPHA).

In the fall of 1971, the Management Committee of the Toronto Board of Education received a brief from a citizens group called People for an Alternative Elementary School, who were requesting the establishment of a subcommittee to devise a plan for the implementation of a new alternative school to open in September 1972. The group proposed an educational environment that would accommodate a variety of instructional methods and different learning styles and support children and adults in their efforts to define, pursue, and achieve their own educational goals; that would offer constant encouragement to allow children to grow in their own direction at their own speed; that would provide a continuity between school and home so that living and learning would not be separate but would be combined in a community school, with greater involvement of the community in the school program and broader use of out-of-school community resources by the children; that would support the child's total experience of himself and his world so that he would be respected as real, viable, and valuable; and that also supported a view of the child as unique and of non-comparable, non-measurable worth. Such an environment required the elimination of arbitrary standards or goals.[89]

The program would be relevant to the needs and values of a geographically dispersed, but psychologically cohesive, community of parents and children seeking to improve the richness and quality of urban life. As an experimental program, it would be evaluated in terms of its own objectives and goals. It was also suggested that the school population be limited to approximately one hundred children, who would normally be enrolled in kindergarten to grade eight, with enrolment being on a voluntary first-come, first-served basis or as a lottery open to all residents of Toronto.

The first brief was later clarified by a more detailed proposal entitled 'The ALPHA Experience' (standing for A Lot of People Hoping for an Alternative), which further stressed the elements of competence in basic skills, personal initiative, self-respect, cooperation, acceptance of diversity, freedom of expression, autonomy, social responsibility, and affiliation within an extended group. The program was envisioned as a learning environment where children, teachers, parents, and other adult volunteers could share knowledge, skills, and life experiences. Resources would also include a variety of learning styles, interpersonal relations, a choice of curriculum materials, and community-related projects.

After the Toronto Board of Education's conditional approval and an extensive search for vacant school space, the ALPHA school was opened in September 1972, utilizing the third floor of the Young Men's Christian Association (YMCA) in the Dundas Street and Broadview Avenue area of east Toronto. Parents (some of whom were architects) had extensive hands-on involvement in creating the space. The fact that the Board required an enrolment of at least one hundred students for the school to open caused the parents to go on a desperate enrolment drive during the spring and summer. The end result was that the ALPHA parental group had only one thing in common – they all hated traditional schooling. Nevertheless, the enrolment number was finally achieved.

Staffing was another major concern. The parents wanted to hire the four teachers assigned to the school, which was against Board policy, and we had to work out a compromise: officials performed the hiring, with strong parental input. Here again I was in the middle as the acting principal. School management was another matter. All parents were welcomed to weekly evening meetings to hammer out program policies and procedures. It soon became apparent that there were strong disagreements concerning such issues as curriculum, learning materials, teaching styles, and discipline. Some parents wanted to volunteer almost full time, and this became threatening to some of the teachers. By Christmas, about one-third of the parents and children had left, threatening to establish a BETA alternative school (Better Education Than ALPHA). However, new parents and students were recruited, and ALPHA continues to this day, occupying space in the former Brant Street School building in the King Street West and Spadina Avenue area.

CONTACT

Not all proposals for alternative school programs came from parents and students. Teachers also brought forward proposals to me as the official responsible for the Board of Education's Alternatives in Education Committee. In May 1972 a group of secondary school teachers (led by Harry Smaller) and graduate students from the Ontario Institute for Studies in Education presented 'A Proposal for CONTACT' to the Alternatives in Education Committee that expressed concern at the increasing numbers of high-school students who were dropping out of their regular programs. They recognized that, while some students in a straight academic program might benefit from more emphasis on technical, commercial, or vocational skills, others might require a different method of teaching while retaining the same program content. Their approach to assist these students would be an alternative school (CONTACT) with the following characteristics.

(a) Students would be drawn from two sources:

   1. Those who had left school before graduation, were presently unemployed, and wished to continue their secondary education in an alternate setting.
   2. Students presently enrolled in Toronto secondary schools but not benefiting from their regular program due to sporadic attendance and/or their behaviour in class.

(b) Students could be referred to CONTACT by teachers, guidance counsellors, and community social service agencies or apply on their own initiative. As the majority of dropouts occur in the inner city, it was anticipated that a larger proportion of students with average or below average achievement levels would be drawn from this area of the City.

(c) The curriculum would consist of two approaches:

   1. Affective Education to develop a feeling of self-worth in each student through cooperation rather than competition, the acquisition of attitudes and social skills to help facilitate the involvement of students in all facets of their community, and achievement based on individual interests, needs, and abilities rather than on group norms.
   2. Cognitive Development, using a problem-directed approach to encourage the development of the skills of innovation, critical analysis, decision making, acting on decisions, and assessing the results of these acts, and to motivate students in more traditional aspects of curriculum, whether remedial work in the basic skills or scholarly presentation in an upper-school discipline.

(d) The program would follow the credit system as outlined in HS1, allow-
    ing a flexibility according to the interests, needs, and past achieve-
    ments of students but still fulfilling the requirements for secondary
    school graduation diplomas.

(e) CONTACT would be ideally located in the inner city, using space oth-
    er than in an existing school, such as a church, YMCA, or community
    hall.

(f) The program would begin with fifty students, four certificated
    teachers, two lay assistants, and resource personnel provided
    by the Toronto Board and outside sources.[90]

CONTACT was approved in principle in June 1972 and began the
following September as an after-school and evening program, using a
portable classroom and a house owned by the Board of Education on
Oak Street in the Regent Park area (formerly occupied by the Task Force
on Education). In September 1973, CONTACT was established as a day
school in vacant classrooms on the third floor of the Duke of York Public School (elementary) in the Jarvis Street and Dundas Street East area
of central Toronto. It later relocated to occupy a building, which had
previously housed a supermarket, adjacent to Regent Park North.

Uniqueness of Toronto Alternatives

The alternatives movement in Metropolitan Toronto evolved quite differently than did the alternatives in education in many American cities.
As the home of two large universities, Toronto was at the forefront of
the Canadian student rights movement of the 1960s. As a major reception area for immigrants (including U.S. war resisters), it was infused
with many differing views and divergent attitudes. As one of the fastest growing and most diverse urban areas in the world, Metropolitan
Toronto had to learn to cope with bigness, while struggling to preserve
the quality of life in its neighbourhoods. These influences combined to
create the climate that spawned a unique alternatives environment in
Metropolitan Toronto.

Several important characteristics seemed to make these programs
different from their American counterparts. One was origin: most programs were established as a result of pressure on a school board from
an external group of parents, teachers, and/or students. In addition,

most programs were quite small in size and enrolment. The variety of programs was also a factor: they were established to relate to the needs of students from differing socio-economic backgrounds at the elementary as well as the secondary school level. Most of the programs emphasized the involvement of teachers and students in day-to-day decision making, with teachers, students, parents, and other interested citizens participating in overall policy development. The common element in all these programs was a commitment to the community-learning-resources concept as the basic focus for curriculum and program development.

Alternative School Case Studies

During the 1970s I was responsible for more than twenty groups of parents, students, and teachers who brought new school proposals to the Alternatives in Education Committee. Following are a few memorable examples.

Wandering Spirit Survival School

In 1976 two Native Canadian families chose to withdraw their children from the public schools owing to perceived racism experienced by their children. Led by Vern and Pauline Harper, they first established a private volunteer school operating out of the Native Canadian Centre of Toronto. When this school proved to be not financially viable, the Harpers approached the Ministry of Education for assistance. Since the Ministry did not provide direct funding to schools, the families were soon referred to the Toronto Board of Education. The sight of Vern and Pauline Harper marching in full Native regalia to the office of Mike Lennox, Superintendent of Curriculum and Program, caused quite a stir on the second floor of the Education Centre at 155 College Street. They demanded full funding for a Native way school that stressed the heritage, spiritual, and cultural aspects of native life. I was responsible for working with the Harpers to develop a proposal for the Alternatives in Education Committee. At first, there was a strong distrust of me as an establishment figure – particularly by Vern Harper, who was the product of the infamous Indian residential schools and had been illiterate until he was in his forties. Finally a mutually acceptable proposal was drafted.

The school was to be named after the famous Cree war chief Wandering Spirit, who was instrumental in the efforts of the Riel Rebellion to protect his people's way of life. However, the real controversy over this proposal centred on the spiritual belief that all objects in nature had life and should be worshipped as the work of the Creator. This focus was opposed by many as religious teaching, including the *Toronto Star*, which published an editorial condemning the proposal.

The school's objectives were to establish standards of behaviour as taught by the spiritual leaders of the Native community; to establish a curriculum that would satisfy the requirements and standards as set forth by the Wandering Spirit Survival Native Council, the Ministry of Education, and the Toronto Board of Education; to utilize materials and resources that were relevant to the Native experiences and acceptable to the Toronto Board; to provide staff and resources in a congenial setting so that each student could work toward his own goals and collectively develop a sense of community; and to provide an understanding of the concept of growth and development from a Native perspective.

The school's policies were to be governed by an all Native council, consisting of an executive council of parents, supporters, and a student representative. Native elders and a shaman were to be active in the school to promote spiritual and cultural values. (I can recall participating in morning exercises at the school where burning sweetgrass was passed around the prayer circle, and confessions and pleas for forgiveness were offered to 'Grandfather.')

In February 1977 the Toronto Board of Education approved the school, and accommodation was found in the basement of the Winchester School Annex in Cabbagetown. Jim Wilkinson, Principal of Winchester School, reluctantly agreed to be Wandering Spirit's principal of record. In one instance, when a Native Canadian teacher could not be found, the Native Council agreed to accept a teacher of Japanese ancestry. One morning during the first week of operations I received a frantic call from Mr Williamson. 'It's about the loud drumming downstairs. What am I supposed to do?' he said. This was but one element of the Wandering Spirit Survival School's heritage and cultural program. Other concerns centred on occasional absences when teachers and students would suddenly depart, without notice, to attend Native powwows elsewhere in the province. The administration of Wandering Spirit was indeed a challenge, but today the first publicly funded Native way urban school in Ontario (if not Canada) still operates, as the First Nations Alternative School in the Dundas Street East and Gerrard Street area.

Inglenook Community High School

A small group of unemployed teachers, including Trevor Owen, had established a private school called Inglenook in North Toronto. When its financial situation became precarious, they approached the Toronto Board of Education for acceptance as a new alternative secondary school. The new Inglenook was envisioned as a community school in that it was to be governed by staff, students, and parents. Through its outreach program it was to involve itself deeply in the life of the community.

The school's objectives were to provide a strong link between academic achievement and activity in the wider world and to provide a solid secondary school education for students whose families desired a direct voice in the daily operations and the long-term goals of the school. The academic program with its four divisions – communications, arts, pure and applied sciences, and social sciences – was scheduled on Monday, Tuesday, Thursday, and Friday. On Wednesday, members of the school were free to explore 'museums, parklands, streets, shops, hospitals, libraries, offices, institutions, alternative communities, theatres, historic properties (and so on), not as artefacts or objects of curiosity but as cells, tissues, and organs of the vast living organism called Toronto' (Inglenook Community High School brochure).

The school was to be governed by the Committee for Evaluation, Academic Standards, and Admissions, with three students and three staff personnel to monitor the quality of academic and community life. A board of directors, consisting of two students, two staff persons, two parents, the principal of record, and one representative of the community at large, would review the policies of the school and make recommendations to the general membership. The general membership would be made up of students, staff, parents, the principal of record, and the community representative. A coordinator would be elected by the staff. Inglenook Community High School was approved by the Toronto Board in 1974 and continues in operation today in the former Sackville School building.

Alternative Primary School

A group of parents in the Forest Hill area of north Toronto, led by Martha Friendly and Laurel Rothman, approached the Board of Education in 1971 with a proposal to establish an alternative primary school (junior kindergarten to grade three). The school was to follow a cooperative model, with parents, teachers, the principal of record, and the school board cooperating to run the program. Full-day kindergartens were to be supplemented by childcare staff (employed by parents) to provide a day of care from 8:00 a.m. to 6:00 p.m.

The philosophy of the school had parents playing an active role in guiding the school's program, selecting its teachers, devising its curriculum, and enriching their children's opportunities. While basic skills were to be stressed, each child would proceed at his or her own pace, either individually or in a group. French, physical education, and artistic development were to be provided at all levels. Parents were expected to contribute to the cooperative's enrichment activities, such as field trips and after-school programming, through volunteer time and voluntary financial donations.

The original Alternative Primary School was approved for operation, in September 1978, and occupied space at Northern Preparatory School in the Spadina Road and Eglinton Avenue West area. Besides the childcare provisions, the original teacher, John Dunlop, introduced learning contracts as an innovation at the primary level. A junior level was later added, and the name changed to Alternative Public School.

Hawthorne II Bilingual School

Another private school stressing a bilingual French and English program, Hawthorne Bilingual School had gone bankrupt. A group of parents, including Michele Leroux, approached the Board of Education to re-establish the program as Hawthorne II Bilingual School. (This proved to be an unfortunate choice of name because creditors of the defunct private school began chasing the Toronto Board to settle outstanding debts.) The objectives of the school were to encourage the development of the whole child, physically, socially, emotionally, and as intellectually, in a bilingual setting with a family atmosphere of small mixed age groups. Key elements of the philosophy were

1. To provide an environment for children to appreciate and learn French as a language and not a lesson.
2. To give each child an education tailored to the maximum degree possible to meet their individual needs, with emphasis on permitting and encouraging each child to advance at their own pace.
3. To emphasize creative activities.

4. To provide an extended hours program for the children of working parents which is both rewarding and enjoyable.
5. To provide an active Parent's Group.[91]

While the basic language of instruction was to be English, oral French was introduced at the junior kindergarten level. The school was to be governed by a board of directors, consisting of five parents, five teachers, and one day-care assistant, in such areas as program planning, staff hiring, and field trips and special projects. Hawthorne II Bilingual School opened in September 1977 and is currently located in the Essex Street Annex at Christie Street Public School in west Toronto.

Spectrum Alternative Senior School

At Deer Park Senior Public School, teachers in a program called Spectrum (Ellen Dorfman, Brian Taylor, and David Clyne) and the students' parents wished to establish the program as the first alternative school at the intermediate level (grades seven and eight). In 1978, teachers and parents presented the proposal to the Alternatives in Education Committee, but it was strongly opposed by the Area 6 superintendent. This placed the teachers in a very awkward position (teachers did not question the wishes of their area superintendent). The Spectrum parents then mounted a political campaign, and when the decision reached the Board of Education's School Program's Committee, they packed the committee room. In came the Canadian Broadcasting Corporation's television videographer (one of the parents) to record the decision-making process. Trustees and officials seemed visibly intimidated by the media attention, and the proposal was approved in spite of the position of the area superintendent. (When I later approached the camera man and asked when the coverage would be aired, he said, 'What coverage? There was no tape in the camera.')

The Spectrum philosophy focused on highly motivated students wishing to have the opportunity to work independently. Program features included

- Small group instruction.
- Individualized goal-setting and evaluation.
- Continuous progress with remedial and enrichment work.
- Instruction and testing to ensure proficiency at grade level in preparation for secondary school.
- Research, field trips, guests, community-based projects.

- Art, emphasizing imagination through a variety of media.
- Stage productions, jug band, art exhibits.
- Physical education activities, games, fitness program.
- Mock parliament and simulations.
- Literary and arts magazine.
- Fund-raising auction for school projects.[92]

Spectrum continues to this day, occupying space at Eglinton Avenue Public School.

The Student School

The Student School was a new alternative secondary school for drop-outs that was proposed by teachers Ken Ellis and John Ruch. Opened in 1979 in space at Eastdale Collegiate (which also housed SEEC), the Student School provided an academic program along with the opportunity for related work experience to persons sixteen years of age and older. A student would have the opportunity, wherever possible, of using the skills and knowledge acquired in class and applying them while working with others in the community who had similar interests, as part of a work experience or community volunteer program.

The most interesting feature of TheStudentSchool was its adventure into true student participation in program planning. Each area of study had a planning committee comprising a teacher, as many students as wished to participate, and, where possible, an outside consultant. The committee would meet, for example, at the end of the first term to discuss plans for all the third term subjects under their area of study. Some students would study the Ministry of Education guidelines for the subject areas, some would work with the consultant, others would solicit information from students interested in taking the courses, and others would look into facilities and space requirements. All would report back and together formulate plans for the third term. Each planning committee then reported to a general council meeting, and a vote on each proposal would ensue. All staff, students, and any person with a long-term interest in the school might vote at these meetings.

At the end of each term there was a week-long tutorial and orientation. The first one occurred in the second week of November and included an intensive evaluation of staff, students, and courses. Other possibilities for these three one-week periods might include special programs such as career choices, post-secondary education possibilities, and week-long trips to areas outside of Toronto.[93]

TheStudentSchool continues as an alternative secondary school of the Toronto District School Board and is now located at Western Technical-Commercial School.

Other Alternative School Programs

There were other alternative school programs that I assisted in establishing during the 1970s.

1. Laneway Community School, a former private elementary school established by the Trefann Court Mothers with a back-to-the-basics curriculum and program. It was the only alternative school to ultimately fail.
2. West End Alternative, a secondary school established by teacher Harry Smaller in the west side of the city and following the same program guidelines as does CONTACT.
3. Beaches Alternative, an elementary school with a program similar to that of ALPHA and located in the Beaches area of east Toronto.
4. Subway Academy II, an expansion, in the west end, of the Subway Academy concept. Two teachers from Subway Academy relocated to occupy space at the non-profit Three Schools in the Brunswick Avenue and Bloor Street West area. This setting also provided a focus for students interested in the visual arts.
5. Downtown Alternative Primary School, a program at the junior kindergarten to grade three level that is somewhat similar in philosophy to ALPHA.
6. Arts Alternative for Adults, a cooperative venture of the Artists Workshop Division of the non-profit Three Schools. Each term, fifty visual arts courses were taught by professional artists. The Three Schools did not mark or grade nor did it issue diplomas, other than a certificate of attendance if requested.
7. Network of Complementary Schools, a consortium of fourteen public and fourteen private secondary schools and school districts in the United States. I was able to have SEED Alternative School admitted as the only Canadian representative in the network, and I later served as its first non-American president. The network program was based on the walk-about concept whereby students pursued their learning interests in a variety of different settings as an aid to career orientation and personal development. Each school offered an area of specialty. For example, the School of Good Hope (Virgin Islands) offered marine biology; Beverly Hills High School

(California) offered television production; and Rabun Gap High School (Georgia), with Foxfire Inc., had cultural journalism. Visiting students could spend four to six weeks (or longer), and the host school provided meals and accommodations. There were also grants available to defray travel costs.

While SEED Alternative School was the Toronto Board of Education's representative in the Network of Complementary Schools, students from other Toronto secondary schools were also welcome to participate. 'Toronto: A City of Neighbourhood Services' was a special one-month intensive course developed for Toronto's participation in the network. Students learned enquiry skills and applied them to an analysis of the human services in a particular neighbourhood. A daily log, plus a major presentation at the end of the course, provided a basis for evaluation. The Ministry of Education accepted this course for credit under HS 1 guidelines.

The network also offered professional development opportunities whereby teachers and staff from member schools could spend one or two weeks at other schools in the consortium and exchange knowledge; where available, subsidies could be acquired by participants to assist with travel, housing, and other expenses.

General Policy for Alternative School Programs

Experience gained in the establishment of alternative school programs during the early 1970s led to my development of a general policy to govern the Board of Education's decision-making process. The following is an excerpt that I prepared to describe the policy to parents, teachers, students, and other citizens of the community.

Alternative school programs in the City of Toronto may be unique in North America because most of them were started by groups of parents, teachers, students, and other interested persons who approached the Board of Education for support of experimental programs within the system. Other school boards have usually designed their own alternative schools with a minimum of community involvement.

The most common characteristic, among the secondary and elementary alternative schools in Toronto, is shared responsibility for major decisions affecting the operation of the school. (This usually includes parents and teachers in the elementary schools, and teachers and students in the secondary schools.) Such vital areas as budget and staffing are shared with Board administrators. However, each alternative school has its own sepa-rate identity and approach to curriculum and program within the guide-lines set by the Ontario Ministry of Education

It takes about two to three months to set up an alternative school. The step-by-step procedure is as follows:

1. The individual or group (parents, teachers, students, and other inter-ested parties) approaches the Curriculum and Program Division infor-mally and inquires about Board policies and operating procedures for alternatives in education.
2. If the individual or group decides to proceed with the application, a letter of intent usually is filed with the Board's Alternatives in Educa-tion Committee. The group in consultation with the Curriculum and Program Division then drafts a proposal. This proposal should include sections on the objectives of the program, educational philosophy, cur-riculum and program, staffing, desired location, accommodation, and budget. A list of prospective students for the new program may also be required. Before the proposal is submitted, the group may be interested in visiting other alternative programs or meeting informally with staff and parents of alternative school programs. All letters of intent with respect to new alternative programs must be received not later than January 31, preceding the year when the program is to be implemented.
3. The application, including the proposal and recommendations, is then placed on the agenda of Alternatives in Education Committee meeting. A report from the Director of Education commenting on the feasibility of the application might also accompany the proposal. Provided that the curriculum and program falls within the Ministry guidelines, the most important considerations usually relate to staffing, location, and accommodations. If all conditions are met, the Committee may then approve the proposal and recommendations for consideration at the next meeting of the School Programs Committee. If there are still unre-solved problems, the Committee might
   a) approve the application in principle subject to the problems being resolved;
   b) refer the matter back to the Director of Education for further study;
   c) formally reject the application.
   All proposals are to be acted upon by the Board not later than March 15 preceding the September of the year when the program is to be imple-mented.

4. The report from the Alternatives in Education Committee is then considered at the next meeting of the School Programs Committee. The Committee may then
   a) concur with the report and recommendations as presented and send them on to the next regular meeting of the Board for final approval;
   b) send all or part of the report back to the Alternatives in Education Committee for further consideration;
   c) amend all or part of the report before sending it on;
   d) formally reject the report and recommendations.
5. The report and recommendations from the School Programs Committee would then be considered by the full Board at its next regular meeting. The Board may then
   a) adopt the report and recommendations as presented;
   b) send the report back for further consideration;
   c) amend all or part of the report;
   d) formally reject the report and recommendations.
6. If the group concurs with the recommendations, as approved, the Curriculum and Program Division will assist in establishing the program, with adequate staffing and an acceptable location and accommodations, under the supervision of a principal and area superintendent.[94]

Outcomes and Reflections

It used to be fashionable to characterize public alternative schools as some fad of the sixties, which would never survive the seventies. Here we are, in the twenty-first century, witness to a so-called flash in the pan that has become a bright flame of innovation sweeping across North America and, indeed, throughout the Western world. What is this movement that has confounded the sceptics and brought some sense of excitement and hope to a system sorely wounded by the twin thrusts of declining enrolment and budget restraint?

The Board of Education for the City of Toronto pioneered the concept of alternative school programs developed through *community initiative* – as opposed to *administrative action* by school-board personnel – either to solve an internal problem or to meet a particular organizational need (for example, declining enrolment, and school leavers). Beginning in 1968, with a secondary school summer enrichment project known as SEED, it established more than twenty alternative schools in response to proposals from parents, students, teachers, and other citizens in the community.

Toronto alternative schools, which cover the complete range of educational alternatives for junior kindergarten children to adult learners, comprise three main types.

Learning Style Alternatives. A group of parents, students, and teachers might be interested in a particular approach to learning that, while not contrary to Ministry of Education guidelines, would provide a different emphasis, such as more artistic enrichment, smaller student-adult ratios, or cooperative decision making. For example, at the elementary level, parents may wish for a smaller, more intimate learning environment that reflects their own lifestyle interests. Alternative schools of this kind most often incorporate school-age day care and educational or recreational enrichment as an integral part of the program. Examples of such parent-led schools have been ALPHA, Beaches Alternative, Alternative Primary, and Downtown Alternative.

At the senior-elementary, secondary, and adult levels it has often been teachers and students who have drafted proposals emphasizing a more individualized program and incorporating the use of community resources and shared decision making. Examples of such have been SEED, Subway Academy, Subway Academy II, Inglenook, Spectrum, and Arts Alternative for Adults.

Socio-Economic Alternatives. Socio-economic alternative programs have grown out of the needs identified by parents and teachers in inner-city, working-class neighbourhoods. The students have usually not had a background of academic achievement nor have they adjusted socially to the organizational demands of a large school. As a result, they have often been labelled as non-achievers, behavioural problems, school leavers, or dropouts. The socio-economic alternative school offers an effective learning environment with a smaller ratio of students to teachers in order to support the needs of students for remedial education and social development. Examples of such schools have been Laneway Community School, CONTACT, West End Alternative, and The Student School.

Cultural-Linguistic Alternatives. Parents wishing to preserve or enhance a particular cultural heritage or linguistic skill have initiated the smallest group of alternatives. A group of Native Canadian parents founded the Wandering Spirit Survival School to integrate aboriginal history, culture, spiritual values, and languages into a regular curriculum. The Hawthorne II Bilingual School provided an education in both French and English while developing an appreciation for the French-Canadian culture.   .   .

The Toronto approach has been unique in North America in that it has followed the community education and development model, that is, a process of social action in which the people of a community organize themselves for planning and action; define their common and individual needs and problems; execute these plans with a maximum reliance on community resources; and supplement these resources when necessary with services and materials from governmental and non-governmental agencies outside the community. Through its Alternative and Community Programs Department and General Policy for Alternative School Programs, the Toronto Board of Education has assisted groups and individuals to identify their needs and to use a combination of Board and community resources in program development. This was particularly the case at the elementary level where the alternative school may combine education, cultural enrichment, recreation, and day care in an integrated program.

The general policy ensured the universal right of parents, students, and teachers to initiate alternative programs that were cooperatively governed and supported in response to perceived local needs. Alternative schools received the same level of Board support as did any other school program; similarly, they also received resources from the non-profit charitable sector. (Some alternative schools became incorporated as non-profit charities.)

The Toronto Board of Education also supported the development of a variety of community resource learning materials and innovative projects in support of alternatives in education. For example, the original Learning Exchange System (Learnxs) Project of 1973 evolved into a non-profit publishing house (Learnxs Press) and an educational foundation (Learnxs Foundation Incorporated) to support innovative practice.

What effect have these alternative programs had on the mainstream of education? After almost forty years of experience with alternatives, a number of positive benefits that could be attributed to the presence of alternative schools in the Toronto system may be identified.

Independent Study. There has been greater recognition of the individual needs of some students for more flexibility in their learning, particularly at the secondary school level. For example, independent study programs in which courses are offered through a learning contract agreement between student and teacher (for example, at Subway Academy) have demonstrated the viability of such programs (especially for enrichment) in large schools.

Greater Mobility. Experience has shown that students can have mobility within a system in order to use a variety of community resources to enrich their programs as well as to take advantage of special interest courses that are only available in other schools (for example, the Subway model). This is particularly important as declining enrolment threatens the continued viability of specialized or limited interest courses.

Small Can Be Beautiful. Alternative schools have demonstrated that it is possible to offer quality education in schools with less than a hundred students through the mobilization of school-board and community resources. This form of education has often proven to be less expensive to operate than are regular school programs.

Unique Needs. There has been recognition that it is not only possible but also often advisable to group together students with similar needs and interests into theme programs, for example, instrumental music and heritage programs.

Prevention of School Closures. Alternative schools bring students back into the system and actually create a demand for classroom space, thus preventing school closures and protecting teachers' jobs. It was the policy of the Toronto Board of Education not to close vacant schools but to use the buildings to house alternative programs.

Alternatives for Teachers. One result of declining enrolment and budget restraint was their effect on teacher mobility. Alternative schools have given teachers the opportunity to have a different type of work experience while remaining within the system.

Program Choice. Alternative schools offer students and their parents the opportunity to explore a variety of different learning environments in order to find the one that meets their particular needs (which may very well be a regular school).

Use of Technology. Owing to their small size and limited resources, alternative schools have experimented with a variety of electronic media aids to strengthen and enrich their programs. For example, they were among the first learning environments to demonstrate the educational value of still photography, film, and video and computer equipment. (A film produced by SEED students was nominated for an Academy Award.)

Visual and Performing Arts. Students from alternative schools have always used such community resources as theatres, galleries, and studios to extend their learning. Regular schools are now beginning to provide similar opportunities for their own students through cooperative education programs.

Research and Development. In a time of austerity, alternative programs provided an opportunity for a school system to experiment with a variety of new initiatives, which could be evaluated on an ongoing basis through a process of action research.

It is my contention that alternative school programs have made an extremely valuable contribution to the mainstream of education through their role as anticipators of (rather than as reactors to) social and economic change. If the future is *process* rather than just *content*, then alternatives will continue to play a leading role in the identification of, and response to, human need, particularly with reference to minority interests. In this age of consumer accountability and a focus on budget restraint, public education must be more communicative, responsive, and effective in its use of resources. These were the fundamental principles on which alternative school programs were founded.

10 Community Service Partnerships

Parallel Use of Vacant Space

In 1975 the Toronto Board of Education approved the Parallel Use of Vacant Educational Space Policy after a process of community consultation, which began in 1973 as an outgrowth of the report of the Task Force on Education. This policy was necessary because the general decline in student enrolments during the 1970s had resulted in vacant classrooms in many schools. During the same period there was an increased demand by citizen groups, organizations, and agencies to improve neighbourhood services. For example, the need for day-care services for working parents had corresponded to the vacancy rate among kindergarten and primary classrooms in some schools. The Toronto Board took the position that, wherever possible, vacant educational space should be made available for neighbourhood service needs.

A procedure known as the Parallel Use Committee (PUC) included representatives from the school staff, citizen organizations, parent groups, and local agencies and businesses in a decision-making process to decide the future use of vacant space in a particular school. A local principal would convene a PUC, with the assistance of my Alternative and Community Programs Department, to review applications from groups and individuals for the use of vacant space.

The Board of Education's policy set a priority for the use of space as follows:

1. Parental groups and other citizen interests from the local school community.
2. Municipal and provincial governments (including the Metropolitan Separate School Board).

3. Non-profit community service agencies and organizations.
4. Commercial interests.

A service fee was paid by non-profit 'parallel users' to cover the costs of utilities and maintenance ($2.14 per square foot in 1980). Commercial operators were required to pay fair market value. I remember receiving a telephone call from a commercial operator wanting to establish a visa school for visiting students from the Far East in Toronto Board of Education premises. When I explained that priority was given to local non-profit and governmental interests, he said that that would not be a problem; he would include me as a silent partner in the new enterprise if I assisted him in getting space. When I said that that would be illegal, he said, 'Not to worry. They could name my wife instead' – my first offer of a bribe in the education business.

In a report to the Board of Education by the Alternative and Community Programs Department in 1980, a total of thirty-eight non-profit groups were listed as having used vacant space under the Parallel Use of Vacant Educational Space Policy. No commercial operators were ever admitted.

School Facilities as Multiservice Centres

In March 1979 the Board of Education received the report of the Work Group on School Facilities as Multiservice Neighbourhood Centres. The report advised that the Toronto Board had had a long history of working cooperatively with departments of civic government, such as Parks and Recreation and Public Health, and with community service agencies offering social, cultural, and rehabilitation programs. Since 1975, the Board policy on parallel use of vacant educational space had provided accommodation for community groups from 8:00 a.m. to 10:30 p.m. in nineteen schools. The groups had included day-care centres, nursery schools, and social, recreational, and cultural organizations.

In 1977 a survey of all elementary schools had indicated that an increasing number of vacant classrooms were available. Unfortunately, the principal and area superintendent sometimes saw the spaces as inappropriate for parallel use. The demand for parallel-use accommodation was exceeding the availability of space, even though elementary and secondary school enrolments had continued to decline. Local communities strongly supported the need to retain their schools as focal points for family life and neighbourhood identity.

The work group's report suggested that an inventory of service needs should be undertaken in each neighbourhood or school area that had significant declining enrolment and the resultant vacant space (three classrooms or more). The survey would be conducted by a neighbourhood services planning committee based on the parallel-use model and including local residents, parents, students, organizations, and school personnel. Characteristics of available space would be suitability, potential for funding and renovations, prospective tenants, and cooperative service relations with other organizations and groups.

The report proposed that several neighbourhood services demonstration projects be implemented as soon as possible in selected elementary and secondary schools to examine the feasibility of smaller educational units as part of the neighbourhood services facilities. The Board of Education approved the report in March 1979[95] – much to the dismay of the YMCA, who was lobbying as the preferred agency to gain control of all vacant space.

Day Care in the School

The need for childcare programs for single mothers and working parents in their own neighbourhoods had been well documented. Educators dealing with the dilemma of diminishing revenues and staff reductions also saw the declining enrolment in the schools as a curse. Principals, traditionally opposed to community use of their buildings, were now faced with classroom and possibly even school closures. When the word got out that having a day-care centre in your school could attract new sources of enrolment, principal opposition just seemed to melt away. I began to get telephone calls asking me if I could please find a day-care centre to occupy vacant classroom space in their school. (Perhaps this was the right thing for the wrong reasons.)

On 13 December 1973, the Toronto Board adopted the report of its Early Childhood Education work group (another task force initiative), which included the first Day Care in the School policy enacted by any school board in Canada. By June 1981, as the official responsible for the development of this policy, I had seen a total of fifty school-based childcare programs licensed under the provincial *Day Nurseries Act*. Some basic elements of these programs were as follows:

Community Development. First priority for the use of school space was given to local non-profit parental interests. Alternative and Community Programs Department staff (including program consultant Julie Mathien) encouraged parents who were in need of a childcare service to form a cooperative group. The group undertook a survey in their local area to assess the need for childcare, whether it be for pre-school children (full or half-day) or for school-age children (six- to twelve-years-old). If the service appeared economically viable, an application, supported by the local school, was submitted to the Board of Education for the use of space to establish the program. Once space had been obtained, an application was made to the Ministry of Community and Social Services for a licence under the *Day Nurseries Act*. (This was also opposed by the YMCA, who wanted exclusive use of space for their First Base programs.)

Once the program was operational, an application could be made to Metro Community Services to receive a subsidy for some of the parents using the centre. The parental group might also decide to incorporate itself as a non-profit charitable organization in order to solicit additional funds and issue charitable tax receipts. As a result of this community development process, a new human services resource was created in the neighbourhood.

Start-Up Assistance. The Toronto Board of Education provided funding to help day nurseries become established during the start-up period. Grants were also available from the Ministry of Community and Social Services for this purpose.

Community Employment. The average day-care centre employed about five persons full or part time. Almost three hundred full or part-time jobs were created, providing a major economic boost to the community.

Work Experience. School-based day care provided an ideal setting for work experience and cooperative education opportunities for secondary school students.

Infant Care. Three infant-care centres were established in Toronto schools to serve the children of teenaged parents while they attended school. This also provided an opportunity for those parents to socialize and learn parenting skills.

Day Care in the Workplace. School-based day care was made available for Board of Education and municipal employees and provided a significant employee benefit, thereby increasing job satisfaction and productivity.

School Benefits. Having a day-care centre in a school acted as a magnet to attract new parents and children and served to offset the effects of declining enrolment. It was found that day-care children were better prepared to start kindergarten because of their early childhood education and socialization to the school environment. Their parents tended to be much better informed and supportive of school programs, as well as being a source of leadership for the development of other school-community activities.

Cost-Effectiveness. As vacant school space could usually be made available to community groups at a reduced cost, school-based day-care fees tended to be significantly less than commercial rates. As a result, available subsidy funding could serve more children, and the moderate-income earners (who did not qualify for subsidy) had more access to a day-care service.

Neighbourhood Security. The fact that both preschool and school-aged programs were located in residential neighbourhoods tended to enhance parental feelings of security for their children and avoid the sense of latchkey guilt suffered by many working parents.

Public Relations. Taxpayers, many of whom had no other contact with the school, might continue to support the existence of the small elementary school as a positive community resource. During the 1970s and early 1980s, the Toronto Board of Education did not take any school buildings out of service.

The implementation of the Day Care in the School Policy was a cooperative venture of the public and voluntary sectors. It turned the negative effect of a change in demography into a positive development in the provision of human services – directly where they were needed. The process also reawakened a sense of citizen participation in social change and reaffirmed the belief that people can make a difference.

Comprehensive Care

During the 1970s the number of women entering the workforce had been increasing steadily. Rising inflation and unemployment had affect-

ed the economic validity of many families, causing financial instability
and marriage breakdown. The number of one-parent families continued to rise. Six- to ten-year-olds were provided for in the *Day Nurseries Act*, in addition to the preschool programs. Under the Board of
Education's Comprehensive Care Policy, school-age centres were established that were complementary to the school day, with care available
before school, at lunchtime, and after school. The initiation procedure
was almost identical to that of preschool, except that accommodations
were not compulsory, and space and facilities could be shared with the
host school. Financial support for the program was derived from parent fees and subsidies. School-age day care provided one solution to
the need for care among latchkey children of working parents. In 1980
there were eighteen licensed school-age programs. There were other
Comprehensive Care initiatives as follows.

Lunch Programs. Lunch programs were developed cooperatively by
the community and school. Lunchroom supervision, already provided
by the Board of Education, was extended through additional Board
funding and parent fees to provide a supervised recreational program
during the entire lunch period. Lunch programs could also be integrated with school-age day-care programs being operated in the school.

After-four Programs. After-four programs were developed to provide educational, cultural, and recreational activities for children after
school. Consultative assistance was provided through the Alternative
and Community Programs Department, as a contract with the YMCA,
to support parents and other citizens in initiating new programs. Financial assistance was received from the Toronto Board of Education, the
City of Toronto, and local fund-raising. The backbone of the after-four
programs, however, was parent volunteers in local schools who provided leadership in developing enrichment programs to complement
the school curriculum. In 1980 there were thirty-eight after-four programs operating as cooperative community school ventures involving
parents, students, and school staff.

Cooperative Learning Centres. Revisions to the Parallel Use of
Vacant Educational Space Policy resulted in the establishment of a new
policy on cooperative learning centres. Parallel users could apply to the
Board of Education's Alternative and Community Programs Committee to have their fees waived in return for providing experiential learn-

ing opportunities for secondary school students in their program. To qualify as a cooperative learning centre, the parallel user would have to work with a local secondary school to develop curriculum guidelines for student participation.

Applegrove Community Complex. The Applegrove Community Complex was a demonstration project under the Board of Education's policy for neighbourhood schools as multiservice centres. In east Toronto, the Duke of Connaught Junior School, the S.H. Armstrong Centre (run by the City of Toronto's Parks and Recreation Department), and the Woodfield Road Senior School were joined together, and a building was added and financed through the federal government's Neighbourhood Improvement program, to create a multiservice centre. The complex provided a full range of educational, recreational, health, childcare, and adult learning opportunities for the Applegrove community. Programs of the Applegrove Complex included

1. Elderaides: The Applegrove community had one of the largest concentrations of senior citizens in Toronto. Students in grades seven and eight would visit older citizens in their homes, deliver meals, run errands, and do minor home maintenance as part of their social studies program. Seniors would also be encouraged to participate as Applegrove volunteers or to take advantage of the adult-learning opportunities.
2. Lifelong Learning Centre: This program was built on the existing continuing-education experience at Woodfield Road Senior School. A learning-needs survey of Applegrove homes was undertaken, using students and community volunteers. A series of adult learning opportunities was organized, using school and community resource leaders.
3. Parent-Child Resource Centre: A joint project of the Social Planning Council of Metropolitan Toronto and the Applegrove Complex created an early-childhood development facility for preschool children. Parents could bring their children for enriched play, while participating in social, recreational, and adult learning activities (for example, life skills and parenting courses). The centre also provided a training facility for private home day-care providers as well as a registry of persons offering this service in the Applegrove community. Funding for the centre, as a demonstration project, was sought from the Ministry of Community and Social Services.

4. Applegrove Day-Care Centre: A day-care facility for children aged two to nine was established by the Applegrove Complex using surplus school space. It was anticipated that this facility would also qualify as a cooperative learning centre.

Work Experience in Education

An outcome of the Cooperative Education work group of the Task Force on Education was policy definition for work experience programs. Work experience is a particular approach to learning that combines classroom study and practical experience in the employment community, according to the following general categories:

1. Career orientation in the workplace: non-paid one- or two-week placement in business, industry, or human services (for example, social, health, education, and recreation) as preparation for graduation or as an aid in career selection.
2. Part-time employment in a career-related setting: paid half time, one day per week, or a three-month block placement (semester system), in business, industry, or human services for the development of skills, employment practice, and/or financial support.
3. Academic credit-related experience: non-paid, one or two half-days per week in business, industry, or human services as an extension of an existing course, as part of an experimental course, or as a special-interest project in the regular school program (for example, urban studies, community services, environmental science, child-care, economics, and marketing).
4. Education on the job: paid full-time employment in business, industry, or human services where educational courses are offered in the workplace, or taken at a neighbourhood school, as an integral part of the work schedule and conditions of employment. Instruction and accreditation would be a shared responsibility of the employer, organized labour, and the Board of Education.

Work Group on Multicultural Programs

In 1970 the Every Student Survey report from the Board of Education's Research Department found that children from recently immigrated low-income families were not succeeding in school. In 1973 the Vocational Schools work group stated that some immigrant groups failed to understand the causes of their children's lack of success in school.

Community groups, encouraged by local activists, were challenging the Board's curriculum and program with regard to the needs of newcomers, especially Italian- and Portuguese-speaking parents, in the west central part of the city. They were particularly concerned about the streaming of immigrant students into vocational programs. In April 1974 the Board's New Canadian Committee issued a resolution that the chairman of the board 'convene a committee of teachers, trustees, parents, administrative personnel, and students to study the philosophy and programs that will be adopted by the Board towards the New Canadian students.[96] When the new committee reported to the Board of Education in June, it requested that it be renamed the Work Group on Multicultural Programs.

The chairman of the new work group was Dan Leckie, who had been elected as a trustee in 1973 as part of the reform movement and had served on the Vocational Schools work group. The new work group decided to operate through a broad consultative process with both the community at large and all parts of the school system. It received written submissions and oral presentations from school and community interests. In May 1975 the Work Group on Multicultural Programs issued a 230-page draft report outlining eight key issues: English as a second language, educational opportunity deficiencies, maintenance of original cultures and languages, the third language, multiculturalism and the curriculum, system sensitivity, community school relations, and responsibilities of senior governments.[97]

In June 1975, on the basis of the draft report, the Board of Education approved new policies regarding a new philosophical base for the teaching of English as a second language, the provision of booster programs for New Canadian children, and the establishment of a school-community relations department to coordinate, on a city-wide basis, the development of school-community relations. John Piper, a loyal supporter of Board Chairman Gordon Cressy, headed the new department.

One of the outcomes of the consultative process was a film made by Earl Grey Senior School's elementary teacher Linda Schuyler and her students entitled *Between Two Worlds*. Ms Schuyler went on to produce the very successful television series *Degrassi Street*, which continues to this day.

Outcomes and Reflections

In recognition that the quality of life in a neighbourhood can have a profound effect on a student's ability to learn, the Toronto Board of Education, in the decade 1969–79, initiated a number of policies and community school programs in response to local needs. These policies and programs were developed and implemented cooperatively with community groups and service organizations. For example, in 1969 a report by the Social Planning Council of Metropolitan Toronto identified the need for after-school programs to provide educational, cultural, and recreational activities for latchkey children. As a result, the Toronto Board established the After-four program, whereby school communities developed and operated their own programs using financial support from the Board, the City of Toronto, and local fund-raising and consultative assistance through a contract with the YMCA. Other such cooperative policies and programs included the Day Care in the School Policy, the Parallel Use of Vacant Educational Space Policy, lunch programs, comprehensive care programs, alternative school programs, and the Neighbourhood Schools as Multiservice Centres Policy.

From January 1978, as coordinator of the Alternative and Community Programs Department, I was responsible for these policies and programs. This position provided a focus for citizens to identify needs and mobilize resources in support of a process of community education and development.

In a time of decreasing revenues and budget restraint it was often very difficult to find continued support for research and development activities. The challenge of declining enrolments in public education was the ability to continue to experiment and innovate while maintaining the quality of existing programs. Alternative and community programs were pioneers during the 1970s in learning to live better with less. This was accomplished through a commitment to the cost-sharing of Board of Education and community resources in terms of financial and voluntary assistance. As previously mentioned, community programs such as After-four, Lunch, and Comprehensive Care encouraged citizen initiative in organizing neighbourhood services. Government grants, and local fund-raising to multiply the value of the dollars invested, matched the financial support from the Toronto Board. The fact that Board of Education contributions remained constant, while the number of programs steadily increased, was a tribute to the strength and vitality of community participation and the value of cost-sharing. During the period from 1 January 1974 to 31 December 1977, through vehicles such as the Learnxs Foundation, I was responsible for raising almost $370,000 in support of innovative school and community programming.[98] Sources of support included federal, provincial, and municipal governments, philanthropic organizations, and publication sales.

The Parallel Use of Vacant Educational Space and Neighbourhood Schools as Multiservice Centres policies provided valid uses for vacant classroom space while generating revenue to offset the continuing costs of maintenance and utilities. As the number of taxpayers with children in school diminished, it was particularly important that these citizens recognized the school building as a source of other services with which they could more readily identify (for example, childcare, health, adult education, and services to the elderly).

Alternative school programs also provided a model to demonstrate the educational viability of small schools. Local fund-raising and volunteer commitment augmented the regular Toronto Board allocations in such areas as staffing, supplies, and equipment. Although alternative schools were sometimes criticized for being more expensive than regular schools, they did in fact generate per-pupil revenues in excess of their actual expenditure on staffing, accommodation, supplies, equipment, and other regular costs.

As of 31 January 1980, there were 961 students enrolled in alternative school programs under the Toronto Board of Education. Student surveys indicated that the majority of these students had been drawn from private schools, other jurisdictions, the dropout population, or those in the process of dropping out. Although the student population in regular schools had been declining, there was an expansion in the number of students served by alternative programs. This expansion was not at the expense of regular schools. In fact, the argument was made that because alternative schools used proportionately fewer resources and created new teaching positions, they were helping to ease the detrimental effect that declining enrolments were having on the rest of the system.

Cost-sharing of alternative and community programs between the Toronto Board of Education and community interests, through local fund-raising and contributions from government and voluntary organizations, also resulted in increased full and part-time employment at the neighbourhood level. It is estimated that 373 full and part-time jobs were created, in addition to regular Toronto Board staff positions, during 1979. Most of these positions employed local people who were then better able to participate in the economy of the community. At a time of large-scale unemployment and nearly double-digit inflation, the effect that this community employment had on the quality of life could not be underestimated.

Alternative and community programs did not continue to prosper without an outstanding commitment on the part of local parents and citizens of the community, who volunteered their time to support these efforts. This was equally true in childcare, after-four, and alternative programs. For example, during the 1978/79 program year, 830 volunteers contributed 12,000 hours in support of the After-four program. If this contribution were costed at even the adult minimum wage of the time ($3 per hour), it would amount to $37,000.

It was particularly gratifying to see the increase of volunteer time among secondary school students. Curriculum changes, which allowed credit for neighbourhood service, and the introduction of the cooperative learning centres greatly expanded this form of participation. As previously mentioned, the community education and development process depended upon citizen participation. Volunteer commitment was at the heart of the ultimate success of that process.

The Work Group on Multicultural Programs represented a further implementation of the community consultative process that had been introduced by the Special Task Force on Education. This process identified the concerns of immigrants that their children were often being streamed into non-academic vocational programs. The work group introduced major policy reforms in such areas as instruction in English as a second language, booster programs for recent arrivals, third-language classes, and a curriculum reflecting multicultural realities.

The establishment of a school-community relations (SCR) department, with its workers assigned to area offices across the city, was seen as another positive outcome to enhance communication among parents, students, and other citizens of the community. There was a danger, however, that these new SCR workers might be seen as political operatives because they owed their appointments to certain reform trustees who were seeking re-election. As a result, many Board of Education staff, conservative and moderate trustees, and other citizens of the community often questioned the motives of the School-Community Relations Department. It is, perhaps, not surprising that when the more conservative trustees regained control of the Board during the 1980s, the department was soon disbanded as a cost-cutting measure ('Those who live by the sword die by the sword').[99]

11 Youth Ventures

The Working Curriculum

In April 1978 the Job Creation work group of the Community Policy Group on Unemployment of the Toronto Board of Education released a report recommending that the Board 'undertake life skills teaching programs in the workplace.' As described in chapter 8, the Board approached the Learnxs Foundation in the spring of that year to assume sponsorship of a feasibility study on the employment of early-school-leaving students (fourteen- and fifteen-year-olds), which was funded by the federal Local Employment Assistance Program (LEAP).

In July, Learnxs received funding from LEAP to establish the Student Employment Experience Centre (SEEC) Project to employ school leavers in a restaurant and catering operation, a woodworking shop, furniture refinishing, and waste-paper recycling. The Toronto Board of Education provided an academic skills coach to the SEEC Project who was 'responsible for developing remedial programs and other educational activities according to the needs of the workers ... All learning activities would grow out of experience in the workplace and would be integrated into the working day.' In November, I submitted a position paper to the Toronto Board entitled 'The Working Curriculum: An Alternative Approach for Dropouts.'

As a result of lessons gained from the SEEC experience, I consulted with Malcolm Roberton of Bread and Roses Credit Union; Bob Doyle, Neighbourhood Services Coordinator, City of Toronto; and Leon Muszynski of the Social Planning Council to identify strategies for creating employment opportunities for disadvantaged youth. One such strategy was community economic development.

Community Economic Development

Community economic development might be defined as 'a plan of action to build new resources which will strengthen the local community internally as well as its relations with the larger world.' The tool of this strategy could be a community development corporation (CDC) that is organized and controlled by local residents to develop the economy of their own community. This third sector not-for-profit enterprise (as opposed to the governmental and private profit-oriented sectors) has the following objectives: to identify and develop local skills and talents; to own and control land and other resources; to start new businesses and industries to increase job opportunities; to sponsor new community facilities and services; and to improve the physical environment.[100]

Community development corporations were first established in the United States in the late 1960s, with support from the federal government, to improve disadvantaged urban and rural communities. By 1975, dozens of communities in at least thirty states had organized community development corporations. These have ranged from such urban examples as the Bedford-Stuyvesant Restoration Corporation in New York City (with assets of thirty million dollars) to the Job Start Corporation in rural Kentucky. An evaluation of CDCs in 1973 indicated that 'they had demonstrated, as contrasted with conventional business, a remarkable level of performance in venture development and profitability in employment related matters and in helping raise the level of confidence and opportunity in their communities.'[101]

In Canada, one of the first CDCs was New Dawn Enterprises in Sydney, Nova Scotia, an area suffering from high unemployment (26 per cent) due to a decline in coal mining, steel making, and fisheries. Incorporated in 1976, New Dawn built and managed several apartment buildings, a dental clinic, and a number of other business enterprises. From these experiences, New Dawn realized that an increase in size and scope required a greater level of sophistication in board of directors' approvals and financial control. As the board, not the staff, was legally responsible for everything that went on in the corporation, the careful recruitment of staff and the active participation of Board members were as essential to a not-for-profit corporation as any other commercial enterprise. New Dawn demonstrated, however, that the social and cultural needs of a community could be strongly addressed with a process of local economic development and job creation. To quote an evaluation conducted in 1979, 'it would be impossible to have contact with the enterprise for any length of time without being impressed by the quality, the dedication, and the energy of both employees and volunteers working with New Dawn.'[102]

As a result of the discussion of possible models to employ youth through community economic development, we convened a planning group to form a community development corporation devoted to youth employment. Representatives from the Learnxs Foundation, the City of Toronto, the Social Planning Council, the Toronto Board of Education, community service agencies, and business and industry made up the membership: John McIninch of Tory, Tory, DesLauriers, and Binnington (a Learnxs board member); John Rothschild of CEMP Investments (a Learnxs board member); Simon Mielniczuk, York Community Services; Bob Doyle, Neighbourhood Services Coordinator, City of Toronto; Al McTaggart, Marketing Director, Toronto Dominion Bank; Leon Muszynski, Program Director, Social Planning Council; Jim Lemon, Urban Geography Department, University of Toronto (a Social Planning Council board member); Malcolm Roberton of Bread and Roses Credit Union; Dale Shuttleworth, Coordinator, Alternative and Community Programs, Toronto Board of Education (in this instance I was also secretary-treasurer of Learnxs and president of the Social Planning Council); and Frank Folz, Equal Opportunity Officer, Toronto Board of Education.

In March 1979, Leon Muszynski submitted a report to the planning group entitled 'Jobs Needed, Community Economic Development: A Job Creation and Social Development Strategy for Metropolitan Toronto.' The report became part of a working draft entitled 'Youth Ventures: A Community Economic Development Plan for Youth Employment in Toronto.' The draft called for a survey of needs and resources in the local area, the creation of a community development corporation, the development of an ongoing evaluation system of cost-effectiveness and social benefit, the establishment of three or four urban cottage industries, the development of an academic skills support system to be integrated into each industry, and the identification of sources of venture capital.

In January 1979 the planning group made a presentation to the Executive Committee of the City of Toronto. In March, Toronto City Council passed a motion endorsing the use of community economic development methods by Youth Ventures as an approach to the problem of unemployment in Toronto. That same month, the first draft of a concrete proposal was produced by the planning group. It was rewritten following feedback from various individuals involved in the field and was submitted in May 1979 for funding consideration to Employment and Immigration Canada under its Local Employment Assistance program. The joint sponsors were the Learnxs Foundation and the Social Planning Council. Signatories were June Callwood as president of Learnxs and myself as president of the Social Planning Council. The Toronto Board of Education gave formal support for this proposal during the same month.

During the summer of 1979, a Youth Ventures management board was formed with representatives from such agencies as Learnxs, the Social Planning Council, the Toronto Board of Education, and the City of Toronto. The management board assumed the responsibility of negotiating with LEAP about the funding for the project and assumed operational control following approval of the proposal in late summer. The sum of $87,000 was ultimately approved by LEAP to launch a professional research and development study.

The research phase of Youth Ventures began in October 1979 with the hiring of a five-person research team consisting of Jack McGinnis (Coordinator), Heather Fisher, Judith Geitzler, Geoff Love, and James Riordan. Four main objectives were established for the research work: the analysis of the feasibility of potential enterprises and the development of business plans for those enterprises recommended for implementation; the development of a working profile of the target group (disadvantaged youth in the sixteen- to twenty-four-year-old range); a review of experience in Canada and the United States with various corporate models, particularly the community development corporation, as the basis for developing the most appropriate legal form for Youth Ventures; and the design of a management structure suitable for the achievement of the balanced social and economic goals of the organization.

Several potential enterprises were investigated, including the following.

Visitors Guide Service. Metropolitan Toronto as an international city of the world has a rich heritage, a strong artistic and cultural tradition, a most attractive natural environment, a vibrant cosmopolitan character, and a very progressive governmental, commercial, and industrial community. However, by comparison to other famous cities of the world, it did not have a professional guide service to acquaint visitors with these amenities. The proposed guide service would have recruited and trained a small group of full and part-time workers, as a one-year demonstration project to test the feasibility of establishing such a service, which would work with existing tour companies and visitor reception agencies in the Metropolitan Toronto region.

Waste-Paper Recycling. Paper mills had expressed an unprecedented need for waste paper from office buildings for remanufacture as fine paper products. Prices paid for this reclaimed material had reached up to $180 per ton, making it economically feasible to establish a service industry to employ youth with limited skills and work experience. The Student Employment Experience Centre (SEEC) Project had demonstrated the viability of such a project through its Paper Chase enterprise. The Education Centre at 155 College Street had introduced desktop holders to sort the most valuable paper at the source. These holders were dumped periodically into jute bags in disposal bins in each department. Project employees made their rounds on a regular basis, and approximately one ton of quality paper was produced each week from the waste paper in this seven-storey building.

It was proposed that Paper Chase demonstration project be extended to add the output of waste paper from other commercial and governmental offices in the downtown area. It was estimated that this enterprise would be cost-effective within its second year of operation and provide employment for ten to fifteen workers of sixteen to nineteen years of age.

Wood Venture. This enterprise would involve the recovery and processing of discarded wood for sale as firewood. As oil prices rose, the use of wood as a fuel became more economically viable. Total discarded wood, within Metropolitan Toronto, was estimated at 70,000 tons per year and included industrial pallets; packaging from glass, furniture, and appliance manufacturing; and various waste from wood processing and tree maintenance. Nine workers would be employed, collecting discarded industrial pallets from local factories. Nails would be removed, and the hardwood cut into sixteen-inch lengths for sale as firewood to households in the community.

Urban Farming. The technology existed, through the use of hydroponics, to produce fresh vegetables on a commercial scale. Large hydroponics operations could be established in urban areas, using vacant space on rooftops. Such systems had been developed and tested in the Toronto area (for example, at Baycrest Hospital), utilizing plastic pipe and an advanced design to reduce the weight of the hydroponics system. It was also possible, through the use of solar energy and reclaimed building heat, to cover the units and support a continuous growing cycle. For example, it could be possible to produce, on a year-round basis, lettuce that would be of superior quality to anything then imported from the southern United States. The fact that hydroponics was a very efficient growing system (with ten to fifteen times the yield of the same area in soil) and that prices for imported produce had risen sharply made it economically feasible to establish a pilot industry in urban farming as a source of youth employment.

It was proposed that such a pilot industry be established on the roof of Eastdale Collegiate on Gerrard Street East, a space originally planned as an outdoor play area but which had not been used for several years. Twenty-nine eighty-foot units could be put into operation in this space, resulting in 4,640 growth feet. The design would be similar to that of the Baycrest Hospital system in North York, and the latter's inventors would be used in a consultative capacity, as would an architect (Lyle Ferguson) and an engineer (Iain Hunter) from the Toronto Board of Education. (Another fanciful recycling feature proposed could have been the raising of carp for sale, using shallow rooftop tanks, with the carp waste serving as part of the nutrients to be fed to the plants.)

A project manager and work force of ten to fifteen unemployed youth would be hired to construct the units and put the system into operation during the regular growing season. Five workers would then be involved in growing and harvesting the crops, while the rest of the employees would work on the construction of a covering and a solar heating unit to allow for year-round operation. The enterprise would concentrate on the growth of cash crops to supply restaurants and specialty fruit and vegetable outlets.

A spin-off from the construction of the hydroponics operation could be the creation of a new enterprise to produce small five-foot units, which could be marketed as teaching aids to schools and retail outlets. As a result, an urban cottage industry with a long-term growth potential would be created.

In June 1980, Youth Ventures' submission for funding over three years was submitted to LEAP. Funding was granted in the amount of $249,711 to establish a paper and wood recycling business.

In October, letters patent were issued for Youth Ventures Developments of Metropolitan Toronto as a non-profit corporation with the
following objects: to create employment opportunities for disadvantaged youth in Toronto by the creation and development of business
enterprises; to create opportunities for imparting managerial and other
work-related skills to disadvantaged youth whenever possible; and to
advance the cause of third-sector business development in Toronto and
elsewhere.

In December, Youth Ventures Recycling Incorporated was established
as a share capital corporation owned by Youth Ventures Developments.
The latter received second-year funding of $112,194 from LEAP, and a
teacher was seconded from the York Board of Education and assigned
as academic and life skills coach at Youth Ventures Recycling Incorporated. In February 1982, York Wood Works was funded in the amount
of $92,438 as a one-year Canada community development project
sponsored by Youth Ventures Developments, to recycle, as firewood,
waste industrial pallets and packaging. Youth Ventures Developments
received third-year funding of $158,325 from LEAP, in September 1982,
to sustain the paper recycling enterprise.

As a third-sector enterprise Youth Ventures targeted, for employment, youth aged sixteen to twenty-four who had poor employment
prospects because of limited education and work experience. Youth
Ventures Recycling employed fourteen staff, of which eleven came
from the targeted group. One target employee served as manager of
supply development, assisted by another target employee who was the
supply development officer and driver.

Youth Ventures Recycling recovered newspapers from households
in Toronto and the Borough of York, and fine papers from offices and
businesses. The collection operation used three trucks driven by target
employees, and warehouse staff members were rotated when needed
as drivers' helpers. The processing operation, which involved sorting,
staging, baling, stockpiling of bales, and shipping, employed an operations manager and seven target employees – a foreman, a lead hand,
two balers, and three sorters or general warehouses workers. Entry-
level employees had the opportunity to advance through the ranks and
eventually assume managerial positions.

Outcomes and Reflections

Youth Ventures had the distinction of being the first youth-oriented community development corporation in Canada. One of the more important innovations to emerge from the Youth Ventures experience was the role of the academic and life skills (ALS) coach. In August 1980, I accepted a position as assistant superintendent of community services with the Board of Education for the Borough of York (one of the municipalities serving the northwest sector of Metropolitan Toronto-). The following is a job description that I developed for the ALS coach, to be approved by the York Board of Education as part of their Education in the Workplace policy.

1. The ALS coach will be employed by the Community Services Office of the York Board of Education and seconded to Youth Ventures to provide individualized instruction in academic subjects, remedial upgrading, technical skills, vocational information, plus counselling and life skills as required.
2. The ALS coach will be employed up to thirty hours per week, Monday to Friday, from the date of commencement of service.
3. The ALS coach will be responsible to management of Youth Ventures regarding duties in the workplace, including scheduling of hours and access to employees.
4. Duties of the ALS coach will include monitoring of performance of employees in the workplace according to credit provisions of HS 1 guidelines of the Ministry of Education.
5. The ALS coach will be expected to be familiar with all elements of the Youth Ventures operation through actual participation on the shop floor and in other work settings.
6. Employees using the services of the ALS coach will be required to register as students under provision of the Education in the Workplace policy of the York Board of Education.
7. The ALS coach will be required to prepare an individual profile for each employee enrolled in the program, documenting needs and prescriptive action.
8. The York Board of Education will provide a complete inventory of learning materials, instructional aids, and vocational information as required by the program.
9. An evaluation of the program will be undertaken cooperatively by the Community Services Office of the York Board of Education and Youth Ventures management for submission to the Youth Ventures board and the York Board of Education.

The following is an excerpt from an article entitled 'What's a Nice Teacher Like You Doing in a Place Like This?' which I wrote concerning the impact of the ALS coach position on the Youth Ventures enterprise.

It should have been a day to be proud. Goodness knows, there hadn't been many in Donny's eighteen years. His family had wandered throughout Northern Ontario, from mining town to lumber camp, until his father just disappeared one day. Before Donny's ninth birthday, his mother took her four children to live in Toronto, where she suffered a nervous breakdown and had to be hospitalized. A series of foster homes and a stint in training school led to his current address in a group home in the east end of the city. No, it hadn't been easy.

He'd never spent that much time in school or been able to find a real job. One day he heard they were hiring in a waste paper recycling plant that was part of a program created to employ disadvantaged youth. He didn't think he'd have a chance but he sure could use the money. To his surprise, he got the job, learned to sort paper, drive a forklift, and operate the baler. He never missed work and felt a sense of accomplishment for the first time in his life.

The previous Friday, after Donny had been six months on the job, the General Manager called him into her office to offer him the position of Warehouse Supervisor. Although he'd always got along well with his workmates, and had even trained new employees, he wasn't sure he could make the grade as a supervisor. But his probation officer encouraged him to give it a try, so he accepted.

The week had gone well. The General Manager was pleased when she handed him the pay cheques to distribute to the workers in the plant. Fifteen minutes later, though, he was still pacing back and forth in front of the office. When asked if something was wrong, Donny hung his head in shame and stammered. 'I'm – I'm sorry, M'am, I can't tell who they belong to.' Only then did the General Manager realize that Donny was one of the five million Canadians estimated to be functionally illiterate, in that their reading problems put them at a distinct disadvantage in our modern society.[103]

The answer did not seem to be to get people like Donny back into formal schooling. Too often they view their original contacts with educational institutions as negative, degrading experiences. In fact, the most effective vehicle for adult basic education may well be an informal, responsive, environment respecting the needs and interests of the learner as a person.

The position of the ALS coach was, indeed, not a traditional teaching assignment. To quote Paul Keleher, reporting after his first three months as ALS coach:

Implementation of the teacher's role was achieved with careful consideration. Suspicious of the formal educational experience, the young people at Youth Ventures took an explorative 'wait and see' attitude towards the academic support person and life skills coach. I saw clearly that if the business was to become a non-traditional learning environment, the 'teacher' must necessarily become thoroughly involved with the day-to-day operations. Accordingly, I began work alongside the young people, sorting, baling and loading in the warehouse and working outside on the trucks. In doing so, I learned from the 'inside' just what the work demanded, how the company operated, and I established positive relationships with everybody. Through these involvements, and a positive projection of my personality, much interest was generated in the possibilities of my functioning also as a 'teacher.'

I began to teach by finding out the educational standards of each individual, and by explaining that my presence at Youth Ventures meant that cooperative educational credit could be gained 'on the job.' The response was gratifying, in that the demands for 'classes' became so high as to challenge my time in accommodating them. Happily, this situation has continued, and my role as teacher has expanded into all aspects of the business and further into the lives of the young people.

The educational and skill-related benefits of the program are many. The following work-related topics were treated formally in small groups and individually on the job:

a) training in safety, sorting, baling, forklift and maintenance;
b) kinesiology – human movements related to work operation;
c) work habits and attitudes;
d) design and technical drawings;
e) communication and social skills;
f) training for supervision.

Academically, I have tested all language skills and numeracy levels, and prescribed and implemented remediation where necessary. I have advised regarding procedures and options for upgrading related to night school, community colleges, correspondence school and individual study, and cooperative education, as well as on continuing education courses and resources.

In life-skills classes, we have dealt with health, communication, interpersonal skills, social attitudes and values, personal financial management, and driver education for classes for G.M. and D. licenses.

In my developing role as counsellor, I have dealt with the following areas: legal, interpersonal, work-related, personal, health, financial, career and educational.[104]

Yet, did the assignment of the ALS coach compromise business objectives at Youth Ventures? This is what Debbie Long, General Manager, had to say to the York Board of Education: 'From a social standpoint the concept of education in the workplace excited me; however, I was admittedly sceptical of the concept from a business point of view. Some of my business concerns were the economic impact on a new business, the possible adverse effects on productivity; the potential increase in absenteeism, turnover, and effects on employee morale; and the possibility of a clash in objectives between the ALS coach and management.'[105]

Despite these initial concerns, dramatic gains were noted in the business operation after the ALS coach had been with Youth Ventures for three months:

1. Productivity: productivity increased by 45 per cent.
2. Employee turnover: prior to the arrival of the ALS coach the rate was 97 per cent; during the first three months, turnover decreased to 35 per cent.
3. Absenteeism and lateness: the incidence of absenteeism and lateness declined from 140 hours in September to 45 hours in December.
4. Literacy and numeracy skills: many employees had experienced difficulty doing fundamental calculations and reading staff memoranda and bulletins; the ALS coach was instrumental in improving this situation.

To quote the general manager of Youth Ventures, 'the ALS coach has managed to prove to the individual employee/students that learning can be enjoyable, a point that failed to get across under the traditional educational system. As for Donny, needless to say he no longer has this problem . . . I believe that education in the workplace has not only had a positive impact on the company, but has also filled an educational void for our staff, specifically, and potentially for young people in general.'

The logistics of establishing Youth Ventures enterprises were always challenging. The site for paper recycling was on Polson Street in the docklands area of east Toronto. For the baling machine to be installed, a pit had to be dug in the floor of the warehouse. Each time, before the footings could be poured, the hole filled up with water – which was not surprising as the plant was built on landfill originally reclaimed from the lake.

The wood recycling project, York Wood Works, occupied part of a warehouse on Rogers Road in west Toronto. Unfortunately, the owner (boxing promoter Irv Ungerman) failed to notify Youth Ventures that there was virtually no heat in the building. Consequently, the workers had to fabricate a tin boiler and use some of the waste wood as fuel to warm the space in the wintertime.

During the 1981–2 recession, Youth Ventures Recycling struggled to survive in a climate of reduced business activity and a depressed price for waste paper in the market place. Owing to Youth Ventures Recycling's having a unique niche position as a small enterprise and providing social as well as economic benefit, Ontario Paper (the primary purchaser of Youth Ventures product) continued to honour its commitments and even awarded extra baling contracts to bridge the difficult times. Youth Ventures Recycling Inc. continued as a worker-owned cooperative.

12 The Communities of York

Organizational Networking

Since the Flemington Road days I had served as a volunteer on the boards of several non-profit community organizations and policy development committees. In addition to the Learnxs Foundation and Youth Ventures, they included North York Interagency Council (founding member); Curriculum Committee on Compensatory Education, Ontario Department of Education (founding member); Metro Toronto Youth Services Study, Ontario Department of Health; Children's Day Care Coalition (founding member); and Task Force on Leisure Education, Ontario Ministry of Culture and Recreation (founding member).

From 1975 to 1981, I was elected to the Executive Committee of the Social Planning Council of Metropolitan Toronto and served as president from 1978 to 1981. It was during this period in the life of the council that the Urban Alliance for Race Relations and Youth Ventures were founded, and Marvyn Novick wrote the influential report 'Metro Suburbs in Transition,' which detailed the inequities in community service provisions in the suburban municipalities surrounding the City of Toronto.

In 1979, I was part of a planning group organizing the 'Education for Community Living for the Eighties' Conference to be held at the Claremont Field Study Centre. The twenty-one persons invited to participate were all recognized as providing innovative leadership in the field of community education and development. The conference focused on three main topics: interpersonal relations, the economy, and the environment. Its purpose was 'to find practical solutions to real problems.' One of the participants who impressed me at the conference was

Harriet Wolman, a trustee with the Board of Education for the Borough of York. Harriet had extensive experience in the areas of multicultural-ism, race relations, immigrant education, alternate sources of fund-rais-ing for community development, and the employment of community liaison officers.

The Borough of York

In 1980 the Borough of York was one of the six municipalities mak-ing up the regional government of Metropolitan Toronto. Located to the northwest of the Toronto city core, York had a population of about 135,000. It also had the lowest levels of income and the highest rates of unemployment in the region. Thirty thousand people, or 27 per cent of the population, had less than a grade-nine education. Forty-two per cent of the residents spoke a language other than English in the home. Traditionally a reception area for southern Europeans, especially Ital-ians, York was now beginning to see an influx of newcomers from the West Indies, southern Asia, and South America. Although located sev-eral miles from the central business district, York had become the inner city of Metropolitan Toronto. However, York was also made up of sev-eral social and economic sectors. Advantaged areas included the former town of Weston in the northwest, the Humbercrest neighbourhood in the southwest, and the Cedarvale-Humewood area along York's eastern borders with the City of Toronto. The central part of the municipality served as a reception area for newcomers with low income and included multi-family dwellings such as Metro Toronto Housing Authority high-rise apartments. (In 1983, York became a city in its own right.)

York Board of Education

In May 1980 the Board of Education for the Borough of York adver-tised the position of assistant superintendent of community services. The qualifications for the position included the ability and experience to establish and maintain good relationships with diverse community groups; the ability to develop and supervise community education pro-grams; the ability to provide leadership for a wide variety of multi-cultural services to schools and the community; the ability to provide support for school and community organizations; the administrative experience and skills to provide supervision for a group of public and secondary schools; the creativity to develop a variety of ways to communicate with a multicultural community; successful experience as a school administrator; and possession of an Ontario supervisory officers' certificate.

Since I had passed my Supervisory Officers' exams in 1972 and had received my PhD in 1978 from the University of Toronto, majoring in community education and development, I thought I might qualify for the position. I was fortunate to be granted an interview and was questioned extensively about my experience with alternative programs, such as the Wandering Spirit Survival School, and my views on such multicultural or multiracial initiatives. I was obviously in favour of such initiatives, but I sensed that some of the interview team were not. The one thing I remember was that after it was over and I was being escorted from the room, the new director designate, D. John Phillips, whispered to me, 'I know what it's like to be a newcomer: I was born in Wales, and my first language is Welsh.'

In June I was notified that I had been appointed to the position, with duties to commence on 1 August 1980. According to former Board of Education chairman Steven Mould, reflecting on the decision, 'everybody was convinced that the Communists were at the gate. No question! Here's the Toronto model ... One of the things John [Phillips] was very good at was selling the Board on the necessity of the whole notion of community education. He had the Welsh model, which was very powerful from his point of view, but he had also served in the west end of the old York Township as a teacher at Humbercrest [Junior and Senior Public School].'

Developing Policies

The York Board of Education, with an enrolment of about twenty thousand elementary and secondary students, was striving to meet the concerns of students with English as a second language and literacy and adult education needs. My responsibilities as assistant superintendent of community services included supervision of seven elementary and secondary schools, in addition to the community services portfolio. My first task in the new job was the drafting of several new Board policies related to community education and development:

Community Use of Space. As had been true with the Toronto Board of Education, the Borough of York was also experiencing declining enrolment, particularly in its elementary schools. At the same time, the

Community Services Office was receiving many requests from agencies, citizen groups, and commercial interests concerning the use of vacant space in the schools during the day. In an attempt to clarify the situation, the office brought forward to the Board a new Community Use of Space policy.

While previous Board policy had stated that profit-making groups must pay rent equivalent to fair market value, there did not appear to be any way to differentiate between organizations in the non-profit sector. For example, if a group of mothers in a neighbourhood got together to establish a nursery program in their local school, should they be treated differently from a large Metro-wide agency or government department? There was reason to believe that the provision of local services helped to stabilize the population of a neighbourhood. In fact, such school-based services might serve as a magnet to attract new students to the school and offset declining enrolment. Therefore, it was proposed that local non-profit citizen groups be given priority over the use of space by government departments, service agencies, or commercial interests.[106]

Preschool Programs. In November 1980 the York Board of Education's Administrative Council (supervisory officers) considered a report from the assistant superintendent of community services, which called for the establishment of a preschool programs work group to draft a policy statement related to programs in the school that involved preschool children, and to develop preschool programs in support of adult day schools at D.B. Hood Community School and George Harvey Secondary School.

In January 1981, I convened the first meeting of the Preschool Programs work group, with membership including the Chairmen's Council, representing school and community organizations; the Ministry of Community and Social Services; Metro Social Services; public school principals; secondary school principals; the Curriculum and Program Department; Multicultural Services (a department of the Community Services Office); the Directors Office; and the Community Services Office. Task groups were formed to investigate childcare support to adult day programs; parent and preschool programs (through the Ministry of Culture and Recreation); licensed programs under the *Day Nurseries Act*; and parenting courses at the secondary school level.

The work group developed the following set of basic principles for the use of school facilities by preschool programs – both those unlicensed programs where parents were present and nursery schools and day-care centres licensed under the *Day Nurseries Act*.

1. That all preschool programs in schools be consistent with the standards for childcare as contained in the *Day Nurseries Act* (1978) and its regulations (for example, with regard to accommodation, equipment and furnishings, enrolment and records, daily procedure, nutrition, fire drill and emergency information, staff and financial records).
2. That all preschool programs satisfy the Board's Policy on Day Use of Vacant Space whereby first priority for use of space is given to non-profit parent cooperative groups in the school area.
3. That a pamphlet be prepared in cooperation with the Ministry of Community and Social Services and Metro Social Services to provide information as follows:
   a) Potential use of vacant school space for preschool programs by non-profit parent cooperatives.
   b) Procedures for the establishment of licensed programs in schools.
4. That school personnel, other board staff, a representative from the Ministry of Community and Social Services, and parent representatives be part of any planning process prior to the initiation of a preschool program in a school.
5. That establishment or renovation costs for such a preschool program be borne by the operator, but that the work be undertaken by the Board of Education's Plant Department.
6. That any preschool program operating on Board premises be required to carry adequate liability insurance.
7. That joint staff development programs be instituted, where appropriate, to bring together teachers, preschool program staff, and volunteers to share information about early childhood education and programs and curriculum in the schools.
8. That secondary schools, where appropriate, assist in the establishment of day-care centres in schools by extending their cafeteria service to these programs on a cost-recovery basis.
9. That the Board endorse the importance of preschool programs in schools and consider providing financial support to assist communities in establishing new programs.
10. That any surplus Board equipment and kindergarten furniture in schools be loaned to preschool programs.

11. That Board personnel be available to provide informal assistance
    in the establishment and ongoing maintenance of these pro-
    grams.[107]

Family Centres. During the 1980s, ten junior public schools hosted
free Family Centre programs designed to serve the needs of parents (or
caregivers) and their preschool children. Parents had an opportunity
to meet informally with other parents to socialize and share information. Children enjoyed a full range of early childhood education activities (including stories, active play, crafts, and music) while the adults
participated in discussion groups on parenting, with guest speakers
(talking about, for example, healthy living, child development, and
budgeting), films, crafts, and community outings. The Board provided
group leaders and instructors for each centre.

Community liaison officers (CLOs) were responsible for the initiation
and ongoing maintenance of the programs. CLO Angela Dozzi at Weston Memorial Junior Public School developed one such family centre:

> Weston was a very tight-knit community with a lot of young parents. One
> of my biggest highlights was opening up the Weston Memorial Family
> Centre ... I will always remember working with a couple of parents with
> small babies. One had an ECE [early childhood education] background,
> and she took over the instructor role. We worked as a committee to start
> it up by word of mouth. When we opened on the first day, it was over-
> whelming. I never had to advertise it. They were loyal and steady and
> came year after year. It was great. The program grew so large that we had
> to open a satellite centre at C.R. Marchant [Senior Public School].
>
> I had to learn to work with the politicians and how to cater to their
> needs and cater to the community's needs and stay within Board guide-
> lines . . . Every politician had their own quirks and ways of doing things
> and philosophies of what the community should have and shouldn't have.
>
> The area trustee, John Gribben, said to me when I first came to Weston,
> 'I don't want you beating the bushes to start all kinds of programs.' But his
> daughter-in-law came to the Family Centre with her young child, and she
> just 'raved' about it and went home and told him what a wonderful pro-
> gram this was. He became one of our loyal supporters. He came to visit,
> had snacks with the little kiddies, and even donated some furniture to us
> from his company. He was a recruit and a convert. From that there were
> lots of before- and after-school programs in that area, which had never
> happened before.'

Community Liaison Officers. The role of the community liaison officer was established in December 1979, as part of a report on long-range
planning for community services. Five functions were identified to promote better communication between school and community:

1. Explaining York Board of Education policies, especially to the families of primary school children and to the new families who moved
   into school communities.
2. Strengthening communication links between the school and community organizations, as well as promoting the general public
   image of schools in the community. In particular, home visits,
   communication with the multicultural community, and assistance
   in the development of school and community organizations were
   examples of current practice in this area. The facilitation of translation services at the school was an important function in several
   parts of the borough.
3. Assisting the principal, particularly in the junior public school
   with minimal support personnel, in the solution of crisis situations
   involving the family and the school.
4. Assisting the regular classroom teacher regarding the identification
   of local community resources that might enrich the school curriculum.
5. Initiating, implementing, supervising, and evaluating community
   education programs at public schools as directed by the York Board
   of Education.

During the 1980–1 school year there was a greater emphasis by community liaison officers on improving communications between the
school, the home, and other community interests (for example, organizations, agencies, and government departments) concerning York
Board of Education policies, procedure, and services. Community liaison officers had also been active in community development by identifying needs in the school and community and mobilizing resources
to help meet those needs. For example, community programs might be
initiated as a result of a documented need for educational, recreational,
cultural, childcare, or youth services that would benefit both school
and community. Sharing expenses with citizen groups and community
agencies minimized the cost of these programs. Costs were also recovered through the continuing education budget formula.

In October 1981 the York Board of Education considered the community liaison officers' annual review for 1980/81 and approved the following recommendation: 'That the priority for the Community Liaison Officer role be (i) improving communications between the school, the home, and other community interests, and (ii) community development using the school as a focal point.'[108]

Community liaison officers most often were appointed to reflect the diverse nature of the York community, including racial and cultural sensitivities and language skills. During the 1980s the five CLOs were each responsible for a family of schools (a secondary school, a senior public school, and its junior feeder school). The policies and programs of the York Board of Education were brought to the community, and, in turn, the community's expectations were related to the school through the CLO. Community development was encouraged through special projects and activities and the working together of agencies, individuals, local businesses, and community groups (for example, community use of space). In particular, each school was required to have a school and community organization (SACO) made up of parents and teachers. The CLOs worked to develop and strengthen the SACOs in each of their schools, and the SACO representatives met monthly at the York Board of Education and formed the Chairmen's Council.

Another major responsibility of the CLO was initiating and administering community education activities in elementary schools. These were supported by funds generated through the Ministry of Education's continuing education budget formula. The Continuing Education Department registers the recorded attendance and hours of instruction for submission to the Ministry as part of the procedure for reimbursement of funds. While non-credit continuing education programs were common in secondary school evening and summer credit classes, York Board of Education was one of the first boards in the province to operate such programs in elementary schools in response to community needs.

Child-centred activities included before- and after-school care programs and general interest activities (for example, computing, dance classes, industrial arts, and music lessons). Activities for adults and seniors included family centres for caregivers and their preschoolers, and programs for seniors (for example, computing, t'ai chi, square and line dancing, arts, and crafts).

Community liaison officers also assisted school personnel by identifying community resources for the classroom teacher that would complement and enrich the school curriculum. One example was intergenerational programs where teachers and children were responsive to the needs of older adults in the community through the twinning of schools to seniors' residences in order to encourage friendly visiting and volunteering. Such an intergenerational program was undertaken in the fall of 1991 as a joint venture of the Community Services Office and the York Board of Education's Adult Day School (ADS). Rose DiVincenzo, Community Services Administrator, partnered with Denise Cross, teacher of an ADS business studies class, to meet the program needs of Silverthorn Place, a new seniors' resident in York. Ms Cross's entrepreneurship course included a market research assignment. It was decided that the ADS students would administer a survey to determine the educational needs of Silverthorn residents. With Rose DiVincenzo's support (she was also participating in York's first teacher-apprenticeship program), the students were guided in the preparation, application, tabulation, and interpretation of the survey. They then visited Silverthorn to administer the survey and conduct personal interviews. For the business studies students it was student-centred learning at its best. For the seniors, it was the opportunity to participate in a variety of education programs that would be offered at Silverthorn Place in response to their needs.

Another example of an intergenerational program was the Angel program at Bala Community School, which was initiated by CLO Angela Dozzi and Principal Jaan Tuju. Senior citizens came in and volunteered to help students who were having trouble, by reading to them, working on their mathematics, or just talking to them if they were having a hard day.

Community liaison officers were active in local fund-raising and in encouraging partnerships among schools, agencies, and community groups. They often served as interpreters, or arranged these services, for school-community meetings. The community services administrator was responsible for coordinating the work of the CLOs and supervising administration of the community education programs. However, it was a most challenging assignment because the role of the CLO was always controversial, with trustees divided as to its importance. In 1987 the York Board of Education approved a review of CLO services system-wide, with a report to be presented in February 1988. A survey conducted of schools, Board of Education departments, and community organizations produced the following results:

1. The services were seen as important by 92 per cent of respondents, and as very important by 81 per cent.

2. The same or more services were requested by 82 per cent of schools and communities, and more services were required by 41 per cent.
3. The services were seen as valuable by 82 per cent of respondents, and were rated as very important by 65 per cent.
4. The valued characteristics of CLOs were the ability to work with people, experience in community work, organizational skills, and willingness to work flexible hours.
5. CLO time should be predominantly devoted to school-community communications and to community education development, in that order.

In 1988 the York Public School Principals' Association strongly supported the CLO's role and responsibilities and requested the allocation of one CLO for each of the six families of schools.

Community School Development. In 1981 the York Board of Education approved my guidelines whereby a school, and its school and community organization, could apply to have its name changed and become a *community school* if the following terms contained in the guidelines were met.

1. A community-related curriculum: education in the school should be enhanced by the use of a variety of community resources (for example, people, organizations, and facilities) to enrich its curriculum and program through students going out into the local community to learn, as well as through the use of community resource persons (for example, volunteers) in the program of the school.
2. A focus for community involvement: parents and other citizens should be encouraged to participate with the principal and staff in the planning process concerning the program of the school and the educational needs of the students.
3. A resource for community development: the school and its personnel (staff and students) should be actively involved with citizens and community groups to identify needs and mobilize resources to improve the quality of life in the community.
4. A community use of facilities: school facilities, when not in use for regular educational purposes, should be available for persons of all ages to pursue community education, recreation, cultural, social service, and childcare needs, both during the day and in the evening.

5. A sense of community partnership: the school should participate with other community service agencies in the planning and delivery of community services according to local needs.

During the 1980s a total of eight junior elementary schools were designated as community schools.

Multicultural Education

During the 1980s the Community and Multicultural Education Department, led by Supervising Principal Rod McColl, provided a variety of programs and services in response to the needs of newcomers to York. Classes in English as a second language and dialect (ESL/D) were offered to all elementary and secondary students entering York schools from many different parts of the world, with increasing numbers from the Caribbean, Latin America, and Asia. These students were helped to adjust to the Canadian way of life and to learn English, or to upgrade their skills, in a supportive, encouraging environment. With newcomers entering York schools throughout the school year, the department provided assessment services to determine their previous academic background and to refer them to the appropriate secondary school. Translation and interpreter services were also offered to meet the needs of parents and teachers.

Heritage Language Programs. Later changed in name to International Language programs, Heritage Language programs were led by Supervisor Giovanni Tullo and provided language and cultural instruction in fourteen different languages, as well as classes in Black heritage, enrolling more than eighteen hundred students. More than one hundred classes in fifteen different schools were offered after school hours and on Saturdays with a staff of more than seventy instructors. A variety of community education programs such as tae kwon do, Chinese brush painting, and folk dancing, as well as adult English as a second language, citizenship, and t'ai chi, were offered to complement the heritage language classes. All classes were initiated in response to parental requests, according to an initiation procedure contained in the York Board of Education's Heritage Programs' policy.

Black Heritage Program. During the 1981/82 school year, 215 students were enrolled in the Black Heritage program. A Black Heritage advisory committee, chaired by Dr Inez Elliston, developed 'Black Heritage Curriculum: A Voyage of Discovery for Children of Afro, Asian, Canadian, American and West Indian Heritages,' which was field-tested by Black Heritage instructors.

Multicultural Learning Materials. The Community and Multicultural Education Department maintained a selection of appropriate multicultural learning materials for both elementary and secondary ESL/D students. ESL/D teacher counsellors (itinerant support personnel for ESL/D classroom teachers) Edda Loffler and Brian Commons published a multicultural novel *We Don't Speak Much English Yet,* and a series of twelve storybook tapes forming activity packages for elementary students were also produced by ESL teachers.

Multicultural Leadership Program. This program provided an opportunity for secondary school students and staff to develop leadership skills and sensitivity for a week during each fall and spring at the York Board of Education's Outdoor Education Centre. Emphasizing the positive benefits of the diversity in York schools, participants learned to appreciate the need for all to feel accepted and valued.

York Italian Language and Cultural Institute. The York Italian Language and Cultural Institute recognized the large proportion of Italian immigrants who had made their home in York. The Board of Education joined with the York University faculties of Arts and Fine Arts, the Italian Consulate, and the Ministry of Education to plan a resource centre at George Harvey Collegiate that would host presentations and display books, magazines, pictures, films, tapes, and art objects related to Italian life and cultural experience. The institute also sponsored successful summer programs in Urbino, Italy. York students were able to earn senior secondary school credits in visual arts and Italian while at the same time enjoying excursions to some of the major cultural centres of Italy such as Rome, Venice, Florence, Pisa, Perugia, and Ravenna.

Network of Complementary Schools. In 1981 the Community and Multicultural Education Department assumed hosting responsibilities, from SEED in Toronto, for the Network of Complementary Schools. This unique student-exchange program provided opportunities for individual students to travel abroad to experience life in various parts of the United States and to study career-related options in selected public and private secondary schools with exemplary programs. During the 1980s, York students studied in the states of New York, Colorado, Michigan, Arizona, and Washington, and in Mexico. In return, students from New York, California, Chicago, and Arkansas visited York schools. All participants felt that they had had invaluable learning opportunities and had made many new friends.

The Community and Multicultural Education Department was responsible for a variety of adult education programs, including the following:

1. Action for Literacy (ALY): an adult ESL and literacy evening tutorial program was offered in homes, libraries, and schools to a wide spectrum of adult learners who were unable to attend more traditional night-school classes.
2. Community ESL/Literacy: classes in English as a second language and in literacy were offered for adults in Metropolitan Toronto Housing Authority buildings and other community locations during the day and evening, with childcare provided where necessary. Other initiatives included ESL for seniors (offered in senior's residences) and ESL prenatal classes (offered in partnership with the City of York Health Unit and the Ministry of Citizenship).
3. Citizenship Preparation: offered in cooperation with COSTI-IIAS (an immigrant aid agency), these classes prepared participants for a citizenship court hearing to become a Canadian citizen.
4. Adult Individual Development: this was a creative response to the need for literacy and life-skills training for slower adult learners, who were encouraged to live independently in the community. In addition to basic education, there was great emphasis on the development of social skills. Highlights of the program, led by Jenny Clark, included a yearly camping trip.

Alternative School Programs

In December 1980 the York Board of Education had requested that the director of education 'take under consideration the matter of the need for the provision of alternative school programs at the elementary school level and report to the Board as soon as possible.'[109]

In March 1981 the Community Services Office received a letter from a group of parents proposing a community alternative elementary school in the Cedarvale-Humewood area on the east side of the Borough of York. This was York's most advantaged neighbourhood, just west of the area from which students were drawn for attendance at the City of Toronto's Alternative Primary School. The parents had conducted a survey, which indicated a strong interest in such an alternative school within the Borough of York. In May the Board directed the Community Services Office to work with the group to develop a proposal. In January 1982 the director of education proposed that a special board committee be established to review the proposal and submit recommendations. Membership on the committee was to be composed of two trustees, the assistant superintendent of community services, two school representatives, and two appointed community representatives from Chairmen's Council.[110]

In March 1982 the York Board of Education approved the following criteria for alternative school programs:

1. Enrolment Base
   (a) The enrolment base for the proposed program shall be within the established class ranges in the current collective agreement according to the age and status of prospective students.

2. Program
   (a) The program shall provide a unique contribution to education in the Borough of York;
   (b) The program shall be consistent with Ministry guidelines and administrative procedures of the Board;
   (c) The group proposing the program shall be involved in the establishment and ongoing maintenance of the program in a consultative capacity.

3. Accommodation
   (a) Accommodation for the program shall be in existing school space in a location acceptable to the proposing group and the local school and community organization, and be in accordance with the Board's accommodation policy;
   (b) The program shall be designated as a separate entity within the host school;
   (c) The Board shall not be responsible for costs of renovations or structural changes to accommodate the program.

4. Staffing
   (a) The allocation of staff shall be according to the Board's collective agreements;
   (b) Selection and placement of staff shall be the responsibility of the principal in consultation with the group proposing the program.

5. Supplies and Equipment
   (a) Supplies and equipment provided to the program shall be according to the Board supplies' allocation procedures, proportional to the number of students enrolled;
   (b) Any additional supplies and equipment used in the program shall be provided at no cost to the Board.

6. Extensions to the Regular Program
   (a) Establishment of a day care centre, as a supplement to the program, shall be according to guidelines contained in the Report of the Pre-School Programs Work Group, and such a facility shall also be open to students of the host school;
   (b) Enrichment activities, which result in costs in excess of the normal transportation and supplies budgets, shall be at no cost to the Board.

7. Accountability
   (a) Under Regulation 262 of the *Education Act*, the Principal shall be the person responsible for the program;
   (b) An Advisory Committee of parents, the Trustees for the area, and the Supervisory Officer for the school, shall assist the Principal in a consultative capacity;
   (c) The Advisory Committee shall have a representative on the School and Community Organization of the host school;
   (d) The Advisory Committee shall be responsible for the provision of funds beyond those recognized as usual Board costs;
   (e) An annual budget, indicating full apportionment of costs, shall be submitted to the appropriate Supervisory Officer by May 31, prior to commencement of the regular school program the following September;
   (f) The Principal and Advisory Committee shall review the progress of the program on a semi-annual basis and report to the appropriate Supervisory Officer by December 31 and May 31 of each year;
   (g) Each proposal shall be dealt with individually by the Board.[111]

These criteria were used to govern the establishment of the following alternative school programs.

Cherrywood Alternative School. In the spring of 1981 a group of parents, mainly from the Humewood Community School area, had made a presentation to the York Board of Education to establish an alternative program at the elementary level. It was later approved, subject to its adherence to the new criteria for alternative school programs. In September 1982 the Cherrywood Alternative School opened, utilizing vacant space in Humewood Community School. Initially, it enrolled children aged four to six years, covering junior and senior kindergarten and grade one. A full day program for kindergarten children and extended day care (8:00 a.m. to 6:00 p.m.) was offered. The school expected to expand by one grade per year up to grade six.

Cherrywood parents believed that the school should be a natural extension of the home, where the parents would take an active role in helping to enrich their children's opportunities. The program was based on a family-grouping model with four-, five-, and six-year-olds sharing space, resources, and teaching staff. It recognized the individual interests, learning styles, and strengths of each child. A lower child-to-adult ratio, and family grouping, allowed children access to a range of materials and opportunities. It was to be an activity-centred atmosphere in which children would be actively engaged with their environment and other people. The program was designed to nurture self-direction and self-discipline, while encouraging enthusiastic learners.[112]

Essential skills in reading, writing, mathematics, social and natural science, and fine arts were emphasized. Exposure to the French language and field visits to historical and cultural centres were also an important part of the program.

Enrolment was open to all children in the greater Metropolitan Toronto area, on a first-come, first-served basis. Fees were required to fund the day-care component. Voluntary donations were encouraged to maintain an enriched program and lower the child-to-adult ratio. Parents were expected to be personally involved with their child's education, as classroom volunteers, in community fund-raising, or as members of the Parents' Executive Committee.[109] By 1986, Cherrywood Alternative School had seventy-five students at the kindergarten to grade-four level.

Program for Academic and Creative Education. An outgrowth of the

Cherrywood experience was the establishment, in 1983, of the Program for Academic and Creative Education (PACE) at Arlington Senior Public School. Arlington, the senior school serving the Cedarvale-Humewood area, was faced with declining enrolment because of losing students to the City of Toronto. PACE emphasized individual learning contracts to encourage students to be responsible for their own learning, through in-depth research and small group presentations. Following its inception, PACE expanded from two teachers and 55 students to six teachers and 180 students in 1986.

INTERACT. The PACE program attracted enrolment from other jurisdictions and private schools. In addition, there had been a recognized need for arts-oriented alternative secondary school programs in Metropolitan Toronto (for example, Claude Watson School in North York and Etobicoke School of the Arts). There was also a need for an alternative program to serve students who were taking private lessons in music, drama, or athletics; these activities – for students who had a life other than schooling – required a more flexible schedule than is normally available in a regular secondary school.

A Toronto parent, John McIninch, approached me concerning his daughter Merryn who had attended Hawthorn II Bilingual School (John and his wife, Michele Leroux, were founding parents of that school). Merryn had decided, at age fourteen, that she wanted to quit school to train full time as an equestrian. I met with Merryn and her father, and she agreed that she would stay in school if there was a more flexible secondary program available that fit her needs.

In April 1985 a proposal was presented to the York Board of Education to establish an alternative secondary school program, tentatively called Program to Encourage Performance in the Arts (PREP), according to the Board's criteria for alternative school programs. The proposal called for the establishment of a program to support the needs of students for enrichment in the performing arts and related areas. It would be hosted by an existing secondary school in order to share facilities, teaching staff, and administrative services. To allow for flexible instruction time so that students could continue their performing arts interests, the program would utilize learning contracts, independent study registers (like Subway Academy), cooperative education placements in performing arts' settings, and other course offerings in the host school. A wide range of community resources, including parental involvement, post-secondary institutions, volunteer organizations, theatre internships, field visits, volunteer tutors, and private lessons, would be encouraged.

Initially, two full-time teachers with particular interests and qualifications in the performing arts would staff the program. Accommodations would consist of two classrooms, with additional facilities to be shared with the host school. The principal of the host school, with an advisory committee of parents, teachers, and students, would administer the program. While the program would be financially supported within the budget of the host school, additional resources could be provided through community fund-raising.[113]

In September 1985, the program, now known as INTERACT, opened its doors at Vaughan Road Collegiate, the school to which Cherrywood Alternative School and PACE would normally send their students. The lead teacher was Elaine Vine, who had excelled as Arlington Senior Public School's drama teacher and was famous for her Gilbert and Sullivan operettas. To be a cast member in one of her multiracial productions was considered more prestigious than making the school's basketball team.

While beginning with only nine students, INTERACT soon grew to an enrolment of more than fifty in grades nine to thirteen. Over the next few years, INTERACT students (in their 'other lives') were to be seen in Hollywood and Canadian films, television series, and plays, with careers in acting, singing, and modelling. Dancers were to be found in national and international ballet companies (including the Kirov in the Ukraine) and musical theatre. Athletes also gained national and international renown in such sports as tennis, swimming, skiing, and figure skating. One INTERACT student, a member of the Mickey Mouse Club in Orlando, Florida, dutifully faxed her lessons and assignments back to Toronto to be graded.

As was true at its inception, INTERACT continued to help relieve the conflicts between parents' and students' aspirations. It was possible for students to continue their education while pursuing a career in the performing arts. Ironically, Merryn McIninch, who became a very successful equestrian on the Pony Club circuit, never became a student at INTERACT; she opted to enrol in the Level Six enrichment program at Northern Secondary School in Toronto.

MacTECH. In September 1986 the Humber College–York Board Liaison Committee proposed the establishment of a new alternative school program in integrated machine technologies, to be known as

MacTECH. It used accommodations at George Harvey Collegiate Institute and Standard Modern Technologies, Canada's last machine-tool manufacturer. The program was jointly sponsored by the York Board of Education, Humber College, Standard Modern Technologies, Weston Machine and Tool, and Magna International. Students used individual learning modules to develop skills in machine-tool operation, electronics, computer control, and microtechnologies, as well as traditional academic skills. After achieving a secondary school diploma, they were able to go on to secure a Humber College machine technologies certificate, offered in the same facilities. The program stressed personal initiative, problem solving, inventiveness, and self-reliance to prepare students for the workplace of the twenty-first century. Leadership for this articulation program came from Marina Heidman of Humber College while I represented the York Board of Education.[114]

Afro-Caribbean Alternative Secondary School. In 1986 the Community Services Office was approached by a group of parent activists led by Jackie Wilson to establish an alternative school for school leavers who had come originally from the West Indies. After much bitter debate, the Afro-Caribbean Alternative Secondary School opened that September, occupying three classrooms at D.B. Hood Community School. The forty-five students were taught by Black teachers who stressed academic skills in the context of the Caribbean region. Ontario's first Afro-centric alternative school, however, proved to be very controversial among some senior officials of the York Board of Education who saw it as a form of segregation. Consequently, the school had to be open to all school leavers and was relocated to George Harvey Collegiate as the Afro-Caribbean Re-entry program. By 1988 the program had been absorbed by the George Harvey Re-entry program and ceased to exist.

Other Programs

Older Adults. During the 1987–8 school year, an older adults committee encouraged the York Board of Education's involvement with senior citizens. Forty-five courses were initiated by community liaison officers at seniors' centres, churches, clubs, schools, and apartment buildings, involving almost a thousand seniors. Activities ranged from quilting, ceramics, t'ai chi, and line dancing to computing, conversational French, and English as a second language. Each June, Rose DiVincenzo, Community Services Administrator, led a group of forty seniors to visit the York Board of Education's Pine River outdoor education centre. Any senior citizen who registered with the Community Services Office received a VIP card to gain free access to programs and services in York schools. Each year, about two hundred seniors would attend an education fair to view displays, demonstrations, and entertainment to inform them about the many learning and leisure opportunities available without cost. (It is not surprising that York senior citizens became a potent political force in support of community education programs and CLO services.)

Volunteers and Education Week. The community services administrator was also responsible for an annual volunteer-appreciation night, which honoured more than two hundred school volunteers each year and gave framed certificates to five outstanding volunteers. Education Week at the West Side Mall demonstrated the excellence of the schools' visual and performing arts and athletics endeavours. Displays and activities included Older Adults Day, Reading Fair, and Technofest.[115]

Continuing Education Funding

In 1988 there were almost twenty-three thousand registrants in part-time programs offered by the Community Services Office through provisions of the continuing education budget formula. This compared to about sixteen thousand regular day students in elementary and secondary schools. Within the Community Services Office the following offered part-time programs: the Continuing Education and Summer School Department, the Community and Multicultural Education Department, and the community services administrator.

Continuing Education and Summer School. The supervising principal of the Continuing Education and Summer School Department was responsible for programs in two categories: evening and summer classes for secondary school credit and general interest offered in community education centres located in secondary schools (600 programs serving 8,300 students); and elementary summer enrichment and remedial classes offered in elementary schools (140 programs serving 3,300 students).

Community and Multicultural Education. The supervising principal of the Community and Multicultural Education Department provided part-time programs for children and adults who were newcomers to Canada and wished to upgrade their academic or language skills or to retain their cultural heritage. These programs were divided into two areas: multicultural programs including English as a second language, literacy and life skills, citizenship, and seniors (80 programs serving 1,200 students); and heritage programs in fifteen languages and cultures (210 programs serving 3,800 students).

Community Education. The community services administrator was responsible for programs initiated by community liaison officers, or local elementary schools, in response to the needs and interests of their communities for part-time learning activities or services, including before- and after-school care, educational and artistic enrichment, parent education, and seniors' activities (300 programs serving 6,400 learners).

Demonstration Projects

The Community Services Office staff initiated several demonstration projects, including the following:

Learning Without Limits. Learning Without Limits was a magazine published by the Community Services Office in the fall, winter, and spring to inform the citizens of York of the many educational opportunities available in their now city. Besides course listings, the magazine included feature articles and advertisements that encouraged participation in the learning process. More than 100,000 copies were distributed by the postal service to homes and businesses in York and surrounding areas.

LWL-TV. In April 1986, I met with David Graham, the owner of Graham Cable, to develop a Cable 10 television version of *Learning Without Limits.* As a result, up to nine hours per week of cable programming was offered, which included literacy and numeracy skills, English as a second language, preparation for citizenship, technical and business education, information about the York Board of Education's programs and services, and leisure-learn activities. Television programs included *Info York* (hosted by Kathryn Cox, the Board's communications officer), *Return to Learn,* the *Home Maintenance* series, and other community education programming and were available from a variety of sources (for example, Magic Lantern Films). McGraw-Hill Ryerson Publishing also agreed to become partners in the production.

The project could reach ninety thousand cable subscribers and provided an advertising opportunity for local business and industry. Operated primarily by volunteers, LWL-TV developed technical production and programming skills among students and teachers, both at the Graham Cable facilities and the studio space operated by Norma Kenny of the Adult Day School.

Parents as Partners. In the spring of 1983, Frank McTeague, the York Board of Education's coordinator of English, approached me concerning two reading projects that served disadvantaged working-class areas in England. The organizers had reported 'a startling improvement by children of all reading levels when they received help at home.' We convened a meeting of principals and community liaison officers from four elementary schools to explore the feasibility of initiating a demonstration project to be known as the Parents-as-Partners Program. A strategic plan was presented, and principals were encouraged to discuss the concept with staff members and make a decision about participating. The goals of the program were to improve the reading performance level of children having difficulty, enable parents to provide informal help at home, and establish support procedures for making a daily school-home connection for problem readers and their parents.

In December 1983, Fairbank Memorial Junior Public School and D.B. Hood Community School agreed to implement the program. Their reading resource teachers, assisted by their community liaison officer, implemented a demonstration project that ran from January to June 1984. Parents of problem readers were invited to attend a meeting at the school. The principal presented background information and proposed a program of parent involvement (of at least twenty minutes per day, listening to the child read). The resource teacher demonstrated nonjudgmental listening skills and how to retell a story. The procedures outlined included the use of a reading record card, and an introduction to basal readers or library books that the child might bring home. Home visits and access to resources for preschoolers were also incorporated into the program.

During the demonstration period a total of eighteen children from fourteen families were involved in the two schools. Fairbank Memorial produced a videotape to help prepare parents for participating in the program. When the project was evaluated in June, it was found that

50 per cent of the children involved in the program made significant progress, but improvement was noted in all children whose parents remained committed throughout the period. As a result, both schools decided to expand the Parents-as-Partners program to regular classes during the 1984/85 school year.[116]

Outcomes and Reflections

Networking has always been an essential component of community education and development. Aside from my duties in alternative and community programs at the Toronto Board of Education, I was able to expand my learning horizons through voluntary participation on several community service committees and advocacy organizations. This also gave me a broader exposure to influential leaders in the field, which ultimately resulted in a new career opportunity in the Borough (later, City) of York.

The position of assistant-superintendent of community services afforded me a chance to continue to explore the concept of community education and development. The York Board of Education was unique in that all its supervisory officers (including the director) were assigned school supervision as well as policy and program responsibilities. This was particularly important to me in developing new community-responsive demonstration projects and other new policy initiatives. The ability to be able to follow through on the implementation phase became part of an action-research process of continuous evaluation and improvement. Naturally, there were some failures as well as successes.

York's Community Use of Space Policy ensured that local non-profit community groups and parental interests, followed by government departments and service agencies, received preferred use of vacant school space. This was particularly important in a community development process, where these resources were made available in order to solve local problems and improve the quality of community life. It also served to bring local citizens together in a collective action plan in response to community needs.

A major beneficiary of the policy was the preschool programs. Parent groups, assisted by community liaison officers, were able to use the York Board of Education's policy to survey their local communities and develop proposals for facilities to be licensed under the *Day Nurseries Act*. A barrier remained, however: the start-up funds to purchase equipment and hire staff for the new centres. Low-income parents were not able to pay per-diem operating fees and required subsidy from Metro Social Services. The York Board was not able to provide start-up funding, and the Learning Enrichment Foundation assumed this responsibility. (The work of this non-profit charity, which was originally established by the Board and its school and community organizations, will be addressed in chapter 13.)

The community liaison officer was an essential component in the community education and development process in the Borough, and later the City, of York. As their job description was to serve both the school and the community, CLOs were instrumental in the development, initiation, and ongoing maintenance of many of the policy and program innovations introduced by the Community Services Office and for which I was responsible. The challenge, however, was to ensure that the role of the CLO did not become politicized. The demise of the School Community Relations Department in the City of Toronto had been a direct result of the perception by right-wing trustees, and some administrators, that this department was 'in bed' with the left-of-centre trustees. When the right-wingers finally gained majority control of the Toronto Board of Education, the days of the School Community Relations Department were numbered.

In York, some trustees saw the community liaison officers as an important communication link with the community in interpreting Board of Education policies and reaching out to parents, especially those with limited English skills. Other trustees sometimes felt threatened if they thought a CLO was not in tune with their political agenda. For example, one Italian-speaking CLO was an interpreter on Kathryn Cox's *Info York* television show until her area's non-Italian trustee demanded that she be removed. The trustee was reported to have said, 'She could be talking about me, and I wouldn't even know it.'

Whenever a new CLO was appointed, the area trustee participated in the interview and selection process. Not surprisingly, the names of former trustee campaign workers found their way on to the short list of applicants to be interviewed. It was often a struggle to ensure that the most qualified and experienced person got the job. I remember one new CLO who was hired at the insistence of the local trustee. The candidate had no qualifying background or experience in the field but was a volunteer at the local mosque. The trustee was counting on the CLO to deliver him the Muslim vote in the next election.

A key resource in York's community development process was access to funding for community education programs through provisions of the continuing education budget formula. Part-time instructors (many of whom were local residents) could be employed to provide essential programs such as preschool and parenting, family centres, before- and after-school care, general interest and remedial programs, and a variety of language and culture classes for newcomers.

Through the York Board of Education's Community School Development policy, schools had the opportunity to change the school name to reflect their commitment to community education and development. This policy also helped to develop leadership skills in teachers and principals who became advocates for more community involvement.

As a reception area for immigrants and refugees, York had a particular challenge in serving their needs. This resulted in the creation of many innovative programs by the Community and Multicultural Education Department such as assessment services, heritage language and culture, special learning materials, multicultural leadership, citizenship preparation, adult individual development, and basic literacy programs for children, youth, adults, and seniors.

To respond to the needs of parents and students seeking diversity in learning styles, the Alternative School Programs policy was created. Beginning in the advantaged east end of the city of York, alternative proposals were approved for primary, junior, senior elementary, and secondary school students through the Cherrywood, PACE, and INTERACT programs. Two alternative programs were established to serve lower-income, and culturally different, students in the central part of the city through the MacTECH and Afro-Caribbean alternative programs.

Communications between school and community were enhanced through the work of CLOs, *Learning Without Limits* magazine, and LWL-TV cable casting. The demonstration project known as Parents-as-Partners got the school and community working together to improve literacy skills among problem readers.

Finally, the innovations in community education and development during the 1980s would not have been possible without the inspirational leadership and ongoing support of the director of education, D. John Phillips. As an immigrant himself, he had a profound understanding and appreciation of the needs of York's impoverished newcomers.

One area of vital importance in developing school-based curriculum and program is relevancy. This is of particular concern for early school leavers and other students who depart secondary school to go directly to the world of work. One approach to bridging the gap between the school and the workplace has been business-education partnerships. Activities have ranged from work experience and cooperative education programs to job-shadowing, mentoring, and adopt-a-school ventures. It has become increasingly apparent that schooling-for-work programs, traditionally offered only to senior secondary school students, may be irrelevant unless the needs of early leavers and non-achievers are addressed as part of a commitment to lifelong learning and industry education restructuring to meet the demands of a new economic age. The next chapter will document a comprehensive social enterprise partnership to begin to address these concerns.

13 Education for Economic Development

Two of the foremost innovations in York, during the 1980s, were the creation of the Adult Day School and the Learning Enrichment Foundation. These organizations formed a social enterprise partnership to address the literacy, language, skill-training, employment, and child-care needs among impoverished adults in the city of York. Many of the adult learners were also parents of children in York schools. Improving the education levels and economic opportunities for these families was seen as a key factor in boosting the achievement among children and youth in York schools.

The Adult Day School

During the 1970s the need was first identified within the Borough of York for more educational opportunities for adults during the day. In fact, the 1976 census had recognized York as having the highest rate of functional illiteracy (less than grade-nine education) in Metropolitan Toronto. In addition, more than 40 per cent of families spoke a language other than English in the home. As a result, community service agencies and interested citizens approached the York Board of Education to offer adult basic education classes (grades one to eight) during the day. One example was the Evelyn Gregory Library, which realized that many of the adults visiting the library were there just to get out of the weather; they could not read. Other groups requiring English language skills were the veiled and burka-clad ladies who were beginning to appear on Eglinton Avenue West, and the Russian school bus drivers who met in Keelesdale Park during the day.

In 1979 the first classes were opened in the library, using provisions of the continuing education budget formula. As the Borough of York was experiencing a steady decline in the number of elementary school students, the program was soon relocated to vacant classroom space – first at Keelesdale Junior Public School and later at D.B. Hood Community School. Classes at the grades nine to ten level were later established at George Harvey Secondary School. In 1981 adult ESL classes and programs for education in the workplace and adult slow learners were added.

By the spring of 1982 more than a hundred and fifty adults were enrolled in day programs, mostly through the continuing education budget, using part-time instructors. It was then that I wrote a proposal to have these adult learners considered as regular secondary school students, generating contract teachers under the collective agreement of the Ontario Secondary School Teachers' Federation (OSSTF). The proposal was not met with favourably by some supervisory officers on the Administrative Council who wished to keep support for education under the limited resources provided by the continuing education budget formula. During the March break, when most of my colleagues were away, I made my pitch to the director of education, D. John Phillips. He listened thoughtfully to the prospect of gaining additional regular secondary students (and increased budget-formula dollars) in a time of declining enrolment and diminishing transfer funding from the Metropolitan Toronto School Board (the source of funds for all area public school boards). He also recognized the importance of meeting the learning needs of our impoverished immigrant community of children, youth, and adults. When my report came to the next meeting of the Administrative Council, the director spoke strongly in favour of my proposal, much to the chagrin of those who opposed it.

In June 1982 the York Board of Education approved the establishment of the Adult Day School program as a department of York Humber High School (I was the school's supervisory officer) under the OSSTF collective agreement, provided that the enrolment reached 168 by the end of September. By 30 September, enrolment in the Adult Day School had risen to more than 265 students, with eighteen teachers, including a major department head. A third vice-principal (Joan Green) was added to the York Humber staff because of the Adult Day School. Accommodation was provided at D.B. Hood Community School for classroom and administrative space, at Fairbank Memorial and Briarhill Junior Public schools for classrooms, and at York Woodworks on Rogers Road for an Education in the Workplace site.

In each instance, adult day classes were initiated according to a process of community development, whereby the identified needs were matched to the available resources (both human and physical) in order to improve the quality of life of citizens in the area. Research in both Britain and the United States had shown that the most effective vehicle for adult basic education was an informal, responsive environment that respected the individual needs and interests of the learner.[117]

The study *Adult Basic Education and Literacy Activities in Canada* observed that 'instructors or coaches need to be emotionally strong, but sensitive people, with good human relations skills, in order to handle the attitudes of students.'[118] The Adult Day School attempted to incorporate these findings into its program development in the following ways:

1. The Adult Day School had a re-entry program for adults and school leavers, including basic education and upgrading, English-as-a-second-language instruction, and Education in the Workplace opportunities.
2. Teachers in the Adult Day School stressed an informal, individualized approach, combining academic instruction, life-skills counselling, and remedial assistance.
3. The curriculum and program were developed out of the life-related needs of learners rather than any predetermined credit guidelines.
4. Classes were located in easily accessible, neighbourhood-based accommodations through the use of vacant classroom space in elementary schools in order to provide settings that were less formal and institutional in nature.
5. Day-care assistance was more readily available in elementary schools to support the childcare needs of adult learners.
6. Volunteers were recruited to assist learners on a one-to-one basis.
7. Education in the Workplace provided opportunities for practical, employment-related experiences through cooperative education placements and training in small business operation.
8. The Adult Day School made extensive use of Board of Education support services, community organizations, and agencies to strengthen the program and assist in communication with the public.
9. Teachers were involved in a retraining process to prepare them better for responding to the needs of adult learners in a re-entry program.

10. The program offered continuous intake to respond to the increasing demand for adult learning opportunities.

Not all school administrators, trustees, and parents were comfortable with having Adult Day School students attending classes in elementary schools. One morning I received a frantic call from the principal of D.B. Hood Community School who had witnessed an adult male student putting his arm around a grade-five elementary student. I raced to the school to confront the offender. The ADS student was shocked to be accused of 'molesting a child.' 'After all,' he said, 'I was just comforting my daughter, who also attends D.B. Hood.' That was the last complaint we ever had of adult students fraternizing with children at school. Many parents and their children shared the same learning environment.

In January 1983 the Adult Day School enrolment had continued to climb, and administrative resources available through York Humber High School were found to be inadequate, particularly in the areas of teacher supervision, appropriate curriculum materials, and budget for supplies, furniture, and equipment. At my insistence, the York Board of Education decided to constitute ADS as a stand-alone secondary school with its own principal, staff, and budget, comprising a secondary educational unit under the Metropolitan Toronto School Board budget formula. At first, District 14 members of the Ontario Secondary School Teachers' Federation expressed their opposition to placing ADS teachers under the collective agreement. This was soon resolved when the federation's president, Marlene Miller, realized how many new members could be added to the district, thereby offsetting the ravages of declining enrolment.

Another major issue was protecting ADS teachers in their jobs. As secondary enrolment declined, other contract teachers declared that the surplus teachers could displace ADS teachers and claim their positions. This would defeat the purpose of having a staff member at ADS who was committed to adult education methodology. I confronted the problem by applying to the Ministry of Education for a new additional-qualifications course in adult education. (I had previously instituted Ministry additional-qualifications courses in compensatory education and community school development.) With the assistance of Professor Jim Wood of the Faculty of Education, University of Toronto, and the OSSTF's Marlene Miller, a course of study for a Part 1 Adult Education additional-qualifications course was developed and approved.

A successful candidate of the course was given an overview of the network of community and social agencies coordinating and providing adult education services; an understanding of Ministry of Education and Boards of Education policies and programs in adult education; an understanding of the characteristics and changing needs of adult learners and the social and psychological factors motivating adult learning; a knowledge of various theories of adult learning with particular reference to the cognitive, affective, and psychomotor aspects of learning; an ability to recognize various adult learning styles and to adjust teaching methods to accommodate the different styles; an ability to assess the cognitive and personal learning needs of adult learners in order to assist them in the development of necessary life skills; a knowledge of the principles of program design and related teaching and evaluation strategies appropriate to adult learners; a knowledge of resources and learning materials; an ability to apply the principles of program design, and related teaching strategies and learning materials, to a selected area of adult education; and knowledge of various modes and aspects of communication, consultation, and cooperative learning appropriate to adult learning.

The York Board of Education's Community Services Office and the Faculty of Education of the University of Toronto offered this course jointly as a basic requirement for teachers at the Adult Day School. Successful completion of this course ensured job protection for new teachers joining the staff and the overall quality of the ADS program.

After its inception in 1983 the Adult Day School continued to expand, both in terms of its enrolment and the number of teaching staff. By 1990, enrolment had grown to more than two thousand students, served by more than 130 teachers – the largest secondary school in York, if not the province of Ontario. What made ADS truly unique was the fact that it had no building of its own, but it shared space in more than twenty sites including elementary and secondary schools, community service settings, business, and industry. During this dramatic growth period, ADS was fortunate to have the inspirational leadership of Principal Carolyn Collyer, working with two vice-principals, some very creative department heads, and extremely dedicated teachers. Organizationally, ADS grew into several departments and programs as described in 'Learning to Ride the Third Wave,' a 1988 report from the Community Services Office.[119]

The following ADS departments and programs were key elements in the school's organization.

Reception Services. New students entering the Adult Day School were greeted by four teachers who had been trained in guidance and counselling and had been assigned to the reception centre at the D.B. Hood campus. They assessed the students' learning needs and placed them in the most appropriate department, class, or location.

English as a Second Language. The needs of more than seven hundred students for basic, intermediate, and advanced ESL and life skills were served by forty-five teachers at five different campuses (Fairbank Memorial and Lambton Park Junior schools, C.R. Marchant Senior School, and Vaughan Road and George Harvey Secondary schools). The focus of the department was one teacher, one class. Effective use was made of computers to enhance the learning process. Programs initiated in response to learner needs included ESL/Literacy for students not literate in their mother tongue; ESL/Writing for students who required advanced writing skills for post-secondary education or employment; ESL/Careers for ESL students who, in order to be ready for employment, required assistance with integrating business skills, cooperative education placements in business, industry, and the professions, work experience, and job readiness training; and afternoon classes that were added at Vaughan Road and George Harvey campuses because of an overwhelming demand for service.

Basic Education and Upgrading. Classes in basic education, upgrading, and life skills were offered at four different locations (D.B. Hood Community School, Roseland and Rawlinson Junior, and Fairbank Senior campuses). The one-teacher, one-class model involved fifteen teachers serving more than 250 students. All basic education and upgrading classes also made extensive use of computer-assisted learning.

Business Skills. The Business Skills Department provided training in keyboarding, word and numerical processing, accounting, and other business-related skills for 140 students and nine teachers at the D.B. Hood, Rawlinson, Briar Hill and C.E. Webster Junior, and Fairbank Senior campuses.

Education in the Workplace. In 1988, ten teachers provided basic education, English-as-a-Second Language instruction, and life-skills, on a withdrawal basis, to entry-level employment and training programs offered by training partners in a variety of business, industrial, and service settings. Training programs included renovation and construction, industrial sewing, childcare assistants, machine technologies, health care aides, electronic assembly and repair, and small business development. All programs were industry driven, responding to the training and recruitment needs of employers in the city of York. Training partners in this community economic development process included Humber College, the Learning Enrichment Foundation, and employers who sat on industrial advisory committees.

Tutorial Outreach. In 1988, the Tutorial Outreach Department served the learning needs of more than five hundred homebound individuals who, owing to physical, emotional, cultural, or employment reasons, could not attend regular ADS classes. Utilizing independent study register programs, thirty-four teachers provided basic educational upgrading, ESL, and life skills, on a one-to-one basis or in small groups, in private homes or community settings (for example, libraries, public housing buildings, and service agencies). In addition, teacher-tutors visited a variety of employment locations to provide educational upgrading and language skills on the job. This service was very popular with companies who employed an immigrant or functionally illiterate workforce.

Adopt an Industry. In 1988, as an outgrowth of both Education in the Workplace and Tutorial Outreach, Adopt an Industry was established as a demonstration project between the employment community and the Adult Day School to increase the potential for educational services in the workplace. Each of a selected group of industries received the services of a full-time ADS teacher on a secondment basis. The teacher was assigned to the company's personnel, or other appropriate department, to perform the following duties: assessing staff development needs; developing a training design; undertaking training programs directly, or through external resources, utilizing education provisions; providing direct service in the areas of educational upgrading and ESL training, as appropriate; and conducting an ongoing evaluation of the overall programs, in response to employer and employee needs.

As a member of the management team, the teacher reported directly to a company supervisor, while maintaining liaison with the ADS project leader and other Adopt-an-Industry personnel. Initial response to the concept among employers was enthusiastic. During the economic downturn of 1981–2, many larger companies had lost their training officers, while small and medium-sized firms could never afford such a luxury. The benefits to the Adult Day School included the professional development of participating staff, as well as a new source of students to serve. Initially, five teachers were placed with the following employers: Facelle, Northwestern Hospital, West Park Hospital, Cadet Cleaners, and Patons & Baldwin.

Media Resources. The Media Resources Department consisted of a department head and an audio-visual technician who were responsible for distance learning, utilizing Graham Cable 10 to reach a potential audience of 100,000 households with at least six hours per week of programming. All media resources created by the department were available as video learning material for use by ADS teachers and students. As previously described in chapter 12, examples of the Adult Day School media resources programming included:

1. *Return to Learn,* a half-hour series shown three times per week, which provided information on ADS and other learning opportunities available for adults in the city of York.
2. *Learning Without Limits* (LWL-TV), a video version of the *Learning Without Limits* magazine, which broadcast for three hours on Saturday mornings. Features included 'Movies and You,' small business creation, basic mathematics, fitness, and nutrition.
3. Continuing education general interest courses, such as How to Start a Small Business (utilizing TV Ontario's *Front-runners* series), which were offered in 1989 as a joint venture with the Continuing Education Department, the York Business Opportunities Centre, and Graham Cable 10.

The Hub. The Hub was an adult learning resources facility staffed by a librarian and a library assistant. It was established at the D.B. Hood campus (and later relocated to the George Harvey campus) to catalogue, display, and distribute a variety of print and visual material for Adult Day School students and teachers.

Mentorship Enhancement and Employment Training. The Mentorship Enhancement and Employment Training (MEET) demonstration project recognized the need of recent immigrants and refugees to maintain contact with their former profession or trade while they were learning English. Contacts were established with mentors in business, industry, and the professions, who agreed to provide an orientation to the workplace and to advise on skill training during this period of adjustment.

Entrepreneurial Studies. In 1988 a new Ministry of Education guide-line on entrepreneurial studies was being field-tested throughout the province. A professional development program was undertaken with a selected group of ADS teachers, utilizing York Business Opportunities Centre personnel and the How to Start a Small Business distance-learning course provided through ADS Media Resources on Graham Cable 10.

Adult Day School Hybrid Programs. Students enrolling in ADS, after the regular contract staff had been assigned at the end of September, were served through continuing education provisions. These included basic literacy and ESL classes, an Action for Literacy in York evening program, education in the workplace, and a summer ADS program. The Adult Day School was unique in that it operated on a twelve-month continuous-intake basis.

Teacher Apprenticeship Programs. The percentage of adult second-ary school students in York continued to grow (more than 40 per cent by the 1990s), requiring a source of qualified teachers with maturity, sensitivity, and a breadth of experience in education and related fields. In February 1990, I proposed the establishment of the Teacher Appren-ticeship Program (TAP) demonstration project to prepare experienced teachers from other countries, and Board of Education support staff, to enter the Faculty of Education at the University of Toronto (FEUT). I had previously provided a two-course package in community edu-cation and adult education for Board support staff so that they could gain two credits from York University's Faculty of Education in order to achieve admittance into the bachelor of arts program at Atkinson College.

During the year preceding their admittance to the University of Toronto, TAP candidates would be assigned educational duties that would prepare them for acceptance and success as students at FEUT. Upon successful completion of their studies to obtain an Ontario teach-ing certificate, TAP candidates could be offered employment with the York Board of Education.

The objective of the project was to recruit ten candidates from Adult Day School ESL students, plus existing support staff, who had the nec-essary qualifications to gain admittance to FEUT. Performance would be monitored through a system of teacher-mentors and staff develop-ment activities. Teacher-mentors were selected to work with each TAP candidate during the 1990/91 pre-admittance year. Appropriate staff development activities were organized for the candidates and teacher-mentors. Candidates for the TAP program were selected by Board of Education and FEUT representatives during the spring and summer of 1990 in order to begin their TAP year in September 1990. Successful TAP candidates would gain admittance to FEUT's bachelor of education (one-year) program for 1991–2.

A TAP advisory committee was convened to meet regularly to monitor the success of the program. Membership on the committee included two teacher-mentors, the principal of ADS, two supervisory officers, a FEUT representative, two candidates from TAP, and a research and planning consultant.

Newcomers Feasibility Study. One of the follow-ups to the 1993 Teacher Apprenticeship program was the Certification and Educational Career Opportunities for Newcomers Feasibility Study, with funding provided by the Access to Professions and Trades Office led by Dr Ari Dassanayake from the Ontario Ministry of Citizenship. The focus of the project was newcomers who faced systemic barriers to teacher certification and employment because they had not been trained in Ontario. Such newcomers included experienced teachers from another country who lacked Ontario teaching certificate (OTC) standing; newcomers who had been granted OTC standing but had not achieved a teaching position because of a lack of Ontario experience; newcomers who were required to complete the consecutive year at a faculty of education but could not gain admittance due to a limited number of places available; newcomers who were required to complete one or more academic courses at a faculty of education in order to qualify for an OTC; and newcomers who were employed as educational support staff in education while attaining their academic qualifications, on a part-time basis, to prepare for admittance to the consecutive year at a faculty of education.

The project recognized the TAP success in gaining admittance for Adult Day School students and Board of Education support staff to the one-year bachelor of education program at the University of Toronto. Both the North York Board of Education and the York Board of Education had staff development programs in place to assist support staff in upgrading their academic skills through York University courses. Faculties at York University had established courses in anti-racism education (for example, at Atkinson College and the Faculty of Arts) at the undergraduate level. Together with methodology courses in the Faculty of Education, programs could be mounted that might be of particular interest to educational support staff, teachers, and administrators in order for them to have a better understanding of the issues related to access to professions and trades.

Membership of the work group that proposed the project consisted of Dean Stan Shapson, Faculty of Education, York University; Bill Hogarth, Superintendent, North York Board of Education; and myself. The coordinator of the project was Lesley Miller, on behalf of the York University Faculty of Education.

The objective of the project was to establish a four-month feasibility study to assess needs, identify barriers, and provide an inventory of resources among the following six partners: York University Faculty of Education, Atkinson College and the Faculty of Arts at York University, the Teacher Education Branch of the Ministry of Education, the North York Board of Education, the York Board of Education, and the Association of Sri Lankan Graduates of Canada.

The outcome of the project was the preparation of a report concerning the feasibility of a demonstration project to improve access to certification and educational career opportunities for newcomers.

The Learning Enrichment Foundation

In 1977, I was approached by three individuals from the York Board of Education concerning the work of the Learnxs Foundation: Bill Bayes (a trustee), Paul Martindale (a supervisory officer), and Alex Gribben a parent from Chairmen's Council (representing school and community organizations). I shared with them the history of Learnxs, including copies of the letters patent and by-laws. They wanted advice on setting up a similar organization at arm's length from the York Board. (Little did I know that I would be going there to work in August 1980 as the assistant superintendent of community services.)

In September 1978 the Learning Enrichment Foundation (LEF) was granted letters patent as a corporation without share capital. The primary object of the foundation was 'the development, support, and advancement of educational programs, experiments, and endeavours of any kind which in the opinion of the directors will promote the cause of education generally and/or benefit the community.'[120]

In its first two years LEF devoted its activities to arts enrichment in the Arlington family of schools. This was possible through a series of government grants supporting arts-enrichment projects, particularly in the more advantaged eastern section of the York Borough. They included a summer theatre program and a touring production during the school year co-sponsored by the Ontario Multicultural Theatre Association.

In January 1980 the foundation employed Eunice Grayson, an east end political activist, as its first administrator, for a six-month period. In December that year I was asked to join the foundation as the fourth member of the board of directors. The following officers were elected: W.W. Bayes, President; J.A. Gribben, Treasurer; D.E. Shuttleworth, Secretary; and P.A. Martindale, Vice-President.[121]

The Learning Enrichment Foundation's revenue for the preceding year had been about twenty thousand dollars. It was made quite clear to me by my superior, the superintendent of program, that my role was to put the foundation to bed. But I had another agenda. It was my intention to expand and diversify the LEF board of directors to be more representative of a broader spectrum of political and organizational interests in the borough. I saw LEF as a potential partner with the York Board to address social and economic needs including childcare, employment, adult education, and multicultural and race relations.

The foundation's by-laws were soon changed to increase the number of directors from four to a maximum of twelve. At LEF's annual meeting in 1982, a new board of directors was installed, consisting of Bill Bayes, President; Paul Martindale, Vice-President; Dale Shuttleworth, Secretary; Steven Mould, Trustee (west area), York Board of Education; Ruth Russell, Trustee (central area), York Board of Education; Panfilo Corvetti, COSTI Immigrant Services; Fergy Brown, Controller, Borough of York; Ian Thomson, Commissioner, York Parks and Recreation Department; Michael McDonald, citizen of Weston area; and Evelyn Pollock, citizen of Cedarvale area.[122]

It was in the early 1980s that LEF programs began to diversify.

Childcare

The York Board of Education's community liaison officers, as part of their community development role, had been responsive to local childcare needs by assisting parents in the establishment of preschool programs. By the spring of 1982 a half-day program, the Mother Goose Nursery, had been established at D.B. Hood Community School, while full-day centres were opened at J.R. Wilcox and F.H. Miller Junior Public schools. However, the Board of Education was not able to provide establishment grants, other than the free use of space, nor were these

programs incorporated as non-profit charities. The Learning Enrichment Foundation took over sponsorship of the centres, working with
parent advisory boards. New full-day centres at Humewood, Fairbank
Memorial, and Cedarvale schools were added later that year. The foundation was able to negotiate subsidy agreements with Metro Social
Services so that children of Adult Day School students could have
access to these centres. The foundation also began sponsoring ten parent and preschool ESL programs in the borough with financial support
from the Ministry of Citizenship and Culture.

Arts Enrichment

Most of LEF's activities remained in the area of arts enrichment, with
sponsorship for multicultural theatre, ballet, and opera performances
and an artist-in-residence program, using mainly short-term government grants. The annual report for 1981 had listed a deficit at the end
of the year of $5,141.[119]

Training and Employment

It soon became clear to me that if LEF were to have any future, it had to
broaden its scope beyond arts enrichment and childcare. In response to
a serious downturn in the economy, the federal government had created
the National Training Program, as a focus for short-term demonstration
projects, to provide training and jobs for the unemployed. I had also
had a wealth of experience with such projects from my Learnxs days.
Beginning in 1983, I encouraged LEF to adopt a new mandate in community economic development. A series of training and job-creation
demonstration projects were launched during 1984 and 1985 through
federal grants offered in partnership with the Adult Day School. These
grants were received primarily through the ongoing support of the
Liberal Member of Parliament for York South–Weston, Ursula Appolloni. Mrs Appolloni recognized that money invested in her riding made
good political, as well as economic, sense. A sampling of LEF job creation and training demonstration projects included:[123]

   A+ Employment Services. A+ Employment Services was a job placement agency established by LEF in February 1983 through the federal
government's Canada Community Development program. The objective of A+ was to serve the temporary or part-time employment needs

of students attending the York Board of Education's Adult Day School. These students were either learning English as a second language or doing academic upgrading. Through the grant, LEF was able to hire placement workers, who in the first ten months were able to place fifty-five ADS students in temporary positions in a variety of job areas, as well as thirty persons in permanent positions. The job placements provided students with valuable skills, as well as recent Canadian work experience to add to their résumés. During the one-year duration of the project, A+ Employment Services successfully addressed the students' need for work experience and the employers' demand for temporary workers. After the grant ran out, LEF, using funds realized from employer service fees, established A+ Temporary Services.

Weston Road Renovations. Weston Road Renovations was a one-year project, also established in February 1983, to train young people in the construction and renovation trades. It started with the restoration and repair of an old fire hall at Eglinton Avenue West and Weston Road, which was to function as the Mount Dennis Community Centre. Tradespeople were hired to serve as trainers for the eighteen young people employed in the project. All were at-risk school leavers, some of whom were living rough because of a lack of housing. An academic skills coach from ADS was added to the project.

The drab front exterior of the building soon gained an attractive Cape Cod facade. (The secretary for Borough of York Controller Fergy Brown told of encountering one of the trainees on the Eglinton Avenue bus, who said, 'See what we did to that old building. It makes us all feel proud.') The work crew soon branched out to complete similar facelifts of storefronts and other businesses along Weston Road – their own contribution to the improvement of a rather depressed neighbourhood. Again, funding was received from the Canada Community Development program (through the advocacy of Ursula Appolloni, MP, I am sure).

Illustrious Restorations. A 1984 training project for eighteen young workers, Illustrious Restorations provided academic and skills training. Five skilled tradesmen and a project manager guided the young trainees through the restoration of HMCS *Illustrious*, a Navy League drill hall on Hickory Tree Road in the Weston area. One of the training consultants was Norm Hunter, a former Glasgow bricklayer who become principal of York Humber High School. Funds for the seven-month project were obtained through the federal NEED program with the assistance of Mrs Appolloni. The *Illustrious* hall later became a site for LEF bingo fund-raising ventures.

Action for Literacy in York. This research and development project offered tutoring on a one-to-one basis to people in the community who could not attend regular ADS classes. I had received a telephone call on one Monday morning in the spring of 1983 from Mrs Appolloni, who said she had one million dollars to invest in a literacy project for unemployed teachers, preferably women. I said, 'I'll give it some thought and get back to you.' 'You don't understand,' she replied. 'I'll need a project submission by Friday.' Thus, Action for Literacy in York (ALY) was born in September that year as a six-month demonstration project with forty-nine teacher-tutors providing literacy instruction to adults in private homes or community settings such as public libraries. Most of the tutors were unemployed qualified teachers who had not been able to secure regular teaching positions. The project was deemed to be so successful that, when the federal grant ran out in March 1984, many ALY tutors were kept on by the Community Services Office through continuing education provisions. In September 1984 most of the qualified ALY staff were hired by the Adult Day School to form the new Tutorial Outreach Department.

Health Care Aides. Health Care Aides was a demonstration project for sixteen ADS students who received academic upgrading while training as health care assistants. They worked at Northwestern General Hospital, learning how to care for the elderly and disabled. Training started in September 1983, with the assistance of Mrs Appolloni and a federal NEED grant. The program was then adopted as a regular credit program by the Adult Day School. It was later expanded to include registered practical nurses training as part of the Education for the Workplace Department. The several on-the-job placements included Northwestern, West Park, and Hillcrest hospitals, and St Hilda's Towers and Villa Colombo nursing homes.

Summer Canada. Summer Canada projects in 1984 included Landscaping Upgrading, which provided skill training and academic upgrading for ten young people in landscaping care and maintenance; the training included laying the front-entrance brickwork at the *Illustrious* hall with instruction from Norm Hunter of York Humber High

School. Another project was Food Service Training, which involved four young people learning food preparation for LEF day-care centres.

Renovation/Construction. This project operated for ten months under the National Training Program. Twenty people received training in carpentry, electricity, plumbing, and masonry, as well as drafting and academic upgrading through the Adult Day School.

Childcare Assistants. The Childcare Assistants project saw fifteen young people trained to assist in LEF childcare centres while receiving academic upgrading through the Adult Day School.

Home Helpers. This project gave fifteen young people academic skills while they were training in such areas as commercial cleaning and home support for the elderly.

Industrial Maintenance. Industrial Maintenance was a six-month Canada Works program in 1985 that trained fifteen young people in maintenance techniques (including painting, minor masonry repair, landscaping, and minor carpentry repair) while they were receiving academic upgrading.

Bus Drivers. Bus Drivers was a ten-week course in bus driving, using a school bus donated by the York Lions Club.

Job Opportunities for Youth. The Learning Enrichment Foundation joined with the York Board of Education and the Ministry of Skills Development to establish the Job Opportunities for Youth (JOY) Employment Centre, serving youth in the Jane Street and Woolner Avenue area of the city. JOY staff provided employment counselling, on-the-job training (through the FUTURES program), and job placement for about one thousand young people in eighteen languages and dialects each year. Upgrading, business skills, and childcare support were provided by the Adult Day School. JOY was acknowledged as one of the most successful youth employment and counselling centres in Ontario.

Food Service Workers. Another LEF training program operated kitchen facilities at Rockcliffe Senior Public School. York Controller Fergy Brown asked the foundation to investigate the establishment of a food services training program in a hall on Weston Road that was operated by an Italian social club. The club was having difficulty maintaining the facility. With federal funding, LEF created a commercial kitchen for the preparation of meals for the childcare centres and trained food service workers. By sharing expenses, the social club was able to continue to operate.

York Community Economic Development Committee

As previously described in chapter 11, community economic development is 'a plan of action to build new resources, which will strengthen the local community internally as well as its relations with the larger world.' In 1983–4, one thousand jobs had been lost in York because of plant closures. Consequently, in August 1984, as secretary of LEF I was approached by the federal Department of Employment and Immigration to convene another social enterprise, a local committee of adjustment under provisions of their Industrial Adjustment Service program. The main objective of the committee was 'to identify local needs and resources in order to develop a strategy to improve the economic well-being of the City of York.'[124]

During that fall, the foundation approached the major governmental, labour, and business interests in the city of York to become financial sponsors in the project. In December a memorandum of agreement was signed by the following partners to create the York Community Economic Development Committee: the City of York, the York Board of Education, the York Association of Industry, the United Steelworkers of America (District 6, Subdistrict 23), the Learning Enrichment Foundation, the Ontario Ministry of Labour, and Employment and Immigration Canada. This was the first such committee to be formed in a large metropolitan area in Canada.

The work of the committee was divided into two main sections: research and development. The Research work group, chaired by Controller Fergy Brown, conducted a survey of existing industries, as well as those that had left the city in the previous two-year period. Key factors drawn from the surveys were as follows:

1. Almost 50 per cent of firms surveyed felt that they could benefit from further training or retraining of staff.
2. Most industries had established in York because of its central accessible location, reasonable rents, available space, good labour pool, and potential for marketing products.

3. Negative aspects of the location included the small size of accommodation, inadequate space for delivery and parking, city building and zoning restrictions, and close proximity to residential properties.
4. Commercial growth had been encouraged, to the perceived detriment of industrial development.
5. Most respondents were able to access city services; however, some experienced difficulty in obtaining information and building permits.
6. Most industries had left York because of a need for more and better space, the high operating costs including taxes and rents, inadequate municipal services, residential versus industrial conflicts, inadequate public transportation, and traffic problems.
7. Suggested areas for improvement included more space for expansion; better public transit; a streamlining of procedures to obtain Planning and Building Departmental approvals; resolution of industrial-residential land use problems; improved access to local employment and training services; better communication between municipal, small business, and industrial interests; and more access to financial and other forms of support.

I chaired the Development work group, which was established to identify and bring a focus to the needs of new industry wishing to locate in York, as well as to assist existing industries with their employment and training requirements. Its membership included persons from the committee and interested individuals from the governmental, commercial, and voluntary sectors. During the period from January to December 1985, contacts were established with potential new employers through a variety of sources:

Real Estate Agents. Liaison was maintained with real estate agents who were showing property in York or who were aware of businesses or industries seeking accommodation. Prime examples of such companies were Faema Company Limited (distributor of restaurant equipment) and Darrigo Foods. In each case, as chairman of the work group, I met with the companies or individuals concerning their needs and was able to offer assistance regarding possible zoning amendments and the requirements of the building code. An updated inventory of vacant industrial space prepared by the committee's research consultant was invaluable in this process. As a result of these efforts, both Darrigo Foods and Faema Company Limited presented offers to purchase the former Hayhoe building at Castlefield Avenue and Caledonia

Road. Although neither bid was successful, Faema Company Limited later purchased a vacant property at 3434 Dundas Street West to found Euro-Milan Inc., a food service and distribution operation scheduled to employ at least fifty workers.

Personal Networks. The Development work group chairman, and other committee members, utilized their own personal network of business contacts to identify potential new employers wishing to locate in York. As a result of this networking process, the following companies were assisted in finding a possible location in the city:

New Line Motors. This company assembled a three-wheeled light delivery vehicle from Italy that was produced by Piaggio Inc., called the Vespacar, and was represented in York by Maurizio Cochi of One Stop Auto. This contact later developed into an LEF federal job-creation and skill-training project called Hornet Express Delivery. A courier service, utilizing two leased Vespacars, employed a group of six women who learned to deliver letters and small packages for business, industry, and other local clients, such as the City of York and the Board of Education. The small vans were painted with yellow and black stripes and even had two antennae on each cab. Their motto was 'Just give us a buzz' (*vespa* means 'wasp' in Italian).

New York Environment and Royal Automobiles. These New York City–based companies, led by George Kryssing, were interested in relocating their operations – the importing and federalizing of luxury automobiles from Europe for sale in the North American market. The relocation would involve the creation of a retrofit and conversion facility and an emission-controls testing laboratory. Significant amounts of time and effort, including visits to Ottawa and New York City, were expended to establish the feasibility of the project. Owing to the decline in value of the United States dollar (versus European currency) and the tightening governmental controls, it was decided that it would not be a viable business venture in the near future.

Youth Ventures Recycling Inc. This worker-owned cooperative that recycled waste paper was formerly established on the Toronto waterfront (see chapter 11). It was interested in relocating to York to avail itself of inexpensive accommodation and employee-training opportunities. The cooperative's sixteen employees collected waste paper from commercial and industrial sources to be sorted, baled, and sold to paper mills for reprocessing. There was also interest in re-establishing a residential newsprint operation to employ another fifteen worker-trainees through the Learning Enrichment Foundation. A suitable space was found on Bertal Avenue. However, City planners and building officials interpreted the by-laws to exclude this industrial use in York, even though the zoning of the area permitted the manufacture of paper, paper boxes, and cellulose, and one of York's largest industries manufactured and stored thousands of tons of paper tissues on the premises. Although Youth Ventures was in the business of processing, not storing, paper, its application was denied. The company subsequently leased a building nearby in North York, resulting in a loss of tax revenue and employment for the city of York.

Saratoga Solar Systems Ltd. and PLP Log Homes. These associated firms in Saratoga Springs, New York, produced and marketed energy-efficient windows and prefabricated log homes. There was potential for the windows, which utilized a new energy-reflecting film developed by the 3M Company, to be manufactured in York for the North American market. Homes constructed of specially machined logs could also be produced.

Bio-Char Inc. This Mississauga-based company, led by Cliff Kerr, manufactured and installed incinerators and waste management systems. In 1984 it acquired a steam plant in Ajax that had been converted to burn waste wood. York and the Downsview area were major sources of waste wood in the region, and there was interest in developing a wood-processing operation to supply the Ajax plant. Agreement was reached to locate such an operation in York, in cooperation with the Learning Enrichment Foundation, and to employ at least fifteen worker-trainees in wood processing and boiler manufacturing.

International Hydro Home Appliances. Discussions were held with this Vancouver-based company concerning the manufacture of the Ecotech dishwasher, a revolutionary new home appliance that won the Daily Mail Blue Ribbon Award in March 1985 at the Ideal Home Exhibition in London, England. The potential to develop a plastic-injection-mould operation to produce this product in the city of York was investigated.

Marilyn Brooks. Investigations were undertaken to develop a computer-assisted design centre in York to serve the fashion industry. Such a facility would require a major investment of venture capital and employment and training funds from senior levels of government.

Non-profit Housing. Discussions were undertaken concerning the possible development of housing on a six-acre site owned by the York Board of Education on Clouston Avenue. Affordable accommodation would be provided for seniors, disabled persons, and families. The building would also house a day-care centre (for infants to five-year-olds), adult education, and recreation space and serve as a training facility for Learning Enrichment Foundation programs in health care aides, day-care assistants, and homemaker services. Area residents, elected officials, municipal departments, and community volunteers were to be involved in the planning process.

Other Contacts. Contacts were also made with the following parties: Yen Tyan Machinery Ltd. (Taiwan), Daihatsu Company (Japan), Magna International, Metro Sportswear, DeTomaso Pantera (USA), and Graham Cable concerning the possible use of vacant industrial space in York.

Entrepreneurial Training Centre

The Learning Enrichment Foundation leased 16,800 square feet of vacant industrial space at 81 Industry Street from Kodak Canada to create the Entrepreneurial Training Centre (ETC), as a small-business incubator. This was made possible through a National Training program grant from Employment and Immigration Canada to train renovation and construction workers. Trainees began renovating the premises, in October 1984, to create small units to be occupied by January 1985. Entrepreneurs were to be offered space at a very reasonable rental rate, clerical services provided by business education students from the Adult Day School, access to computers, and the services of a small-business consultant. The ETC would provide support to the new businesses during their crucial first twenty-four months of operation. The businesses would then be encouraged to relocate to other vacant industrial spaces in York.

After the program had been established, the City of York Building and Planning departments made a decision that rezoning of the site was necessary for a training facility, even though Humber College operated a branch across the street and had never been required to rezone.

It was not until 11 July 1985 that the rezoning was finally approved. Building permits, which could not be applied for until after rezoning, were then requested. However, on picking up building permits at City Hall, the project manager was informed, for the first time, that Ontario Ministry of Labour must also approve the site because the ETC was to be located on the second floor of the building. Then, inspection by the Ministry of Labour revealed that the building had a wooden roof, which limited the building's use. Space for each entrepreneur would require a separate application to the Ministry of Labour as each business had different standard building requirements. Finally, the building was judged unfit for an entrepreneurial training centre, and new premises had to be found. As a result, the Learning Enrichment Foundation lost thousands of dollars of potential revenue to operate the centre, and seventy entrepreneurs trained in the ETC program were denied space to establish new businesses.

York Business Opportunities Centre

The Learning Enrichment Foundation applied to the Ontario Ministry of Industry, Trade, and Technology for a grant to establish a small-business incubator in York as a result of its previous experience with the Entrepreneurial Training Centre. In December 1985, the foundation was granted $585,000 by the Ministry to establish 20,000 square feet of accommodation in a building that would house a small-business information centre as well as incubator space for forty small businesses, creating 160 jobs over the next three years. It was hoped that the Humber College Innovation Centre might also occupy space in the new facility. Business education students and teachers would provide clerical and administrative support services for York Business Opportunities Centre (YBOC) tenants through the Adult Day School.

A challenge for YBOC was the provision of childcare services for workers and trainees. The optimum space for the facility was the former office suite at the front of the building. This decision was opposed by York Mayor Alan Tonks and YBOC Manager Bram Zinman (a Tonks campaign worker), who felt that having a day-care centre at the front of the building was unbusinesslike. They used zoning restrictions to block the building permit, because childcare was not allowed in industrial areas.

The Learning Enrichment Foundation launched an appeal and began a campaign to raise public awareness of the need for childcare in the workplace. When the issue came before York Council, many childcare advocates were assembled, including Child-in-the-City researchers from the University of Toronto and a reporter from the *Globe and Mail*. Not only was the LEF building permit for the YBOC childcare centre approved, but the by-law was also revised to allow childcare in the workplace throughout the city.

Support for Existing Employers

As Development work group chairman, I sent out a letter of introduction to 378 businesses and industries in York, offering assistance with identifying sources of venture capital and financial investment, applying for zoning and building permits, arranging training and educational programs for employees, finding accommodations to expand or relocate existing businesses, and starting new enterprises. As a result, responses were received from twenty-two businesses requesting some form of assistance. Following are examples of the assistance provided:

Standard Modern Technologies. This well-known industry in the machine technology field had the dubious distinction of being the last machine-lathe manufacturer in Canada. Its lines of training lathes were sold to schools and colleges across the continent. In December 1984, Standard Modern Technologies experienced severe financial problems, which affected the continuing viability of the company. As work group chairman, I met with the president of Standard Modern concerning additional sources of financial support as well as the training needs of his employees for their future opportunities in the machine maintenance service area. As a result of these discussions, a Machine Technologies Training (MacTECH) project team was established, consisting of representatives from Humber College, the York Board of Education, and Standard Modern Technologies. A new certificate program in machine technologies for secondary school and Adult Day School students was offered in September 1986 by Humber College, utilizing space at George Harvey Collegiate Institute and Standard Modern. A description of the MacTECH alternative project is to be found in chapter 12. Standard Modern also started to quote to school boards on the machine maintenance and retrofitting of machine shop classrooms, with very encouraging results.

Italian Food Services. The City of York and the Metropolitan Toronto region accommodated about one thousand food-service outlets (restaurants, cafes, banquet halls, and catering firms) specializing in Italian cuisine and employing more than five thousand persons. There was no food-service training program for persons working in this industry, who required a specialized set of skills in such areas as food-equipment operation, restaurant service, fast-food service, catering, and banquet service. In Italy, such skills are taught through an apprenticeship program in the private sector. As Development work group chairman, I met with proprietors of several restaurants and banquet halls to discuss their needs for sources of trained personnel. As a result, a submission was made to Employment and Immigration Canada by the Learning Enrichment Foundation to establish an Italian Food Services Training program, utilizing available space in the Dufferin Street and Eglinton Avenue West area.

Bauhaus Designs. The rapidly expanding upholstered-furniture manufacturer Bauhaus exported to both the United States and Europe. The firm had an ongoing need for persons to train as upholsterers and had difficulty acquiring such trainees. Through cooperation with the Learning Enrichment Foundation's JOY Employment Centre, A+ Employment Services, and the Adult Day School, prospective employees were recruited, and a six-week in-house training program established. Bauhaus trained to its own specifications, while the Adult Day School provided educational upgrading, ESL, and life-skills instruction in the workplace.

Industrial Sewing. In the previous few years, the city of York had become known as Spadina North because of the number of companies relocating from the traditional garment district in the Spadina Avenue area of the city of Toronto. Manufacturers were concerned that many of the southern European women who had been the backbone of the industry were reaching retirement age. As a result, the Industrial Sewing Advisory Committee was established in cooperation with the Learning Enrichment Foundation. The following industries participated on the committee: Nash Pant, Metro Sportswear, Cambridge Clothes, and Banff Wear. An application was subsequently approved by Employment and Immigration Canada for LEF to provide an Industrial Sewing Training program in straight needle and surger operation.

LEF Employment-Training Programs. Through training funds provided by federal and provincial governments, the Learning Enrichment Foundation mounted entry-level training programs, according to the needs identified by local employers, for renovation and construction workers, industrial maintenance workers, home helpers, health care aides, courier and light delivery workers, clerical service workers, food service workers, bus drivers, and childcare assistants. The JOY Centre and A+ Employment Services handled recruitment for the programs in consultation with local employers, and the Adult Day School provided academic upgrading, ESL, and life skills in the workplace. During 1985, 275 worker-trainees were employed in these programs.

Weston Machine & Tool Limited. This auto parts manufacturer, associated with Magna International, hoped to expand its operations in the city of York. The work group made representation to try to keep the company in the city and to provide trained machine operators and apprentice toolmakers through the previously mentioned Machine Technologies Training (MacTECH) project.

Venture Capital and Other Assistance

Extensive work was carried out to find sources of venture capital for new and expanding businesses. Examples of such initiatives follow:

Government Grants and Loans. An inventory of existing federal and provincial grants and interest-free or low-interest loans was developed. Consultations and referrals were undertaken with several business ventures concerning their qualifications for such assistance.

Small Business Development Corporation. The Province on Ontario maintained a program whereby investors could receive tax credits of 30 per cent on investment in a new small business development corporation (SBDC). This seemed a very attractive way to secure a pool of investment capital for new local businesses in the manufacturing and resource industries. The feasibility of establishing an SBDC in York in cooperation with the municipal government was investigated.

Entrepreneurial Skills. As previously mentioned, the LEF Entrepreneurial Training Centre, in cooperation with the York Board of Education, provided two ten-week courses in 1985, How to Start a Small Business, which attracted seventy participants. As well as learning to develop a business plan, trainees received individual assistance from a business consultant concerning their proposed ventures. In addition, a training program in worker-owned cooperatives was undertaken, utilizing the resources of the Worker Ownership Development Foundation.

MICROTRON Centre

The MICROTRON Centre was a demonstration project resulting from my administrative exchange in 1985 (see chapter 14) that was sponsored by the Ministry of Education, the Ontario Association of Education Administration Officers, and the United Kingdom Society of Education Officers. My exchange partner was Norman Dennis, Deputy Director of Education for the Borough of Bury in Manchester, England. During the three weeks I spent in Bury, I was most impressed by their staff-training program for teacher computer literacy. The program included a large fully equipped mobile training unit who moved from school to school, instructing teachers in the use of computers in the classroom.

When I returned to York, I began working with Geoff Day, the Board of Education's Computers-in-the-Classroom consultant, and Norm Dale, Technical Education Consultant, to establish a microelectronic training facility. The MICROTRON Centre opened in 1986 as a training centre for microcomputer skills; word and numerical processing; computer-assisted design, graphics, and styling; and electronic assembly and repair. The Board of Education, Commodore Business Machines, Comspec Systems, Corel Systems, the Learning Enrichment Foundation, York Business Opportunities Centre, and Humber College jointly sponsored the centre.

The MICROTRON Centre occupied three classrooms at Vaughan Road Collegiate, which had been renovated and equipped (including air conditioning) for year-round use during the day and evening. The facility served York Board employees, small business and industry (as identified by the York Community Economic Development Committee's survey), government departments, voluntary organizations, and the community at large. Operating funds were provided through professional development and continuing education provisions. The Adult Day School provided an academic skills coach for students in the microelectronic assembly and repair program.

MICROTRON Bus

The MICROTRON Bus was the outreach strategy for the MICROTRON

Centre. The Learning Enrichment Foundation provided a school bus that had been originally used for driver training (the million-miler from Humber College was donated by the York Lions Club). A local boat-building firm undertook the bus conversion during slow times, with the help of funds donated by Comspec Systems. The result was a gleaming white covered van with red-and-blue graphics and sponsor logos prominently displayed.

The eight workstations in the bus used equipment and software donated by Commodore Business Machines and Corel Systems. It functioned as a mobile community education facility, with operating expenses borne through the continuing education budget formula. The bus visited schools, business and industry, service organizations, and public housing projects to provide training in information technology, robotics, computer-assisted design, and desktop publishing.

Each employer or organization using the service was responsible for hydro hook-ups, including heat and air conditioning, and a fee for instructional hours. After each day's activities and on weekends, the bus was secured within the heated interior loading dock of the York Business Opportunities Centre.

Outcomes and Reflections

While York had long been a reception centre for newcomers, especially after the Second World War, it was during the 1980s that a concentration of impoverished immigrants from southern Europe, particularly Italy, began to have a profound impact on the nature of the education service in the borough. Most of these newcomers resided in the central section of the municipality, but the political power base was to found in the eastern area along the Cedarvale Ravine, sometimes referred to as Forest Hill West. (Forest Hill is an exclusive enclave in Toronto.) Other influential political areas were located in the northwest, which encompassed the former town of Weston, and to some extent in the southwest sector near the Humber River. Mostly long-time residents of Canada populated all of these economically advantaged areas, which made for a struggle between the needs of the haves and the have-nots.

The Community Services portfolio was seen by the progressives as a means to address these disparities. Participants in the traditionally more advantaged power structure seemed more resistant to the changes required to address the diverse needs of the poor. The situation became further complicated when the Italians and other Europeans began to move north and west, to be replaced by West Indians, Latin

Americans, and South Asians – people of colour. Nor were the trustees, senior officials, and other administrators very reflective of the changing demographics.

It was the mandate of the Community Services Office to create policies and programs that could make a difference in these new realities. One approach was to strengthen community and multicultural education services for the regular students. Another was to embark on new service strategies designed to address social and economic inequities across the municipality. Providing disadvantaged adults with better access to literacy, language, and employability skills was seen as a means to improve the quality of family life. The Adult Day School and the Learning Enrichment Foundation were vehicles to begin to achieve these objectives.

The original proposal to expand and enrich adult education opportunities was not supported, at first, by my supervisory officer colleagues. It was due to the intervention and leadership skills of Director John Phillips that the Adult Day School was approved as a regular secondary school under the Ontario Secondary School Teachers Federation contract. He was also the champion in gaining approvals at the Metropolitan Toronto School Board and with the Ministry of Education. Other strong supporters of ADS were found among trustees such as Steven Mould and Harriet Wolman.

Another essential factor contributing to the success of the Adult Day School was the truly inspirational leadership provided by principals Norm Hunter and Carolyn Collyer during the 1980s and Milan Crepp in the 1990s. Following ADS's lead, regular secondary schools began to establish adult classes to offset declining enrolments. By the mid 1990s, almost 45 per cent of York secondary school students were adults – by far the largest proportion of any school board in Canada.

The Adult Day School's strategic partner in combining education and economic development was the Learning Enrichment Foundation. Although LEF was originally established in 1978 as an arts enrichment organization, mostly serving the more advantaged eastern section of York, it blossomed in the 1980s to join with ADS in serving the diverse needs of York's impoverished families. However, LEF had had difficulty getting off the ground. In the beginning it was seen as an alien body, particularly among some supervisory officers, school administrators, and some trustees who were not proponents of more school-community involvement. I certainly felt an lack of support for continuance when I arrived in 1980. Again with the support of Director Phillips and Trus-

tees Wolman, Mould, and Beyes, I was able to encourage the enlarge-
ment and diversification of the LEF's board of directors, while adding
more political strength.

What began to make a difference for the Learning Enrichment Foundation, aside from its arts enrichment activities, was the school-based
childcare centres, which helped the elementary schools that were facing declining enrolment and provided subsidized spaces for children
of ADS students. The foundation also opened infant-care centres in
secondary schools (for example, Vaughan Road and George Harvey
schools) to complement the family studies programs. By 1992, there
were thirteen LEF centres in schools, and the York Business Opportunities Centre.

Other important features in what became known internationally as
the York Model combining community education and economic development were the employment and training programs, most of which
had an ADS academic skills component. Utilizing a series of short-term
federal and provincial job-creation and training grants, LEF was able
to respond to community needs, such as those identified by the York
Community Economic Development Committee. As a third-sector
social enterprise, the Learning Enrichment Foundation became one
of the largest employers in the city, with a projected budget of more
than $15 million in 1994, providing more than one thousand full and
part-time jobs. Credit for these accomplishments must be given to LEF
Administrator Eunice Grayson, her creative staff, and the dedicated
board of directors.

Surviving in a challenging political environment was not easy. As
LEF's contribution to the community expanded from revenues of less
than $20,000 in 1981 to more than $10 million ten years later, some
municipal politicians and officials often viewed the foundation as a
threat. The York Model was gaining publicity and praise throughout
Ontario, Canada, the United States, Europe, and even Asia because
of a series of articles that I had written in journals and periodicals. Its
high profile was not always appreciated by some of my senior official
colleagues and trustees at the school board and some civic politicians
(including the mayor) and department heads.

In the case of the York Community Economic Development Committee (which I had helped to create), some City officials viewed the
Development work group (which I chaired) with distrust and hostility. When efforts were made to gain cooperation and assistance for
such projects as the Entrepreneurial Training Centre, Youth Ventures

Recycling Inc., and Bio-Char Inc., the officials' reaction was most often defensive with marginal cooperation and, in some instances, outright harassment. Another example was the childcare facility at the York Business Opportunities Centre. Although strongly opposed by Mayor Tonks, the Learning Enrichment Foundation and the Development work group were able to mount sufficient political pressure to have the by-law changed at city council to allow childcare in all industrial zones throughout the city. As a result, the mayor addressed the York Board of Education in a private session (aided by at least one of my supervisory officer colleagues) in order to try to gain control of LEF and discredit my role. Thanks to the strong intervention of Trustee Steven Mould, the Board of Education chose not to accept the mayor's recommendations.

As previously mentioned, the York community economic development committee became a model for similar projects, both in Canada and beyond. We held consultations with groups in Sudbury, Kirkland Lake, Cochrane–Iroquois Falls, London, Kingston, Peterborough, Windsor, Ottawa-Carleton, as well as in other municipalities in Metropolitan Toronto. The York Model was also influential in Victoria and Nanaimo (British Columbia), Winnipeg (Manitoba), Montreal and Québec City (Quebec), and Halifax-Dartmouth and Lunenburg (Nova Scotia). I gave addresses in London and Manchester, England. In 1986 the concept was featured in Chicago at a major conference on literacy that was sponsored by the United States government. Finally, the government of Ontario asked me, as the Development work group chairman, to prepare a strategy to extend community economic development to municipalities across the province.

York was the first municipality, within a large metropolitan area, to be chosen by Employment and Immigration Canada to host an industrial committee of adjustment. This gave us the opportunity to bring together, for the first time, the key players in the governmental, commercial, and voluntary sectors. As each of the partners was also required to invest in the enterprise, there was a much stronger sense of commitment. Unfortunately, it also occurred during a time of unprecedented federal, provincial, and municipal upheaval, resulting in a continuing sense of uncertainty and instability, which did not help the developmental process. In spite of all these frustrations, the committee survived and prospered as a model for others to emulate.

There was a new sense of cooperation among the three economic sectors, resulting in such accomplishments as the York Business Opportunities Centre, joint education and training initiatives, a more productive use of industrial space, and the creation of new enterprises, which resulted in increased tax revenue and a much better sense of hope and well-being for the future of York.

What were the implications of such social enterprise activities to contemporary education? The York Board of Education during the 1980s was faced with several challenges, including a large, impoverished, ESL immigrant and refugee population to be served; declining enrolment and residential tax revenue, which was particularly affected by the potential transferral of Catholic students to the Metropolitan Separate School Board; a continuing decline in the number of industrial and commercial ratepayers whose taxes were essential to the City's economic well-being, including its education budget; and a declining manufacturing and service sector in the city, resulting in a corresponding decline in job opportunities for residents – both school leavers and their parents.

Social enterprises such as the partnership of the Adult Day School and the Learning Enrichment Foundation, and the York Community Economic Development Committee, helped to attract and retain students to the school board; they attracted new employment opportunities to the city, while retaining existing jobs, and stabilized the tax base needed to maintain municipal services, including schooling. However, there was always a danger that such social enterprises could become politicized and used as vehicles to enhance the personal political ambitions of individuals rather than the interests of community social and economic well-being. The fact that social enterprise works 'both sides of the street' can be an advantage as well as a disadvantage.

14 Building an Enterprising Culture

British Connections

The York Model combining community education and economic development was beginning to be recognized both nationally and internationally. I had also written a number of articles published in journals and periodicals, and several chapters in books, relating to the York experience. One outcome (as previously described in chapter 12) was an administrative exchange between the City of York and the Metropolitan Borough of Bury (Greater Manchester), Lancashire, England. The Ministry of Education, the Ontario Association of Education Administrative Officials, and the Society of Education Officers in the United Kingdom sponsored the exchange. During the month of June 1985, I spent three weeks in Bury and one week in London, studying innovative practice in community education and economic development. My exchange partner, Norman Dennis, Deputy Director of Education in Bury, visited York in the spring of 1986 to complete the exchange.

Bury, the smallest of the ten metropolitan boroughs in Greater Manchester, had a population of about 176,000. During the late nineteenth and early twentieth centuries Bury was a centre for the spinning and weaving of cotton. With the decline of cotton mills, Bury became a centre for the manufacture of paper products, using pulpwood from Scandinavia. This industry had also declined, and the borough had many vacant industrial sites and a serious problem of unemployment, particularly among youth (not unlike the City of York).

My exchange visit to the United Kingdom included some of the following learning highlights:

Secondary Education. While the Bury Local Education Authority (LEA) maintained fifteen comprehensive high schools (for ages twelve to sixteen years), of which four were denominational, 69 per cent of students did not continue on to sixth-form colleges to prepare for university or polytechnic entrance.

Youth and Community Services. The Local Education Authority employed a number of youth and community workers, who staffed full-time youth and community centres or operated part-time programs in various locations throughout the borough. The service provided financial assistance to voluntary organizations and individuals, maintained central equipment stores, provided training courses for adults and young people, and organized various activities and projects. The staff also had a major responsibility to serve young adults without permanent employment.

By comparison to the work of York's community liaison officers, the Bury service was not related to school and community development, and included many of the activities undertaken by the Recreation Department in York. It was interesting, however, that the service was the responsibility of the education authority.

Youth Training Scheme. The major source of innovation and funding in British education appeared to be the Manpower Services Commission (MSC), not the Department of Education and Science. The Youth Training Scheme was introduced in 1983 to provide high-school leavers with employment experience in business and industry or the public sector. The scheme guaranteed thirty-nine weeks of planned work and practical experience as well as thirteen weeks of off-the-job training and education. Trainees received a training allowance, holiday entitlement, travel expenses, and, at the end of the program, a Youth Training Scheme certificate.

All funding from the Manpower Services Commission went to the employer, not the education authority. The employer could choose to contract with a Local Education Authority for the training and education component, use a private sector organization, or undertake this responsibility itself. In many ways, the York Board of Education had a parallel to the Youth Training Scheme through the Learning Enrichment Foundation employment-training programs in cooperation with the Adult Day School. However, the Youth Training Scheme in the United Kingdom represented a comprehensive alternative preparation system for youth that did not necessarily involve schooling or the education authority.

Technical and Vocational Education Initiative. The Technical and Vocational Education Initiative (TVEI) was another major innovation introduced by the Manpower Services Commission in 1982 to provide vocational education across the curriculum. Local Education Authorities had to compete for funding from MSC on a contractual basis.

Bury had established a TVEI project in four high schools, one sixth form college, and the College of Further Education. In general, students could choose the TVEI option, which included the core academic subjects and technological training in such areas as craft, design, and technology (CDT), computing, control and modular technology, and microelectronics. The CDT program, which replaced industrial arts at the high school level, was a multidisciplinary approach that focused on individual projects. It required students to invent, design, and fabricate a product using a variety of materials and technology (for example, hydraulics, pneumatics, and microelectronics). Students also received dramatic arts and experiential learning components, including work experience and outdoor education, through Project Trident, a joint undertaking of private industry and the Local Education Authority. This became a model for York's MacTECH project.

Innovation and Technology Centre. The Local Education Authority established the Innovation and Technology Centre (Itech Centre) in a vacant primary school. The Itech Centre offered three main areas of training: microcomputing, word-processing and business skills, and electronics and microcomputer repair. With reference to the latter, the Authority awarded the contract for the maintenance of its microcomputer equipment to the Itech Centre. The centre served the training needs of the TVEI and YTS programs, as well as the retraining of employees from local business and industry. The Itech Centre influenced the creation of York's facility for community education and staff development, the MICROTRON Centre, with its microelectronic assembly and repair training program.

Professional Development. A teachers' centre was established to provide a variety of short in-service training courses for teachers, in addition to giving support to schools through the loan of instructional materials and audio-visual services. A microelectronics centre provided courses related to microcomputers, electronics, and control technology. Teachers in craft, design, and technology received retraining in a microtechnologies van operated by a local polytechnic. Application was made to Manpower Services Commission in June 1985 to establish the TVEI-related In-service Training Scheme (TRIST), which greatly increased resources for professional development. It should be noted that these provisions related to teaching, not to support staff. The microtechnologies van provided inspiration for the MICROTRON Bus as a mobile community education and economic development initiative serving the city of York.

Arts Enrichment. For several years Bury had operated a very successful instrumental music program on Saturday mornings, using facilities in a vacant primary school. Students from across the borough attended these classes, which were offered by regular teaching staff. The program had been an important source of enrichment for talented students and for those from low-income homes where private lessons were not possible. It provided the impetus in York for integrated arts programs on Saturday mornings at George Harvey Collegiate and during the summer at the Pine River Outdoor Education Centre.

London Visitations. During the week spent in the London area, I visited a number of agencies serving unemployed youth, which included Project Full Employ, Business in the Community, and the National Council of Voluntary Organizations. In particular, at the Centre for Employment Initiatives I had a meeting with the director, Colin Ball, which resulted in an article in their journal *Initiatives* concerning the York Model. Colin later nominated me to represent Canada on a youth employment study group being formed at the Organisation for Economic Co-operation and Development in Paris. Other visits included the Open University in Milton Keynes, the National Extension College in Cambridge, and the British Broadcasting Corporation to learn more about distance education and the use of television to promote adult basic literacy and numeracy. This visit was particularly relevant to the Adult Day School's *Return to Learn* and LWL-TV projects.

Community Education Development Centre. A colleague, Wally Coulthard, who was a supervisory officer with the East York Board of Education, had also been involved in a study tour to Britain to learn more about community education. I had suggested that he see the

Community Education Development Centre (CEDC) in Coventry. In March1986,JohnRennie,CEDC'sdirector,visitedToronto.Wally,John,and I met over lunch to discuss experiences in community education and development. I was impressed and inspired by the work that John and the CEDC were doing in England and Wales. An ongoing personal and professional relationship was forged between the CEDC, the Community Services Office, and the Learning Enrichment Foundation in the city of York. We continued to meet regularly during the 1980s and 1990s through conferences of the National Community Education Association in the United States, the International Community Education Association (which was hosted by the CEDC), and ongoing exchange visits.

One With Nature Society. During subsequent visits to Britain I met with Dom Gregson, Chief Executive Officer of Robermap UK, and John Rennie, Director of the Community Education Development Centre, to found a new British not-for-profit society to address such environmental issues as the availability of landfill space and air quality and, in particular, the recycling of household waste. Based on technology and procedures perfected in Ontario, the One With Nature Society (OWN) promoted the adoption of the blue-box recycling system to sort household waste (for example, paper, glass, and metal containers and plastics) at the source. Composters provided an alternative for the disposal of vegetation from gardens and lawns. An extensive community education campaign was envisioned to involve householders, schools, business, and industry in each municipal authority implementing the OWN system. Youth employment was encouraged in developing and maintaining the system and in the manufacturing of boxes and composters. The OWN system was to be developed in cooperation with the Community Education Development Centre in Coventry, municipal councils, trusts, local voluntary organizations, business, and industry.

Sri Lankan Experience

In September 1986, I was notified by the Académie Diplomatique de la Paix (World Diplomatic Corps) in Brussels that I had been awarded the 1986 Dag Hammarskjöld Gold Medal for achievements in the fields of education and science. The Académie Diplomatique de la Paix had been founded in 1963 'to honour and promote the ideals embodied in the United Nations charter and the work of the late revered Secretary

General of the U.N., Swedish diplomat and recipient of the 1961 Nobel Prize, Dag Hammarskjöld. The basic purpose of the Academy of Peace is to further the cause of world peace and human progress by encouraging and recognizing individual achievements in diplomacy, arts, letters, science and cultural relations that enhance the goal.'[125]

Made up of diplomats from more than seventy countries, the Académie Diplomatique is a private, non-governmental, non-profit organization dedicated to the welfare of human kind. Past recipients of the gold medal had included Dr Christian Barnard, Peter Ustinov, Neil Armstrong, Bob Geldof, Leonard Bernstein, Harry Belafonte, and Lech Walesa. The 1986 recipients included Brian Urquhart, former United Nations secretary general; Olaf Palma, former prime minister of Sweden, posthumous; Maurice Strong; Mother Teresa; and Dr Haing Ngor, Oscar winner from the film *The Killing Fields*.

Another former recipient, Professor Dr Anton Jayasuryia, Chairman of the Sri Lankan delegation, put my name forward as president of the Learning Enrichment Foundation. I am sure, however, that Dr Ari Dassanayake of the Ontario Ministry of Citizenship originally nominated me. The presentation was made during the twenty-fifth anniversary celebration of the awards on 20 September 1986 at the Bandaranike Memorial International Conference Hall in Colombo, Sri Lanka.

During the week spent in Sri Lanka, I met many diplomats, government officials, and other delegates from around the world, including a very prominent Sri Lankan industrialist, D.B. 'Buddy' Wethasinghe, Chairman of Electro-Plastics Limited. Buddy Wethasinghe was most interested in replicating the York Business Opportunities Centre and the MICROTRON Centre in Colombo. Besides his industrial interests, he was an active volunteer in the Buddhist community and a leading member of the Colombo Lions Club.

When I returned to Toronto, I approached the Canadian International Development Agency (CIDA) concerning a possible technology-transfer Starter Study between Colombo and York. The objectives of the project were to explore the feasibility of establishing the Colombo Business Opportunities Centre as a small-business incubation and training facility based on the LEF model; to explore the feasibility of establishing a free trade zone in the city of York based on the Colombo model; to visit business and governmental contacts related to the above objectives; and to explore other trading and technological transfer opportunities that might exist in Sri Lanka related to Canadian goods, services, and technical expertise (for example, industrial sewing; furniture; machine technologies; electrical, plastics and computer products; and educational, health, and childcare services).

Arriving at Canadian International Development Agency offices in Ottawa, as a representative of the York Board of Education I first approached the institutional grants officer. I was told, politely, that all funding for institutional applicants had already been expended. When I went down the hall to the non-governmental organizations office, I changed hats to become the president of the Learning Enrichment Foundation. Alas, I received a similar response – all the money had been taken. 'What is left?' I pleaded. 'The Commercial Section,' I was told. When I got to meet Lance Bailey at that office, the first question he asked was, 'Who are you?' 'I'm a business,' I replied. 'Well, let's sit to discuss your proposal,' said Mr Bailey.

The result was a Starter Study grant of $13,000 to the Learning Enrichment Foundation for the York-Colombo Business Opportunities Training Project. This involved a ten-day exploratory visit to Colombo in June 1987 by Dr Dassanayake and me, followed by a twelve-day visit to York in July by Buddy Wethasinghe and Thilan Wijesinghe, a consultant from Coopers & Lybrand in Colombo.

There was a strong interest, among Sri Lankan government officials and the business sector, in the York Model owing to the influx of unskilled, unemployed workers migrating to Colombo from rural areas. The project would offer training in entry-level skills, and small-business incubation, to provide employment opportunities for the migrant workers. Experience gained from the ADS-LEF training programs, such as the MICROTRON Centre and the York Business Opportunities Centre, was seen as a key component of a similar community education and economic development facility for Colombo.

The City of York hoped to gain from studying the Colombo free trade zone and from other trading and technological transfer opportunities between the two cities. Unfortunately by the beginning of the 1990s, the increasing number of terrorist attacks within Colombo by Tamil separatists made the future viability of the project seem untenable.

Organizing Technology Transfer in Ontario

In 1984, I was elected president of the Ontario Community Education Association (OCEA). The association was a bilingual, non-profit, province-wide organization comprising volunteers from all walks of life who believed that education, our most valuable resource, is not only synonymous with schools but also a lifelong process that is based on a broad sense of learning and an abundance of untapped resources in the community, and that community education is a process through which citizens can determine and meet their educational, recreational, cultural, and social needs.

In 1986 the Ontario Community Education Association and the Learning Enrichment Foundation made a joint submission entitled 'Organizing Technology Transfer in Ontario (OTTO)' to the Honourable Sean Conway, Ontario Minister of Education, under his Miscellaneous Grants program. The objectives of OTTO were to develop an integrated strategy to improve educational opportunities related to distance education and technological training, particularly in northern and rural areas and including francophone and Native Canadian populations, and to utilize existing demonstration projects, government departments, education providers, and voluntary organizations to enhance the strategy.[126]

The OTTO program was to be established as a voluntary sector enterprise convened jointly by the Ontario Community Education Association and the Learning Enrichment Foundation. The City of York's programs in distance education, technological training, adult basic education, and community economic development would serve as a model to be extended to other parts of the province. Components of the strategy were to include the establishment of a community education and development network to involve local citizens in OTTO, utilizing existing OCEA directors and members across the province; television applications including cable, narrow band, and satellite dish transmission, utilizing the LWL-TV demonstration project in York, TV Ontario, and community college facilities; small-business incubation and entrepreneurial training based on the York Business Opportunities Centre model in York; technology buses to visit northern and rural communities to demonstrate and train in microelectronic, pneumatic, and hydraulic technological applications (for example, the MICROTRON Bus project in York); and an approach compatible and supportive of new Ministry of Education technological studies, entrepreneurial studies, and science curricula.

Centre FORA

One of the outcomes of the OTTO project was Le centre franco-ontarien de resources en alphabetisation (Centre FORA) that was established in

Sudbury in September 1989 by Yolande Clément, Secretary of OCEA-AECO. The association made representation to the Honourable Alvin Curling, Minister of Skills Development, on behalf of the literacy needs of francophones throughout the province. Centre FORA would involve a library of resource materials as well as the development of new programs and publications. The centre was jointly funded by the Ministry of Skills Development and the federal Secretary of State for five years. The OTTO project had been instrumental in advocating the creation of such a centre in northern Ontario.

Provincial Education Project to Promote Economic Renewal

Another proposal compatible to OTTO was a submission I made to the Ministry of Education in 1986, on behalf of the York Board of Education, which focused on the changing nature of employment in the province of Ontario. Manufacturing and resource industries were declining, while the services sector was growing (for example, private profit-oriented, private non-profit, and governmental services). One of the fastest growing employment areas had been the voluntary, not-for-profit sector. To compete in the post-industrial age, there was a need to strengthen our innovative and entrepreneurial skills to access world markets and decrease economic dependencies. Future attitudes and the skills engendered would become part of the cultural fabric if this process of economic renewal were to begin in the local microeconomic sphere. Combating large-scale unemployment and underemployment among youth required an educational strategy to bring together the private for-profit, not-for-profit, and governmental sectors in a joint strategy to promote social and economic renewal.

The objectives of the Provincial Education Project to Promote Economic Renewal (PEPPER) were to design and implement a local economic development process for communities in the province of Ontario; to involve local school boards, municipal governments, business and industry, and the voluntary sector in the implementation of the process; and to develop and implement curriculum guidelines at the primary/junior (P1.J1.), intermediate/senior (OSIS), and adult levels to encourage the acquisition of the following attitudes and skills at the local level – self-reliance, cooperative planning, microeconomic theory and practice, marketing and entrepreneurism, innovation and problem-solving, microelectronics, voluntarism, community development, small business management, and information technology.

Proyecto Surco

During the 1990/91 school year, an English-as-a-Second-Language teacher at the Vaughan Road campus of the Adult Day School encouraged two of her students to develop a program proposal as part of their language studies. Sandra Mena and Maria Marin, immigrants from Guatemala and Venezuela, respectively, were concerned that children coming from Latin America often lacked knowledge of the history and culture of their native land. They also suffered from low self-esteem because the media image of Latin America was often negative. Studies had shown that immigrant youth had a higher dropout rate than had students native to Canada. To quote Sandra and Maria: 'This program will give us the opportunity to preserve our roots by providing our children with cultural knowledge so that they will develop love and respect for their countries of origin. These would be elements needed to build the cultural identity they need and increase their self-esteem. It also provides an ideal setting within which to reinforce their native tongue. This would not only help in their communication with their parents, but would also increase their language skills, thus broadening their future horizons.[127]

In March 1991, Sandra and Maria were referred by their teacher to the York Board of Education's Community Services Office to explore possible sources of funding for a demonstration project. As the superintendent of community services, I met with Joan Milling, the executive director of York Community Services, an agency serving our Spanish-speaking community. After consultation with the local office of Employment and Immigration Canada, a letter was sent to the Minister of Employment and Immigration seeking support for the project to be known as Proyecto Surco (the Spanish word *surco* means 'furrow,' as in ploughing a furrow in the soil). During the spring and summer of 1991, Sandra and Maria, with the assistance of their teacher, continued to refine their proposal and to develop their word-processing skills. They also joined the Multicultural Access Committee at York Community Services and met with a group of local artisans from Latin America.

In September, information was received concerning the START Option, a stay-in-school initiative from the Minister of State for Youth. The focus of the program was twelve- to eighteen-year-olds in senior public and secondary schools who were at risk of dropping out. The local Employment and Immigration Canada office, however, wished to concentrate on the twelve- to fourteen-year-old age group as a preventative measure. After considerable discussion with the York Board of Education's Career Centre, Guidance Department, and community liaison officers, and revision of the original proposal to fit START guidelines, an application was submitted by York Community Services to Employment and Immigration Canada in November 1991. In December, it was learned that the proposal had been funded to employ Sandra and Maria from January to June 1992.

The objective of the Proyecto Surco was to provide appropriate cultural interventions to ninety Latin American students, aged twelve to fourteen years, who had been identified as potential early school leavers by the York Board of Education and school guidance counsellors. Project activities were establishing a community needs assessment and developmental model to ensure target group participation in project planning and interventions, including an inventory of available resources, parent-student interviews, and a self-evaluation survey; setting up interactive group and classroom format teaching settings for at-risk students including the use of traditional Hispanic crafts and history resource people, permanent in-school displays, and special events promotion and interchange; providing one-to-one individualized counselling; and offering intercultural staff development with school educators.

In January 1992 an advisory committee, consisting of personnel from York Community Services, Opportunities for Advancement, and the York Board of Education, assisted Sandra and Maria with the implementation of the program. In February they met with the senior public school principals as part of their needs assessment process.

Black Youth and School Completion

In February 1991, I was approached by Employment and Immigration Canada to convene a seminar focusing on early school leavers, particularly West Indian youth. The bottom line was that it had to happen by 31 March, the end of the federal budget year. I said that I was willing to work with other community agencies to prepare a proposal but that the actual planning and implementation would have to be done by the youth themselves. What emerged was 'Black Youth and School Completion – Accepting and Sharing the Challenge,' a one-day seminar held on 31 March 1992 at the York Memorial Presbyterian Church and sponsored jointly by the Learning Enrichment Foundation's Job Opportunities for You (JOY) Employment Counselling Centre and York Community Services. A steering committee consisted of representatives from the Keele Street Youth project of York Community Services; the JOY centre; the Cooperative Resources Centre of OISE; the York Board of Education's Change Your Future program; and our Community Services office. In about three weeks a program including speakers, discussion groups, and catering had been organized by the youth themselves – both school attendees and dropouts.

More than 150 young people and adults representing at least fifty different organizations attended the seminar. The result was a detailed inventory of social and educational needs and resources. In particular, I remember the discussion following a panel presentation that had been led by a Black former Toronto Argonaut football player. One young man from the audience came to a microphone and said, 'I live in the Jane-Woolner apartments (public housing) on the fourth floor. I've never done very well in school. The guy down the hall quit and now he drives a new 4 x 4 (he sells drugs). On the first floor another guy has the most expensive shoes and the best clothes to wear (he's a pimp and sells girls). I just want to join the economy.'

As a follow-up to the seminar, a work group of youth and service providers was convened in August 1992 to discuss an implementation plan to respond to the educational, social, and employment needs of disadvantaged youth, particularly in the west section of the city near the Jane Street and Woolner Avenue housing project. Meeting regularly at the nearby Rockcliffe Senior Public School, the work group agreed that a community youth project should focus on all disadvantaged youth between the ages of twelve and twenty-four. The project itself should be youth driven so that young people would derive a greater sense of ownership and self-esteem and develop their organizational and decision-making skills. This might be accomplished through the creation of a youth focus group to identify needs and develop leadership capabilities. Parents and other community members would serve in an advisory capacity. Agencies and organizations would provide resources and advocacy for the project. Following are three initiatives undertaken by the work group.

West End Tutorial Program. The West End Tutorial program was a Saturday morning tutoring program for students in the Jane-Woolner area, offered at George Syme Community School. It was modelled on a very successful program that had been offered for the previous eight years at Vaughan Road Collegiate in the east end of the city by the Canadian Alliance of Black Educators, including community liaison officer Ruth Wiggins and the York Board of Education. Initially, the West End Tutorial program operated with volunteers from the Jane-Woolner Neighbourhood Association and staff from both George Syme and Rockcliffe schools. It was hoped that paid instructors could be provided once the viability of the program had been assured. There were no additional accommodation costs for the program as the school was already open for heritage classes on Saturday mornings.

Black Heritage. A survey at Rockcliffe Senior Public School indicated that thirty students were interested in a Black heritage program. An instructor was made available to offer the program through the Heritage Languages program of the Community Services Office.

UJAMMA. A joint project of Goals for Youth Ontario, Junior Achievement Canada, the Jane-Woolner Neighbourhood Association, and Rockcliffe Senior Public School, UJAMMA provided life skills and employment training for disadvantaged twelve- to fourteen-year-olds in the Rockcliffe-Jane-Woolner area. School staff, community mentors, and parents participated, with funding provided by the START Option of Employment and Immigration Canada.

Youth Enterprise Summit

Another outcome of the 'Black Youth and School Completion' seminar process was the Youth Enterprise Summit (YES). Original planners for the summit were York Community Services, the York Board of Education, and the York Community Agency and Social Planning Council (YCASP). Other sponsors included the International Community Education Association (of Coventry, United Kingdom); Kiwanis Club of Casa Loma; Levi Strauss & Co. (Canada) Inc.; Ontario Ministry of Citizenship; the Community and Partnership Initiatives Program; and Shaw Cable Television.

To quote from 'YES – Report of the Youth Enterprise Summit':

> On the weekend of April 23, 1993, thirty-seven young people from the City of York met at the Claremont Field Centre to debate their future in a rapidly changing economy. Their goal was to find creative initiatives to solve problems confronting young people today, to accept responsibility for personal growth, and to assume some leadership on the road to building an 'enterprise culture.'

Earlier that spring thirty-five youth groups in York were approached to select participants for the Youth Enterprise Summit. Volunteers were elected from those intrigued by a unique opportunity to express their concerns and aspirations, and to learn to work for change. These eager young people recognized that, not only were former employment possibilities no longer available, but because of race, economic status or education, existing employment opportunities would be exceedingly difficult for them to access.

At the opening of the Summit, organizers used examples and simulation exercises to encourage participants to get to know one another, think creatively and become 'enterprising individuals.' Enterprising people work on collaborative strategies to initiate and assume responsibility for change. They:

- See change as an opportunity rather than a problem;
- Develop the self-confidence to become planners and organizers.

No one anticipated that these young people, aged 17 to 20, would so quickly take the initiative, exhibiting an exciting, high level of enthusiasm and energy. A framework was established and a common language was developed by the end of the first session. Adult observers caught up in the excitement had to hold back and resist the temptation to 'help.'

The group focused on five areas – family, education, environment, employment and communications – and developed action plans. Specific proposals recommended a reality-based TV series to be produced by young people; school curriculum that gave students a voice on content; a community awareness program on dysfunctional families; a youth enterprise centre; and a community composting program.

Young people made plans to continue work after the Summit. They recognized the need to get the message out to other youth – to involve as many as possible. All enterprises were to be youth-driven. Adults were invited to become partners.

Our challenge today is to assist these young people to secure funds and resources to gain the skills and develop the enterprises that will really work for youth in the City of York. Youth who participated in the Summit are committed to improving life in the City of York for themselves and their peers, for the broader community, and for the next generation of young people.[128]

Following the Summit, youth set up a hiring committee and a building committee to look for space to house a youth enterprise development corporation (YEDCO).

York Community Services created nine summer positions for youth from the summit. Eleven young people received employment and researched enterprises. Youth workers visited forty youth-serving agencies and interviewed dozens of people. They quickly learned about gaps and needs and received practical advice on starting youth-led enterprises. Key visits and meetings included a visit to Focus: Hope, an inner-city youth initiative in Detroit; a visit to a mid-scale community composting project in Guelph that could be replicated in the city of York; meetings with representatives from the Ontario Ministry of Environment and Metropolitan Toronto Works Department about community-based composting initiatives; meetings and tours at Shaw Cable Television, Global Television, City-TV, and CBC Television concerning youth programming; a meeting with Metropolitan Toronto Youth Council staff and the City of York Community Agency and Social Planning Council regarding City of York representation; a meeting with officials from the York Board of Education regarding planning student input to curriculum and school operations; a meeting with the provincial Ministry of Municipal Affairs regarding the *Community Economic Development Act* and potential youth enterprise projects; visits to eight youth counselling centres about sharing resources and setting up a peer counselling and education program in the city of York; and site visits to several vacant properties in the city of York, followed by preparation of a detailed plan for co-locating several youth enterprises in a central site.

Other activities included making contacts with local politicians, presentations to youth groups, and a youth petition on the need for improved youth services and for research on non-profit incorporation of the summit group. The achievements and the professionalism with which this work was carried out were exciting and very rewarding. The youth employed during the summer also participated in completing grant proposals for funding to build upon their summer research and maintain their momentum.

Outcomes and Reflections

As previously described in chapter 13, I was experiencing increasing opposition from some administrative colleagues and trustees while the profile of the Community Services Office continued to rise. The York

Model of community education and economic development had gained prominence both nationally and internationally. As a result, I was in demand to prepare publications, speak at conferences, and participate in study groups both in North America and overseas. By the late 1980s, I was being increasingly asked to justify these activities, which some saw as detracting from my role as a supervisory officer in the city of York. Although I tended not to take lieu time (compensatory time for numerous evening meetings) or all of my allotted vacation days, and I clocked more hours on the job than most of my colleagues, my immediate superior worried about me short-cutting my local responsibilities. Fortunately I was able to retain the support and trust of the director of education, John Phillips, and some influential trustees, such as Steven Mould. Raising the profile of the City of York Board of Education was not seen as a political negative. In an organizational restructuring in 1990, my position was upgraded to that of superintendent of community services.

Another issue was the impending retirement in 1990 of Director Phillips. There had always been a divergence of leadership styles between the people coming from the elementary and the secondary panels. Elementary administrators tended to be curriculum · leaders with stronger ties to children, parents, and community. Secondary administrators were often more bureaucratic in their managerial styles, with an authoritarian control hierarchy of principal, vice-principal (with specific duties such as timetabling and discipline), department heads, assistant heads, and teachers. Their relationship to community was much more obscure.

John Phillips had an elementary, community-involved leadership style. The conservative, secondary school–oriented lobby among some supervisory officers and trustees favoured Norman Ahmet, Senior Superintendent of Personnel and the former principal of Vaughan Road Collegiate, to replace Mr Phillips. Leading the political process to gain trustee support was Mr Ahmet's close friend, Personnel Superintendent Barry Rowland. Mr. Rowland, son of the legendary former pastor of York Memorial Presbyterian Church, was a long-time resident of the Greenbrook area of York and a City of York councillor. Ultimately, Mr Ahmet was chosen as the new director.

The Community Services Office became an ongoing target for attack and emasculation. The community-responsive leadership style of John Phillips seemed no longer to be valued in the new regime. So, by 1994, I felt that my days as superintendent of community services were numbered. Consequently, I announced my early retirement, to take effect on 31 December that year.

In 1995, the Mike Harris Conservatives swept to power in Ontario with their 'Common Sense Revolution.' The neoconservative policies implemented included a 21.6 per cent reduction in the allowances to social assistance recipients. Funding for public education was centralized according to a provincial education equalization formula, which drastically reduced the power and influence of school trustees and led to service cuts, particularly in Toronto and other urban centres. Funding ceased for community education programs under provincial continuing education provisions. Adult education was also decimated because adults could no longer be accepted as regular secondary school students beyond the age of twenty-one. By 1998, the City of York Board of Education and its Community Services Office were no more, as the six public boards in Metropolitan Toronto were forced to amalgamate to form the Toronto District School Board.

15 Training for Social Enterprise

Having taken my leave from the City of York, I was now seeking new career opportunities in the voluntary sector. At fifty-six years of age I was not ready to sit home and collect my pension. Previous experience in creating not-for-profit enterprises, such as the Learnxs Foundation and the Learning Enrichment Foundation, seemed to me the way to go. Both organizations, originally, had no endowment or ongoing stable source of core funding. Aside from some in-kind support from their arm's-length association with the school boards, they were special-purpose entrepreneurial bodies depending, for the most part, on a series of short-term demonstration projects for their continued survival. In this regard, they were third-sector enterprises carving out a service niche between the commercial and governmental sectors. (The term in common use today is *social enterprises*.)

Centre for Community and Economic Renewal

My experiences with the Adult Day School, and with the Learning Enrichment Foundation in particular, offered some potential areas of need to be explored. My previous association with the Adult Education Department at the Ontario Institute for Studies in Education represented a possible hosting arrangement. I had maintained close contact with my former thesis committee members James Draper (committee chair) and Alan Thomas and had gained respect for the work of Jack Quarter who specialized in cooperative enterprise. In the fall of 1993, Jack and I had drafted a proposal for the Centre for Community and Economic Renewal (CCER), to be located at the Ontario Institute for Studies in Education. The centre's mandate was to establish programs and to grant certificates to adults desiring to learn about social (or third-sector) enterprises, such as non-profits, cooperatives, and other community ventures, as well as to offer training programs for small business and other employer and employee groups. The centre would link education to practice insofar as the courses would attempt both to create a better understanding and to prepare its participants for roles within the social sector and other sectors of the economy. These roles could range from paid employment to self-employment to voluntary roles, or some mix of the two.

Programs would be designed individually for each student, using a combination of activities (including practicums) offered by the centre and courses already available through OISE. Programs offered by the centre would be taught by some combination of its own staff, instructors on stipend who would contract with the centre, and through sub-contractual arrangement with other organizations. The participants would be adults with appropriate interests, including those who had lost their jobs, and those desiring to renew their employment skills. One of the initial tasks would be to do a market assessment and to prepare a promotional piece for the target market.

The centre would operate with a small staff, from an office at OISE. There would also be an advisory board (that is, ourselves and a few other people with an interest in the project). In order to get the centre underway we would attempt to raise funds externally so that a staff person could be hired to manage it and non-personnel costs could be covered. However, once the centre started enrolling people into its programs, it would be financed through a combination of contractual income and the fees paid by its participants. With respect to the fees, the arrangement that we proposed was that the participants would pay fees to OISE, and a portion of these would be transferred to the centre in order for it to cover its costs. Therefore, the arrangement could be viewed as a partnership between OISE and the centre, insofar as OISE would provide some financial administration, certificates, its name and space, the availability of courses, and some faculty time (a small amount of Jack Quarter's time). The centre would be responsible for promotion, arranging programs for its participants, contracting with extramurals, and administering its own budget. It might derive income also from service contracts as well as some external fund-raising. For that purpose, the centre might want to be able to use the OISE Foundation for contributors desiring a tax benefit. In this regard, Jack Quarter and I met with Arthur Kruger, Director, and Angela Hildyard, Assistant

Director of OISE. They agreed that the centre would be established as part of the Business Development Office at the institute.

Members of the centre's advisory board consisted of Marina Heidman, Manager, Peat Marwick Stevenson & Kellogg; Sandra Wedlock, Program Development Consultant, Faculty of Administrative Studies, York University; Laurence D. Hebb, Managing Partner, Osler, Hoskin, & Harcourt; Steven Mould, Managing Partner, Moffat, Morgan & Mould Inc.; D. John Phillips, Director, Supervisory Officers Qualifications Program, Metropolitan Toronto School Board; Jack Quarter, Professor, Adult Education Department of OISE, and Chair, Advisory Board of the Centre for Community and Economic Renewal; Julie White, Executive Director, Trillium Foundation; Dale E. Shuttleworth, initially Superintendent of Community Services, City of York Board of Education; Judith Gabor, Educational Consultant; Angela Hildyard, Assistant Director, OISE; Jean Bouchard, Cooronnateur RUISSO (representing Centre FORA in Sudbury); John Howley, Director, Employment and Training Services, Metro Toronto Community Services; and Lisa Avedon, Senior Manager, Ontario Training and Adjustment Board.

I became the Executive Director of the Centre for Community and Economic Renewal in January 1995.

Training Interns in Education

The first demonstration project undertaken by the new Centre for Community and Economic Renewal, in 1994–5, was Training Interns in Education (TIE), with $82,000 in funding provided by the Canadian Jobs Strategy program of Human Resources Development Canada. In June 1994 the *Toronto Star* reported that a 'Sri Lankan immigrant dishwasher' had been brutally beaten by 'a racist skinhead.' The assault left the forty-five-year-old former math teacher with brain damage and a paralysed left hand, arm, and face. Behind the horror of the attack was the story of a highly qualified professional who, to support his family, had been compelled to take a job washing dishes and mopping floors in a rough inner-city neighbourhood and working long hours. Leaving work late one night, he had run into a vicious gang of white supremacists who were combing the alleys of Toronto, looking for victims.[129]

The Teacher Certification and Career Opportunities in Education for Newcomers feasibility study (see chapter 13) had identified the need for newcomers who previously had a career in public education to gain supervised field placements in a school setting and to be assisted in finding employment or in reviewing their professional qualifications. The Training Interns in Education project, coordinated by centre's Judith Gabor and myself, provided employment experience and vocational training for unemployment insurance and social assistance recipients who were unable to achieve a letter of eligibility to teach in Ontario because of insufficient academic or professional qualifications, who were unable to be admitted to a faculty of education because of a lack of appropriate Ontario education–related experience, or who were unable to find employment as a teacher, teacher aide, or other support staff because of a lack of general knowledge concerning methodology and practice in the Ontario educational workplace.

The TIE staff, through the Centre for Community and Economic Renewal (CCER), worked with the boards of education from North York and the City of York and a number of individual principals in other boards in the Greater Toronto Area, to secure in-school practicum placements for four days per week for TIE participants. One day was spent at OISE, studying the theory and practice of public education in Ontario.

The TIE staff screened several hundred unemployment insurance and social assistance recipients to select seventy participants, the majority of whom were women (74 per cent) and visible minorities (13 per cent). The project was twelve months in duration (October 1994 to September 1995), comprising two school terms. Successful participants were awarded a certificate of completion and formal evaluations by the host schools. Ninety-three per cent of the total intake of seventy people completed the program successfully. With the assistance of TIE, participants were able to achieve a letter of eligibility or a letter of standing from the Ministry of Education and Training or to develop a plan to qualify for employment in the field of education or related areas. Eligible TIE participants were also offered a Teaching English as a Second Language (TESL) course, in July 1995, by CCER in partnership with the Ontario Ministry of Citizenship and Culture. Successful graduates received a Ministry TESL certificate qualifying them to teach in any community-based English as a Second Language program. CCER remained in contact with TIE graduates, offering leadership, organizational help, networking direction, office support, information sharing, and volunteer coordination for mutual assistance. Metro Toronto Community Services provided additional support for social assistance recipients.

To quote the final report to Human Resources Development Canada:

The Training Interns in Education project has been successful in a variety of ways.

- According to student feedback, over 90 per cent felt their chances of finding their way into an education-related field had been improved by participating in the TIE program.
- The partner boards of education found the presence of the TIE students helpful in the schools and allowed them to become familiar with potential staff members of a wide variety of cultural backgrounds. The Ontario Ministry of Education is presently considering the accreditation of the TIE training program to facilitate the Ontario certification of internationally trained educators.
- The children in the Greater Toronto Area, who interacted with the TIE participants, gained significantly from seeing additional adult role models from a wide variety of cultures in their schools. TIE participants brought over 35 languages and the cultural understanding of 34 different countries to their in-school classroom assignments.
- Of a group of 70 unemployed, and often unemployable education-related workers, the large majority are either actively working on a part-time or full-time basis, or continuing their education and nurturing their TIE-related networks to gain employment in the future.[130]

General Educational Development Pilot Project

In 1994 thousands of unemployed workers descended upon Oshawa, Ontario, in hopes of landing a job at General Motors. Despair, however, awaited those in the long line who did not have a high school diploma. They did not even receive an application form, let alone an interview.

During my years as supervisory officer of York's Adult Day School, I had become increasingly concerned about the plight of immigrants, refugees, and migrants who lacked a high school diploma because they had failed to finish secondary school, were unable to produce a graduation certificate (because they had fled from a war zone, for example), or did not have credentials that were recognized in Ontario. They could not afford to spend two to three years gaining enough credits to be granted an Ontario secondary school diploma.

During a visit in 1993 to the Focus: Hope project in Detroit, as an outcome of York's Youth Enterprise Summit, I became aware of the General Educational Development (GED) high school equivalency program.

In particular, I learned about the availability of computer software that was being used to assist students in preparing to challenge the GED exams.

The General Educational Development test is a standardized high school equivalency test for adults (nineteen years and over) that was created in 1947 by the Education Testing Service for the American Council on Education. During the Second World War there was a need by the military to classify the academic skills of new recruits and draftees to the armed forces from across the United States. This classification was essential because each state maintained its own academic standards. The tests covered what high school graduates were supposed to know about writing, science, mathematics, social studies, and literature, and the arts. They also measured reading comprehension, analytical skills, writing ability, and other important skills.

After the war, the GED testing program spread across the United States. By 1992, twelve million adults had earned GED diplomas. In 1967, the GED test came to Canada, beginning with the armed forces in Nova Scotia. In the following years a Canadian test with Canadian or neutral content, which was normed across the country (administered to a sample of graduating senior secondary students) and updated regularly, was available. By 1992 the governments of all provinces and territories, except Ontario and Quebec, were licensed to administer the GED tests. That year, 23,000 Canadian adults wrote the tests, and 15,000 received a high school equivalency certificate.

While the Ontario Ministry of Education and Training did not currently recognize the GED test, an increasing number of Ontario residents were leaving the province to take it. For example, to secure an apprenticeship position, or to gain employment in the police or fire departments, a high school diploma or equivalency certificate was mandatory. A study in the United States found that fully 98 per cent of employers accepted the GED as the equivalent of a high school diploma.

In exploring the feasibility of bringing the GED qualification to Ontario, I was fortunate to make the acquaintance of Peter Kilburn, Director of Educational Services for the New Brunswick Community College. Peter also represented Canada on the GED Testing Service in Washington, DC. His mentorship was invaluable in informing me about the GED tests and the steps required to introduce the program to Ontario. The first step was political. In 1994, while still the superintendent of community services, I approached Tony Romano, Constituency Assistant to Premier Bob Rae, to set up an appointment with the premier in order to discuss the merits of bringing the GED to Ontario. It did not hurt that the premier was the Member of Provincial Parliament for York South and his constituency office was on Eglinton Avenue West, directly across the street from my office in the York Board's Education Administration Centre. I had also known Premier Rae during the 1970s when he was the federal MP in East Toronto, and he had supported the Student Employment Experience Centre demonstration project.

When I presented the GED concept to the premier, his first reaction was, 'Charles will like this!' (referring to Deputy Minister of Education and Training Charles Pascal). His second reaction was, 'We can support this as a pilot project in the city of York [his riding],' provided that it did not cost the Ontario government 'one thin dime.' (The Rae government was shouldering a large budget deficit inherited from its predecessors.)

Who would fund the pilot project? On behalf of CCER, I drafted a proposal entitled 'GED Pilot Project in the City of York' to be submitted to the Canadian Jobs Strategy of Human Resources Development Canada (HRDC). The project would be a joint venture funded by HRDC, with the Ministry of Education and Training, Metropolitan Toronto Community Services, and the Centre for Community and Economic Renewal at OISE as partners.

The Ministry of Education and Training was prepared to sign a one-year contract with the GED Testing Service in Washington, DC, to administer GED tests through its Independent Learning Centre. The Centre for Community and Economic Renewal would operate the GED Preparation Centre, with candidates referred by Metro Social Services Offices (70 per cent) and Canada Employment Centres (30 per cent). Components of the project were as follows:

Preparation. Those persons referred to the GED Preparation Centre would receive a diagnostic pre-test of their literacy, language, and mathematical skills. On the basis of these results they would be enrolled in the preparation centre for an average of sixty hours (six hours per day for ten days) or be referred to another more appropriate program for remedial assistance (for example, adult learning centres, adult ESL, and literacy programs). The preparation process would incorporate four different methods: computer-assisted learning software (available from the United States, for example Josten's or CENTEC); print materials (GED texts by Canadian publishers, for example Barron's); audio-visual lessons (for use at the preparation centre or at home, for example by TV Ontario and the Kentucky Department of Education); and individual tutoring and mentorship.

Testing. At the end of the preparation period, candidates would receive a post-test and, if they were successful, would be referred to the Ministry of Education and Training's Independent Learning Centre to take the GED exams, which consisted of a seven-and-one-half- hour battery of tests over two days in writing skills, social studies, science, mathematics, and literature and the arts.

Certification. Candidates who were successful in each of the five subject areas would receive an Ontario high school equivalency certificate. Those missing one or more subjects could be retested at a later date.

Evaluation. The Field Services and Research Department at OISE would have a separate arm's-length contract to follow up on GED candidates and provide a detailed description of the results of the referral, preparation, and testing phases of the pilot project. An advisory committee to assist OISE in the research study would include representation from the Ontario Teachers' Federation, the Metropolitan Toronto Board of Trade, the Ontario Chamber of Commerce, the Continuing Education School Board Administrators, and the Ontario Council on Adult Education.

Implementation. The GED Preparation Centre, administered by CCER, would be located in the city of York on a main transportation line accessible to the handicapped. A GED learning systems coach, a counsellor, and an administrative assistant would staff the centre for each seven-hour shift (two shifts per day). The centre would be equipped with twenty networked computer-learning stations, a file server, appropriate GED software (for example, Josten's system), texts and diagnostic tests (for example, Barron's), a videocassette recorder, a library of videotapes (for example, from the Kentucky Department of Education), and furnishings for independent study.

Based on the average of sixty hours of preparation time, it was estimated that, during the pilot project, 1,100 candidates could be trained using a fourteen-hour day. The project would provide the Ministry of Education and Training with the necessary information and experience on which to base a decision regarding the future implementation of the

GED throughout Ontario, as well as the best method to prepare for the tests.

On 6 February 1995 the GED Preparation Centre, located at 2700 Dufferin Street in the city of York, was officially opened by Dr Charles Pascal, Deputy Minister of Education and Training; Dr Angela Hildyard, Director, OISE; and Joe Volpe, MP for Eglinton-Lawrence. Human Resources Development Canada's JobLink approved $349,000 for the Centre for Community and Economic Renewal at OISE to fund a one-year pilot project that would prepare one thousand unemployment-insurance and social-assistance recipients for the GED tests, which would to be administered by the Independent Learning Centre. Successful candidates would receive the Ontario high school equivalency certificate from the Ministry of Education and Training. A separate research contract of $50,000 was granted to OISE to provide an arm's-length assessment of the success of the GED Preparation Centre.

During the period from May 1995 to January 1996 the Independent Learning Centre tested a total of 218 candidates from the preparation centre, with 81 per cent earning an Ontario high school equivalency certificate (versus a national average of 63 per cent). This success rate was attributed to the preparation centre's computer-assisted FASTRAC system, which utilized the Josten's Invest Learning Star 2010 software, and computer hardware and software provided by Toronto Datacom. Other essential components were the services of the GED coach, the counsellor, the administrative assistant, and volunteer tutors.

Obstacles. The pilot project, and the continued viability of CCER, faced some obstacles. Its mandate had been a preparation system for GED tests, leading to high school equivalency certificates for Ontario's adult learners. This direction was not supported politically by the Ontario Secondary School Teachers Federation. To achieve a high school equivalency, in about sixty hours of preparation, meant that these adult learners would not be spending as much as two to three years to gain regular secondary school credits leading to an Ontario secondary school diploma. Many Ministry of Education and Training officials had been, or continued to be, members of the teachers' federation.

The Ministry had required that a research study be undertaken to provide an objective evaluation of the pilot project. OISE's Research Department was to conduct this study, which was to be monitored by an advisory committee of key stakeholders. In January 1996, OISE's research officer reported that not only was no research being done but the advisory committee had not been convened, in spite of the fact that both the assistant deputy minister of education and training and the director of GED Testing Service (United States) had written to OISE concerning the status of the research study. The results were required before the pilot project could be considered for an extension across the province.

In June 1995 there was a general election in the province of Ontario. The Conservatives, led by Mike Harris, defeated the New Democratic Party government of Premier Bob Rae. The new minister of education and training was John Snobelen. Coincidentally, Mr Snobelen had not graduated from secondary school. We immediately began a lobbying campaign to inform him about the GED pilot project and to gain his approval for an extension across the province. The Board of Trade of Metropolitan Toronto and the Ontario Chamber of Commerce also approached the minister, strongly supporting the GED for Ontario.

Provincewide Testing. On 9 September 1996, Minister Snobelen announced that a new service for adults who want to be tested and earn the equivalent of a high school diploma would now be available across the province. To quote the minister: 'The Ministry of Education and Training is committed to both training for basic literacy and GED testing. With six new test sites underway in Sudbury, Toronto, Mississauga, Ottawa, Thunder Bay, and Windsor, more people will have the opportunity to take GED tests and break through any barriers that not having finished high school may have caused for them.'[131] Needless to say, the Centre for Community and Economic Renewal and its GED Preparation Centre were overjoyed at what they had achieved.

Visitors' Guide Service

In response to the employment needs of Training Interns in Education graduates and Adult Day School ESL students, the Centre for Community and Economic Renewal prepared a proposal for submission to Canadian Jobs Strategy entitled 'Metropolitan Toronto Visitors' Guide Service Training Project.' The proposal recognized that more than 28 million persons either visited or passed through the Metropolitan Toronto area each year; the assets of Metropolitan Toronto included a rich historical heritage, a strong artistic and cultural tradition, a most attractive natural environment, a vibrant cosmopolitan character, and a very progressive governmental, commercial, and industrial community; by comparison to other famous cities of the world, Toronto did not have a professional guide service; unemployed immigrants and refugees who were ESL students could be trained as visitors' guides and be provided with a career path or a source of part-time employment; a demonstration project that trained newcomers with linguistic skills to be visitors' guides could provide a new source of employment for the trainees as well as a service to non-English-speaking visitors; besides skill training, the program might also result in four secondary school credits in guiding and tourism services being granted under provisions of the Ontario Schools Intermediate Senior (OSIS) guidelines.

The objective of the project was to recruit and train a total of sixty Adult Day School ESL students to serve as visitors' guides, or in other hospitality-related vocations, in Metropolitan Toronto. Trainees would qualify for four secondary school senior credits in guiding and tourism services and cooperative education, as well as a certificate from the Centre for Community and Economic Renewal. The project would also act as a source of recruitment and placement for tour companies, visitor reception agencies, and other employers in the hospitality industry wishing to employ multilingual guides and other service workers. Trainees would be drawn from unemployment insurance and social assistance recipients.

The response to the proposal, from Canadian Jobs Strategy, was to provide research funding for three unemployment-insurance recipients to conduct a preliminary research study on the feasibility of a visitors' guide service. The Centre for Community and Economic Renewal joined with the Ontario Tourism Education Council to implement this project. The result was the employment of three adult ESL students, who designed a curriculum for a training plan for visitors' guides. The study also led to standards being applied across Canada for tour operators, tour directors, and tour guides. The original Visitors' Guide Service proposal was resubmitted to Human Resources Development Canada, the Ontario Training and Adjustment Board, and other potential funding sources.

Executive Service Corps

The Centre for Community and Economic Renewal proposed a demonstration project in response to the social and economic needs of older workers. The rationale for the Executive Service Corps (ExecuSERVE) was that during this age of employment restructuring, many managerial or other highly skilled personnel might be facing early retirement, job loss, or a change in career path, and as part of their relocation and adjustment process, these persons might make an outstanding contribution as community service volunteers. In particular, the fields of education, health, social service, and community economic development could benefit greatly from the part-time or short-term commitments of such knowledgeable and experienced personnel. A non-profit program specializing in their recruitment and placement could assist business, industry, and the professions by providing a source of meaningful volunteer employment for early retirees and dislocated and severed staff during their period of adjustment. In addition, such a program could contribute to the emotional health and well-being of such people in transition, while providing a vital service to the community in a time of diminishing resources and fiscal restraint.

The objectives of the one-year demonstration project were to assist business, industry, and the professions in serving the needs of relocated, severed, and early retired managerial and highly skilled professional personnel; to recruit such personnel and secure volunteer placements in the fields of education, health, social service, and community economic development; to provide an evaluation of the effectiveness of the program through ongoing monitoring of both ExecuSERV volunteers and their placements; and to make the project self-sufficient after year one through fees-for-service from corporations and individuals, as well as memberships in ExecuSERV.

Candidates for the project would be recruited from business, industry, and the professions and interviewed by the project coordinator and a volunteer. A placement officer and volunteer staff would contact educational, health, social service, and community economic development organizations to identify potential candidates, who would then be matched to appropriate community service vacancies. ExecuSERV staff would continue to monitor the performance of volunteers in the workplace, suitability of placements, and levels of employment satisfaction and prepare progress reports to the CCER advisory board and funders.

The ExecuSERVE proposal was ultimately submitted to the Trillium Foundation (distributor of lottery proceeds) for funding. It was anticipated that employers might provide financial support to the project as an alternative placement for employees during the relocation, severance, and early retirement process. Unfortunately the Trillium Foundation chose not to fund the proposal.

Youth Enterprise Learning

During the early 1990s there had been a series of community development projects by York Community Services and the York Board of Education's Community Services Office, including PROYECTO SURCO
(for Hispanic youth), the 'Black Youth and School Completion' seminar,
the Black Heritage program, the Rockcliffe START project, and Youth
Enterprise Summit.

In June 1995, York Community Services secured funding from JobLink
Ontario. The goal of the project was to initiate educational alternatives
and leadership training to enable disadvantaged youth in the city of
York to develop a Youth Enterprise Learning (YEL) Centre aimed at creating new economic development alternatives and employment opportunities. The Centre for Community and Economic Renewal provided
coordination, resource development, action research, and evaluation
services.

The JobLink funding assisted in employing a teacher and an outreach worker for one year (1994–5) at Archbishop Romero Catholic
High School (the York Board of Education chose not to participate)
to support the development of an alternative educational program
that would ensure that project trainees stayed in school while gaining
credits according to their academic and enterprise learning needs. The
teacher and outreach worker assisted twenty-five trainees in achieving
credits related to academic upgrading and enterprise learning skills
(for example, personal life management, entrepreneurship, and business skills).

It was anticipated that viable new enterprises would emerge that
could be incubated in the project until they became financially sustainable. Small group and independent learning strategies were employed
in the hope that, if the project were successful, the Metropolitan Separate School Board might adopt it as an alternative education program.

During July 1995, Youth Enterprise Learning students gained an
Introduction to Business credit, and in August each was assigned a
small-business mentor. The Centre for Community and Economic
Renewal continued to provide consultation assistance in support of
the three-credit entrepreneurship skills package, including school
and community sites, from September 1995 to January 1996. During
the term, YEL students operated a successful snack shop at the school.
Other enterprises being researched included a composting system for

apartments, a poop-and-scoop device for canine waste recovery, and 'dry dog' bags (a zippered cloth enclosure to dry wet or muddy pets).

Study Tours

The Centre for Community and Economic Renewal hosted the following European professional development tours.

Early Childhood Education. In April 1995 the Centre for Community and Economic Renewal joined with early childhood educators to organize 'a comparative study of European early childhood educational methodology and practice.' A group of thirty-three educators travelled to France and Italy for two weeks of professional development to compare childcare and preschool programs in Paris and Bologna. Led by early childhood consultant Julie Mathien, participants visited group and family home childcare, écoles maternelles and scuola materné (full-day preschool programs for three- to five-year-olds), and school-age programs. They met with government policy staff, including Peter Moss, Coordinator, European Community Childcare Network, who presented a special seminar.

The enthusiastic response to the study tour resulted in the Centre for Community and Economic Renewal organizing an international early childhood education conference at OISE in November 1995, with Peter Moss addressing about one hundred participants.

Cooperative Economic Development. In May 1996 the Centre for Community and Economic Renewal partnered with the Canadian Cooperative Association (Ontario Region) to sponsor a study tour of community and cooperative economic enterprises in the Emilia-Romagna region of Italy. In the early 1970s factories in the area between Florence and Venice had begun to close under the dual impact of exploding oil prices and double-digit inflation; in response, cities, unions, and trade associations came together to establish a large number of small, flexible firms that depended on cooperative business networks for success. The twenty participants on the study tour visited manufacturing, agriculture, food, craft, training, financial, and public service sectors. Materials and presentations by experts, concerning ways in which the cooperative and private sector manufacturing networks could be applied in Canada, supplemented the tour.

The Training Renewal Foundation

In October 1995, Angela Hildyard, OISE's new director, informed the Centre for Community and Economic Renewal's advisory board that any further funds awarded to CCER would be subject to a 40 per cent administrative fee payable to OISE. In February 1996, CCER was also told that it was not allowed to charge user fees to GED Preparation Centre trainees, which had become one option for raising funds when the federal funding had ceased. The provincial government had also decided to merge the University of Toronto's Faculty of Education and OISE; the new venture, to be headed by Dean Michael Fullan of the Faculty of Education, was to be known as the Ontario Institute for Studies in Education of the University of Toronto (OISE/UT).

The advisory board of CCER was faced with a real dilemma. Few funders would agree to sign contracts with CCER if 40 per cent of the funds were to be taken from CCER's budget and given to OISE/UT. The GED Preparation Centre had to have the option of charging user fees if it was to survive beyond the pilot project.

The Centre for Community and Economic Renewal sought alternate accommodation, which was found without cost in the Faculty of Education at York University. Dean Stan Shapson had been a partner in the Certification and Educational Career Opportunities for Newcomers feasibility study that was funded by the Ministry of Citizenship (see chapter 13). On 1 July 1996, CCER relocated to York University.

The advisory board decided to seek incorporation and charitable registration for CCER as the Training Renewal Foundation, with the legal assistance of board member Larry Hebb of Osler, Hoskin, & Harcourt. Federal incorporation under the *Canada Corporations Act* was granted on 18 April 1996. Signatories of the letters patent were Lisa Avedon, Jean Bouchard, Laurence Hebb, John Howley, Steven Mould, and Sandra Wedlock. On 15 September 1997 the foundation received notification from Revenue Canada that it had been granted status as a registered charity. (Larry Hebb and I had finally achieved this after an excursion to Ottawa to seek direct advice from government officials regarding the wording of the submission.)

Prior Learning Assessment Partnership

In an attempt to extend the life of the GED Preparation Centre beyond the federally funded pilot project, the new Training Renewal Foundation (TRF) explored several options. One was a partnership with the Metropolitan Separate School Board's Monsignor Fraser College to offer GED preparation as part of a secondary school credit.

Monsignor Fraser College had developed for adults a secondary school guidance credit in Career Development, as part of an articulation agreement between the Metropolitan Separate School Board (MSSB) and Seneca College of Applied Arts and Technology. It was decided to include a standardized challenge test as a component of the prior-learning assessment (PLA) portfolio developed within the Career Development credit. The standardized test chosen was the GED exam, which also prepared students for the mature student exams at Seneca College. Upon completion of the 120 hours of instruction, students might receive a Career Development credit, a high school equivalency certificate, and entrance into Seneca College (or another college) as a mature student. The course had several components, with exam preparation representing about 40 per cent of instructional hours.

Prior to the course being offered, the Central Region Office of the Ministry of Education and Training was consulted. The consensus was that using GED exams as part of the PLA portfolio was acceptable. Since the career development course had been taught within the Metropolitan Separate School Board for four years (and other boards across the province), it was considered to be approved.

Candidates for this course would be social assistance recipients (referred by Metro Community Services) and family benefits and unemployment insurance recipients. An adult returning to school after a number of years of absence traditionally required four to six credits after maturity evaluation to graduate with an Ontario secondary school diploma. The Career Development course prepared adults in less time, and at less expense, than if they had followed the traditional path. This was of particular importance for social assistance recipients, who could not afford the time or the fees charged by private training agencies.

On 28 November 1996 the Metropolitan Separate School Board approved the following motion: 'That the Director be authorized to enter into a partnership on a pilot basis for a one year renewable term with the Training Renewal Foundation at York University (The GED Preparation Centre) to provide one credit in Career Development for adult candidates through Monsignor Fraser College.'[132] The new Career Development course was offered at the GED Preparation Centre, with the school board assuming operating costs, including staffing, accommodation, and equipment rental. The Training Renewal Foundation contributed the FASTRAC system and consultative assistance.

The Training Renewal Foundation invited Minister John Snobelen to witness an official signing ceremony for the agreement between the Metropolitan Separate School Board and TRF, which was scheduled for 27 February 1997. However, a telephone call and a letter from Mariette Carrier-Fraser, Assistant Deputy Minister of Education, to Norm Forma, MSSB Director of Education, stated that the Career Development guidance credit did not meet Ministry guidelines. Further, she stated that 'any change in the Ministry position will have to take into consideration the impact on private training agencies offering GED preparatory courses and the impact on students enrolled in such courses. Consideration must also be given to the most effective method of delivering this type of course.'[133] It became apparent that OSSTF supporters within the Ministry and for-profit GED training agencies, which had sprung up when GED testing was expanded, had formed a very effective lobby. The signing ceremony had to be cancelled.

The Training Renewal Foundation countered with an appeal to John Weir, Executive Assistant to Minister Snobelen, in response to the letter from Ms Carrier-Fraser and asked for a meeting with Ministry officials to resolve any misunderstandings about the nature and legitimacy of the course. On 3 December 1997, I received a letter from Michael O'Flanagan, Superintendent of Education at MSSB, terminating the agreement effective 31 December 1997. A second letter from Mr O'Flanagan, dated 11 February 1998, contained the following comments:

I'm pleased to comment on the partnership between the Metropolitan Separate School Board (MSSB) and the Training Renewal Foundation to operate the GED Preparation Centre from November 1, 1996 to December 31, 1997. This adult education partnership involved a credit in Career Development (NGD 4G0), which included academic assessment and preparation to write the Ontario High School Equivalency Certificate (GED) exams as part of a Prior Learning Assessment Portfolio leading to College entrance (e.g. Seneca) or employment.

There were clear social, economic and academic benefits for students. Feedback from both teachers and students indicated that the program was extremely successful in meeting the needs of the adult population. Given a choice, students prefer the 60 hours GED preparation route to an Equivalency Certificate instead of the traditional delivery of credit courses over one to two years leading to an Ontario Secondary School Diploma (OSSD). The Career Development course with the Prior Learning Assessment Portfolio including the GED Preparation Component has also been of great benefit to students' self-esteem, enhancing their opportunities for job placements, job advancement and access to post-secondary institutions. Social Services Offices across Metro have demonstrated an appreciation of the partnership by referring hundreds of their social assistance clients to participate in the program at no cost to the student.

Unfortunately, the Ministry of Education and Training has directed MSSB to terminate the partnership as it is seen to be in conflict with current grant provisions.

The Training Renewal Foundation and MSSB were both encouraged that Ontario Works may provide funding for such a needy clientele.[134]

Community Services Appeal

The Training Renewal Foundation was now looking at other sources of support to continue the operation of the GED Preparation Centre. Since its inception the centre had assisted more than one thousand social assistance recipients, at no cost to Metro Community Services, to achieve an Ontario high school equivalency certificate. In November 1997, the foundation approached Shirley Hoy, Commissioner, Metro Community Services. A possible source of funding seemed to be the Ontario Works program through the Ministry of Skills Development option of employment supports. However, in late December, Heather MacVicar, General Manager, Social Services Division, informed us that the GED Preparation Centre did not qualify under Ontario Works or previous employment programs.

As the future of the preparation centre was in serious doubt, the Training Renewal Foundation decided to take political action. On 8 January 1998, Laurie Monsebratten, the *Toronto Star*'s social policy reporter, wrote a major article on the front page of the Greater Toronto section, entitled 'Loss of program may dash dreams – Funding cuts may doom welfare recipient program.'[129]She told the story of Desiree Bennett, a thirty-year- old grade-eight dropout who could not even get work as an office cleaner. For her, the thought of going back to the classroom for two to three years was daunting, but, to quote Bennett, 'thanks to this program I'm going to write my [high school equivalency] exam at the end of the month and make something of my life.'

On 14 January, I wrote a letter to Dr Gordon Chong, Chair, Toronto Community and Neighbourhood Services Committee, asking for the opportunity to meet the committee as soon as possible to discuss 'arbitrary decisions which will have such a devastating impact on disadvantaged adult learners in Toronto.' On 12 February, I appeared before the Community and Neighbourhood Services Committee to seek funding under Ontario Works for the foundation's GED preparation program. The response from Shirley Hoy and her staff was that, first, the GED Preparation Centre program did not qualify for funding under Ontario Works provisions (which was ironic since a letter was later received, dated 2 March 1998, from the director of social services of the County of Hastings stating that they were funding GED preparation under Ontario Works); and second, since adult basic education was the responsibility of the Ministry of Education and Training, the Ministry should be responsible for funding GED preparation. (On 27 February 1998, Dr Chong wrote a letter to Dave Johnson, who had replaced John Snobelen as minister of education and training, pressing this point.)

A second *Toronto Star* article, by education reporter Peter Small, entitled 'Dropouts realizing they face bleak future,' detailed how federal and provincial cuts were decimating programs meant to aid dropouts. Examples given included the threat to adult day schools, the upgrading courses offered at community colleges, and GED preparation. In spite of lobbying by the Metropolitan Toronto Board of Trade and the Ontario Chamber of Commerce, the question of who should be funding GED preparation for social assistance recipients was never resolved.

Another example of the government fighting its deficit on the backs of the poor was soon to follow. In a follow-up article on 12 March 1998, Peter Small reported on 'expected provincial slashing of funding for 13,000 people enrolled in adult day programs in Toronto. The Tories have already chopped $150 million from adult education. Toronto was spared because it did not rely on provincial grants. But that will change September 1 when the province sets new per pupil spending levels.'[135]

Immigrant and Refugee Partnerships

After the demise of the Metropolitan Separate School Board funding and the refusal of Metro Community Services to provide assistance because of their interpretation of Ontario Works guidelines, the GED Preparation Centre at 2700 Dufferin Street was closed. In August 1997 the Preparation Centre reopened in new shared accommodation at 75 Ingram Drive to reduce expenses. Fortunately, two new GED preparation partnerships were on the horizon.

Maytree Foundation. In March 1998, I approached Ratna Omidvar, Executive Director of the Maytree Foundation (formerly Executive Director of Skills for Change), about entering into a pilot project with Maytree to provide GED preparation training for immigrants and refugees. Maytree would initially support fifteen places at $300 per trainee. Each candidate would receive sixty hours of FASTRAC multi-media GED preparation, including computer-assisted assessment and training, print and video materials, and tutorial assistance according to individual needs.

Candidates would be referred from Davenport Perth Neighbourhood Centre, Rexdale Community Microskills Development Centre, Skills for Change, and Canadian African Newcomers Aid Centre. These organizations would also be represented on an advisory committee to guide the implementation of the pilot project. The committee would conduct a follow-up survey with reference to the success rate of candidates in achieving their Ontario high school equivalency certificate, as well as their future prospects for employment and training.[136] On 14 April 1998, a letter was received from Ms Omidvar, confirming a grant of $4,815 for the GED Preparation for Immigrants and Refugees (GEDFIR) pilot project.

On 15 July 1998, the Training Renewal Foundation submitted a final report to the Maytree Foundation. In general, it recognized the difficulty in recruiting candidates whose level of English proficiency was such that they could not successfully complete the sixty-hour preparation program leading to the GED exam. It was determined that only individuals with advanced English skills would be successful in the FASTRAC sixty-hour preparation format.

Davenport Perth. In January 1999, the Training Renewal Foundation was approached by the Davenport Perth Neighbourhood Centre to enter into a partnership to operate a GED preparation and prior-learning assessment and recognition project at 21 Randolph Avenue, a high-need newcomer reception area in west Toronto. In February, a contract was signed with Manager Barb Taylor of HRDC's Toronto Lakeside Office to operate the Skills Building for Employment facility, serving 250 participants from March 1999 to February 2000. The foundation's

GED software, videotape library, prior-learning-assessment curriculum, computer equipment, and furniture from 75 Ingram Drive were transferred to the new facility at 21 Randolph Avenue. Training Renewal Foundation staff trained the new Skills Assessment for Employment Centre personnel and served in an advisory capacity.

An important outcome of the new partnership was the recognition by Human Resources Development Canada that the department could enter into service agreements to fund projects that utilized a self-directed, computer-assisted assessment tool (for example, the foundation's GED software) by which an individual could gain information about his or her educational level. HRDC could also provide subsidy for individual clients to access GED preparation training under Ministry of Skills Development employment benefits. This decision had major positive future implications for Training Renewal Foundation's provision of learning assessment and GED preparation services.

BEST Institute of Technology

In 1984, during the days of the York Community Economic Development Committee, I met Mike DiDonato, owner of Faema Company Limited, who was looking to expand his operations beyond its location in a building on Davenport Road. Faema imported espresso coffee machines and other food service equipment from Italy. There had been a rapid growth in the specialty coffee industry in North America since the Second World War. First, Italian and then other European-style restaurants offered espresso and cappuccino on their menus. Later, chains of specialty coffee cafés, such as Starbucks and Second Cup, sprang up across the continent. The demand for new espresso equipment – at first imported mostly from Italy – grew exponentially. Mike DiDonato, a pioneer in the field, wanted not only to sell more equipment to restaurants and the home market but to begin roasting his own coffee beans. He needed more space and was interested in the former Hayhoe Foods factory in York. Unfortunately his wife and sons, who jointly owned Faema, were not in favour of the idea, and the deal fell through.

I kept in touch with Mike, and ten years later Faema had purchased a multistoreyed building on Dupont Street in Toronto. However, there was going to be a problem. The original technicians working for the company had, like Mike, been immigrants from Italy, and they were getting ready to retire. The business was expanding, and Faema needed more and more skilled technicians to repair, install, and service equipment in the field. Another concern was the changing nature of the technology. Machines, once mechanically operated, had become electronic with digital controls and were beginning to revolutionize the industry. With immigration from Europe declining steadily, Mike wondered where the new café equipment technicians would come from.

In 1996, with the assistance of Ratna Omidvar, I approached Pat Fia, Manager of HRDC's Dufferin office, to propose a Café Technician Repair and Installation training program. Four groups of eight unemployed persons would receive thirteen weeks of training in the repair and installation of café equipment. At the request of HRDC, the Training Renewal Foundation established the BEST (Barista Equipment Skill Training) Institute of Technology to provide training for the food equipment and other industries on a tuition or fee-for-service basis. This would also allow the foundation to apply to HRDC to be certified as an educational institution and provide tuition tax credit receipts. (The Training Renewal Foundation was duly certified in December 1997.)

Café Equipment Training

In February 1997, HRDC approved a sum of $243,600 to train a total of thirty-two unemployment insurance and social assistance recipients. The objectives of the project were to provide participants with basic skills and knowledge in the areas of café equipment installation, repair, and maintenance; to review accepted quality assurance practices and develop quality control and self-management skills; to develop participants' teamwork skills, through training and application in a working environment; to enhance participants' self-esteem and self-confidence through planned activities, acquisition of knowledge and skills, and team support and through on-the-job application of skills learned; to increase the long-term employment possibilities for participants by increasing their educational levels to that of high school graduate or equivalent (for example, GED preparation); to provide participants with technical skills in the installation, repair, and operation of café equipment; and to provide opportunities for participants to increase their interpersonal skills, as an aid to enhancing their value as an employee in the hospitality industry through contact with other trades people and the public.

The project was industry driven in that an advisory board of employers helped to develop the curriculum and monitored the ongoing implementation and evaluation of the project.

Potential candidates recruited from Canada Employment Centres and Social Services Offices attended an information session in which the foundation and advisory board members provided an overview of the industry, the thirteen-week program, and future employment opportunities. Those submitting application forms were screened for suitability and then interviewed by a team made up of the advisory board of employers and Training Renewal Foundation and HRDC personnel. The first group of eight began the training process on 1 April 1997.

Although Faema had been the original proposed training host for the project, problems emerged. There were continuing disagreements among Di Donato family members concerning the location of the project at 672 Dupont Street, and no lease was provided. Without a lease, no liability insurance could be secured; therefore the availability and security of accommodation could not be confirmed. Although Faema had promised to provide a trainer from its staff for the program, such a person had not been identified. The ability of Faema to provide employment opportunities and adequate wages for project graduates was also questionable.

At the eleventh hour, the foundation had to find a new training host. In desperation I visited David's Import, a neighbour of the then GED Preparation Centre at 2700 Dufferin Street. David's Import specialized in small espresso pod machines particularly for the home market. David suggested that I contact Andy, 'the service expert' at Alfa Food Machinery, which was a larger distributor of espresso machines and other equipment such as granita (slush) machines and panini (sandwich) grills. I called Andy and left a message about what I was seeking. Soon I got a rather irate return call from Ross Cammalleri, Alfa's chief executive officer, who accused me of trying to raid his staff (a common practice in the industry). When he had calmed down, I assured him that I was looking for a company to act as a training partner for the new Café Equipment Technician program. We got together and negotiated a joint venture agreement.

Alfa Food Machinery agreed to make available for lease a training space and equipment at their location at 231 Cartwright Avenue. The thirteen-week training process would incorporate an apprenticeship format, with ready access to the Alfa repair facility and the assistance of Vladimir Martinov, Alfa's director of technical services, as a training instructor.

Alfa itself required additional technical staff to accommodate the expanding demand for its services. They agreed to assist in approaching other companies, both locally and across Canada, to secure future employment of our successful graduates. The availability of skilled technicians was essential for the growth of the industry, and Alfa was prepared to form an association of Italian food service machinery distributors.

Barista Training

In October 1997, HRDC provided $51,000 to fund a six-month Café Equipment Operator (Barista) program for thirty-two employment insurance recipients. They were to receive two weeks of barista training in the operation and maintenance of café equipment at Alfa Food Machinery, which had relocated to 75 Ingram Drive in August 1997. The Training Renewal Foundation left its premises at 2700 Dufferin Street and York University in order to combine café equipment training, GED preparation, and the foundation office in one location, 75 Ingram Drive, as a tenant of Alfa.

In April 2000, the foundation formed a partnership with the Specialty Coffee Association of America (SCAA), the world's largest coffee trade association, to be its training representative in Canada. The first joint venture was offered in conjunction with the Canadian Coffee and Tea Expo in Toronto in September 2000. Eighteen participants were transported to the Training Renewal Foundation's training facility, where they ate lunch and spent an afternoon preparing to be baristas (coffee bar tenders), using the standards and curriculum pioneered by the SCAA. Trainees learned the basics of making a perfect espresso, fantastic cappuccino, and delightful iced drinks. Each of the participants gained enough knowledge and skill to receive a barista training certificate, which was presented jointly by TRF and the SCAA.[137]

Youth International

In September 1998, the foundation embarked on a Youth International project with $300,000 of HRDC funding, to provide up to twenty disadvantaged young people (aged eighteen to twenty-nine) with employment skills that would lead to jobs as café equipment technicians. The training format consisted of two months of skills orientation at Alfa's new location, followed by a two-month placement with an employer in the United States in order to learn more about digitally controlled equipment, and a further two months of work experience with a potential employer in Canada.

By this time, with Alfa's assistance, we had developed a network of industry employers who served on our advisory board or provided jobs for graduates. Several of these companies were either subsidiaries of U.S. firms or had business contacts south of the border. Placements for Youth International trainees included New Jersey, New York City, Buffalo, Minneapolis, Madison (Wisconsin), and Los Angeles. Two trainees were assigned to each location. The foundation provided a training allowance, which was deposited for each trainee in a bank in Toronto. Once in the United States, the trainees would access funds by using a credit card at an automated teller machine, because they were not allowed to be paid employees in that country.

The American companies assisted in finding temporary housing and transportation during the placement. While this turned out to be a personally enriching life-skills experience for participants, it was not without incident. Norman, an African Canadian (more than half of the trainees were visible minorities), had been placed at McCullagh Coffee's headquarters in Buffalo, New York. Late one evening he went to a local convenience store for snacks. Upon leaving the store, he was confronted at gunpoint by what turned out to be plain-clothes police officers. He was assaulted and handcuffed and soon found himself in jail, charged with murder. Fortunately McCullagh Coffee officials and John Campbell, the chief executive officer of McCullagh Coffee in Mississauga (Ontario), were able to secure Norman's release after about twenty-four hours. Was this just a case of mistaken identity or was it racial profiling? Regardless, Norman, who always seemed to be smiling, survived the experience to become a valued employee of Ambassador Coffee in Mississauga. Eighty per cent of Youth International graduates found employment in the coffee industry.

Another outcome of Youth International was a draft proposal to the Youth Entrepreneurship program of HRDC, entitled 'Young Entrepreneurs in Coffee and Vending Industries.' The proposal recognized that while most Youth International graduates found employment in the industry, there was also a strong interest, among some graduates, in setting up their own entrepreneurial ventures. To test the potential of a new entrepreneurship training program, a prototype portable coffee cart was designed and built by Milvan Food Equipment; Alfa Cappuccino Imports donated a Blitz pod machine, while Timothy's World Coffee and Ambassador Coffee provided consumables. The feasibility of the cart as a business enterprise was successfully demonstrated at the skating rink at Harbourfront by David Pontello.

Industrial Adjustment

The primary mandate of the Training Renewal Foundation has been 'to prepare the unemployed for new careers in a post-industrial economy, based on consumer-related services and knowledge-driven enterprise and globalization.' TRF recognized that future employment opportunities for its trainees would be in the personal services sector as opposed to traditional manufacturing or natural resource industries. Employers who approached the foundation for assistance with their human resource needs identified two of these personal service niches and training needs. With the assistance of HRDC's Industrial Adjustment Service, the Training Renewal Foundation was able to convene the following industrial adjustment committees.

Dry-cleaning and Laundering

Some employers in the dry-cleaning and laundering industry became aware of the fact that TRF was training technicians in the repair and maintenance of Italian-made espresso equipment. As most dry-cleaning equipment was also manufactured in Europe (especially Italy), they felt that we might have something in common. With funding provided by HRDC, the Dry-cleaning and Laundering Industry Adjustment Committee was established, consisting of industry employers, the Training Renewal Foundation, and Nancy Green from HRDC. A requirement of the industrial adjustment process was that the committee be chaired by an individual who was at arm's length from the industry and the foundation. Lesley Miller from York University was chosen to chair the committee, which operated from April 1998 to August 2000.

Issues facing the industry included an aging pool of skilled workers in the industry, particularly in the pressing and spotting areas, and a shrinking pool of garments to be dry-cleaned, owing to consumer preferences and societal trends towards casual dressing. In addition, several home dry-cleaning products had come into the marketplace; although the results of use had not yet been thoroughly tested, the short-term effect was the further erosion of the public's use of dry-cleaners. Furthermore, a number of new cleaning technologies (for example, wet cleaning) were now available for use by dry-cleaners, and these technologies required an exceptional refinement of skills. There was an urgent need for the small and medium-size enterprises making up this service industry to remain competitive, pay attention to training, and ramp up for new technology.

The final report of the Dry-cleaning and Laundering Industry Adjustment Committee contained the following summary:

Over the past two years, the Drycleaning and Laundering Industry Adjustment Committee has worked hard to become a cohesive group focused on assessing and addressing the human resource implications associated with changes in the fabricare industry. As of August 2000, the Committee has an active membership of over 15 individuals involved in all aspects of the project. The Committee has taken responsibility for undertaking actions that will benefit this large (over 2,000 drycleaners employing at least 7,500 individuals in Ontario), highly fragmented industry that has great difficulty in speaking with one voice.

Over the initial period that the Drycleaning and Laundering Industry Adjustment Committee was in existence, its work focused on outreaching to, and building a trust relationship with, key individuals within the drycleaning industry. One of its first steps was to undertake a Needs Assessment survey within the industry.

During the first year, the Committee explored ways of meeting the needs identified in the Needs Assessment including raising the profile of the industry and offering on-site training programs, particularly in the areas of spotting and pressing. A great deal of feasibility work was undertaken during this phase, yet each possible training solution proved extremely difficult and costly to implement.

As the Committee moved into its second year, it officially established a joint project with the Ontario Fabricare Association (OFA), building an industry membership organization, to achieve goals in two priority areas: mentorship/training and profile-building.

During the past year much effort and vision have gone into achieving the goals established by the combined Industry Adjustment Committee and the OFA. The two priority areas have provided an opportunity for the industry to:

– Introduce technology;
– Build capacity and knowledge
– Enhance skills;
– Build partnerships and networks.

Highlights of the accomplishments of the Industry Adjustment process include launching of the fabricare.org website in November 2000, curriculum development for a Pressing and Spotting Course and a Customer Service Representative Training Course, and the initiation of a number of potential partnerships with organizations and associations with similar interests.[138]

Coffee and Vending

During the spring and summer of 2001 the foundation convened meetings between the Ontario Coffee and Vending Service Association (OCVSA) and Human Resources Development Canada to investigate human resource needs in the office coffee and vending industry. OCVSA is a not-for-profit organization whose membership consists of operators and suppliers of coffee and vending services.

On 1 October 2002, OCVSA signed an agreement with the Labour Market Partnerships program of HRDC to establish the Ontario Coffee and Vending Labour Adjustment Committee with the following objective: 'to undertake an industry-wide needs assessment that will form the basis for determining the short- and long-term human resources requirements and for developing plans to meet these needs.' The committee was chaired by Dr Ari Dassanayake of Canadian Offshore Investments, and participants included representatives of Heritage Coffee, Mother Parker's Tea and Coffee, Speedy Vending, Olympia Coffee, Vending Products of Canada, Kingsmill Foods, Coffee Association of Canada, HRDC, and the Training Renewal Foundation.

The Ontario Coffee and Vending Labour Committee met from December 2001 to March 2002 to develop, distribute, and analyse the results of an industry needs assessment survey that was circulated by mail and through an insert in *Canadian Vending Magazine*. The final report of the committee, which was prepared and published by the foundation with funding provided by HRDC and in-kind support from OCVSA, was officially presented on 31 March 2002. Conclusions and recommendations dealt with the additional sources of both pre-service and in-service training for route drivers, sales staff, and technical personnel. In this regard, a training resource library of print and audio-visual materials was assembled. Strategic alliances were recommended between OCVSA and such organizations as the National Automatic Merchandizing Association, the Specialty Coffee Association of America, the Canadian Automatic Merchandizing Association, and the Training Renewal Foundation.

Office Coffee and Vending Equipment Training

In August 1999, the Training Renewal Foundation's landlord and training partner, Alfa Food Machinery, decided to purchase its own premises at 750 Millway Avenue, Unit 6, north of Toronto in the city of Vaughan. While this meant another move for the foundation's offices and training facilities, it also extended our service network to the rapidly expanding Greater Toronto Area. In 1999–2000, TRF formed a new partnership with the Region of York's Community Services and Housing Department to provide BEST Institute of Technology's Café Equipment Technician skill training for the region's Ontario Works clients. Vladimir Martinov, Director of Technical Services for Alfa, and Ann Bradfield, TRF's administrative assistant (and a BEST graduate), provided ten weeks of theoretical and skill training, which was followed by four weeks of on-the-job placement with industry employers.

Two training sessions were completed from December 1999 to March 2000 and from May to August 2000, and a total of twenty graduates received BEST Café Equipment Technician certificates, which led to jobs in the coffee industry or related fields. Since its inception in 1997, more than ninety unemployed persons had graduated from BEST training programs to secure positions in the food services sector, many with office coffee and vending equipment employers.

As a result of the success of the Café Equipment Technician programs, the Training Renewal Foundation was becoming known throughout the coffee industry. Espresso-based specialty coffee represents about 20 per cent of industry sales. Eighty per cent of Canadians still prefer traditional brewed coffee (such as Tim Hortons). In 2000, Sam Silvestro, the chief executive officer of Topeco Coffee and Tea in Cambridge and the past president of OCVSA, approached the foundation. Sam wondered whether TRF might consider offering a training program for office coffee and vending equipment technicians and service workers. Topeco and several other employers in the Waterloo region were experiencing difficulty in filling openings for technicians and route drivers in their brew coffee service and vending machine operations.

The foundation approached Garry Springer, Employment Support Programs Supervisor for the Region of Waterloo Social Services and Housing Department, to determine the feasibility of offering such a program, utilizing Topeco as the host company. The source of trainees would be Ontario Works and active employment insurance recipients. Early in December 2000, TRF met with local employers, HRDC, and the

Waterloo Employment Support Program to establish an advisory committee and develop a curriculum for training. The new program was to
be fourteen weeks in duration: ten weeks of theory and hands-on training at Topeco followed by four weeks of work experience placement
with a prospective employer.

Two job fairs were held in January 2001, resulting in forty-eight applications received. Waterloo Social Services selected twenty-five applicants to be interviewed by the advisory committee, who chose fifteen
candidates for the program. Training was offered from February to May
2001, and by July a total of twelve trainees were employed, two were
being interviewed, and one was forced to withdraw for health reasons.
This was believed to be the first office coffee and vending equipment
technician and service worker training program in Canada.[139]

The Training Renewal Foundation has continued to train social
assistance recipients each year for careers as coffee and vending equipment technicians and service workers. In August 2001 the foundation
partnered with the Region of York Community Services and Housing
Department and Coffee Delight in Vaughan to provide ten weeks of
training in brew coffee service and vending machine operation followed by four weeks of on-the-job experience with a potential employer. In November 2002 the program was repeated, with Red Carpet Food
Services in Markham acting as host employer and the Ontario Coffee
and Vending Service Association joining the partnership.

April 2003 saw the Region of Peel Social Services join TRF and McCullagh Food Services to offer the program. It was repeated in August 2004
with one week of pre-employment preparation, prior to the ten weeks
of theoretical and hands-on skill training, added to the format. In September 2005, the foundation, with support from the York Region Community Development and Investment Fund, delivered the program in
partnership with Alfa Cappuccino Imports. Then in June 2006, it was Peel
Social Services, with Van Houtte Inc. as host employer. Since 1997, more
than two hundred unemployed persons have trained with the Training
Renewal Foundation and its partners for careers in coffee and vending.

Industrial Warehousing

In August 2001, TRF was asked by the Region of York Community
Services and Housing Department to assist in establishing a training
program for lift truck operators. The foundation approached Hewitt
Material Handling, the Ontario sales and service dealer for Caterpillar

lift trucks, located nearby at 425 Millway Avenue in Concord. Hewitt's Rick Dawe provided one week of theoretical, hands-on, and safety training for ten trainees at its plant, and TRF organized an additional week of on-the-job experience with warehouse employers. In December, nine trainees received their Lift Truck Operator certificates.

As a result of the success of the Region of York programs, Garry Springer of Waterloo Social Services approached TRF in February 2002 to coordinate a series of industrial warehouse training programs for eight groups of ten social assistance recipients. Following information sessions in different Waterloo Region locations, and a interview selection process, candidates received one week of employment-readiness training from Waterloo's Experience Matters program, which included attendance, motivation, dependability, and teamwork. Hewitt Material Handling provided one week of lift truck operator theory and safety instruction, plus hands-on training at their Trillium Drive branch in Kitchener. As well as sourcing the lift truck training opportunity, TRF organized on-the-job work experience with placement partners in the region.

At the completion of the program in April 2003, the Region of Waterloo estimated that more than 85 per cent of the trainees had achieved employment in the industrial warehousing field. Despite this success, one of the placement employers, the Food Bank of Waterloo, lobbied vigorously among regional politicians to take over the contract. (The Food Bank's executive director was a regional politician.) TRF was portrayed as an outside interloper, and even though the foundation had originated and perfected the program, it lost the contract.

Nevertheless, this did not mean the end of industrial warehouse training. Beginning in April 2005, the Training Renewal Foundation partnered with the Region of York, Hewitt Material Handling, and Safety One Inc. to train seven groups of ten Ontario Works clients as industrial lift truck operators. One week of pre-employment training was followed by a week of lift truck operator theory and safety instruction, plus hands-on experience. A third week of job-readiness training prepared graduates for employment.

From the Grounds Up

In January 2001, TRF joined with Turning Point Youth Services and Operation Go Home to establish a combined GED learning assessment centre and barista training café at 95 Wellesley Street East in Toronto.

Called From the Grounds Up, it served the academic upgrading and employment skill training needs of homeless youth who were referred by agencies in the downtown area. The foundation donated computers, furniture, software, training, and materials. Turning Point Youth Services provided accommodation, and Starbucks Coffee donated an equipped espresso cart, tables, and chairs.

Functional Literacy Forum

The Training Renewal Foundation was originally instrumental in bringing the adult General Educational Development (GED) program to Ontario. A pilot preparation project in 1995–6 had led to the introduction of the Ontario high school equivalency certificate, with test centres operated by the Ministry of Education across the province. In June 2001, TRF convened the 'Invitational Forum for Functional Literacy in a Knowledge Economy' in the Torstar board room at the *Toronto Star* offices. Chaired by Dr Charles Pascal, Executive Director of the Atkinson Foundation, the forum brought together key leaders of the commercial, governmental, and voluntary sectors including TV Ontario, Prime Restaurants, Rogers Cable, Centre FORA, NCS Learn, Ontario Works, the National Literacy Secretariat (of HRDC), TDL Group Ltd., City TV, Statistics Canada, Glen Ardith Frazer Group, Toronto Board of Trade, Ontario Chamber of Commerce, Conference Board of Canada, Ontario Secondary School Teachers' Federation, Computers for Schools Ontario, *Toronto Star*, Ministry of Correctional Services, and the Independent Learning Centre of the Ministry of Education.

The purpose of the forum was to address the learning needs of the 3.5 million Ontario citizens (per Statistics Canada) who had some degree of difficulty with literacy and numeracy skills and accreditation, so that they would be better able to compete in today's new social and economic environment. An outcome of the forum was to be a series of planning and implementation working groups in the following areas: literacy training and labour adjustment in the hospitality industry; a pilot project for eighteen- to twenty-one-year-old graduates of the Ontario Works' Learning, Earning, and Parenting program; ways to promote and publicize better the availability of GED testing; the Ontario high school equivalency certificate and preparation and remediation services; and an expansion of the use of the Internet to deliver the above programs.[144]

Learning, Earning, and Parenting

In March 2002, as an outcome of the functional literacy forum, the foundation formed a joint venture to create the Learning, Earning, and Parenting (LEAP) Demonstration Project with the Region of York Community Services and Housing Department; the Ontario Works branch of the Ministry of Community, Family, and Children's Services; the Ontario Early Years Challenge Fund; Tim Hortons; and TV Ontario. To quote the Training Renewal Foundation's annual report of 2002–3:

> The first phase began with ten 18- to21-year-old social assistance parents for whom traditional high school completion was not an option due to childcare responsibilities. Objectives for the project included the achievement of the Ontario High School Equivalency Certificate, through GED preparation training utilising home instruction via the Internet, and preparation for post-secondary education and employment. The Workplace Skills Training Partnership, LearnScape.com and the Education Network of Ontario (ENO) provided software and Internet access. Tim Hortons and Prime Restaurants offered employment assistance. York Region's Ontario Works program contributed transportation, childcare and training expenses. TRF was responsible for: overall orientation; computer equipment; arranging software and Internet access; and ongoing academic support. Overall, the Ontario Early Years Challenge Fund and the Rotary Club of Toronto–Forest Hill, provided financial assistance for the demonstration project.
>
> The participants in the first phase were joined by another group of ten young women in April 2003. As of July 2003, seven participants were planning to write their GED examinations prior to September 2003. One participant has written her GED examinations and passed them successfully. Of the total group of twenty participants, ten were already enrolled or planning to enrol in post-secondary programs and five are working full time. Of participants enrolled in this demonstration project, fifteen of twenty (or 75 per cent) should no longer need the support of Ontario Works within a year of starting the program. A further three are uncertain of their plans about post-secondary programs, but are investigating options. This has been a positive outcome for the participants. Most of them have gained the skills required to live independently of social assistance and have gained the skills needed for future success. It is hoped that these skills and aspirations will be shared with their children.[140]

Your Choice Learning Centre

In December 2000, TRF responded to a Request for Proposal from the Ontario Ministry of Education for demonstration projects to address provisions of the *Safe Schools Act* related to Strict Discipline programs for expelled students. *The Safe Schools Act* (2000) required that a student be expelled for committing any of the following infractions while at school or engaged in a school-related activity: possessing a weapon, including possessing a firearm; using a weapon to cause or to threaten bodily harm to another person; committing physical assault on another person that causes bodily harm, requiring treatment by a medical practitioner; committing sexual assault; trafficking in weapons or in illegal drugs; committing robbery; giving alcohol to a minor; and engaging in another activity that, under a policy of the board, is one for which expulsion is mandatory. A fully expelled student was not allowed to enter a school premises in the province until the expulsion order had been lifted. This meant that an alternative learning site had to be created to accommodate these students.

I approached two of my former colleagues from my schooling days, Bill Hogarth, Director of Education, York Region District School Board, and Charles McCarthy, Superintendent of Education, York Catholic District School Board, as partners in the development and submission of an application for funding. The twenty-seven-month project would provide academic, social, and fitness skills for up to ten fully expelled students from York Region at a time. In January 2001, notification was received from the Ministry that a demonstration project had been approved to take place from April 2001 to June 2003.

The public board provided financial administrative services and accommodation at its Jefferson site, 11570 Yonge Street, which was a former school building that the board rented for professional development activities. The Catholic board was responsible for the services of a full-time teacher, a child and youth worker, and a part-time principal, as well as assessment and learning materials, furniture, and equipment (for example, computers and fitness gear).

On 1 April 2001, the project opened as the Your Choice Learning Centre (YCLC). The teacher chosen for the centre was an amateur bodybuilder who was skilled in the use of the project's weight training and fitness equipment. The weight training and fitness activities proved to be very popular with the students, particularly in building self-esteem.

The responsibilities of the Training Renewal Foundation as part of the management team included the initial contact, pre-admission, and application process for parents and students interested in applying to YCLC; liaison with the student's former school, as well as community service agencies, resulting in the preparation of a student profile; and ongoing consultative assistance to YCLC staff, students, parents, and community service agencies regarding academic and behavioural assessment.

Owing to the demand for services in the Georgina area of the region, the foundation was also responsible for the initiation of a northern satellite facility in Sutton. Space was acquired at the Georgina Arts Centre to accommodate up to four students. A part-time teacher and a full-time child and youth worker were allocated to this facility.

The first student was admitted to the YCLC demonstration project in December 2001. As of June 2003, a total of twenty-eight applications had been received for admission to YCLC. Ten students successfully completed the program and were approved for re-entry to a regular school. Twelve students either did not proceed to be formally admitted to the centre or left before completing the requirements of the Strict Discipline program.

When the demonstration project was completed, the Training Renewal Foundation applied to the Ministry for an extension of funds for an additional year. This was opposed by the York Region District School Board who resented the fact that the original funding had gone to the partnership and not to support their own needs, such as their ACCESS program for suspended students. Although the foundation had conceived the project, written the proposal, and formed the YCLC partnership, the Ministry chose to direct future funding to the public board, leaving the other two partners out of the project.

Meeting the Gap

In July 2003, Karen Glass of the Ministry of Community, Family, and Children's Services approached TRF to investigate the feasibility of introducing to Ontario the Welfare-to-Career (W2C) program pioneered by Cascade Engineering in Grand Rapids, Michigan. Cascade and its chief executive officer, Fred Keller, had received numerous national and community awards for encouraging the unemployed and underemployed to make a successful transition to long-term, sustainable employment. Their workforce of 1,100 included about 100 former social assistance recipients.

The Cascade W2C experience resulted in many benefits, including the realization of a competitive advantage by utilizing an untapped pool of human resources (the unemployed) and drastically reducing recruitment costs. Perhaps most important, the program afforded the company an opportunity to provide leadership in illustrating how both social and private sector goals could be reached simultaneously.

In August 2003, I travelled to Grand Rapids to meet with Ron Jimmerson, Cascade's human resources manager of community partnerships and workforce diversity. Key to the success of the program had been a partnership with the State of Michigan's Family Independence Agency whereby the agency's caseworkers were placed on site at Cascade to assist W2C clients to become valued employees. The costs of the caseworker service were shared between Cascade and the Family Independence Agency. The success of the W2C program at Cascade had led to the establishment of the Southwest Organizations Unifying Resources for Our Community and Employees (SOURCE). Ten local Grand Rapids employers had joined with Cascade and the Family Independence Agency to replicate the W2C model through the SOURCE Resource Centre.

In the fall of 2003, the Training Renewal Foundation established a working group with several employers and representatives from the Ontario Works branch of the Ministry of Community and Social Services and three Ontario Works delivery agents for the regions of York, Peel, and Brantford-Brant. In February 2004, TRF convened 'Meeting the Gap,' an employer information forum to secure support for creating provincially tailored, industry-specific skill and pre-employment training opportunities within the Ontario Works framework. Ron Jimmerson provided an overview of the W2C-SOURCE model to an audience of fifty, including approximately twenty-five employers and industry associations in such fields as transportation and logistics, coffee and vending services, construction, heating and air conditioning, and building maintenance.

In May 2004 an advisory committee of employer and governmental representatives was established to guide the development of a framework for adapting the W2C-SOURCE model for Ontario.

Pre-employment Partnership

In March 2004, the Training Renewal Foundation was informed that its proposal for the Pre-Employment Partnership (PREP) had been approved by the Region of York under its Community Development and Investment Funding strategy. The PREP Project in the Region of York would replicate the W2C-SOURCE model to serve the needs of Ontario Works recipients. The foundation would partner with employers and the Social Services Department to identify key employment sectors in the region where there was an ongoing labour shortage for skilled, job-ready personnel (for example, in building trades, coffee and vending, and industrial warehousing); to recruit and convene employer networks in each sector according to labour adjustment needs; to develop job-readiness, pre-employment, and skill training courses of study for each of the employment sectors; to establish ongoing procedures for sourcing appropriate Ontario Works participants to receive pre-employment and skill training according to sectoral needs; and to identify sources of financial support to cover the costs of the above training.

It was anticipated that the PREP Project would build and strengthen a strategic alliance of commercial, governmental, and voluntary partners to address social and economic needs in the region of York while serving to demonstrate the feasibility of the W2C-SOURCE model in Ontario.

Construction Craft Worker

In June 2001, Local 183 of the Universal Workers Union had partnered with management contractors and the Ministry of Training, Colleges, and Universities to launch the Construction Craft Worker (CCW) as an apprenticeship trade in Ontario. The new trade established standards for excellence and province-wide certified training. Construction craft worker apprentices who enrolled in the two-year program were instructed in a wide range of skills including blueprint reading, operating hand tools and stationary equipment, form setting and placing concrete, using rigs and hoists, selecting and installing scaffolding, and protecting the natural environment.

In May 2004, the Training Renewal Foundation was a partner in a pilot project to recruit, select, and train social assistance recipients from the region of York as CCW apprentices. The foundation provided, as a field test of the PREP curriculum, seven trainees with three weeks of pre-employment training before they commenced their eight weeks of construction craft skill training at the Life Long Learning Centre in Vaughan. The Universal Workers Union's Local 183 and management contractors jointly operated this centre. The Training Renewal Foundation was responsible for a further two-week job trial placement and the ongoing monitoring of trainees for the six months after they had secured employment as paid construction craft worker apprentices. The project was repeated again in February 2005.

Unfortunately in 2006 the Universal Workers Union, Local 183, was forced into receivership by its original parent, the International Labourers' Union in the United States, which resulted in the termination of the Construction Craft Worker partnership.

Employment Assistance and Retention Network

During the period from 1 January to 31 December 2006, TRF initiated the Employment Assistance and Retention Network (EARN) demonstration project with financial assistance from the Region of York's Community Development and Investment Fund. The project served social assistance recipients and their families who were immigrants or refugees. EARN was designed as a holistic approach to assist internationally trained professionals, trades people, entrepreneurs, and managers to secure employment in their previous vocation, in a related field, or in a new career based on their knowledge, skills, and experience.

A total of fifty referrals were provided from social service centres in Vaughan, Richmond Hill, and Newmarket. Thirty-six per cent of the newcomers were from the Middle East, and 28 per cent from eastern Asia and Africa. Highlights of the program included a two-week pre-employment training program that focused on confidence building, interpersonal skills, goal setting, team problem solving, résumé preparation, computer literacy, and educational upgrading, as well as child development and parenting skills as required. The foundation provided laptops to twenty-nine participants who lacked home-based computers (each laptop had software programs installed), and fourteen families received Internet connections.

EARN resources consisted of employers, professional and trade organizations, education service providers, community service organizations, and volunteer groups and individuals. They provided cooperative education placements, mentorships, qualifications, skills, assessments, job referrals, vocational information, career path clarification, and employment opportunities.

Of the fifty original EARN participants, seven were deemed to be unemployable because of health concerns or childcare responsibilities. Two disappeared or were unreachable, and two were referred to the Ontario Disabilities Support Program. That left a total of thirty-nine (78 per cent) who were capable of benefiting from EARN. Of this group, twenty-nine (75 per cent) received placements in cooperative education settings or mentorships. Nineteen (49 per cent) participated in job-search activities, which resulted in fourteen (36 per cent) securing employment. A further nineteen (49 per cent) were enrolled, or were in the process of enrolling, in further education or training. Therefore, a total of thirty-three (85 per cent) of EARN participants were either employed or would be employable after further education and training.[141]

Outcomes and Reflections

For many years I had been working 'both sides of the street.' While earning a living in the governmental institutional schooling sector, I was also active in the voluntary sector creating community education and economic development programs. Often the two sectors overlapped through my involvement in developing such organizations as the Learnxs Foundation and the Learning Enrichment Foundation. These activities were often influential in the creation of new policies and programs locally, provincially, and even nationally. In fact, such innovations as the educational foundation, alternatives in education, and community education and economic development gained widespread exposure for Toronto on the international stage.

In 1995, I found myself for the first time solely in the non-profit voluntary sector. As far as the governmental and commercial sectors were concerned, I was for the most part on the outside, looking in. The Training Renewal Foundation, however, as a special-purpose body (as opposed to a philanthropy) still had the capacity through its demonstration projects to encourage change and influence policy development. Financial support for its operations has come from all levels of government – municipal, provincial, and federal. The primary recipients of TRF services have most often been the disadvantaged, the unemployed, and the alienated, many of whom were newcomers to Canada. Yet, my life as a change agent and social entrepreneur continued to be an intensely political struggle, with both successes and failures.

The forerunner of TRF, the Centre for Community Education and Economic Renewal, sought a hosting relationship with the Ontario Institute for Studies in Education. This was important because it gave the fledgling organization credibility in seeking demonstration-project funding from the federal government. OISE also offered access to valuable resources including personnel and space. However, all the funds (about $750,000) flowed through OISE and were subject to its relatively high administrative fees, its requirement to place otherwise redundant staff, and a tendency to 'back-seat drive' the centre. Nevertheless, it was a positive experience thanks to the initial support of Professor Jack Quarter and Assistant Director, and later Director, Angela Hildyard.

I believe that participants in the Training Interns in Education project gained much from their association with OISE. Being able to secure placements and mentorships with schools in Metropolitan Toronto was a definite asset in helping TIE graduates to gain certification and future employment. I would like to think that TIE also helped policymakers to focus on reducing barriers for foreign-trained professionals (for example, with the Access to Professions and Trades program of the Ontario Ministry of Citizenship). I am not sure, however, that shifting responsibility for accreditation from the Ministry of Education to the College of Teachers was a step in the right direction.

The GED Preparation Centre pilot project represented a policy milestone for aid to the disadvantaged adult learner, particularly newcomers to Canada. It was also a political exercise in which gaining the support of Premier Bob Rae and Deputy Minister Charles Pascal was an essential component. The GED Preparation Centre pilot project eventually achieved about an 85 per cent success rate in preparing social assistance recipients for the Ontario high school equivalency certificate using the FASTRAC computer-assisted system. Unfortunately we continued to struggle with certain Ministry of Education and Training bureaucrats and Ontario Secondary School Teachers' Federation operatives who were trying to undermine the GED and the Ontario high school equivalency certificate process and helping to keep it Ontario's best kept secret. (This became particularly evident later when the Ministry forced the Metropolitan Separate School Board to terminate the Career Development–GED Preparation project.)

The forced merger of the Faculty of Education of the University of Toronto and OISE proved to be fatal to the hosting agreement for the Centre for Community and Economic Renewal. The 40 per cent overhead levy and CCER's inability to collect fees for service meant that this relationship could not continue. We were fortunate to gain, through Dean Stan Shapson, a temporary home at York University until the Training Renewal Foundation could be legally incorporated as an independent charitable organization. Special tribute must be paid to CCER advisory board volunteers and, in particular, Larry Hebb, Steve Mould, and John Howley, whose leadership helped to make it all possible.

Another milestone in the history of the Training Renewal Foundation has been our involvement with the coffee industry. Responding to industry needs, in first espresso and later brew coffee and vending equipment, TRF has become a major source of trained personnel for the industry. Since 1997, more than two hundred unemployed persons have been prepared for careers in this industry. Special appreciation must be extended to such industry leaders as Ross Cammalleri and Vladimir Martinov, Alfa Cappuccino Imports; John Campbell, McCullagh Food Services; Murray Schelter, Ambassador Coffee; Fritz Kugler, Timothy's World Coffee and Zavida Coffee; Ted Fusee, Van Houtte Inc. (and also a current TRF coffee and vending trainer); and Sam Silvestro, Topeco Coffee. These were the pioneers, who along with TRF Associate Director Murray Shukyn and myself made it all possible. Another key source of support has been the Ontario Coffee and Vending Service Association and, in particular, its past presidents Sam Silvestro, Sam Neill, and Peter Wilson. The foundation has established the first espresso and brew coffee equipment training programs in North America.

With the support and guidance of Human Resource Development Canada's Industry Adjustment Service staff, including Tony Melino, Nancy Green, and Maged Daoud, the Training Renewal Foundation was able to mount effective industry-driven labour adjustment demonstration projects for at-risk youth, for dry cleaning and laundering personnel, and for coffee and vending equipment technicians, respectively. Each involved research and development activities to investigate how to meet present and future human resource requirements.

The provision of industrial warehousing training was in response to requests from York Region, and later Waterloo Region, to train and place social assistance recipients as lift truck operators. However, after designing the program and successfully preparing about 150 new lift truck operators for the warehousing industry, TRF found itself a victim of political manoeuvring as non-profit and commercial trainers (Food Bank of Waterloo and Safety One) moved in to take over the training contracts.

Another area of innovation was the Your Choice Learning Centre for fully expelled students in York Region. The foundation had responded to a Request for Proposal by forming a partnership with the two York Region school boards and writing and submitting an application for funding to the Ministry of Education. When the application was approved, TRF itself did not have the financial resources required to administer the project over the twenty-seven-month period. Money had to be available upfront to purchase furniture and equipment and to pay staff until transfer payments from the Ministry were received. So the York Region District School Board became 'the bank' for the project.

Although initially an acceptable stand-alone storefront had been found by TRF, ultimately the school board insisted that the centre be located in a building that it was renting on Yonge Street in Richmond Hill. Fees paid by the centre would significantly reduce the rental cost of the building for the school board. The building also housed the school board's ACCESS program for suspended students. However, the proximity of the two programs, and their different operating styles (ACCESS was more freewheeling with less supervision), caused conflict between students and staff of the two programs. It is not surprising, perhaps, that when the twenty-seven months ended, the York Region District School Board lobbied vigorously (and successfully) with the Ministry to gain sole access to the funding, much to the dismay of both TRF and the York Catholic District School Board.

One lesson learned from the Employment Assistance and Retention Network (EARN) project was that there appears to be an incentive for some service providers to keep newcomers in their programs as long as possible. This makes sense if the programs are funded based on the number of registrations achieved each year. But what of the newcomers who wish to gain skills and be employed as soon as possible? They seem to be caught in a perpetual revolving door of assessment, résumé writing, job readiness, and job-finding courses, with little connection to marketable skills and employment.

In summary, being a small fish in a big pond continues to be a struggle. A small organization (like TRF) with low overhead and infinite flexibility has to be very entrepreneurial and creative to survive. It reminds me of the old saying 'Success has a thousand parents; failure is an orphan.' A small non-profit social enterprise might be more responsive to the needs of the population it serves and more creative in its problem solving, but too often, it seems, the older, well-established, and more politically connected A-list agencies swoop in to seize the funding (and the credit) once a service pattern has proven itself. The small organization soon finds itself on the outside, looking in. Having said that, the Training Renewal Foundation in its first ten years of operation has been justly proud of what it has accomplished, as an advocate of community education and social enterprise, in serving the needs of the disadvantaged and the employment community in the Greater Toronto Area.

16 What Is Old Can Be New Again

Gaining a Global Perspective

In 1973, I had submitted an action profile to the Inner City Schools work group entitled 'Cultural Immersion Program for Teachers in Immigrant Areas.' It resulted in a series of professional seminars on Italian social, cultural, and political life offered during the fall of 1973 and winter of 1974. During the winter break a nine-day study tour was organized for seminar participants to visit schools, day nurseries, homes, and historic and cultural sites in cities, towns, and villages in the Abruzzi region. This area, on the Adriatic Sea in central Italy, had been a major source of newcomers emigrating to Canada, and Toronto in particular.

A detailed itinerary, including air and land transfers and hotel accommodations, was the responsibility of Fernando Caligiuri of the International Cultural Exchange. Fernando, a former Alitalia executive, had extensive experience in organizing student travel to Europe, particularly during the winter break. I had never before been outside of North America, and this study tour proved to be a life-altering experience for me.

I will always remember visiting the Italian village of Castelli on the slopes of the Gran Sasso, the highest mountain in the Apennines. Above Castelli had been a monastery whose monks for centuries produced exquisite ceramic artefacts. Boys from the village traditionally had trudged up the mountain to be educated and trained as artisans by the monks. The original monastery was now a museum, but boys (and girls) from the village still learned to manufacture ceramics, while attending the local school. Some graduates had established cottage industries, selling ceramic craft to support the local economy. An addi-

tional vital source of revenue was the many families who had immigrated to Toronto and were sending money back to help their relatives
in Castelli.

Another memorable experience occurred during a visit to monu-
ments in Rome. One of the participants was Crawford Murphy, Principal of St Gaspar School in North York. While touring the area around
the Trevi fountain, I discovered a small church containing the tomb of
St Gaspar. Needless to say, when Crawford returned to school with
photos taken in front of the tomb, he became an instant hero among the
Italian parents whose children attended St Gaspar.

I also realized that many people from the generations before the
advent of the jumbo jet had never had access to relatively inexpensive
travel overseas. This was not true for the young people of the seventies
who were backpacking around the world. As someone committed to
experiential learning, I felt there should be a better way to serve the
needs of 'leisure learners' such as myself. It was then that my wife,
Marilyn, and I created Can-Learn International as a program-planning
enterprise to assist universities, colleges, school boards, voluntary
organizations, business, and industry to address the unique experiential learning needs of their staff and clientele.

Over the years, Can-Learn, in partnership originally with the International Cultural Exchange and later Ontario Sarracini Travel Service,
has assisted educators in planning a great variety of educational-travel
opportunities. Some have been general interest or professional development activities for adults, while others involved academic credits
for university and senior secondary school students. Programs have
included artistic and cultural interests, historic and archaeological
themes, environmental and wellness experiences, and new service patterns. In each instance, they have been custom designed to meet the
unique needs of groups of learners according to our motto 'Stretch
your mind, not your budget.' Personally, Can-Learn International has
afforded me opportunities to travel and to gain a cross-cultural global
perspective on community education and economic development.

Another such profound learning experience was the time spent in Sri
Lanka with Ari Dassanayake. Ari, the consummate networker, introduced me to the social and cultural realities of a country teetering on
the verge of civil war. The beauty of the natural and built environment
was complemented by the warmth and friendship of the people. To be
treated as a colleague rather than just another tourist was a revelation.
My two trips to Colombo and the surrounding countryside included

visits to industrial sites and tea and rubber plantations to understand the nation's economy better. In the spiritual city of Kandy, I had the honour to worship at the temple devoted to the adoration of Buddha's tooth. As a result of these experiences, a series of proposals for cultural and economic ventures were drafted, linking Colombo and Toronto.

Centre for Educational Research and Innovation

During my study leave to England (primarily Bury, Manchester) in 1985, I walked in off the street to visit the offices of the Centre for Employment Initiatives in London. Their journal *Initiatives* showcased community education, training, and economic development innovations for at-risk youth. There I met Colin Ball, the editor, who soon was eager for me to write an article on the York Model to be published in the journal. Colin was in the process of being named a lead author at the Organisation for Economic Co-operation and Development's (OECD's) Centre for Educational Research and Innovation (CERI) in Paris. This began my own involvement in a series of OECD-CERI projects, expert meetings, and symposia in several different countries.

Enterprise Learning

In 1987, Colin Ball nominated me to represent Canada as a country expert in a new CERI project of inquiry directed at '(a) how young people can be enabled to develop employment initiatives and entrepreneurial skills as an important ingredient of their education and training; (b) what changes are needed in educational curricula and school practices designed to strengthen young peoples' capacity to assume responsibility and initiative in a situation where labour markets and skill requirements are rapidly changing.'[142]

The experts' group for the project, led by CERI's Jarl Bengtsson, held several meetings to present clarifying reports concerning practice in their respective countries, including Australia, Canada, Ireland, Japan, the Netherlands, Sweden, United Kingdom, Greece, Italy, France, Spain, and Denmark. The process of preparing the final report entitled 'Towards an Enterprising Culture' represented a profound learning experience for me, working closely with colleagues on the international stage.

One outcome of the project was a definition for *enterprise learning*, which may be described as 'a project or task centred process: (1) which is defined entirely by the learner; (2) which is centred on real projects or tasks of a problem-solving, need-meeting, responsibility-discharging or opportunity-seizing nature; (3) which is supported and facilitated by teachers/trainers/others and not organized or directed by them; (4) which produces outcomes additional to gaining academic and/or experience, for example, in the form of a greater understanding of the values and benefits of being enterprising, for the individual and/or society more generally.'[143]

Another outcome for me from the experience was my authorship of a book entitled *Enterprise Learning in Action: Education and Economic Renewal for the Twenty-first Century*, published by Routledge in London in 1993. It drew upon case studies in community and enterprise learning from around the world, showing how young people can be taught the enterprise skills that will enable them to survive in an uncertain world.

Riding the Third Wave

A further source of innovation in Ontario had been the Sheridan College Video Conferencing Group led by Peter Mallett. Satellite videoconferencing involves three elements: production, distribution, and communication facilities. Production facilities are often commercial television stations, which have the studio and equipment for live and pre-recorded segments. Distribution facilities take care of moving the programming from the studio to, in effect, a launching point into space as well as handling the telephone communication between participants. The space segment, utilizing a satellite uplink facility, beams the program back to earth over a wide geographic area, where locations or sites interested in that particular program receive it.[144]

In March 1987, I proposed to the OECD study group that a satellite video production be convened in Europe, highlighting exemplary projects from the preliminary study, and beamed to interested parties in North America. In particular, the video production would become the keynote plenary session of the biannual Ontario Community Education Association conference to be held on 26 May 1988 at Carleton University in Ottawa.

The program would be produced by Peter Mallett of the Sheridan Video Conferencing Group and sponsored by the Ontario Community Education Association (OCEA), the Board of Education for the City of York, the Learning Enrichment Foundation, the Organisation for Economic Co-operation and Development, and other interested governmental, commercial, and voluntary sector partners. A budget of $20,000 was developed to cover the costs of studio facilities, satellite time, and pre-production and post-production expenses. As it turned out, the major source of financial support for the program was the OCEA's Organizing Technology Transfer in Ontario (OTTO) project, which was funded by the Ontario Ministry of Education and Magna International, a large North American auto parts manufacturer, through its chief executive officer, Frank Stronach.

It was originally intended that the video conference be centred in Paris; however, when adequate facilities were not available, the program was moved to London, England. The OECD subsidized the travel costs of participants, and a private television studio was rented to stage the event. Chris Searle, a British media personality, was enlisted to host the conference. There were four other participants interviewed during the program. Colin Ball, principal author of the OECD's preliminary study, presented an overview of enterprise learning. Dr Joyce O'Connor, Director, Social Research Centre, National Institute for Higher Education in Limerick, Ireland, presented *Enterprise: The Key to the Future*, an innovative resource package for young people. Erick Wallin, Department of Education, University of Upsala in Sweden, described the Värmlands Cooperatives, a foundation that encourages young people to take action to create jobs through cooperative activity. Stuart Plant, Chief Executive, ENTRAIN Limited in Sheffield, England, provided an overview of a major new initiative to introduce enterprise training into the Youth Training Scheme in the United Kingdom.

The video conference entitled 'Enterprise Skills for a Changing World: Riding the Third Wave' was scheduled from 9:00 a.m. to 10:30 a.m. Eastern Daylight Time. The program was uplinked from London, via Internet transatlantic satellite, and was downlinked to Washington, DC. The signal was then uplinked again to Westar IV satellite and broadcasted throughout North America.

In addition to the individual interviews of participants, prerecorded inserts were used to provide variety and enrich the case studies. The seventy-minute presentation of content was followed by an eighteen-minute question-and-answer period and a two-minute wrap-up to conclude the videoconference. After a one-half-hour intermission, North American participants were able to join those in London in a one-hour audio conference, utilizing a telephone bridge. Sites receiving the program were provided with handout material giving additional information about the OECD project and the case studies presented.

The OCEA biannual conference at Carleton University in Ottawa entitled 'Community Education: A Lifelong Enterprise' utilized the video conference for its keynote plenary address. I chaired a response panel, which included Dr Janet Eaton, Director of the Community Education Research Centre at Dalhousie University, and Alan Clarke of the International Joint Commission. In addition, the availability of the video conference was advertised through *NUTN NEWS*, a newspaper of the National University Teleconference Network (NUTN) that is distributed to colleges and universities. Distance educators throughout North America, as suggested by Peter Mallett, were also contacted. As a result, on 26 May 1988 more than 140 groups interested in community education, economic development, and entrepreneurship in locations as diverse as Toronto (Ontario), Milwaukee (Wisconsin), Holland (Michigan), Fort Lauderdale (Florida), Prince Albert (Saskatchewan), and Sydney (Nova Scotia) received preconference materials. Several of these centres also participated in the one-hour interactive audio conference.

For the Ontario Community Education Association, the video conference demonstrated the expanding nature of community education in the information age, and the potential to extend learning opportunity beyond traditional institutional boundaries. The other centres throughout North America were asked to return evaluation forms, and the response was universally positive. To quote a letter (printed in the NUTN newsletter) from Shirley M. Davis, Director of Media-based Programs at Purdue University: 'Thank you very much for taking the trouble to make your London-to-Ontario teleconference available to NUTN members. We had eight people watching here, and they were very excited about the message delivered. From the production perspective, let me add my personal applause for the style of production you chose, the choice of host, and the success of your presenter coaching. Again you have given us a model of good, honest, person-to-person communications without the concerns of show biz and commercial-level production quality. As a result, you created an environment where the presenters were relaxed enough to do their best, and they had a lot to offer.'[145]

The follow-up to the video conference was two-fold. The OECD monograph *Towards an Enterprising Culture: A Challenge for Education and Training*, originally issued in June 1989, was republished in a perfect-bound, graphically designed format by Creative Printing Services, an entrepreneurial training program of the Adult Day School, located at the York Business Opportunities Centre. The original video conference, *Enterprise Skills for a Changing World*, was edited down to a twenty-minute training video to accompany the above publication. Both the publication and the video were marketed as 'an action kit for the twenty-first century' from ADS Press, York Business Opportunities Centre.

Enterprise Development Video Network

The success of the video conference and post-production process spawned a new Learning Enrichment Foundation project entitled the Enterprise Development Video Network (EnDevNet) to enhance communications in Europe and North America concerning social, economic, and natural environmental issues and programs. A series of eight three-hour video conferences was proposed, linking Europe and North America, to showcase exemplary programs in enterprise development that mobilized the combined resources of the governmental, commercial, and voluntary sectors.

In June 1989 the European Space Agency launched Olympus, then the most powerful communications satellite in the world. On its high-power European direct broadcast beam were nine hours per day of education and training programs, originated by over three hundred organizations from sixteen countries in Europe. These organizations came together to form the European Association of Users of Satellites in Training and Education Programs (EUROSTEP), with Canada included as a signatory to the agreement. In April 1990, Peter Mallett and I were part of the Canadian delegation attending 'Distance Learning by Satellite in Europe,' the first EUROSTEP conference held in Leiden, the Netherlands. As a result, EnDevNet was granted satellite time by EUROSTEP, and transatlantic link-up through the Department of Communications in Ottawa. The value of these contributions was in excess of $40,000. In addition, EnDevNet received financial support from Cable-casting Limited (North American and European cable systems) and the promise of funding to prepare post-production materials from Levi Strauss & Co.

Business-Education Partnerships

In 1990, I was asked by Jarl Bengtsson of CERI to participate in an experts' group to explore 'the widespread increase in the amount of contact between education and business in OECD countries.' The group

consisted of experts from both private companies and public organizations. In addition to Canada, the twenty-four members were drawn
from the United Kingdom, the United States, the European Union,
France, Japan, Sweden, Australia, Finland, Italy, and the Netherlands.
The author of the report from the experts' group was Donald Hirsch of
the CERI secretariat.

The resulting OECD publication, *Schools and Business: A New Partnership*, attempted, for the first time, to document the explosion of contacts
between schools and businesses in recent years at the international
level. It illustrated twenty-four case studies in nine OECD countries.
Activities ranged from mini-enterprises and teacher retraining to curriculum reform. The study analysed the motives behind such links and
looked at what they could achieve. It concluded that partnerships with
businesses would become an increasingly central part of school systems and of attempts to reform them.

Yet, partnerships beyond the school should be a two-way process that
benefits both business and industry. The level of cooperation between
partners, however, may vary widely. The first dimension identified
were simple links that involved no more than a joint activity, which one
or both participants pursued out of self-interest, with no shared goals.
Partnerships involved an arrangement between the participants to do
one thing in exchange for another. *Strategic coalitions*, however, involved
genuinely common goals and a range of committed partners to, in this
case, improve the education system.[144] There has been a concern, especially in the United States, that for-profit companies are moving in to
operate school systems. This contracting-out of service, supposedly to
save money, has a neoconservative scientific-management agenda.

In June 1991 the York Board of Education received a report concerning a publication from the Conference Board of Canada entitled *Profiles of Partnerships: Business Education Partnerships That Enhance School
Retention*. The Board of Education, as a partner in the York Community
Economic Development Committee, was recognized as one of the thirty exemplary partnerships selected from across Canada.

In January 1992, the York Board of Education received a draft report
entitled 'Partners in Education: The New Partnership Between Business and Schools' from the Organisation for Economic Co-operation
and Development in Paris. The Board of Education's partnership with
the Learning Enrichment Foundation was recognized as an exemplary
project for inclusion in this report, which was later published by the
OECD and distributed throughout the world. As superintendent of

community services and an expert consultant on enterprise learning and business-education partnerships since 1986, I had represented the Board of Education at the OECD.[146]

In April 1992 a letter was received from the Council of Ministers of Education, Canada, requesting that I, as superintendent of community services, represent Canada at an international conference on business-education partnerships to be held in May 1992 at Philips Stadium in Eindhoven, the Netherlands. The Dutch ministry of education, Philips BV, and the OECD jointly sponsored the conference. A highlight of the conference was the launching of the OECD publication *Partners in Education*.

As superintendent of community services, I was also asked to represent the Conference Board of Canada at the International Partnerships Conference in June 1992 at the National Exhibition Centre in Birmingham, England.

Innovations in School Management

In 2000, I was contacted by Motoyo Kamiya, a former member of the Training Renewal Foundation's board of directors, who was now employed as consultant with OECD-CERI in Paris. Motoyo asked me to be the lead author and expert consultant for a study of innovations in school management, to be conducted by OECD-CERI. (I had originally served as a reference for Motoyo in her gaining the position in the CERI secretariat.) Nine OECD member countries made an investment to be part of the study: Sweden, Belgium, Greece, Hungary, Japan, Mexico, the Netherlands, the United Kingdom, and the United States.

The study was to focus on new school management approaches at the primary and secondary school levels within the broad context of the educational system. Beginning in June 2000, my wife, Marilyn, and I spent three months in Paris, working on the study. This involved the editing of background reports prepared by the experts who had been appointed by each participating country, and visits to the nine countries by the OECD secretariat and/or consultants to the study. In addition to my role as lead author, I was responsible for making field visits to the Netherlands, the United States, and Mexico. In August, I delivered a draft report to the secretariat, which employed Donald Hirsch (an independent consultant from the United Kingdom) and David Walshe (a journalist with the *Irish Independent*) to prepare the final report, entitled 'New School Management Approaches.'

Part 1 of the report provided a synthesis of the main developments and issues concerning school management that had emerged from the country studies. Part 2 consisted of nine country chapters that contained background information on national policy approaches as well as descriptions of the innovative work being undertaken in the case visited.[147]

In December 2001, I delivered a keynote address to an OECD-Hungary seminar on managing education for lifelong learning. The paper, consisting of my personal conclusions on my participation as lead author and expert consultant on the OECD-CERI school management study, included the following excerpts.

The first task was to ask myself the question: What is innovation? The overall objective of our study was to identify innovation in school management in the nine countries, for a sense of conflict seems to exist between the languages of top-down educational reformers, who promote an industrial age scientific managerial style, as opposed to that of bottom-up renewers, who advocate knowledge leadership for the 21st century learning organisation ...

In the face of the global tendencies to force educational change to externally impose restructuring and reform, we should emphasise the parallel and often greater importance of improving the internal interactions and relationships of schooling. But schools are one facet of an essential public service infrastructure that has been struggling with decentralisation, taxpayer accountability, restructuring and privatization, with diminishing financial support. This is an organic, politicised service, which must continually respond to diverse consumer needs. Public service cannot pick and choose its clients or manipulate its outcomes. It has a universal mandate to serve virtually all members of society. In a service economy, it is the most accountable sector within the social order. If we are to retain and improve the standard of excellence our society deserves, we must invest in renewing the self-esteem, learning capacities, problem-solving abilities and leadership skills of our public service professionals. Schooling by test scores, threats of sanctions, chronic criticism and employment insecurity are devaluing our human and social capital and are poor sources of motivation for improving performance among students, teacher and school managers. Our future social and economic well-being and quality of life are clearly at stake.[148]

As a result of my work on the OECD-CERI school management

project, I prepared a manuscript entitled 'School Management in Transition: Schooling on the Edge.' It was published in 2003 by Routledge Falmer in London.

A Growing Morality Gap

After the Second World War, industrialized nations, particularly the United States and the United Kingdom, experienced a growing disillusionment with big business, big labour, and big government. In the 1970s, Margaret Thatcher led the movement in the United Kingdom to liberate the economy of what she saw as negative influences of government ownership, union domination, and regulation, in order to release the drive and ambition of individual entrepreneurs. In 1984, Ronald Reagan in the United States joined the movement when he argued that government had pre-empted the family, the neighbourhood, and church and school organizations that acted as a buffer and a bridge between the individual and the naked power of the state. Thus, the neoconservative revolution was born with Thatcherism and Reaganomics demanding and securing a downsizing of government spending, particularly on essential human services such as health and education. As a result, the call for lower taxes, a balanced budget, and debt reduction became the pathway to political power across the Western world.

The Province of Ontario, beginning with the election of the Mike Harris Conservatives, became a case study in neoconservative opportunism. In 1995 the Conservatives were elected on the basis of a platform of tax reduction known as the Common Sense Revolution. In 1996, the provincial government radically reduced the number of municipalities through regionalization. Financial transfer payments were restructured: the Province assumed responsibility for schooling, while the costs for social services, housing, and transit were passed down to the local ratepayers. (One result was the reduction of social assistance benefits by 21.6 per cent.) The new municipalities were faced with increasing local taxes because deficit financing was forbidden.

The number of civil servants and administrative officials, both provincially and locally, was drastically reduced to balance the provincial budget and allow for provincial income tax reductions. Services were contracted out at both provincial and municipal levels, causing shortfalls in essential areas, which endangered such services as public health care and water quality (hence the Toronto SARS infection and the Walkerton E. coli contamination, respectively).

As a result of the assumption of provincial financial and budgeting control, a central funding formula was imposed on each school authority. The number of locally elected trustees was dramatically reduced, and their roles emasculated. Per-pupil spending was reduced, with fewer supervisory officers at the local level, thereby placing more pressure on school principals. Ancillary staff was drastically cut, including guidance counsellors, social workers, psychologists, librarians, remedial teachers, community and youth workers, educational assistants, secretaries, caretakers, and maintenance workers.

A scientific-management performance model was introduced with a more rigid curriculum and standardized testing at the level of grades three, six, and ten. Mandatory competency assessment for all teachers to retain certification, and the removal of all principals from the teachers' union, was enacted. The government proposed that non-teachers fill these administrative positions.

There was a shift from the approach of a strong learner-centred teacher as facilitator towards an approach of more teacher-directed time on task . This became particularly apparent following the advent of standardized testing whereby some teachers felt compelled to 'teach to the test.' Test scores were published in local media, and parents often compared performances among schools. In the areas of literacy and numeracy, a strong back-to-the-basics approach (for example, phonics versus whole language) became more pronounced. The government also ended the entitlement of adults (aged twenty-one years and over) to attend secondary or adult day schools as regular students. School boards drastically reduced their services to these students, including ESL learners. (York's Adult Day School ended.)

Budgeting cutbacks forced school boards to close schools, levy exorbitant user fees for community use of space, and reduce administrative and support staff. Teachers were reluctant to apply for principal positions, which resulted in an impending shortage of experienced school managers. Schools were not being adequately cleaned and maintained. There was a shortage of instructional materials and supplies. Mandated curriculum reform, standardized testing, and teacher assessment resulted in serious morale problems among many teachers, support staff, and school managers. Many parents had the perception that schools were failing and teachers were lazy.

During the twentieth century, community education theory, as espoused by John Dewey and Edward Olsen in the United States and Henry Morris in the United Kingdom, had an increasingly strong philosophical and programmatic influence on the nature of schooling in the

Western world. It ranged from community-focused curriculum to the school as a multiservice centre for human development to the school as a focal point for social and economic renewal in order to improve the quality of community life. The rise of the neoconservative political agenda, however, often resulted in a dismantling of the community education infrastructure. Severe budget cuts and a back-to-the-basics mentality often resulted in the sacrifice of school- community partnerships. The school was often reduced to a custodial testing clinic rather than a centre for community education and development. Those most harmed by this shift in social and economic priorities have been impoverished parents and their children, many of them being our most vulnerable newcomers from diverse racial and cultural backgrounds. The dawn of the twenty-first century has indeed exposed a growing morality gap between the needs of the rich and the poor.[149]

In November 2007 the United Way of Greater Toronto published a report entitled *Losing Ground: The Persistent Growth of Family Poverty in Canada's Largest City.* It found that in 2005 almost 30 per cent of Toronto families were poor, with a median income that was $10,000 lower than in the rest of Canada. Poverty was defined as a family whose after-tax income was 50 per cent below the median in their community. Toronto families were losing ground on every measure: median incomes ($41,000), the percentage of low-income families, and the sheer number of families living in poverty. This decline was attributed to three factors: Toronto is a magnet for both immigrants and the disadvantaged; high-paying manufacturing jobs have been replaced by lower-paying and temporary service jobs; and the rules for unemployment insurance discriminate against inhabitants of Toronto as compared to those of other major Canadian cities.[150]

In 2008, the maximum monthly social assistance benefit for an individual was $572, or an annual income of $6,864. A single parent with two children received $984 per month, or $11,808 for the year.

The Toronto District School Board published the results of a 2006 survey of 105,000 students in grades seven to twelve. It found that almost 70 per cent of students were non-white. Half the high school students said they were not taught about different cultures. Yet, two-thirds thought that learning about their own race would make school more interesting, and almost half felt it would help them do better in school. Ironically, a proposal by some Black parents and educators to establish a Black heritage–focused alternative school has been met with strong disapproval by some politicians, educators, journalists, and the public at large. They see it as a return to racial segregation – despite the fact that the First Nations Alternative School (formerly Wandering Spirit Survival School) has successfully served the needs of aboriginal parents and students for the past thirty years.[151]

Reflections for the Future

Reflecting on a career as a community educator, which has spanned more than forty years, from 1966 to 2008, I have endeavoured to act as a change agent, introducing the principles of community education and economic development as policy and program alternatives. The first thirty years were spent in public schooling, where I was employed as a teacher, consultant, principal, coordinator, and superintendent. The past twelve years have been spent as a social entrepreneur trying to make a difference while partnering with the governmental, commercial, and voluntary sectors. In each instance, the vehicle has been the demonstration project, promoting change through a system of action research; that is, each project was initiated in response to an identified community need. An organic strategy was conceived to address that need, and the resulting service was modified in response to an ongoing process of participant and external evaluation.

What has been learned during these years that might have relevance to the concerns of today and tomorrow? Here are a few reflections, which might be used to address these concerns.

Sheltering the Poor

No new public housing has been built in Toronto for about thirty years (65,000 applicants are on the waiting list), and existing buildings are badly in need of maintenance and repair. Current thinking in the housing field favours a community with a mix of income levels, combining both condominiums and rental units. Indeed, Regent Park is being redeveloped to reflect this reality, but most poor people are still accommodated in large social housing ghettos. My tenure in both Lawrence Heights and Regent Park, however, demonstrated that there can be a sense of community with local residents and service providers working together to make a difference – provided the resources are available.

Community Outreach

The local community school can act as a focal point for parents, service organizations, and citizen groups to respond to local needs, to solve problems, and to contribute to community betterment – the basic elements of community education and development. What it takes are community development workers, as part of the local education team, projecting the learning environment outside the traditional confines of institutional schooling. This will require the financial resources to employ school and community workers, such as the social services consultant in Lawrence Heights during the late 1960s and the community liaison officers serving the City of York in the 1980s and 1990s. Unfortunately, ceilings imposed on educational spending in the early 1970s, and the neoconservative political agenda in Ontario beginning in 1995, brought an end to these innovations. Isn't it time for a community education renaissance to improve the quality of life for newcomers and other low-income urban dwellers?

Learning for Life

The provision of additional funding allowed community schools to offer extended day programs to meet the social, cultural, recreational, and remedial needs of school-age children, youth, adults, and seniors. In Lawrence Heights it was a special budget allocation provided by the school board to assist residents of an impoverished community. In the city of York the Ministry of Education placed participants on a continuing education register for reimbursement. In both cases, neoconservative political policies ended this form of entitlement.

Childcare

In 2007, the Organisation for Economic Co-operation and Development released a study, which found that affordable preschool care was vital to the quality of family life. 'For single mothers . . . trapped between governments that require them to work and daycare centres that charge more than they can afford, they make tenuous babysitting arrangements or find ways to stay on welfare.'[152] This has been shown to be particularly true for the working poor and those receiving social assistance.

A variety of school-based childcare services was created through the community-education partnerships. In Lawrence Heights in the 1960s an emergency childcare service was established in response to needs identified by the Community School Advisory Council. The partners, in addition to the Flemington Road Community School, were the Mennonite Brethren Church, North York's Welfare and Parks and Recreation departments, the Family Service Association, and the National Council of Jewish Women. This service, which later evolved into a licensed pre-school centre, was the first of its kind in Metropolitan Toronto, if not the province.

Early childhood education work groups in Toronto in the 1970s and York in the 1980s resulted in board of education policies to create child-care services in vacant classroom space through parental initiative and social service subsidies. In Toronto it was the school board that finan-cially assisted with the start-ups, while in York the school board part-nered with the Learning Enrichment Foundation to establish preschool and infant-care centres. York also provided school-age care through the work of the community liaison officers and the continuing education budget formula.

Another outcome of the childcare initiatives was the nutrition pro-grams in both Lawrence Heights and York, which through the creation of community kitchens provided catered meals to the childcare centres. This was the beginning of the recognition of the importance of break-fast, snack, and lunch programs for school-age children. All of these services proved to be vital in enriching the learning environment and strengthening the quality of family life.

School-Community Partners

The Social Services project at Flemington Road Public School respond-ed to concerns about children whose disruptive behaviour was detri-mental to both school and community. Social Development groups, the Special Adjustment Centre, the Interdisciplinary Team, and the Com-munity School extended day programs were services that helped to decrease behavioural problems in the classroom and delinquency in the community. Even former young offenders from the youth drop-in cen-tres became positive role models for the younger children. I believe that this focus of the school as an extension of the community it serves could still be relevant in responding to the concerns of today's low-income areas that are beset by bullying, street gangs, and violent crime. What is missing is the type of community-school services and partnerships that once proved so effective in responding to the needs of at-risk children and youth in Lawrence Heights.

Youth Enterprise

A continuing crisis in impoverished neighbourhoods is the number of unemployed school leavers congregating on street corners or shopping plazas. Without sufficient education and employability skills, their future is bleak; they are destined for unstable minimum-wage jobs or social welfare assistance. It is not surprising that many such youth, especially racial minorities, are easy prey for criminal gang activity. As the young Black male stated at York's 'Black Youth and School Completion' forum in the 1980s, 'I just want to join the economy.'

In Lawrence Heights during the 1960s the Community School drop-in centres were one response to this concern. These activities gave at-risk youth a positive place in which to 'hang out,' where they had a sense of ownership. One spin-off was the Job Improvement Corps demonstration project, which successfully found jobs and school re-entry opportunities for participants.

In the 1970s it was the Oak Street portable in Regent Park that became a focus for youth activity, including a successful drama program and an entrepreneurial venture, the youth-operated Green Summer Day Camp. The Learnxs Foundation sponsored both the Student Employment Experience Centre and Youth Ventures, providing jobs and workplace education for school leavers.

In the 1980s the Learning Enrichment Foundation created a variety of demonstration projects for unemployed youth, including Mount Dennis Developments and Illustrious Restorations, each with an academic skills coach on staff. Another project was the Job Opportunities for Youth Employment Centre, providing pre-employment preparation, counselling, and job search services to minority youth.

In the 1990s York Community Services joined with the school board, and later the Centre for Community and Economic Renewal, to sponsor the 'Black Youth and School Completion' forum, PROYECTO SURCO, the Youth Enterprise Summit, and the Youth Enterprise Development Corporation to encourage enterprise learning among racial minority youth. The Training Renewal Foundation's Youth International project successfully trained at-risk young people, in Toronto and in placements in the United States, to be café equipment technicians and entrepreneurs.

These demonstration projects have provided ample evidence that early school leavers and minority youth, if given access to alternative education and skill training opportunities, can find successful career pathways. In 2005, Toronto experienced the 'Year of the Gun' when more than fifty young people (mostly Black males) were shot and killed, often as a result of criminal gang activity (and the influx of guns from the United States). Isn't it time that we rediscovered some of the community education and economic development strategies that could save at-risk youth in poor neighbourhoods from becoming the discarded generation?

Alternatives in Education

The Toronto Board of Education was unique in North America in its bottom-up process for creating alternative school programs. It recognized that students had different learning styles that cut across socio-economic lines. Groups of parents, students, and teachers made applications, according to Board of Education policy, to establish programs at the primary, junior, intermediate, and senior levels in both advantaged and disadvantaged areas. Some programs called for more flexible, individualized learning using community-based resources, while others offered re-entry opportunities for school leavers from the inner city. One school, Laneway Community School, even had a back-to-the-basics structure.

A common element among students in alternative programs, whether school or community-based, was a sense of identity. This was particularly true for cultural and linguistic alternatives such as Hawthorn II, with its bilingual French-English focus, and the Wandering Spirit Survival School. Wandering Spirit, created to serve poor aboriginal children, was certainly the most controversial; it embodied a Native-way spirituality, which raised cries of racial segregation and religiosity, including an opposing editorial in the *Toronto Star*. Yet, Wandering Spirit, now known as First Nations Alternative School, has prospered as a transition program for Native students.

In 2008 the Toronto District School Board and the community at large find themselves bitterly divided over a proposal to create an African Heritage alternative school in response to the 40 per cent of Black students, especially males, who are not finishing secondary school. As previously mentioned, there has been a surge in youth gang violence, and the death toll among young Black males continues to climb.

Proponents of an alternative school with a Black-focused curriculum and teaching staff argue that Black males, many from poor single-mother-led families, lack positive masculine role models. Without education and vocational skills they are easy recruits into criminal activity and youth gang membership. The traditional school system is obviously not serving the needs of these vulnerable young people.

The importance of a positive identity in the pursuit of human fulfilment cannot be underestimated. Culturally specific alternatives, such as Wandering Spirit in the 1970s and the Afro-Caribbean Alternative School in York in the 1980s, have demonstrated the potential effectiveness of such programs in raising self-esteem while improving academic performance among at-risk young people.

The current neoconservative social and economic climate has had a negative impact on the alternatives-in-education movement. This began with the Harris government seizing control of educational spending in large urban centres. As a result, alternative school programs were required to be accommodated in regular school buildings, and some of the innovative program direction and flexibility was curtailed. During the 1970s and 1980s the socio-political climate was much more supportive of experimental initiatives (such as an African heritage–focused alternative school) in response to a demonstrated need. In 2008, as a result of considerable lobbying from the Black community and other progressive political activists, the trustees of the Toronto District School Board narrowly approved an Afro-centric alternative elementary school, to be opened in 2009 in a wing of Sheppard Avenue Public School. This decision was taken in spite of the strong opposition of Liberal premier Dalton McGuinty. Mr McGuinty had recently won a provincial election partly based on his opposition to public funding of faith-based private schools (for example, Christian, Jewish, Muslim, and Sikh).

Adult Day School

The Adult Day School in the city of York was established according to the principles of community education. It was responsive to the needs of an impoverished newcomer population, focusing on educational upgrading, language skills, and preparation for employment or post-secondary education. The Adult Day School was unique because it had no single institutional base but utilized available space in elementary and secondary schools and community-based locations. When its enrolment reached about 2,400, it was probably the largest secondary school in Canada.

York had long been a reception area for immigrants and refugees. Many newcomers, often with post-secondary education in their native lands, desperately needed English-language skills to secure employment and become fully functioning members of Canadian society. The Adult Day School offered these services in neighbourhood schools, with parents often sharing a learning environment with their own school-age and preschool children. Employment preparation consisted of a variety of training programs and cooperative education placements in a variety of business, industrial, and service settings. Partnerships enabled training programs in renovation and construction, industrial sewing, childcare assistance, machine technologies, health care aid, registered practical nursing, electronic assembly and repair, and small business development. All programs were industry driven, responding to the training and recruitment needs of York's employers. Training partners in this community economic development process included Humber College, the Learning Enrichment Foundation, and employers who sat on industrial adjustment committees.

Cooperative education matched Adult Day School students with on-the-job placements in their former professions and trades. This was more than a simple orientation to the workplace, because employers had a chance to see the students demonstrating their knowledge and practical skills. Many ADS students were employed as a result of these co-op placements.

Other innovative ADS programs included:

Alternative Studies. Also known as Tutorial Outreach, this program saw ADS outreach teachers providing individualized community-based programs for students who were unable to attend regular classes owing to physical, emotional, employment, or childcare concerns, or cultural barriers. Teacher-tutors also visited a variety of employment settings to provide educational upgrading and language and work-related skills on the job. This service was very popular with companies that employed an immigrant or functionally illiterate workforce.

Adopt an Industry. Adopt an Industry was a joint venture between employers and the Adult Day School. Each of a selected group of employers received the services of an ADS teacher to assess staff learning needs and implement remedial services. In addition to being a source of professional development for ADS teachers, this service helped to retain employers in York who might have otherwise relocated.

The Adult Day School, as a key component of the York Model for Community Education and Economic Development, influenced innovative practice in adult education provincially, nationally, and even internationally. However, sadly, the election of the neoconservative Harris government in 1995 meant the end of adult access to regular secondary school programs, including ADS. Now, almost fifteen years later, the devastating impact that this policy has had on the lives of newcomers and other disadvantaged adults is being fully realized.

The Education Foundation

During a period of austerity and fiscal restraint, an education foundation, such as the Learnxs Foundation, the Learning Enrichment Foundation, and the Training Renewal Foundation, can be an important source of support for demonstration projects. These initiatives, in turn, may be influential in policy development with public bodies. The flexibility and cost-effectiveness of the arm's-length education foundation allows for experimentation with relatively limited risk for the municipal authority. This research and development function, through the pooling of public and private resources, can ensure creative activity and program excellence when public organizations are facing new challenges as they struggle to maintain service patterns.

A private foundation associated with a public body can also provide the opportunity for committed persons from the public body and citizens at large to participate in joint problem solving and collective action. To ensure a sense of objectivity and avoid the danger of politicization, the majority of directors should be citizens of the community who are not affiliated with the board of education or municipal council.

The education foundation can provide a vehicle to tap those sources of funding (for example, senior levels of government, private sector corporations, and philanthropies) in support of innovative practice that are not readily available to the municipalities. It can also create wealth and employment through the sale of goods and services, while involving the community as a joint partner in the social enterprise.

Experiences in Toronto, the former city of York, and more recently York region suggest that an education foundation should ideally include the following characteristics:

1. Focusing on a small-business or entrepreneurial design in job creation, training projects, and support for private sector enterprise.

2. Emphasizing the future, including waste recovery, energy creation, and conservation and support services that do not compete with existing private sector businesses and that offer potential for long-term employment.
3. Employing teachers to provide basic education, English as a Second Language, and life skills, or to arrange a cooperative education placement.
4. Featuring on-the-job training and worker participation in the management function through cooperative enterprise or advisory committees.
5. Incorporating a community development process allowing local citizens to be active in needs assessment and resource development.

In 1991, the Organisation for Economic Co-operation and Development, in recognizing the partnership of the Learning Enrichment Foundation and the York Board of Education as a case study in exemplary practice, made the following observation:

> In fact, the foundation has been remarkably successful in maintaining links between its various interests, and in particular between its interest in community development and work force preparation. Each of its activities seems to reinforce another. For example, the daycare centres simultaneously teach a vocational skill to trainees, allow parents to study other courses while their children are being looked after and are themselves helped by other training schemes such as carpentry (which makes their furniture) and catering (which makes their lunch). Similarly, the co-existence of an office skills training course and a small business incubator on the same site allows fledgling companies to use secretarial services provided by trainees.
>
> This is a highly sophisticated coalition, which manages to reconcile the various interests of a number of actors at community, enterprise and individual level. In some cases this involves building on shared goals: the pool of goodwill towards the daycare centres, for example is an important source of motivation. In other cases, goals can be very individualized and specific. When one of the city's hospitals seconded a teacher under the 'adopt-an-industry' scheme, it aimed specifically to find a way of bringing the literacy skills of its auxiliary staff up to scratch to enable them to recognize and safely handle dangerous substances. A unifying theme is the foundation's commitment to ensure that adult education and training is made directly relevant to workplace requirements.[153]

Economic Renewal

In 1956, the city of Modena in Italy's Emilia-Romagna region was faced with layoffs in major industries in the area. Through the active involvement of government, artisans' organizations, educational and financial institutions, labour unions, planners, and architects, Modena established its first artisans' village. Unemployed workers were encouraged to set up their own shops with the assistance of readily available venture capital loans. As a result, seventy-five small firms occupied space on the ground floors of buildings and had apartments on the second floors. These workshop-homes on city-owned land were municipally financed and sold to the new entrepreneurs on long-term contracts. This was one of the models we studied in creating the York Community Economic Development Committee.

York was the first municipality in a large metropolitan region to be selected by Employment and Immigration Canada to host an industrial committee of adjustment. By the bringing together of key economic participants in the governmental, commercial, and voluntary sectors, a new unity of purpose was achieved. The York Model demonstrated the potential of community economic development as an important strategy to address local social, industrial, and employment needs.

Both the Modena and the York experiences demonstrated the potential for a new microeconomic model for survival in a post-industrial era that was characterized by plant closures, industrial dislocation, and offshore sourcing. While the information age may have also encouraged the development of some new low-wage business and personal service employment, the traditional industrial heartlands continue to be beset by an abundance of vacant industrial space and a redundant workforce. Local economic renewal will require a new consortium of city government, small business, large industry, educational and training resources, labour unions, community groups, and public-spirited investors. Essential components in this renaissance might include the following:

1. Local self-sufficiency: wherever possible, enterprise should be developed to satisfy the needs within the local area in order to improve employment opportunities and develop new products and services.
2. Affordable space: cities should enter the real estate market by developing public lands for small-business accommodation or

subsidizing space costs in the private sector to encourage industrial development.

3. Entrepreneurial and skill training: public education and commercial and voluntary sector interests should join together to organize educational and training programs in the workplace that encourage inventiveness and the acquisition of entrepreneurial and worker ownership skills.

4. Shared resources: to survive in the global marketplace, manufacturing should adopt the most productive technologies available. By sharing equipment, expertise, and software, firms could reduce capital expenditure and share in research and development of new designs and products.

5. Marketing cooperatives: companies within a similar field could form marketing cooperatives to promote their goods and service. Sales representatives from each cooperative would market a full line of goods and services and seek opportunities for export to anywhere in the world.

6. Venture capital: local sources of private investment, and more supportive lending policies among banks and credit unions, should be encouraged to help to ensure the viability of local enterprises.

Economic renewal should begin at the local level where government, commerce, and the voluntary sector can combine their resources to create an entrepreneurial support system and generate the essential education and training opportunities to maintain that system.

Community Education and Diversity

What does the history of community education and development tell us about the current challenges that we face in Ontario's increasingly diversified society? As previously stated, social diversity is not limited to race, religion, or culture; it also encompasses differences in learning styles, beliefs, patterns of thought, gender, sexuality, and the ways in which we deal with change. Historically the first phase in the process of community education and development begins with a needs assessment within a geographic area or community of interest. By seeking to involve all community members, including minorities, in the assessment process, the needs of all participants are recognized and valued.

The next phase in the process involves a resource inventory whereby the skills, talents, monetary, and in-kind resources of participants, including the commercial, governmental, and voluntary sectors, are mobilized to solve problems and create sources of innovation to improve the quality of community life. This dynamic also tends to enrich personal and collective self-esteem. In every instance it is a learning process that builds social capital and a sense of human fulfilment.

What is required in our diverse social and economic communities, therefore, is access to resources that empower citizens to influence their own destinies better. This was demonstrated in the previously described impoverished urban areas that were populated by diverse racial, religious, cultural, and socio-economic minorities. It was also true among those pursuing alternative learning styles and entrepreneurial ventures. While governmental support for these innovations has drastically declined in the last ten years, the potential still exists to reinvest our human and financial resources in a renewed commitment to community education and development policies and programs.

A Community Education Renaissance

A non-traditional role for school principals would be to see the school as an extension of the community it serves. Instead of being a clinical institution sheltered from the realities of community life, the school becomes a focus for community living and human fulfilment. This has been the community school model originally envisioned by John Dewey and Edward Olsen. In the community development process, the school, as the major human and physical resource in the neighbourhood, provides leadership by helping to bring citizens together to assess local needs, mobilize resources, and improve the quality of life in the community. The principal of the community school is an integral leader in a community development process. This has been of particular relevance to impoverished rural and urban areas.[154]

The impact of the industrial age on parenting and the decline of the influence of religious institutions have extended the role of the school beyond academics to encourage social, cultural, and values integration. Schools represent a primary service of childcare, safety, and security in the community.

To begin to address the challenges to our diverse newcomer populations, especially in our impoverished urban areas, I believe that the lessons learned from more than forty years of community education and economic development can be of vital importance. However, this renaissance will require some fundamental policy changes and a reinvestment of the funding provisions sacrificed by the previous Ontario government's neoconservative agenda. I hope that the preceding chapters might serve as a blueprint for such a renaissance.

Raging Boomers

As the baby boomers enter their retirement years, many enjoy good health and physical vitality. From my own experience, I know how important it is to remain an intellectually challenged contributor to community well-being. The fact that many boomers, especially teachers, may benefit from the security of an indexed pension plan raises some options for their continuing to be productive in the so-called golden years.

For example, the work of the Training Renewal Foundation is really underwritten by the participation of my colleague Murray Shukyn and myself as retired members of the Ontario Teachers' Pension Plan. This role has allowed us to continue to be advocates in a social enterprise that promotes social justice, community problem solving, and responsiveness to the social and economic needs of less advantaged members of society. It has allowed us to use our new-found discretionary time to work with a volunteer board of directors to try to make a difference in improving the quality of community life by harnessing the resources of the commercial, governmental, and voluntary sectors – the essence of shared ownership. As an increasing proportion of our boomer generation enters the retirement years, the cause of community education and social enterprise might be an alternative pathway for personal fulfilment and renewal. What is old can be new again!

17 Blueprint for Renewal

My introduction herein outlined two provocative reports that were released in 2008. The McMurtry-Curling report addressed the issues of impoverished children and families, segregated social housing, racial conflict, youth violence, mental health problems, and lack of recreation and employment opportunities. The Campaign 2000 report focused on the inadequacies of social assistance and childcare, affordable housing, education, and training.

My first stated objective was a historic overview of the impact on public education of theory and practice in the fields of community education, community development, community economic development, and social enterprise creation.

The previous chapters have dealt with ways and means to address the concerns raised by the McMurtry-Curling and Campaign 2000 reports, through a chronology of events that occurred during the forty-year span from 1966 to 2006. Some of these initiatives have been incorporated into current policies and programs, but others have either been discarded or emasculated because of the following factors.

Neoconservative political theory and scientific management methodology have changed the nature of public schooling by centralizing financial control, curricular development, and, increasingly, the labour relations with the Province. Pedagogy has been affected by the introduction of standardized testing and time-on-task strategies in the classroom. This top-down restructuring has had a profound impact on the potential for bottom-up reforms and innovations influenced by students, parents, teachers, and other citizens of the community. One approach to remediate these concerns would be a return to a more decentralized, learner-centred governance style in our schools and communities. Without a sense of openness to community needs, one cannot begin to address the issues raised in the McMurtry-Curling and Campaign 2000 reports.

My second objective called for the provision of a political insight into the decision making concerning policy and program development. The 1960s and 1970s saw the beginning of more citizen involvement in shaping the nature of theory and practice in public education. Parents, other citizens, students, and teachers became more active in electing school trustees and influencing decision making at the school-board level. This resulted in new policy and program initiatives related to impoverished children, race and cultural relations, school-based child-care, alternatives in education, services for at-risk youth, economic development, and social enterprise. While some of these initiatives still have limited currency in the system, others were discarded when grass-roots political influence began to be curtailed after 1995.

The third objective dealt with the role of the internal change agent or social entrepreneur. Beginning in the late 1990s, revenue available to school boards decreased when the control of school funding was taken over by the Province. The role of the local school trustee was diminished, and participation of parents, teachers, and students was discouraged. As budgets tightened, personnel who were not directly related to classroom practice were sacrificed. Positions such as the school-community worker, youth outreach worker, resource librarian, and a variety of other student service personnel became redundant. Without these resources, the role of the innovative school administrator or change agent became very difficult.

The fourth objective concerned the nature of social and economic renewal and its potential impact on public education in the twenty-first century. The preceding chapters have dealt with the attempts to introduce community-based resources and influences in order to change the nature of institutional schooling. These attempts included opening up the school system to the needs of impoverished communities, and mobilizing resources – both human and physical – to not only improve the learning process but begin to change both the social and the economic environment. This involved innovations in the delivery of education and skill training to persons of all ages. It also focused on the role of such education and training innovations in attacking the root causes of poverty and alienation. Institutional schooling and training provisions, however, have traditionally been inward-looking and self-serving systems that are somewhat insulated from social and economic realities. The centralization of government control, budgetary restraint, and declining enrolment in urban areas have further exacerbated this situation.

The experiences and interventions described in the preceding chapters may be applied to a blueprint to meet the current needs of alienated and impoverished children, youth, and families. An essential determinant throughout has been the influence that leadership roles have had on the outcomes. The nature and impact of this leadership may be seen in the following profiles.

School-Community Worker

The causes of youth violence and other forms of antisocial behaviour may often emanate from struggling families living in impoverished neighbourhoods. Interventions could begin in the early years, using the community school development models as described in the chapters devoted to Lawrence Heights and the City of York.

Community education defines a new partnership between school personnel, students, parents, other citizens, social service agencies, community organizations, and employers who come together using the resources of the local school as a focal point. This is of particular importance in schools serving low-income areas and social housing communities. In particular, the Flemington Road Community School Advisory Council became the vehicle for collective action. Preschool and school-age childcare and nutrition programs were pioneered. Therapeutic services for troubled children and families were initiated. Extended-day recreational, artistic, and cultural enrichment programs were undertaken for children, youth, and adults. A variety of other community services including mental health, legal, medical, and other family-related programs were established.

The key component in this process of community education and development was the position of the *school-community worker*, who operates in both environments, bringing together the disparate individuals, groups, and other interests to form the community school development partnership. The investment in such a position at the elementary school level is essential if impoverished communities are to begin to resolve local educational, social, economic, and political problems.

Another type of school-community worker at the secondary level, the *youth outreach worker*, can play a similar role. Working both in the school and in the community this person brings together the resources

to serve the needs of alienated youth in their total learning environment. Such a person acts as a liaison with other community-based services and employers to develop alternative programs for young people
who are not benefiting from traditional schooling. These programs can
integrate academics with out-of-school experiential learning opportunities. Individual mentoring and group work help troubled youth to
find pathways of expression other than criminal gang activity.

Community outreach workers have not traditionally been players on
the institutional schooling team. However, community education offers
a redefinition of the nature of overall learning beyond the chain-link
fence. A new training process needs to be developed to prepare candidates for these positions.

Political Change Agent

Schools by their very nature have tended to be insular, inward-looking,
and self-serving institutions. School governance has been traditionally
mandated both by local school boards and the provincial government,
which controls overall financial policy (especially since 1998) and program guidelines. As political bodies, the school boards and the government have tended to focus on their own self-interests. While teacher
unions have exerted some influence on policy and program, they too
have been most concerned with their own salaries and working conditions. Where do students, their parents, other citizens, and ratepayers
fit in?

Beginning in the 1960s, citizen activists and other advocacy groups
began to lobby the school boards and the provincial government for
a more open and transparent decision-making process. In particular,
there was a call for more flexibility and diversity in policy and program
development to reflect different learning styles and curriculum content.
The experience of the Toronto Board of Education, particularly around
the Special Task Force on Education process in the 1970s, was reflective of this movement for change. During the period, such innovations
as inner-city compensatory education, experiential and community
resource learning, community schools, alternatives in education, multiculturalism, race relations, and cooperative education were introduced.
Advocacy groups and progressive educators within the system had a
major influence on the development, initiation, and implementation of
these policy and program innovations.

The role of the *political change agent* or social entrepreneur was an important part of this transformation. As was true for the school-community worker at the local level, the change agent as a middle management activist who understood the nature of both internal and external political decision making was an essential component of the change process. There is a need for the role of such a change agent who can work with both sides of the political divide to encourage, initiate, and nurture policies and programs that are responsive to current and future societal needs, in both public education and its interface with the community.

An institutional schooling environment devoted primarily to systems maintenance can be a very challenging assignment for a middle manager with a change agent agenda. Learning to work both sides of the street is not something that is taught at faculties of education. A syllabus devoted to the politics of education should be part of school-administrator training.

Diversity Leader

A student-centred curriculum and program demands sensitivity to the diverse needs of all learners. This is particularly true for newcomers whose first language is neither English nor French. Comprehensive programs for both reception and ongoing remedial support for students with a different cultural background, mother tongue, or dialect are essential. The *diversity leader*, working as a teacher, consultant, or line administrator, becomes an advocate to meet the needs of these students. Such a person would also be an advocate for programs and services designed to encourage a positive race relations environment among staff and students. The City of York's Multicultural Leadership program is one example of a community development program to meet this need.

The diversity leader might also work actively with parents and students to initiate demonstration projects reflecting minority interests, such as heritage-language, aboriginal, or Afro-centric cultural programs. Such a position, however, can be a challenging assignment when one is caught in the middle between conflicting political agendas. Toronto's Wandering Spirit Survival School, York's Afro-Caribbean Alternative School, and the recently proposed Toronto District School Board Afro-centric elementary programs are examples of controversial initiatives. Preparation and in-service training for the diversity leaders is a priority.

Alternative Education Advocate

In the late 1960s there was the beginning of a political movement in Toronto for more flexibility and choice in learning opportunities at the elementary and secondary school levels. The focus was often on shared decision making and learning outside of the classroom. Activist trustees, parents, teachers, and students began petitioning for new alternatives in education – both schools and programs – to reflect different learning styles and artistic, cultural, and linguistic interests. The result at the school-board level was a general policy to guide the establishment of such alternatives in education. By the 1990s, more than thirty such schools and programs had been initiated. Recently, new initiatives for school leavers and suspended and expelled students, as well as race and gender specific programs, have been introduced.

It has always been a challenge to find teachers and administrators to staff alternate programs. *Alternative education advocates* are personnel who can work effectively with the disparate interests involved in the operation of these schools and programs. Such interests may include students, parents, teachers, trustees, and citizen activists. Alternative education advocates are leaders who must walk the line between institutional and community expectations. They require political skills that are not currently taught at faculties of education but that should be an integral part of teacher and administrator preparation.

Adult Educator

The experience with the Adult Day School in the city of York produced a profile of the successful *adult educator*. This is a professional who is committed to an individualized student-centred style of instruction, which begins with an initial holistic assessment of a learner's needs. Such an assessment is not limited to the academic domain but also includes the social and economic environment. Skills of teachers and administrators at ADS included teaching basic literacy and numeracy, English as a second language, and employment-related skills, as well as regular secondary credits. Cooperative education, entrepreneurship, and life skills were also part of the curriculum and program.

As many students were immigrants and refugees receiving social assistance, ADS staff had to have a special empathy for their social and economic realities. The fact that ADS teachers were spread over about twenty community-based locations avoided any sense of institutionalization. They formed partnerships with community agencies, citizen groups, employers, and media interests to serve the academic, social, and economic needs of their learners better. Many had had experience working in the private sector or as community volunteers before beginning their careers as teachers. They were truly community educators devoted to improving the lives of their impoverished students and families.

Unfortunately, the change of political party after the 1995 election in Ontario meant the end of ADS as a demonstration project in community education. By 1998, adults could no longer be financially supported as regular secondary school students. This, along with the almost 22 per cent decrease in social assistance income, had a profound impact on impoverished families. Symptoms of this impact can be found in the rising incidence of child poverty, youth violence, and mental and physical health concerns.

As we approach the end of the first decade of the twenty-first century, Ontario along with most other governments is sliding into a economic recession that will further exacerbate the plight of the poor. Besides a major boost in financial assistance for children and families, a reinstatement of financial support for adults as regular secondary students served by trained adult educators is essential. Again, there is a need for the pre-service and in-service training of teachers and administrators to enable them to focus on the specific needs of adult learners.

Community Economic Developer

As previously described in chapter 13, community economic development was defined as 'a plan of action to build new resources which will strengthen the local community as well as its relations with the larger world.' The vehicle for the promotion of community economic development related to public education has been the educational foundation. This non-profit charitable organization combines the resources of the governmental, commercial, and voluntary sectors to launch a series of demonstration projects to enhance educational and training opportunities in the interests of social and economic well-being. The key element in the initiation of this foundation is the services of the *community economic developer*. This community educator, while employed by a school board, is able to combine the resources of the three sectors to form a political action plan for school and community renewal.

One Toronto outcome, in the case of the Learnxs Foundation, was the creation of such innovations as Learnxs Press, which was an alternative source of community-focused learning materials, and both the Student Employment Experience Centre and Youth Ventures Inc., which served the educational and training needs of at-risk youth. The community economic developer worked both sides of the street to mobilize and combine the necessary resources.

Another outcome of this form of leadership was the Learning Enrichment Foundation. This non-profit charity combined the resources of a school board, other levels of government, and the commercial sector to create educational, childcare, skill-training, and job opportunities for thousands of immigrants, refugees, and displaced workers in the city of York. The foundation's partnership with the Adult Day School was essential to the success of both services in meeting the educational, social, and economic needs of the community. Again, the community economic developer was the catalyst in bringing these resources together. For example, the Learning Enrichment Foundation provided primary leadership in the creation of the York Community Economic Development Committee, which sought to improve employment and training opportunities in a city that was facing ongoing deindustrialization and soaring unemployment.

Yet, the role of the community economic developer has never been a part of the skill set for a teacher, consultant, or educational administrator, in spite of the fact that the educational foundation model has been emulated provincially, nationally, and internationally. This is another leadership role that needs to be added to the preparation and in-service training of teachers and administrators.

Social Enterprise Trainer

Social enterprise has been previously defined as a non-profit organization or venture that advances its social mission through entrepreneurial resource strategies. According to this definition, both the Learnxs Foundation and the Learning Enrichment Foundation would qualify as social enterprises combining resources of the governmental, commercial, and voluntary sectors. Another social enterprise has been the Training Renewal Foundation, whose mandate is 'to serve disadvantaged youth and other displaced workers, including immigrants and refugees, seeking skills, qualifications and employment opportunities.' As a result of human-resource needs assessments among employers in such service sectors as coffee and vending machines, industrial warehousing, laundering and dry-cleaning, and construction craft, the

Training Renewal Foundation has prepared hundreds of social assistance recipients for employment. Most were at-risk youth, immigrants and refugees. The foundation's innovation is to locate training in the workplace, partnering with employers and different levels of government. These short-term projects – three to fifteen weeks – represent a cost-effective, fast-track strategy for participant employability.

The Training Renewal Foundation's *social enterprise trainers* provide an alternative to the institution-based training that is usually offered over many months by the college system or traditional large A-list agencies. The foundation's unique outreach strategy, partnering directly with employers and government departments, has been a key determinate in achieving an 80 per cent rate of employment among graduates.

The leadership roles described above have several common elements, including:

1. The ability to work simultaneously in both an institutional setting and the community at large.
2. A partnership that brings together resources of the governmental, commercial, and voluntary sectors as part of a problem-solving process.
3. The ability to find a political consensus among sectors and divergent interests of participants while working across sectors in initiating and implementing policies and programs.
4. Their introduction of the theory and practice of community education and development, community economic development, and social enterprise to the field of public education, which represents a major source of diverse intervention.
5. Their concern for the impoverished, immigrants, refugees, migrants, and those seeking new learning and skill-training opportunities, which provides a focus for this intervention.

In summary, I believe that the focus for renewal in impoverished, racially diverse communities should begin with children in the early years. The community school concept provides a multiservice resource partnership to encourage a quality education experience with essential supports to family life including childcare, nutrition, physical and mental health, and social, recreational, and legal services. However, in every instance, the process must be developed, maintained, and supported by citizens of the community, assisted by service professionals and volunteers.

A similar focus should be found at the secondary school level with students themselves as active participants in the process. Alternative programs that focus on different learning styles and cultural and racial identities should be encouraged at both levels.

The needs of school leavers and unemployed adults should not be neglected, with community-based skill-training and job-readiness programs as an outgrowth of a community economic development process. In particular, the specific needs of newcomers to the community should be addressed. It is only through such holistic collective action that the challenges of poverty, violence, and racism can begin to be met at the local level. This is not to imply, however, that senior levels of government should not be attacking the root causes of poverty, homelessness, and social insecurity.

Finally, the leaders previously described are *agents of change*. But their leadership skills will never make a difference if there is not a politically active climate within public education and the social and economic environment that encourages and supports these changes. To ensure that such leaders will continue to emerge, theory and practice in community education and development, community economic development, and social enterprise creation should become part of the preparation and in-service training of teachers, administrators, and other human service professionals. These leaders represent the architects of an educational blueprint for social, economic, and political renewal – the true essence of schooling for life.

References

1 Toronto Board of Education. 1976. *We Are All Newcomers to This Place.* Report of the Multiculturalism Work Group.
2 Shuttleworth, D.E. 1993. *Enterprise Learning in Action.* London: Routledge.
3 Dewey, J. Quoted in Kilpatrick, W.W. 1933. *The Educational Frontier.* New York: Appleton Century.
4 Fantini, M.D. 1973. *Public Schools of Choice: A Plan for the Reform of American Education.* New York: Simon & Schuster.
5 Ontario. 1968. *Living and Learning: Provincial Committee on Aims and Objectives in the Schools of Ontario.* Toronto: Newton Publishing.
6 Ontario. 1972/73. *Secondary School Organization and Diploma Requirements.* Circular H.S. 1. Toronto: Ministry of Education.
7 Ontario. 1972. *The Learning Society: Commission on Post Secondary Education.* Toronto: Ministry of Government Services.
8 Carter, G. 1973. *Dictionary of Education.* New York: McGraw Hill.
9 Dewy, J. 1915. *The School and Society.* Chicago: University of Chicago Press.
10 Olsen, E.G. 1945. *School and Community.* New York: Prentice Hall.
11 Minzey, J. 1972. Community Education: An Amalgam of Many Views. *Phi Delta Kappan* 54, no. 2 (November).
12 Biddle, W.W., and L.J. Biddle. 1965. *The Community Development Process.* New York: Holt, Rinehart & Winston.
13 International Co-operation Administration. 1956. Community Development Review, no. 3. December.
14 Shuttleworth, D.E. 1978. The Learning Exchange System, LEARNXS: Analysis of a Demonstration Project in Community Education. PhD thesis, University of Toronto.
15 Delagran, W. 1967. Life in the Heights: The Tenants' Viewpoint, North York. Unpublished research study.

16 Oliver, G. 1968. Adopting Agency Structure and Program to Offer Co-operative Outreach Services. Paper presented to the Canadian Conference on Social Welfare, Ottawa, 19 June.

17 North York Board of Education. 1966. Report re: Flemington Road Public School. Office of the Director, North York, 19 May.

18 Shuttleworth, D.E. 1970. Education for Community Living: A Human Development Process. In *Poverty and Social Policy in Canada*, ed. W.E. Mann. Toronto: Copp Clark.

19 Shuttleworth, D.E. 1966. The Role of the Social Service Consultant in Flemington Public School. Draft proposal to the North York Board of Education.

20 Shuttleworth, D.E. 1971. Flemington Road Community School: A Process in Community Development. In *Citizen Participation Canada*, ed. J.A. Draper. Toronto: New Press.

21 Helling, R. 1965. Address to School and Community Seminars, Flemington Road Public School. North York, 2 November.

22 Shuttleworth, D.E. 1966. A Survey of Social Attitudes and Occupational-Educational Expectations in Culturally Different Areas. Unpublished research study.

23 Shuttleworth, D.E. 1968. *The Effect of the Multi-Problem Family on the Education Process*. Toronto: Ontario Educational Research Council.

24 Shuttleworth, D.E. 1971. *The Life Style of the Pre-Adolescent in Public Housing*. Toronto: Ontario Educational Research Council.

25 *The North York Mirror*. 1968. Educators clash on damage. 18 December.

26 Special Senate Committee on Poverty. 1970. Minutes of a Meeting at Flemington Road Public School. North York, 10 March.

27 Oliver, G. 1968. Adapting Agency Structure and Program to Offer Co-operative Outreach Services. Paper presented to the Canadian Conference on Social Welfare, Ottawa, 19 June.

28 Shuttleworth, D.E. 1968. Volunteers Unlimited. Report to North York Board of Education.

29 Shuttleworth, D.E. 1969. Junior Big Brother Experimental Project. Report to North York Board of Education.

30 *Community-on-the-Move*. 1969. Housing Tenants Urged to Unite. Lawrence Heights, 24 February.

31 Thomas, R.A.L. 1968. Correspondence to D.E. Shuttleworth. 29 August.

32 Lee, L. 1969. Ontario teachers study families of pupils from inner city areas. *The Globe and Mail*. July 10.

33 Tough, A. 1971. *The Adult's Learning Projects*. Toronto: Ontario Institute of Studies in Education.

34 *The Globe and Mail*. 1969. Articles of 21 July, 18 August, and 25 August.

35 Toronto Board of Education. 1969. Minutes of Management Committee Meeting. 2 September.
36 Toronto Board of Education. 1970. Minutes of Committee of the Whole. Report 12, Part 1. 15 July.
37 Toronto Board of Education. 1971. Interim Report of the Special Task Force. 25 February.
38 Toronto Board of Education. 1971. Task Force Progress Report. 25 February.
39 Toronto Board of Education. 1972. Progress Report of the Special Task Force. 22 March.
40 Notes from meeting with Gordon Cressy. 1972. Task Force House, 14 February.
41 Ontario Ministry of Education. 1972. New Dimensions. April.
42 Toronto Board of Education. 1972. Report of the Work Group on the Use of Volunteers in Schools. 24 October.
43 Toronto Board of Education. 1973. Report of the Work Group on Early Childhood Education. 28 May.
44 Shuttleworth, D.E. 1973. Action Profile No. 3: Day Care Centre in an Elementary School. Early Childhood Education Work Group. 28 February.
45 Shuttleworth, D.E. 1973. Action Profile No. 1: Funding and Co-ordination of Extended Day Programs for Adults in Elementary Schools. Community-School Development Work Group. 12 February.
46 Shuttleworth, D.E. 1973. Action Profile No. 2: School Development Fund. 4 February.
47 Grande, T. 1973. Action Profile No. 4: A Transition Program for Young Children. Inner City Schools Work Group. 19 February.
48 Novick, M. 1972. Action Profile No. 5: Social Policy Sub-Committee. Inner City Schools Work Group. 18 December.
49 Johnson, R. 1973. Action Profile No. 6: A Plan to Use Out-of-School Indigenous Youth as Lay Assistants in Working Class School Class Rooms. 19 February.
50 Shuttleworth, D.E. 1973. Action Profile No. 7: A Cultural Immersion Program for Teachers in Immigrant Areas.
51 Toronto Board of Education. 1972. Progress Report of the Special Task Force. 7 April.
52 Toronto Board of Education. 1972. Report of the Riverdale Youth Project. 29 May.
53 Toronto Board of Education. 1972. Final Report of the Special Task Force. 27 July.
54 Cooperative Education Work Group. 1972. Minutes of Meeting. 30 October.

55 Cooperative Education Work Group. 1972. Minutes of Meeting. 21 November.

56 Toronto Board of Education. 1973. Report of the Sub-Committee on Work Experience. 3 May.

57 Borowsky, G. 1972. *Yellow Pages of Learning Resources*. Cambridge, MA: MIT Press.

58 Cooperative Education Work Group. 1972. Minutes of Sub-Committee on School-Community Learning Resources. 18 December.

59 Cooperative Education Work Group. 1973. Minutes of Meeting. 25 January.

60 Toronto Board of Education. 1973. The Learning Exchange System. Report to the School Programs Committee. 15 May.

61 Toronto Board of Education. 1973. Learnxs Foundation. Report to the School Programs Committee. 16 June.

62 Toronto Board of Education. 1973. Minutes of Meeting. 24 May.

63 School Programs Committee. 1973. Report on the Learnxs Project. 23 October.

64 Learnxs Task Group. 1973. Minutes of Meeting. 11 December.

65 Local Initiatives Proposal. 1973. Resource Bank for Community Learning.

66 Learnxs Task Group. 1974. Minutes of Meeting. 8 January.

67 Learnxs Task Group. 1974. Minutes of Meeting. 21 January.

68 Volunteers in Education. 1974. Produced with cooperation of the Volunteers in Education Work Group.

69 Toronto Board of Education. 1974. Report of the Learnxs Task Group. 28 February.

70 Learnxs Task Group. 1974. Minutes of Meeting. 8 March.

71 Toronto Board of Education. 1974. Minutes of Meeting. 19 September.

72 Learnxs Foundation. 1974. Learning Exchange System: Learnxs. Local Initiatives Program proposal. 1 October.

73 Learnxs Task Group. 1975. Minutes of Meeting. 13 June.

74 Learnxs Task Group. 1975. Meeting re: Publishing Policy for Learnxs. 16 July.

75 Learnxs Foundation. 1975. Community as Classroom Publications. Application to Local Initiatives Program. 11 September.

76 Learnxs Staff. 1975. Minutes of Meetings. September to November.

77 Project 121. 1976. In *Volunteers in Education*. Toronto: Learnxs Press.

78 Young, V., and C. Reich. 1974. Patterns of Dropping Out. Research

79 Department, Toronto Board of Education. December.

80 Social Planning Council of Metropolitan Toronto. 1978. *The Problem Is Jobs, Not People*. October.

81 Koulack, E., and V. Young. The Student Employment Experience Centre Project for Out-of-School Young Adolescents, Child in the City Program, University of Toronto.

82 Kozol, J. 1972. *Free Schools.* NewYork: Bantam Books.

83 Illich, I. 1971. Education Without School: How It Can Be Done. *New York Review of Books* 15, July.

84 Bremer, J. 1970. *Some Thoughts on Education.* Philadelphia Parkway Program Brochure, 4th edition.

85 Moore, D.R., et al. 1971. *The Metro School: A Report on the Progress of Chicago's Experimental School Without Walls.* Chicago: Urban Research Corp.

86 Edmonton Board of Education. 1974. Community Oriented Education: M.E. LaZerte's Core Project. Report of a Preliminary Inquiry.

87 Yip, D. 1971. SEED: A Preliminary Report No. 93. Toronto Board of Education Research Department.

88 Etobicoke Board of Education. 1971. A Proposal for the Establishment of an Alternative Education Program for Senior Secondary School Students. Ad Hoc Committee on Half-Way Schools.

89 North York Board of Education. 1971. A Feasibility Study Program at the Senior High School Level. An Interim Report. 22 March.

90 Toronto Board of Education. 1971. People for an Alternative Elementary School and the ALPHA Experience. Report of the Management Committee.

91 Toronto Board of Education. 1972. Proposal for CONTACT. Alternatives in Education Committee. 4 and 15 May.

92 Toronto Board of Education. 1980. Hawthorne II Bilingual School brochure. December.

93 Toronto Board of Education. 1981. SPECTRUM Alternative Senior School brochure. January

94 Toronto Board of Education. 1979. *THE STUDENT SCHOOL,* Another Way Newsletter. October.

95 Toronto Board of Education. 1979. Alternative Schools brochure. May.

96 Toronto Board of Education. 1979. Report of the Work Group on School Facilities as Multi-Service Neighbourhood Centres. 1 March.

97 Toronto Board of Education. 1974. Minutes of the New Canadian Committee. 17 April.

98 Toronto Board of Education. 1975. Draft Report of the Work Group on Multicultural Programs. 20 May.

99 Toronto Board of Education. 1977. Memo to the Superintendent of Curriculum and Program. 14 December.

100 A favourite quotation of D. John Phillips, Director, York Board of Education, referring to the politicization of the education process.

101 Centre for Community Economic Development. 1975. Community Economic Development brochure. Cambridge, MA.

102 Stein, B. 1973. How Successful Are CDCs? *Review of Black Political Economy*, Spring.

103 Stein, M. 1979. *Evaluation of New Dawn Enterprises Ltd*. Sydney, NS: College of Cape Breton.

104 Shuttleworth, D.E. 1983. What's a Nice Teacher Like You Doing in a Place Like This? *Orbit*, Ontario Institute for Studies in Education, February.

105 Keleher, P. 1982. Education in the Workplace Report, York Board of Education. 11 January.

106 Long, D. 1982. Education in the Workplace Report, York Board of Education. 11 January.

107 York Board of Education. 1981. Procedures for Community Use of Space. Report of the Assistant Superintendent of Community Services. February.

108 York Board of Education. 1981. Pre-School Programs Work Group Report.

109 York Board of Education. 1981. Report of the Assistant Superintendent of Community Services. 7 December.

110 York Board of Education. 1980. Minutes of Meeting. 15 December.

111 York Board of Education. 1982. Report of the Director of Education. 25 January.

112 York Board of Education. 1982. Minutes of Meeting. 29 March.

113 York Board of Education. 1982. Cherrywood Alternative Primary School brochure. Spring.

114 York Board of Education. 1985. Report of the Assistant Superintendent of Community Services. 1 April.

115 Shuttleworth, D.E. 1993. *Enterprise Learning in Action*. London: Routledge.

116 York Board of Education. 1988. Learning to Ride the Third Wave. Report of the Community Services Office.

117 Shuttleworth, D.E. 1986. Parents-as-Partners. *Orbit* 78, April.

118 St. John-Hunter, C., and D. Harman. 1979. *Adult Illiteracy in the U.S. Report to Ford Foundation*. McGraw-Hill.

119 Thomas, A.M. 1976. *Adult Basic Education and Literacy Activities in Canada*. Toronto: World Literacy of Canada.

120 York Board of Education. 1988. Learning to Ride the Third Wave. Report of the Community Services Office.

121 Learning Enrichment Foundation. 1978. Objects of Incorporation. 27 September.

122 Learning Enrichment Foundation. 1980. Board of Directors meeting. 1 December.

123 Learning Enrichment Foundation. 1982. Annual Report. 7 June.

124 Learning Enrichment Foundation. 1983. Administrator's Report. December.

125 York Community Economic Development Committee. 1986. Community Reports. 29 April.

126 Académie Diplomatique de la Paix. 1986. Correspondence. 1 September.

127 Ontario Community Education Association. 1986. Education as a Community Enterprise. Submission to the Hon. Sean Conway, Minister of Education.

128 York Board of Education. 1992. PROYECTO SURCO. Report of the Superintendent of Community Services. 10 February.

129 City of York Youth Enterprise Summit. 1993. YES Report. 23–25 April.

130 Monsebratten, L. 1998. Loss of Program May Dash Dreams. *Toronto Star*, 8 January.

131 Training Interns in Education. 1995. Final Report to Human ResourcesDevelopment Canada. September.

132 Tests for High School Certificate Expanded Across the Province. 1996. New release communiqué, Ontario Ministry of Education and Training. 9 September.

133 Metropolitan Toronto Separate School Board. 1996. Minutes of the Board Meeting. 28 November.

134 Ministry of Education and Training. 1997. Correspondence from Mariette Carrier-Frazer to Norm Forma. 28 February.

135 Metropolitan Toronto Separate School Board. 1998. Letter from Michael O'Flanagan, Superintendent of Education, Secondary.11 February.

136 Small, P. 1998. Firm Fears Cut to Adult Classes. *Toronto Star*, 12 March.

137 Training Renewal Foundation. 1998. Letter of Intent to Ratna Omidvar, Maytree Foundation. 23 March.

138 Training Renewal Foundation. 2000–2001. Annual Report.

139 Miller, L. 2000. Drycleaning and Laundering Industry Adjustment Committee: Local Labour Marketship Partnership Project. September.

140 The Training Renewal Foundation. 2000–2001. Annual Report.

141 The Training Renewal Foundation. 2002–2003. Annual Report.

142 The Training Renewal Foundation. 2006–2007. Annual Report.

143 Organisation for Economic Co-operation and Development. 1989. Towards An Enterprising Culture. CERI Monograph. 4 November.

144 Shuttleworth, D.E. 1987. *The Social and Economic Integration of Young People in North America*. Paris: OECD Qualifying Report.

145 Mallet, P. 1989. *The Book*. Oakville, ON: Sheridan Teleconferencing Group.

146 *NUTN NEWS*. 1988. A newsletter of the National University Teleconference Network, vol. 5, no. 6, May.

147 OECD. 1992. *Schools and Business: A New Partnership.* Paris: Centre for Education, Research & Innovation.

148 OECD. 2001. *New School Management Approaches.* Paris: Centre for Education, Research & Innovation.

149 Shuttleworth, D. 2001. *Managing Schools for Complexity.* A paper delivered to OECD-Hungary Seminar, Budapest, 6–7 December.

150 Shuttleworth, D. 2003. *School Management in Transition: Schooling On the Edge.* London: Routledge Falmer.

151 Monsebratten, L., and R. Daly. 2007. Canada's Poverty Capital. *Toronto Star*, 26 November.

152 Brown, L., and K. Rushowy. 2007. Teach Us About Us: Students. *Toronto Star*, 28 November.

153 Quoted in C. Goar. 2007. Nations Thrive by Helping Families. *Toronto Star*, 30 November.

154 OECD. 1991. *Partners in Education: The New Partnership Between Business and Schools.* Paris: Centre for Education, Research & Innovation.

155 Giles, G. 1992. Defending Community Education in Schools: An LEA Strategy. In *Education and Community.* London: Caswell.

Index